W9-AOD-728

# JEAN RHYS

Jean Rhys has long been central to debates in feminist, modernist, Caribbean, British and post-colonial writing. Elaine Savory's study, which incorporates and goes beyond previous critical approaches, is a critical reading of Rhys's entire oeuvre, including the stories and autobiography, and is informed by recently released unpublished manuscripts by Rhys. Designed both for the serious scholar and those unfamiliar with her writing, Savory's book insists on the importance of a Caribbean-centred approach to Rhys, and shows how this context profoundly affects her literary style. Informed by contemporary arguments on race, gender, class and nationality, Savory explores Rhys's stylistic innovations – her use of colours, her exploitation of the trope of performance, her experiments with creative non-fiction, her use of humour and her incorporation of the metaphysical into her texts. This study offers a comprehensive account of the life and work of this most complex and enigmatic of writers.

ELAINE SAVORY teaches at the New School for Social Research in New York. She has written extensively on African and Caribbean literatures, especially women's writing. She is co-editor of *Out of Kumbla: Caribbean Women and Literature*.

CAMBRIDGE STUDIES IN AFRICAN AND CARIBBEAN
LITERATURE

Series editor: Professor Abiola Irele, Ohio State University

Each volume in this unique series of critical studies will offer a comprehensive and in-depth account of the whole *œuvre* of one individual writer
from Africa or the Caribbean, in such a way that the book may be considered a complete coverage of the writer's expression up to the time the
study is undertaken. Attention will be devoted primarily to the works
themselves – their significant themes, governing ideas and formal pro-
cedures; biographical and other background information will thus be
employed secondarily, to illuminate these aspects of the writer's work
where necessary.

The emergence in the twentieth century of black literature in the
United States, the Caribbean and Africa as a distinct corpus of imaginative work represents one of the most notable developments in world
literature in modern times. This series has been established to meet the
needs of this growing area of study. It is hoped that it will not only
contribute to a wider understanding of the humanistic significance of
modern literature from Africa and the Caribbean through the scholarly
presentation of the work of the major writers, but also offer a wider
framework for the ongoing debates about the problems of interpretation within the disciplines concerned.

*Already published*

*Chinua Achebe*, by C. L. Innes
*Nadine Gordimer*, by Dominic Head
*Edouard Glissant*, by J. Michael Dash
*V. S. Naipaul*, by Fawzia Mustafa
*Aimé Césaire*, by Gregson Davis
*J. M. Coetzee*, by Dominic Head

# JEAN RHYS

ELAINE SAVORY

CAMBRIDGE
UNIVERSITY PRESS

PUBLISHED BY THE PRESS SYNDICATE OF THE UNIVERSITY OF CAMBRIDGE
The Pitt Building, Trumpington Street, Cambridge CB2 1RP, United Kingdom

CAMBRIDGE UNIVERSITY PRESS
The Edinburgh Building, Cambridge, CB2 2RU, UK    http://www.cup.cam.ac.uk
40 West 20th Street, New York, NY 10011–4211, USA    http://www.cup.org
10 Stamford Road, Oakleigh, Melbourne 3166, Australia

© Cambridge University Press 1998

First published 1998

Printed in the United Kingdom at the University Press, Cambridge

Typeset in 11/12½ pt Baskerville No. 2    [GC]

*A catalogue record for this book is available from the British Library*

ISBN 0 521 47434 5 hardback

*To Robert*

# Contents

| | | |
|---|---|---|
| *Preface* | *page* | x |
| *Acknowledgements* | | xvii |
| *List of abbreviations and note on the text* | | xix |
| *Chronology* | | xxi |

1   Living on both sides, living to write — 1

2   Registering protest: *The Left Bank* and *Quartet* — 36

3   A Caribbean woman lost in Europe?: *After Leaving Mr MacKenzie* and the question of gender — 57

4   Writing colour, writing Caribbean: *Voyage in the Dark* and the politics of colour — 85

5   Dangerous spirit, bitterly amused: *Good Morning, Midnight* — 109

6   People in and out of place: spatial arrangements in *Wide Sargasso Sea* — 133

7   Brief encounters: Rhys and the craft of the short story — 152

8   Performance arts: the theatre of autobiography and the role of the personal essay — 177

9   The Helen of our wars: cultural politics and Jean Rhys criticism — 196

*Notes* — 226
*Select bibliography* — 271
*Index* — 297

# *Preface*

Jean Rhys and her texts have been interpreted by different critics and theorists in strikingly different ways. She and they are in those readings: Caribbean, English, European; feminist and anti-feminist; elite, working class, marginal; white and white Creole; outsider and insider; ageless and of her time. But one identity can hold all of these contradictory facets: Rhys is a Caribbean writer. In her very complexity and contradictoriness, in important aspects of her writing style and in her fictional portrayal of race, ethnicity, class, gender and nationality, she is best understood within the richly diverse tradition of Caribbean literature and culture. The scribal aspect of this tradition has largely come into being as part of local and global anti- or post-colonial movements but equally as much as an important component of nation-building. At this time, almost the turn of the century, Caribbean writing reflects both the extensive migration of Caribbean peoples to Europe, America and Canada and also the need to confirm and define nationality and regional identity.[1]

Rhys reflects two major facets of Caribbean culture: a multi-faceted cosmopolitanism which searches out complexity and a desire for home and belonging which seeks an uncomplicated self-definition. Like Caribbean culture, her writing is both metro-politan and anti-metropolitan, both colonial and anti-colonial, both racist and anti-racist, both conventional and subversive. In the best and most creative ways, her textuality demonstrates a refusal to be absolutely coherent and therefore an acceptance of unresolved ambiguity, ambiguity which permits creative innovation and which is in effect politically anarchist, in the sense of resisting centralised and authoritative readings of experience.

There are controversial questions with which I am very much concerned. The first is the old chestnut question of whether Rhys is a Caribbean writer. This may appear to have been largely resolved already: my own statement of Rhys's affiliation is unequivocal. But there are still those who either deny Rhys's Caribbean identity or are largely ignorant of it. However most controversy about Rhys's placement derives from Caribbean discourse which is not only about Rhys, or writers, but about the major work of defining still developing identities in the face of an increasingly international world. Recently, as I discuss in chapter 9, the major Barbadian poet and cultural theorist Kamau Brathwaite has called Rhys the 'Helen of our wars', meaning the contemporary intellectual culture wars in the Caribbean which are fought to determine which affiliations and directions will predominate as the Caribbean moves towards the next century. Rhys then is absolutely at the centre of these major questions: her importance, like Helen's, has as much to do with geopolitical relations as with her indisputable talent and literary contribution.

The second question is closely related to the first: it asks what exactly we mean if we say that Jean Rhys is a Caribbean or West Indian writer.[2] Caribbean identity is various and political in especially complex ways. It is not monolithic but infinitely various and located not only in the region itself but importantly elsewhere: Canada and the United States both have important West Indian communities. Each major literary talent contributes to her or his culture but also helps to redefine it. Considering Rhys has made critics more aware of the complexities of white Creole identity.

Despite Louis James's very early placement of Rhys as Caribbean (1978), a good many critics have chosen to ignore this, though Brathwaite (1974), O'Connor (1986); Emery (1990) and Gregg (1995) as well as post-colonial scholars such as Peter Hulme and Sue Thomas have sought to demonstrate that understanding Rhys's Caribbean affiliation is critical to realising her project. It is only recently that the various camps of Rhys criticism, feminist, British, Caribbean, post-colonial, have begun to converse.

My own interest in Rhys is a writerly one, and I am primarily concerned with the ways in which Rhys's Caribbean identity translates into textuality, especially given her isolation from Caribbean cultural locales after her teens. She began to write well before decolonisation movements became evident and Caribbean literature in English established its canon.[3]

I write also as a feminist critic informed by the Caribbean.[4] I know that a woman writer, as the twentieth century closes, still often writes outside or across cultural borders, and the more information we can acquire about how she writes and where and when, the more strength we give to women writing: this means I am very much interested in the context of the Rhys texts, i.e. in Rhys's writing life. But I have used biographical material about Jean Rhys cautiously, always with an awareness that when the source is Rhys herself it is wise to remember that she created the narrative of her life, in her autobiography, letters or articles, as an ongoing fictional text. It was true in the sense of being honest in its interpretation, its reading, of her experience: it did not attempt to be literally faithful to small details and to the shapelessness of actual life. It is mostly a mistake to *simply* conflate Rhys's life and her texts.

Though I do agree with Veronica Gregg (1995) that Rhys's account of her writing experience is a structured narrative, I see in it two levels: on the relatively coherent official version which Rhys left as finished or near-finished text and the other, which ruptures the first, a fragmented series of much less edited statements. In chapter 1, I trace these levels of the story of writing, especially the importance of Rhys's formative years in Dominica and the ways in which these informed her mature self-construction. There follow seven chapters which each deal with an important issue in relation to Rhys's textuality and its Caribbean identity: her characteristic writing style; her construction of gender and sexuality; her use of colours as a fictional code and its connection to her construction of race; humour and the spiritual or metaphysical; landscape; story-telling; autobiography and performance. The argument of each chapter is organised around a specific text or texts, but applies generally to all of Rhys's writing. The last chapter is concerned with variant readings of Rhys by critics and scholars working out of different ideological and cultural locations and is framed by the recent important exchange between Kamau Brathwaite and British post-colonial theorist Peter Hulme.

Rhys's early instinct as a writer was for poetry and drama. Her fictional texts, spare and economical, often containing elision, are connected by a series of images or technical devices which function as sustained codes, as is common in the work of major poets. Rhys saw theatrical possibilities in some of her texts, which has been borne out by the effectiveness of various radio, stage and film adaptations.[5] She first wrote *Quartet* as a play.[6] Dramatic dialogue, like poetry, works as much by omission as by explicit statement: pauses and silences are extremely important in the meaning of the whole. Rhys's style matured over the length of her career but did not substantively change. Therefore I have set out the major contributing elements of it in the chapter on her early work.

In a departure from other Rhys criticism, I have separated the short stories from what I regard as personal essays or creative non-fiction, and have discussed the latter along with Rhys's auto-biography *Smile Please* (1979). I link her whole writing career to her love of the theatre and argue that writing became a substitute milieu for the stage and that autobiography became performance.

Despite my deep interest in Rhys, I have at times felt some difficulty during this project. There has been such an enormous amount of writing on her, that taken in the context of Caribbean literary scholarship, this is an embarrassment of riches as well as a welcome tribute to Rhys's importance, because the fact is that there are few substantial studies of other major anglophone Caribbean writers, such as Brathwaite, Lamming, Walcott, Selvon, Naipaul, Harris, many of whom began to publish their major work before Rhys completed *Wide Sargasso Sea*. In 1979, at Rhys's death, only two book-length studies had appeared, James (1978) and Staley (1979). By 1998, as I complete this, there is an enormous amount of work: a good number of full-length studies all or partly devoted to Rhys's work, a biography, numerous unpublished dissertations, several important bibliographies and a collection of critical essays. There are also many chapters in books on Rhys as well as hundreds of articles, reviews, interviews and profiles. Scholars exchange views via the *Jean Rhys Review* and the

University of Tulsa's Rhys Listserve. In short there is a Rhys industry: certainly enough to make a full-fledged conference on Rhys alone a feasible proposition.

In understanding this, it is not enough to recognise Rhys's outstanding writing ability. There are also some historical and political factors at work. Rhys was, as I will discuss later, fortunate to be encouraged and first published by Ford Madox Ford, then a very powerful literary figure, a man who could open doors. He ensured her important reviewer attention by writing a lengthy preface to her first collection of stories, *The Left Bank and Other Stories* (1927). Many artists discovered Paris was an aesthetic and social haven in the 1920s, including many marginalised in their own country, like Josephine Baker (Benstock 1987: 13).[7] For women artists in general, Paris provided a creative space: but Rhys was herself very isolated for the most part from that community.[8]

By the time *Wide Sargasso Sea* was published (1966), the feminist movement was gaining ground following on the civil rights movement, and by the height of the feminist movement in America and Europe (c. 1970–85), Rhys aroused much feminist interest. Finally, in the past twenty years or so, the development of postcolonial studies has meant that Rhys has again become a central literary icon.

I do think it is imperative that there be a much greater balance between criticism on Rhys and that devoted to other major Caribbean writers. But Rhys deserves to be read as an early professional Caribbean writer, experiencing exile well before the first major generation of Caribbean literary exiles of the 1950s. Like Rhys, I have both a healthy scepticism towards borders, boundaries and nationalities and a resistance to strategies which reduce human complexity. The Caribbean, at best, offers a space within which conventional identities are both subverted and restored, in which both the impulses to leave and to come home are equally understood.

Reading Rhys through the lens of the Caribbean intensifies an awareness of the complexity and variety of Caribbean literature: Rhys is clearly part of the family, not the lost relative living away. Like V. S. Naipaul and Jamaica Kincaid, she provokes radically different responses in readers of different cultural and political

locations. Naipaul has a tendency to criticise all but the British
and Kincaid to criticise mainly the British: both deconstruct their
immediate cultural community with razor-sharp intelligence but
their polemical texts frequently stereotype those they marginalise.
Like Naipaul, Rhys can at times use her skills as a writer to portray in disturbing ways how a prejudiced consciousness works;
like Kincaid, Rhys relies on the voice or consciousness of a young,
extremely clear-sighted woman in most of her fiction. But Rhys's
contradictions prevent her fiction from becoming polemical: in
the end she disturbs in more interesting ways.

Like Kamau Brathwaite, Sam Selvon, Paule Marshall and
Nourbese Philip, she explores her own particular racial and ethnic identity. Like Derek Walcott and Michelle Cliff, she textualises
a pained but powerful affiliation with Europe, source of both literary recognition and the damage caused by colonialism. Like George
Lamming and Erna Brodber,[9] she conveys a culture through the
journey of a child to adulthood. Her concerns about insoluble
divisions caused by race contrast with Wilson Harris's challenge
to essentialisms in his mythic construction of liminal identities,
but in writing, controversially, the first-person narrative of a black
woman, in 'Let Them Call It Jazz' (first published 1962), she
opened the door to the idea that a Caribbean writer can attempt
to cross over racial and gender boundaries, something which
important Caribbean writers of the next generation, Robert Antoni
and Caryl Phillips, have claimed and used themselves.[10] Antoni
spent the five years it took him to write his second novel, *Blessed
Is the Fruit* (1996), with a copy of *Wide Sargasso Sea* on his work
table.

Caribbean texts clearly read differently to insiders, those who
know the culture and thus can understand nuances, but all readers
are biased, partial and contradictory in their expectations: all readings are to some extent flawed by the shortcomings of the reader.
Mine are no exception. I have tried to read Rhys in the context
of the Caribbean, as I read the Caribbean.

I think no apology is needed for the fact that I have written
this study because I admire Rhys as a working writer: nor because
I have tried to hold a careful balance between the academic and
the writerly in my style. Jamaican poets Olive Senior and Lorna

Goodison have produced elegies on Rhys, Senior's about a pilgrimage she made to Rhys's grave in England. Both poets wish
their literary ancestor peace and express their affection. In that
spirit, and as a poet myself, I offer this work in gratitude for
Rhys's discovery that it is possible to defy prescriptions and to
find home in writing itself.

# Acknowledgements

I must first thank Francis Wyndham, Rhys's literary executor, for permission to quote from her published and unpublished texts, as well as the University of Tulsa, where the largest collection of Rhys's papers is housed.

The following list is inadequate testament to the variety of ways I have been helped: at the University of Tulsa, Curator Sidney Huttner and his staff, Lori Curtis, Milissa Burkart and library staff member, John Hodge – Lori Curtis, especially, helped enormously; in Tulsa, Peggy Keller, for shelter and nurture, especially, also Liluah Seifried and Martha Beard; at the University of the West Indies, Cave Hill, especially Jeniphier Carnegie and also Alan Moss, Carlyle Best and Nell Bretney; in Barbados, Alfred Pragnell; at the University of the West Indies, St Augustine, Sandra Barnes; in Dominica, especially Lennox Honychurch, for sharing his knowledge and lending me the 1894 Royal Commission report on Dominica; Pat Honychurch, who arranged for me to trace Rhys's family journey from Roseau to Bona Vista; the late Ena Williams and her daughter Myrtle MacIntyre, Daphne Agar and Gerry Aird; in New York, Nicole Phillips, for the gift of Honychurch's history of Dominica, and being a believer; in Canada, Irving Andre for the gift of his book on Dominican literature and my brother Michael, for reviews and articles; at the British Museum in London, staff at the Colindale newspaper library and the Manuscript Room; in London, especially Maggie Butcher and in Oxford, Lynette Lithgow and Dominic Pearson both for shelter and support; for the generous sharing of their own work on Rhys, Sue Thomas, Martien Kappers-den Hollander and Erica Waters; for the invitation to share a draft of

xvii

chapter 9 at a Departmental Seminar, Professor Christopher Sten of George Washington University's English Department; also my insightful and supportive colleagues at Lang College, The New School for Social Research, with whom I shared chapter 9 in our faculty research seminars. I thank: for access to a 1920s map of Paris, La Maison Française, New York University; for sharing work and encouragement, Kamau Brathwaite; for faith, Ronnie Pardo and J. B. Keller; for the fellowship of Dominican scholarship and the delight of exchanging resources, Lisa Paravisini. Nora Gaines, remarkable editor of the *Jean Rhys Review*, searched out and shared material, constantly encouraged, read some early draft, introduced me to Rhys scholars Peter Hulme, Teresa O'Connor, Bianca Tarozzi and, by mail, Martien Kappers, and published earlier versions of chapters 5 and 6.

I must give very special thanks to Elizabeth Wilson, who read the manuscript with her usual wisdom and grace. Abiola Irele, the series editor, has been a source of constant support, encouragement and excellent advice. My editor at Cambridge University Press, Ray Ryan, has been patient and so I was able to work on newly released Rhys papers. I thank my long-suffering immediate family especially Austin (for his constantly expressed desire to see this done), Stacy, Todd, Vincent, Jeannie, Daphne and Colin, and above all, Robert, whose love and support has been the same as always, entirely generous and loyal, even after he discovered through bitter experience why acknowledgements pages always so praise a writer's mate.

Finally, I am immensely grateful that over many years, the Caribbean has adopted me, kept me challenged, alert, usefully conflicted, silenced productively at times. It was in the Caribbean, naturally, that I first recognised I needed to pay more attention to Jean Rhys. It is to the Caribbean that I bring my work always, with many, many thanks.

# Abbreviations and note on the text

PUBLISHED TEXTS

| | |
|---|---|
| *ALMM* | *After Leaving Mr MacKenzie* |
| *CSS* | *Collected Short Stories* |
| *GM, M* | *Good Morning, Midnight* |
| *L* | *Letters* |
| *Q* | *Quartet* |
| *SIOL* | *Sleep It Off Lady* |
| *SP* | *Smile Please* |
| *TAB-L* | *Tigers Are Better-Looking* |
| *TLB* | *The Left Bank* |
| *VITD* | *Voyage in the Dark* |
| *WSS* | *Wide Sargasso Sea* |

UNPUBLISHED MANUSCRIPTS

| | |
|---|---|
| BEB | Black Exercise Book |
| GEB | Green Exercise Book |
| OEB | Orange Exercise Book |
| REB | Red Exercise Book |
| 'TS' | 'Triple Sec' |

LOCATION OF RHYS MANUSCRIPTS

University of Tulsa, Special Collections, is always indicated as UTC. I have, at the request of the Tulsa Collection curators and archivists, not indicated file numbers as the collection is likely to be constantly reordered and refiled for some time.

The term 'coloured' as used in this study in relation to race is a West Indian usage signifying a person of mixed race.

The term West Indian is used to signify the anglophone Caribbean. The term Caribbean signifies the the whole region.

Rhys's diaries, letters and unpublished manuscripts have unusual punctuation when they are punctuated at all. When quoting from these documents, I have been faithful to Rhys's original texts.

# Chronology

| | |
|---|---|
| 1824 | James Potter Lockhart, Rhys's maternal greatgrand-father, buys 'Genever' (now spelled Geneva) plantation in the British colony of Dominica. |
| 1831 | Legal discrimination on the grounds of skin colour abolished in Dominica. |
| 1833 | 29 August slavery abolished in British law. This was effective from 1 August 1834 in West Indian territories. |
| 1838 | Coloured majority in Dominica House of Assembly, which would control the legislature until the introduction of Crown Colony government in the late 1890s. |
| 1881 | Williams Rees Williams, Rhys's father, arrives in Dominica from Britain to practise medicine. |
| 1882 | Marriage of Rhys's parents, William Rees Williams and Minna Lockhart. |
| 1890 | Ella Gwendoline Rees Williams born in Roseau, Dominica, 24 August, fifth child and fourth surviving child of the family. |
| 1901 | Colonial Office approves Administrator Hesketh Bell's plan for an 'Imperial Road' to open up the interior of Dominica for development into plantations. |
| 1907 | Ella Williams leaves Dominica for England and attends the Perse School, Cambridge. |
| 1909 | Leaves Perse School for Tree's School, now RADA. |
| 1910 | William Rees Williams dies. |
| 1909–10 | Joins chorus of *Our Miss Gibbs*. Calls herself Ella Gray. |
| 1910 | Meets Lancelot Grey Hugh Smith. |
| 1912 | End of the affair with Smith. |

| | |
|---|---|
| 1913 | Writes her account of the affair in diaries, which will eventually become raw material for fiction. |
| 1914–18 | First World War. |
| 1919 | In Holland, marries Willem Johan Marie (Jean) Lenglet, 30 April. |
| 1920 | Rhys's son William Owen dies, three weeks old, Paris, 19 January. |
| 1922 | Rhys's daughter Maryvonne born 22 May, Ukkel, near Brussels. |
| 1924 | Meets Ford Madox Ford in Paris. Lenglet is arrested for misappropriation of funds; serves time in prison in France. Rhys's relationship with Ford Madox Ford begins. Ford Madox Ford publishes Rhys's short story 'Vienne' in *the transatlantic review*.[1] |
| 1927 | *The Left Bank and Other Stories*, with a preface by Ford Madox Ford. Leaves Paris for London. |
| 1928 | *Postures* (later titled *Quartet*). |
| 1931 | *After Leaving Mr MacKenzie*. |
| 1933 | Divorce from Jean Lenglet. |
| 1934 | *Voyage in the Dark*. Marries Leslie Tilden Smith. |
| 1936 | Returns to Dominica for a three-week visit. |
| 1939 | *Good Morning, Midnight*. |
| 1939–45 | Second World War. Rhys is separated from her daughter from 1939 until 1945. |
| 1941 | Edgar Mittelholzer, *Corentyne Thunder*. |
| 1945 | Leslie Tilden-Smith dies. |
| 1947 | Marries Max Hamer. |
| 1949 | Vic Reid, *New Day*. Rhys charged with assaulting neighbours; spends a few days in Holloway Prison. |
| 1950 | Max Hamer tried for misappropriation of funds: serves time in England. |
| 1952 | Sam Selvon, *A Brighter Sun*. |
| 1953 | Roger Mais, *The Hills Were Joyful Together*. Phyllis Shand Allfrey, *The Orchid House*. |

|       | Phyllis Shand Allfrey returns to Dominica from England to co-found the Dominica Labour Party. |
|-------|---------------------------------------------------|
|       | George Lamming, *In The Castle of My Skin.* |
| 1957  | V. S. Naipaul, *The Mystic Masseur.* |
| 1958  | Jan Carew, *Black Midas.* |
|       | Federation of the West Indies established: Phyllis Shand Allfrey becomes Minister of Labour and Social Affairs. |
| 1959  | Paule Marshall, *Brown Girl, Brownstones.* |
|       | Race riots in Britain in Nottingham and Notting Hill, London. |
| 1962  | Sylvia Wynter, *The Hills of Hebron.* |
|       | Derek Walcott, *In a Green Night.* |
|       | Wilson Harris, *Palace of the Peacock.* |
|       | Federation of the West Indies collapses. |
| 1965  | Max Hamer dies. |
| 1966  | *Wide Sargasso Sea.* |
| 1967  | Edward Kamau Brathwaite, *Rights of Passage.* |
|       | Dominica becomes an Associated State of Britain. |
| 1968  | *Tigers Are Better-Looking.* |
| 1975  | *My Day.* |
| 1976  | *Sleep It Off Lady.* |
| 1978  | Dominican Independence celebrated, 3 November. |
| 1979  | Jean Rhys dies, 14 May, Dorset, England. |
|       | *Smile Please.* |
| 1984  | *Letters.* |
| 1987  | *The Collected Short Stories.* |

CHAPTER I

# Living on both sides, living to write

> With this eye I see & no other . . . I had two longings & one
> was fighting the other.
> I wanted to be loved & I wanted to be always alone.
>
> (GEB)

It is crucially important to explore the contexts of Rhys's work, especially her placement of the role of writing in her life and of race, class, nationality, gender and religion. She was interestingly contradictory on these subjects, and inclined therefore to tell a story which was Janus-faced, capable of capturing opposing readings of the world which usually failed to communicate well with one another.

Rhys had a well-developed instinct for the submerged pattern within the raw material of life, she also, as a writer, created her own history, not only in her autobiography, but less guardedly in letters and fragments of unfinished autobiographical manuscript. Emotional honesty was her touchstone, selectivity and clarity her writing mantras. Honesty does not mean disclosure has to be complete: selectivity does not mean anything important has to be left out. Rhys chose to tell a very edited version of her life in *Smile Please* (1979) and left, in her will, an injunction against anyone writing her biography: she wanted to insist that attention be paid only to the work. There were clearly episodes in her life which she preferred not to discuss and which she argued were irrelevant to her literary achievement. Naturally such an attempt at censorship has not been entirely successful, given the fact that Rhys had a particularly interesting career as a writer which clearly drew closely on an unusual life experience, though it is important to

I

acknowledge Rhys's profound feeling 'all of a writer that matters is in the book or books' (*SP*: 136). She thought it 'is idiotic to be curious about the person' (*SP*: 136).

Rhys has successfully thwarted the biographical scholar to some extent: given the many moves and the intense poverty which she suffered for long periods of her life, it is remarkable that we have any manuscripts at all before the period of high public and literary interest in Rhys which followed the appearance of *Wide Sargasso Sea*.[1] By the time Carole Angier did research for her 1990 biography, many of the people who might have provided crucial information were also dead or very old. In the end, Angier sometimes tried, to her detriment, to utilise Rhys's fiction to fill gaps in the life. Because Rhys preferred to erase her private life, it is not surprising that so many of the unpublished essays, fragments of fiction and exercise books filled with early rough drafts and sometimes autobiographical entries are concerned with the writing, with the story of the artist as working professional woman. This is the story she left, though even here we have highly contradictory and fragmentary and often self-censored comments by Rhys on how the work came about. The issue of how women write is a topic which many feminists still find compelling: the means of production of women's texts is often a critical issue in understanding their cultural identity and placement.

The narrative of Jean Rhys's life is, since Angier's biography, fairly well understood, though further work clearly remains to be done. My purpose in reinterpreting the story is to point out the centrality and specificity of her Caribbean experience, particularly for those readers unfamiliar with the region, and/or unaware of the developing scholarly map of her life and work. Given the fact that many critics have effectively marginalised Rhys's Caribbean origins (this even to an extent in Angier's work, since she did not visit Dominica), it is important to make quite sure Rhys's Caribbean childhood and her views on race, class and nationality which began to be formed there are understood as the doorway into my readings of Rhys texts. Her conceptions of gender and her religious affiliations, both of which mark her fiction powerfully and both of which also owe a good deal to Rhys's Dominican years, are included in subsequent chapters.

I have another important reason for interest in Rhys's life, especially, in this chapter, the importance of the formative years, and that is to explain the complex cultural identity which so informs her textuality, not just in theme but in the multi-voiced narrative she gradually developed in her long fiction. As Veronica Gregg has noted (1995), citing Jean D'Costa (1986), Rhys was self-contradictory and ambiguous about many issues of identity. She had an intense ambivalence towards both the Caribbean and England and was, in her culturally complex identity as she grew older, unable to entirely belong anywhere. To the writer David Plante she was unable or unwilling to answer when asked if she was a West Indian or a French writer and responded quite vehemently when asked about her English literary affiliation:, 'No! I'm not! I'm not! I'm not even English' (1984: 44).

Whilst Gregg acknowledges Rhys's capacity to change position on a given topic, she also constructs her as 'the white Creole', following the tendency of post-colonial theory to address general cultural identities.[2] But as Lizabeth Paravisini-Gebert points out, in her biography of Dominican politician and novelist Phyllis Allfrey (1996), not all white Creoles feel alienated in Dominica.[3] Nor do they all have the degree of Rhys's ties to and alienation from England. Her father was Welsh, but that was complicated by his sense of rejection by his father.[4] Rhys lived in England most of her life and married two English men. Her immediate white family migrated successfully to England during her adult life,[5] but she never felt at home there.

Her childhood was in the small white community of Dominica, but nevertheless gave her experience of different races (black, white, mixed, Carib), languages and cultures. It evidently taught her that meaning and truth can be multi-layered. But if she had stayed in the region, in my view she would not have been able to fit in any better than she did anywhere else: her country was essentially the page and her most important personal connections often other writers or her characters, including her fictional versions of herself. Though her adult life in Europe contributed much profoundly influential experience, her personal narratives of writing and cultural identity begin with her Caribbean childhood: Dominica is of central importance in reading Rhys's life and work.

Rhys was born in Dominica in 1890 (though she encouraged confusion about her birthdate and much early scholarship accepted 1894).[6] She was named Ella Gwendoline Rees Williams, though the spelling of Gwendoline during her lifetime and in critical studies is diverse.[7] Her mother was white Creole of Scottish ancestry, a Lockhart, and her father was Welsh and had come to Dominica in 1881, shortly before his marriage, to practise medicine.[8] Gwen Williams grew up in the enclave of white Anglican Roseau, still now a small town sitting between the dramatic forested escarpments which characterise Dominica's interior and the huge horizon of the almost always deserted Atlantic Ocean and Caribbean Sea. Much of the island was impenetrable in her childhood as it is now. Governor Hesketh Bell tried to open up a road to facilitate colonial settlement: it was never completed.[9] Rhys used the idea of this Imperial Road in a piece of unpublished creative non-fiction.[10]

Most of Dominica's people are of African descent and had in 1890, the year of Rhys's birth, still vivid memories of the slavery which had ended in 1834. In 1890 many were also Catholic (as is true today) and spoke a distinct French patois. The Anglican hierarchy attempted to be dominant as a representation of the religious wing of British possession and white hegemony. Rhys's response to Catholicism is, as I shall argue later, very important.

The context of Rhys's childhood can be pieced together by studying Dominica's history, reading the surviving newspapers of Rhys's childhood years, and then interpreting Rhys's heavily self-edited published account of her young life (*Smile Please*), along with surviving drafts, letters and notebooks. Indeed Rhys cannot be seriously read without the context of Dominican life in the late nineteenth century, from which we can extrapolate the class, race, religious and gender formations which were laid on Rhys at birth and which she both contested and accepted at different times.

Dominicans of colour resisted colonial injustice when they could. The Report of the Royal Commission (1894) on the condition of Dominica is important. Lennox Honychurch (1984) describes a heavily taxed peasantry, more burdened by a tax increase in 1888. In 1893, the village of La Plaine, in one of the poorest and least accessible areas of Dominica for produce markets, strongly resisted when one of their community was evicted from his house so the Government could sell it for non-payment of taxes. The resistance turned violent and police and naval forces opened fire: several were killed or injured. The incident became known as the La Plaine Riots. The Commission's report includes notes on the views of Rhys's father, Dr W. R. Williams and her uncle, Acton Don Lockhart.

Gwen Williams's maternal family, the Lockharts, were in a very powerful position in Dominica in the late nineteenth century: Rhys was 'that Lockhart girl' in her youth to members of her family's circle, signifying the relative unimportance of her father's name on the island.[11] Her mother had grown up on the lovely and important estate in the south of Dominica called Geneva, which had been owned by the family since 1824. Acton Lockhart, Rhys's mother's youngest brother, took over the running of the Geneva Estate from his widowed mother sometime in the 1880s, by Carole Angier's estimate (1990: 8). Both men had been Government-appointed, 'nominated' members of the Assembly, part of the machinery of white colonial control of island affairs. In 1894, Williams expressly did not want to see elective seats increased in the Assembly, i.e. he appears to have been on the colonial, white side of Dominican politics.[12]

When Williams arrived in Dominica from Britain and married Minna Lockhart a year later, in 1882, he entered an intensely political, competitive, small world in which the white, colonial and so-called mulatto or coloured intelligentsia debated the issues of the day in both the legislature and the local press. Dominica, as Lennox Honychurch points out (1984), was the only island in the West Indies where white power was successfully challenged. Dominica's elite of mixed-race landowners, ancestrally from French territories, uneasily co-existed with white political appointees and professionals from Britain.[13] In 1831, the so-called 'Brown Privilege' Bill made discrimination in political and cultural life on the basis of race illegal. Three members of colour were elected to the House of Assembly in 1832 and by 1838, there was a majority of colour.

One of the most controversial figures in Roseau life when Williams arrived was Dr Henry Nicholls, originally English and married into a prominent Dominican white family.[14] In the 1880s, he was at the height of his influence as doctor, horticulturist and literary and political personality. Rees Williams was not the ambitious, political and social star that Nicholls was, although he made his own social connections, such as his bridge playing (*SP*: 57). He was first nominated to the Assembly for a period in the mid-1880s.

In my reading of the Dominican newspapers, I concur with Sue Thomas (1996c) that Williams's colonial affiliations seriously and justifiably irritated the coloured intellectual elite of Roseau. However I think Lennox Honychurch's view of him as complex is convincing.[15] If he was both liberal (in relative terms) and critical of the mulatto elite, then he was both at one with his wife's family interests (Thomas 1996c) and also at times a mildly dissident Celt on the subject of race or religion, just as his daughter was capable of holding both liberal and racist views. Williams certainly understood, in his testimony to the Royal Commission in 1894, that taxation was the root cause of general unrest and that elective members of the Assembly 'know they can be out-voted' and 'discount the value' of votes of Government nominees (Report of Royal Commission, 1894: 21). Nevertheless, he seems to have thought that more Government projects and control of the Assembly would be the solution.

Williams was often attacked in the feisty local press, including the *Dominica Dial*. On Saturday, 31 May 1884, it was implied that his fondness for alcohol got in the way of his professional duty, the editor calling him 'a convivial practitioner'. On Saturday, 30 August 1884, the *Dial* editorial was a little sharp about Dr Williams's sweet potato farm at Bona Vista, in the hills above Roseau, since it was outside the district under Williams's medical jurisdiction: enjoyment of his farm might therefore prevent the doctor's prompt attendance to his patients. Williams had negotiated, early in his time in Dominica, and with the help of Dr Nicholls, to shift his medical responsibilities closer to Roseau so as to become part of town society and enjoy a larger income (see also Thomas 1996c).[16] The *Dial* went on to comment sardonically that in a crop of sweet potatoes grown at fifteen hundred feet above sea-level 'lay the foundation of the fortune which every emigrating Briton expects to extract from the colony of his choice'.

On 29 November of the same year, Williams was described as 'the professional man who was lucky enough to jump from the post of medical attendant on board a telegraph repairing steamer', thereby increasing his salary from sixty to two hundred and fifty pounds a year.[17]

The tone of these comments is quite characteristic of the rough and tumble of the Dominican press in the late nineteenth and early twentieth centuries and entirely recognisable in Rhys's short fiction.[18] Nicholls, who had also passed through a process of being presented in the press as upstart foreigner and then as important, if often maddening, local dignitary, was eventually said to have received the task of heading a Commission on Yaws as a compensation for some loss of his income and practice.[19] A letter to the editor of the *Dominica Dial*, 20 August 1886, says bluntly, 'We all are alive to the fact that Dr Nicholls is the most prejudiced white man in the island.' Nicholls was inclined to engage in protracted skirmishes in the newspapers when he was attacked.[20] This was often: he clearly had both political and social ambitions, was evidently both pompous and had great status (Lizabeth Paravisini-Gebert describes him and his wife as 'the equivalent of a Dominican royal couple' (1996: 12)), and was gifted with words as well as in medicine and horticulture. He was also quite willing to be provocative. Williams however seems to have remained silent in the face of verbal attacks, unusual in the world of educated Roseau in the late nineteenth century.

Sue Thomas goes further and argues Williams transformed from first appearance in the island as 'European exotic' to final development into a 'full-blown planter' (1996c). By the late 1890s, Thomas points out, he was a vocal member of the lobby for Crown Colony Government, perceived as a tributary of British control in that it resisted relative political autonomy for Dominica because of the power, political and economic, of the coloured elite in the island.[21] Perhaps most importantly, Thomas challenges Carole Angier's explanation of the reason why Rhys's eldest sister Minna went to live with relatives: instead of financial woes, Thomas suggests that Minna needed to complete her education at a higher level than was available in Dominica at the time. Thomas argues that Dr Williams was listed in the 1910 electoral register for the

Roseau Town Board as one of the seven richest men in the community so he could not have been financially fragile in the 1890s and early 1900s. Yet Rhys noted in *Smile Please* the loss of the two estates her father owned when she was small, Bona Vista and Amelia, explaining that they were not profitable because her father could not spare enough time from his medicine to farm them.

However, Lennox Honychurch describes an important economic change between the 1890s and the years before the First World War (1984: 113–21). Williams got out of agriculture just before an upturn in Dominican revenues from crops. He clearly, if we accept Thomas, became affluent again after his daughter left for England in 1907.[22] No doubt Rhys had the selective memory of her family history which we all do: she always told the story of her leaving theatre school in London concealing her failure to be able to continue her acting course, as Angier points out (1990: 49): she claimed the cause was her father's financial difficulties. She did not deny memory is selective and often self-protective: in *Smile Please*, a note of self-interrogation sounds in her admission that she probably romanticises her father, perhaps as she saw little of him (*SP*: 57). She did remember her mother crying to a coloured Dominican woman friend, maybe about money (*SP*: 34).

Veronica Gregg also questions Rhys's *Smile Please* account of a riot when she argues that there is no record of a riot in Roseau in 1902 or 1906 (*SP*: 37–41). Gregg ascribes 1902 or 1906 depending on whether Rhys's birth is calculated at 1890 or 1894. But according to Irving Andre, William Davies (the *Dial* owner, whom Andre identifies as a wealthy plantation owner as well as political leader and newspaper proprietor) declared in 1898 that 'race war' would be waged against the British if they introduced Crown Colony government (1995: 74ff). The actual unrest, which Rhys remembered as 'the Riot' from her childhood was provoked according to Andre by rumours that the Presbytery and Catholic cathedral were to be burned down by members of the coloured community. Rhys would have been eight, though she says in *Smile Please* she was about twelve, perhaps the age she gives Antoinette at the time of the riot in *Wide Sargasso Sea*. For Rhys, the cause was a local newspaper editor's article attacking the power of Catholic priests in Dominica. André comments that the black community would at times riot in defence of the whites and against the coloured community: coloured elites had by no means always been supportive of the black majority and were often distrusted, sometimes even more than the white colonials.

The tensions between white, coloured or brown, and black people dominated the Dominica of Rhys's childhood and early adolescence, at the end of the nineteenth and first years of the twentieth century during which the country moved slowly away from the memory of slavery and towards a modern state: James (1978) claims Williams received the respect of many poor people when he died, signifiying he must have had some racial sensitivity and kindness. That this could be the same man who offended the anti-colonial middle class is not in the least unbelievable: the strength of internalised colonialism and the extent of racism could, for some people, make the slightest humane response on the part of the white doctor a matter for gratitude. For those however who had a critical and resisting eye on colonialism and racism, Dr Williams might easily have been just another opportunistic white migrant from Britain.

The Commonwealth of Dominica obtained independence from British colonial rule in 1978, after a period of Associated Statehood from 1967. The young high-colonial child Gwen Williams lived mainly in the family house on Cork Street in Roseau, a corner property with a courtyard and a large mango tree, stables and Dr Williams's surgery, holidaying on one of her father's small estates in the hills.[23] She was a Lockhart, a doctor's daughter, white and Anglican. Her father's mother, 'Irish Granny', sent gifts from England. In Dominica, a relatively modest income by the standards of Britain gave whites a life-style which was in caste and pattern much higher than their station. Rhys's family escaped the heat and dust of the town for holidays, most memorably at Bona Vista, where servants attended their needs. The slim margin by which such privilege was maintained is indicated by the sale of Bona Vista and another small estate, Amelia, both sold by Rhys's father when she was fairly young (*SP*: 16–17).

Rhys's ambivalence about race has to be understood in the light of her early memories of the times at Bona Vista, set against her growing realisation as she grew older of the grim facts of racial tension and white isolation which informed her Roseau life. The family's journey was from Roseau along the coast to the fishing village of Massacre, then up inland along a narrow trail, set with stones to assist the horses and make the trail more durable, along a ridge line and up into the hills, across a valley to higher ground and the house, sitting on a gentle slope of hillside, overlooking the distant but still vivid sea: it was a journey of escape from the pressures of town to the holiday world of the hills. Amelia was on a slightly lower hillside not far from Bona Vista. Though the Bona Vista house has disappeared, except for some tell-tale pieces of foundation stone and roof, the site is immediately recognisable from Rhys's terse descriptions of the location and passages in her fiction and drafts.[24]

It is virtually impossible to overestimate the formative years in Dominica as shaping the idea of language Rhys worked with. The tension between the West Indian, white Creole accent she had as a young woman and could produce even in old age and the middle-class English voice she mainly used towards the end of her life reflects her response to British middle-class, largely literary connections. But her Caribbean childhood must have taught her that language is almost always a layered means of communication, with hidden codes and contrasting registers. It is very evident in her letters that French was an important linguistic resource for her throughout her life. She must have originally understood it not only as something learned at school but as living patois in her Dominican years. Later she learned different registers when she married Jean Lenglet, himself a French speaker who was not fluent in English, and she lived and worked in Paris.[25] Peter Roberts, in his history of West Indian language (1988), points out that plantation whites did not have to strive for formal language and slaves were denied language education, so that standardised forms of language were less significantly established in the Caribbean than in societies where a middle class struggled to become acceptable by adopting the formal language structures of their superiors. The very linguistic inventiveness which so marks Caribbean writing and performance was made possible by the history of lack of extensive imposition of formal language structures in plantation society for either white or black culture. By Rhys's day, a rather ponderous anglicised tone was adopted in the Dominican newspapers, especially by Dr Nicholls, one which fortunately seems to have entirely failed to influence her writing voice. In the *Dominica Dial*, 31 March 1888, there was an attack on English patois as 'an ignoble travesty of the mother tongue', an attitude which extended to French patois as well. This local (and colonised) attitude towards Creoles was generally pervasive until well into the twentieth century. Major work by Caribbean and African linguists has begun to establish a much more precise understanding of the roots of Caribbean Creoles (Roberts 1988). In the forced union of European and African languages during slavery lay the beginnings of new language structures, syncretic and creative, which ultimately became Creoles, or as Kamau Brathwaite has said, 'nation languages'.[26] One of the most obvious established characteristics of Caribbean writing is linguistic multi-valency, a characteristic shared in some ways by other literatures of resistance, such as Irish, African-American and African writing and subtly present in Rhys's texts.

In going to the Perse School in Cambridge, the city where her Welsh grandfather had been to university, Rhys effectively left her mother's world for her father's. In 1909, after she left school, she entered a drama course at Tree's School (so named after its founder, subsequently known as the Academy of Dramatic Arts and ultimately the Royal Academy, or RADA). She always said that she left Tree's School because her father died and her mother could not afford to keep her there. Angier's version is that Rhys was rejected by the theatre school because of her West Indian accent and failure to accommodate to the expected standard British voices then thought essential to an actor's employability (1990: 49). If anything would have impressed upon Rhys her colonial and marginal status it would have been this painful failure to achieve her dream of acting because of her accent (though it is not clear that Rhys had much performance talent, from her own account of her chorus girl days).[27] She excised the truth about the rejection from her story in *Smile Please* of Aunt Clarice taking her shopping to buy clothes for the return to Dominica, and Rhys going into a theatrical agent's office and getting a job in 'in the chorus of a musical comedy called *Our Miss Gibbs'* (*SP*: 85).

Rhys's journey from instinctual to professional writer seriously began in Paris in the years of High Modernism. From her comments on writing we can see how writing itself became in effect the country she knew best. Her comments on writing very often stress its enormous centrality in her interior life:

I can't remember feeling much pity I was too young My pity was for imaginary people not real ones. (BEB)

In fact, I'm certain I was often disagreeable whenever I was interrupted in the effort to get down and shape the flocks of words which came into my head, I didn't and don't know why. (*SP*: 128)

My will is quite weakened because I drink too much but even this lunatic writing is better than the blank blank days and the feeling that they have won. (GEB)

Trying to piece together Rhys's narratives of self means stitching together manuscript fragments, published or unpublished, autobiography, letter, draft or reported conversation or interview: these are either the edited version which Rhys intended to be made public or the series of revealing ruptures in unedited writing of that controlled series of statements.

Jean Rhys was always a writer, that is, the name Jean Rhys came into being as the signature on a piece of achieved writing. The other adult women who inhabited her body are not Rhys's concern in the writing: Ella Gray, Ella Lenglet and Ella Hamer, about whom we know comparatively little. In old age, Rhys signed an envelope containing manuscript material in the presence of David Plante as both Jean Rhys and E. G. Hamer (Plante 1984: 44): no doubt this was a legal necessity but it is also a powerful symbol of Rhys's knowledge of the power of names, and also the fact that her private name signified a self unavailable through the writing.

We have, beyond the published novels, stories, autobiography and essays: a few notebooks, with drafts ranging between fiction-alised diary and rough draft; a reasonably large quantity of letters, mostly to editors, publishers, agents, and literary friends and associates which deal with her writing or with writing and reading in general and a number of interviews or profiles which contain statements by Rhys. These are invariably about her writing. David Plante's profile of Rhys (1984) tries to balance the writer with the frail old woman who also inhabited the same body, but his unsettling narrative makes Ella Hamer even more fugitive. Plante further complicates Rhys's autobiography by claiming he seriously collaborated with her on it (1984: 42). Nevertheless *Smile Please* is the major source for Rhys's writing narrative. Perhaps, when she was old, there was little left except the writer: this is not unusual in any seriously committed artist who receives late recognition.

Certainly Plante's ambivalence, at the beginning of his essay, about becoming involved in Rhys's private space makes it clear it was only the writer who had attracted his interest, and at intervals he returns to this theme: 'You are attentive to her, not as Mrs Hamer but as Jean Rhys' (1984: 25). But Plante also clearly found exposure of the fragile woman behind the writing too tempting to resist: his shameful betrayal of an old woman's trust to his writing ambition is well known.[28]

Despite Rhys's comment to David Plante that she wondered 'if it was right to give up so much of my life for writing' (1984: 31), there were many years, especially between 1939 and 1966, when the writing was largely a personal commitment, that is, though Rhys continued to write, her work remained mostly unpublished. Her private life was painful: during 1939–45, she struggled with not knowing what had happened to her only living child, Maryvonne, who disappeared in Holland after working for the Resistance, as did Maryvonne's father.[29] In 1945, Rhys's husband Leslie died suddenly of a heart attack in immensely stressful circumstances.[30] She wrote this into a story, 'The Sound of the River' (*TAB-L*, 1968; *CSS*, 1987). But the relationship with Maryvonne, the experience of motherhood, is almost entirely missing from Rhys's texts: even as raw material for fiction she largely censored it. Her major protagonists are either young and unmarried, with pregnancies terminated early or resulting in the loss of a very young child, or they are older and childless.

If it is true that, as Rhys said, 'Writing took me over. It was all I thought of. Nothing and nobody else mattered much to me' (*SP*: 128), it might be assumed there should be more finished

work than the relatively slim, though finely finished, shelf of books
Rhys completed. David Plante reported that Rhys's response to
his comment that writing was her life was 'My life has been
turbulent and very boring' (1984: 53). This is a chilling comment,
which does not quite make clear whether it was the turbulence or
the surrounding calmer time when she was able to write which
was boring. It is of course one of the paradoxes of the writing life
that large stretches of lonely, uneventful time are essential to the
achievement of finished work. The raw material of experience
which informs that work does not necessarily need to be exciting
or unusual.

First and foremost Rhys was a professional writer, then a
professional writer whose consciousness was centrally shaped by
her Caribbean childhood, as Gregg has also argued (1995). In
Dominica, writing in the newspapers was a vital part of local
middle-class culture and reading was of course a part of that
tradition. We do not know for sure whether Rhys discovered
any of the narratives of women travellers or residents in the
Caribbean or of early Caribbean-born women writers.[31] But she
acknowledged the idea of the book as immensely powerful in her
formative years in *Smile Please*: 'Before I could read, almost a
baby, I imagined that God, this strange thing or person I heard
about, was a book' (*SP*: 20). Nancy R. Harrison (1988: 115 reads
this as a 'father-text' and opposed to the 'mother-book' which
became Rhys's model for writing, represented by her mother's
sewing book with needles flashing in the sun (*SP*: 20). In *Smile
Please*, her mother gives her a book as a consolation when one of
her brothers ruins a little play the children were putting on for
the family: the account ends, 'Now I was alone except for books'
(*SP*: 19).

Not only published books, but the oral tradition played an
important part in Rhys's childhood. Her nurse Meta reiterated
the common Caribbean folk concern that too much book-reading
would cause illness or madness, especially threatening fertility in
girls: in this case, Meta threatened that reading would make eyes
drop out. The young Rhys had two story-telling companions,
fictionalised as Meta and the much more pleasant and friendly
Francine (*Smile Please* and *Voyage in the Dark*). Rhys claimed the

emotional impact of Meta's stories was greater: 'Meta had shown me a world of fear and distrust, and I am still in that world' (*SP*: 24).

Equally importantly, Meta connected reading for Rhys with defiance of authority and pursuit of stubborn self-assertion:

Also I was always reading I don't mean at all that I was beaten for reading but only that it added to the general irritating effect. My nurse Meta could not bear the sight of me with a book she could not bear the sight of me anyway but complete with book it was too much. (BEB)

Even in her story of the Geneva Estate, which was owned by members of her mother's family, Rhys mentioned magazines which warned against using makeup and how she still felt she was defying them when she wore it. Rhys's account of her life in *Smile Please* shows how powerfully her experience connected emotional intensity and working with words.

The role of books changes in the section describing Rhys's arrival in England at the age of sixteen: 'In England my love and longing for books completely left me. I never felt the least desire to read anything, not even a newspaper . . .' (*SP*: 90). There was only one book she remembered *Forest Lovers*, a popular romance.[32] The degree of alienation from print here reveals how seriously a first experience of England depressed her. England would continue to be a source of serious conflict: in a draft manuscript 'Essay on England' (UTC), Rhys declares herself very badly educated, but nevertheless admits to avid reading: 'All the books I read were English books and all the thoughts that were given me were English thoughts, with very few exceptions' (p. 1). Her child's sense of social hierarchy and anxiety was shaped by novels about 'ladies and gentlemen'.

Variant versions exist of what she remembered as books in her childhood home, mentioned both in *Smile Please* and an untitled manuscript 'It had always been like that . . .' (UTC). Despite her clear, openly expressed ambivalence about England, Rhys lists major and minor English texts she remembers seeing at home: mythology sent by her 'Irish Granny', the Bible, Milton, Byron, Crabbe, Cowper, Swift, Defoe, Bunyan, Stevenson. She would say to Plante, during the period of working on *Smile Please*, that she had never read Balzac, Proust, Fielding, Trollope, George

Eliot, James, Conrad, Joyce.[33] She said she failed to enjoy Austen
but had read Dickens, the English Romantic poets and Shakespeare as well as enjoying some melodrama in her youth and
thrillers throughout her life (*SP*: 45). That she was extensively
self-educated is clear: that she was as badly educated as she sometimes suggested is doubtful, given her evidently quick mind and
willingness to read. When she was still an impressionable young
woman, Ford Madox Ford set her to read French literature, beginning a life-long pleasure and a life-long influence.

Rhys's strong sense of colour (see chapter 4) was applied to her
conception of books. In *Smile Please* Rhys includes the detail of
loving the colours of the books 'Irish Granny' sent, 'the red, the
blue, the green, the yellow' (*SP*: 20), a detail which connects with
the narrative of the 'red, blue, green, yellow' quill pens she bought
on the day she began to write the diaries which would one day
contribute draft material to *Voyage in the Dark* (*SP*: 103). This relation of primary, jewel colours to books and writing situates those
colours as positives in Rhys's personal palette.

Rhys grew up in a colonial culture where books were assumed
to be written overseas, in England, and where women, especially
at that time women of African descent, might be excellent story-
tellers, but not writers. Yet she has become, along with a few
other writers, such as her friends Eliot Bliss (*Luminous Isle*, first
published 1934) and Phyllis Allfrey (*The Orchid House*, first published 1953), an ancestor of contemporary Caribbean women
writers. No doubt living in France, especially Paris, and in England, where the profession of writing was well established, was
a help, as it was to other Caribbean writers who left the region
in later generations.[34] But Rhys wrote plays as a child, 'nearly
always dramatisations of the fairy stories I loved so much' ('Then
came the time . . .', UTC). Poetry became a sustained source of
comfort and verbal play early in adolescence. *Quartet*, Rhys's first
novel, was first written as a play.[35] But it was only fiction to which
she gave the dedicated willingness to draft and redraft until her
voice became clear, though she incorporated both dramatic and
poetic elements into her fictional technique: she never fully
expressed whether she understood that her poetry was inferior to
her fiction because she generally did not work professionally at

it.[36] The account in *Smile Please* of the enormously traumatic ending of her first serious affair opens with a very short poem she wrote: 'I didn't know / I didn't know / I didn't know' (*SP*: 92), suggesting that writing poetry had, like her first diaries, a therapeutic rather than a professional purpose. She made a strong assertion in what seems to be a rare directly personal comment in the Orange Exercise Book: 'As I was saying I dont give a dam (sic) for the novel. Only to make money the novel is / What I like is Poetry what I really like: you know some poetry my hands go quite cold when I read it.' She loved French poetry and copied it out.

If poetry was her love and her amateur writing project, fiction was her means to earn a living. But Rhys expressed contradictory views on writing for money: she said in 1949 that she was '*dragged* into writing by a series of coincidences . . . need for money' (*L*: 65) and in 1959 that she could only write for love (*L*: 171). But then Rhys often expressed contradictory views: this capacity no doubt helped her create dramatic, conflicting voices so well. In the end, writing helped her endure a good deal:

My dear, I had a horrible war . . . we got back to London in time for the V bombs and all. My daughter, Maryvonne, joined the Resistance in Holland (at 14) & except that she'd been in trouble with the Germans I heard no more until 1945.
Then Leslie died.
Well all those years are gone. I try to forget them . . .
I remember Great is Truth.
Oh yes. I used to write it up with lipstick all over the place.
What a tiresome creature I was, & still am. But if I can do this book it wont matter so much will it? (Letter to Eliot Bliss, 13 October 1947)

Rhys thought of writing at the end of her life as an autonomous and irresistible power: as David Plante reported, 'My books aren't important . . . Writing is' (1984: 57) and 'You see, I'm a pen. I'm nothing but a pen . . . You're picked up like a pen, and when you're used up you're thrown away, ruthlessly, and someone else is picked up' (*SP*: 31). She conceived of writing as a 'huge lake' fed by 'great rivers' like Tolstoy or 'trickles' like Jean Rhys (Plante 1984: 22). Like many writers, she established a legend of her beginnings as a writer (*Smile Please*) and starts with the story of a walk in London in late autumn, when the last dead leaves on the trees look like birds: Rhys thought like a poet does, in images. Here, seeing a stationer's shop with brightly coloured quill pens displayed in the window, she thinks they will cheer up an ugly table in her newly rented room. After buying a dozen and some exercise books, her favourite nibs, ink and an inkstand, to decorate her table, she experiences a kind of catharsis:

... after supper that night – as usual a glass of milk and some bread and cheese – ... it happened. My fingers tingled, and the palms of my hands. I pulled up a chair to the table, opened an exercise book, and wrote *This is my Diary*. But it wasn't a diary. I remembered everything that had happened to me in the last year and a half. I remembered what he'd said, what I'd felt. I wrote on until late into the night, till I was so tired I couldn't go on, and I fell into bed and slept. (*SP*: 104)

The next day, she continues, after the landlady asks her not to walk up and down crying and laughing late at night and disturbing the tenant below. She fills three and a half of the exercise books, ending with a bitter sentence, 'Oh, God, I'm only twenty and I'll have to go on living and living and living' (*SP*: 105). Then she puts the exercise books in the bottom of her suitcase, under her underclothes. They stay with her through moves for seven years without being reread, the surest sign that at this time she was not a professional writer but an amateur diarist using writing as therapy. But the important elements in this story are that the writing seems to be signalled by a physical sensation which almost suggests possession, and is something which happens to Rhys as opposed to something she absolutely controls. It is evidently a catharsis and results in a rough draft (one which we know from other evidence contributed to *Voyage in the Dark* years later). It leads her into anti-social behaviour and isolation and distracts her from eating and sleeping. Rhys's papers and letters contain several versions of this story of emotional catharsis through writing, which would eventually be followed by her professional writer's care over reworking a rough autobiographical draft into polished final form. Ironically, this story of the beginnings of serious writing comes in the part of *Smile Please* which Rhys did not finish: it is interesting to speculate whether she would have cut more out of this before letting it go.[37]

Nora Gaines, editor of the *Jean Rhys Review*, has drawn my attention to the similarity between Colette's narrative of her writing beginnings in *Mes Apprentissages* (1936; 1973) which is quoted in Colette's preface to her Claudine novels, and Rhys's narrative.[38] Colette finds school exercise books in a stationer's and buys them, giving her fingers 'a kind of itch' for writing lines, in the sense of school exercises or punishments. After finishing some work which the notorious Willy rejects, she puts the exercise books away for two years 'At the bottom of a drawer' (1987: Preface n.p.). Rhys may have kept the Colette text near her because in the Rhys papers there is a copied out paragraph from *Mes Apprentissages* with a note explaining it was very helpful.[39] It is very likely that familiarity with the Colette passage informs Rhys's story of writing origins, but Rhys's account is most interesting for its reflection of what became her essential mode of work, from autobiographical confession to rough fictional draft to tight editing through version after version until the stylistic identity of the piece satisfied her.

Rhys's statements that she only knew her writing was true 'Not really true as fact. But true as writing' (Plante 1984: 31) and that 'I think and think for a sentence, and every sentence I think for is wrong, I know it. Then, all at once, the illuminating sentence comes to me. Everything clicks into place' (Plante 1984: 30) are important here: what she composed as her official history of her writing life would not have to attend to detail but rather be written in such a way that it revealed the inner contours of remembered experience. The final shape erases the clutter of actual sequential events and cuts them down to the bone to expose an underlying structure. It also conveniently omits extraneous and surface details which might have been too personal or confessional. Rhys constructed *Smile Please* the way she constructed all of her texts: patiently cutting, reshaping, ordering and balancing until the satisfactory shape is finally achieved. Sometimes, it is clear she overly cut, especially in the composition of *Smile Please*, but mostly the evidence of her good judgement lies in the quality of her finished texts.

Evidence of Rhys's working methods can be seen by examining multiple drafts which exist for several of her short pieces of fiction. It is also very evident when we examine the process which turned the rough drafts of the Exercise Books[40] or of stories into final published form. In this Rhys is a writer's writer: it is a pleasure to study her techniques as much as to read her finished texts.

The effect of such spare, emotionally taut writing as Rhys's mature style favoured is seen in the extraordinarily moving piece called 'From a Diary: At the Ropemaker's Arms' (*SP*: 129–41). This has some of the same legendary elements as the story of the first writing episode. Rhys is alone, in this case after her third husband's incarceration in prison for fraud. It is a time of serious emotional trauma and the writing again takes place in a rented room which is unfamiliar. It is again a diary. Angier thinks this piece so important that without it Rhys could not have written *Wide Sargasso Sea*, because it 'put her back in touch with the deepest source of her art – the lucid honesty and self-understanding which drink drowned and degraded' (1990: 460).

It is also clear however that Rhys needed alcohol to carry her beyond merciful forgetting and sane self-protection into first draft intensities which her professional writer self then took and reshaped and refined. She wrote to Selma Vaz Dias in 1959 that her struggles to finish the first draft of 'Mrs Rochester', later *Wide Sargasso Sea*, had to be fuelled with 'the help of very bad drink. One day drunk, two days hangover regular as clockwork' (*L*: 159). The intensity of frightening and immobilising feelings which the writing process could release as essential raw material is chillingly recorded in the first few lines of the Black Exercise Book, an arresting rough fictional draft which includes signature initials which were Jean Rhys's own original name: 'In bitterness & loneliness so complete . . . My heart is all . . . in my throat & tasting bitter . . . Lord save me I perish – Somebody had chalked on the wall – Lord save me I perish and underneath SOS SOS SOS signed GEW . . . Smith thought feel as I feel I'm not alone.'

There is a stunning distance between the writer of Rhys's first drafts, often highly emotional, fragmentary, cryptic as well as vivid and emotionally precise, and the meticulous and canny last editor she was, even, when the chance arose, sternly reviewing previously published work when republished.[41] 'From a Diary', the very title using Rhys's oldest and most instinctive writing format and suggesting revelatory material, begins with a direct instruction to herself to write everything down directly, no revisions, 'no second thoughts' and 'no tools of my trade', including drink, allowed. In the mock trial which follows, the Rhys persona attempts to refuse a question on the grounds that she 'cannot say it', she does not 'have the words' (*SP*: 131). But after a good deal more trenchant self-analysis, she comes to this conclusion:

I must write. If I stop writing my life will have been an abject failure to myself. It is that already to other people. I will not have earned death . . . But I have not written for so long that all I can force myself to do is to write, to write. I must trust that out of that will come the pattern, the clue that can be followed. (*SP*: 133)

The last line in this section is a finely ironical piece of advice from the interrogator 'be damned careful not to leave this book about' (*SP*: 133). The book, then, is a difficult and contradictory passage, a kind of necessary purgatory or cleansing, but with the power to reveal too much.

It was through Diana Athill's careful and loving editing that this extraordinary piece of writing was published in *Smile Please* after Rhys's death: not only does Athill give details of Rhys's desire to have absolutely every syllable fine-finished before letting a manuscript go, but she makes clear that the second half of *Smile Please* in which 'From a Diary' appears consists of what Rhys would have called drafts (*SP*: 5–6).

A typed manuscript fragment preserved in Tulsa, quoted in full below, has the date 14–9–38 and adds another detail to Rhys's almost metaphysical story of writing:

I have typed out all the stuff I wrote when I was drunk. I crumpled the pages up and threw them into the dustbin. But one escaped through the railings and down the steps, rolling along like a snowball, a butterfly, a dead leaf. I went [*down* deleted] after it, smoothed it out and read in a strange handwriting: ――――

David Plante records Rhys asserting that she had no imagination, in the sense that she wrote out of her own experience, but the imagined life she created is evident, especially in *Wide Sargasso Sea*. As Veronica Gregg points out, Rhys ended this assertion with 'the invention is in the writing' (1995: 53). Rhys's explanation that when she was trying to create the Caribbean of 1840, for *Wide Sargasso Sea*, it was '*nothing to do with me. It is imagination*' (*L*: 162), however denies her customary disclaimer of imaginative skill. Rhys was however perhaps trying to explain that in this case her life was not the only major source of fictional raw material, for she was revisioning another fiction, Charlotte Brontë's *Jane Eyre*. Brontë's novel appeared in 1847; slavery ended in the Caribbean in 1833: the two dates must have connected in Rhys's imagination.

The most important of Rhys's cultural placements is that of writing itself, and in that culture, the Caribbean was the original formative space. In her maturity, she belonged to a writerly culture, one which she fashioned for herself, rather than a school or community of writers. In many ways she belonged nowhere else, feeling different and alone within her family, instinctively at war with much of the tenets of the small, embattled white Anglican community in Dominica into which she was born and despite her mentor Ford Madox Ford's attempts in 1924 to introduce her to the Parisian literary set, a loner there. In England, where she lived before she became a writer and also for most of her life afterwards, she was thought to be dead during the long break between *Good Morning, Midnight* (1939) and its dramatisation by actress Selma Vaz Dias in 1949, so reclusive had she become.[42] It was as if she died to the world when she didn't write, and came alive again only as a writer. It is therefore interesting that Rhys's protagonists mostly do not write, though their insistence, after *Voyage in the Dark* (1934), on telling their stories does make them story-tellers. Sasha, in *Good Morning, Midnight*, does a little ghost-writing but is not the fully professional writer Rhys was herself.

Gregg comments on *Smile Please*: 'The reader, seeking a mimetic representation of the essential Jean Rhys, is deceived, comes away empty-handed' (1995: 71). Yet perhaps this heavily edited, no doubt largely fictional legend of Rhys is in fact the essential Rhys, whilst not the essential Gwen Williams, Ella Gray, Ella Lenglet or Ella Hamer, in the sense that what Rhys chose to remember, to construct textually as her life, was only the story of her writing.

Rhys's attitude to race, class and nationality was also extremely complex, to judge from her published and unpublished comments: 'As far as I know I am white . . .' (letter to Francis Wyndham, *L*:

172). She was sometimes markedly contradictory about her relation to black and white racial identities in Dominica:

Maybe I do have black blood in me. I think my great-grandmother
was coloured, the Cuban. She was supposed to be a Vatican countess.
I think she was coloured. Where else would I get my love for pretty
clothes? And oh how I envied them, in their clothes, dancing in the
street. But what have they done to Dominica? What? It's all gone.
I don't ever want to go back. (Jean Rhys as written by David Plante
1984: 17)

She remembered having strong sympathies for the underprivil-
eged. But she had strong contradictions there as well: 'When I
was a little girl I was always saying, "That's not fair, that's not
fair," and I was known as socialist Gwen. I was on the side of the
Negroes, the workers. Now I say, "It's not fair, it's not fair",
about the other side, because I think they *aren't* treated fairly'
(Jean Rhys as written by David Plante 1984: 50).

Her conception of her national status was equally complicated.
She talked about that in the context of writing itself, a transnational
condition:

I have not met other writers often. A few in Paris. Ford of course. Even
fewer in England. That does not matter at all, for all of a writer that
matters is in the book or books . . . It was Jack, who is a writer, who told
me that my hatred of England was thwarted love. I said disappointed
love maybe. (*SP*: 136)

It was out of her love of writing, and her shrewdness about
what good writing might be, that she also noticed the advent of
West Indian literature:

I am very sold on the poems of a man called Derek Walcott (I think)
from St Lucia coloured I believe or a negro. Read some & was delighted.
Cape has brought out a new lot, *In a Green Night* which I'm trying to get
hold of . . . Do you know I believe the West Indies may produce artists
and poets – the climate, atmosphere & mixture of races all exactly what
is wanted. (Letter to Eliot Bliss, August 1962)

In the end, she believed in cultural relativism, although she
would not have called it that: 'What you see depends upon what
you are' (OEB). I do not mean to infer that Rhys was frivolous
about her views on race, class and nation (also gender, discussed

in chapter 4, and religion, discussed in chapter 6), or double-
dealing in her protestations. Rather that she did play on two
teams in every case: she was born white, upper-class and Dominican; she became effectively working class for a formative period
and poor thereafter, and English as far as the literary world was
concerned. In Paris, in the 1920s, she moved from being a penniless mother with a husband in prison to promising writer and
protégé of the powerful writer, editor and cultural baron Ford
Madox Ford. Class and money are not quite the same thing,
especially in England, but in terms of the England and the France
she encountered, lack of money as well as her West Indian accent
kept her out of the middle class. As she said wryly of herself, 'as
a well trained social animal I'm certainly not the goods' (*L*: 30),
thus denying in one sentence the whole effort her elite white
culture in Dominica made to acculturate her creative, anarchic
spirit to their racial and class privilege and their construction of
obedient female.

When Rhys had to leave the Academy of Dramatic Arts
because her accent was considered inadequate, this was in effect
a rejection of her on a class basis by the serious English artistic
world (Angier 1990: 49–50). Talented and attractive lower-class
English girls had few options for a career, but they had the stage
or they could let their beauty be objectified by artists as a mute
female body, or model clothes. Jean Rhys, known in England
and on stage as Ella Gray, shared this world. Her first serious
love, Lancelot Smith, was clearly incapable of a fully committed
relationship with any woman, but no doubt he constructed her as
West Indian and a chorus girl, and therefore out of the question
as candidate for wife in his terms and his culture. Rhys's political
response to class seems to have been in effect anarchist, for she was
most comfortable living outside the conventions of any society.
She was conflicted about both the working and middle classes.
She began by feeling both alienated from and comfortable with
her privilege and she was to live through hard times and know
what it was to have to ask for financial help:

Peggy if you know of a cheap room, & by cheap I mean *cheap* about
30/- I'd be saved. I've sheets and things. Also if one of your pals could
say I was their companion or maid or something I'd be more saved still.

I could live cheaply in this cheap room and write . . . (Letter to Peggy Kirkaldy, 28 May 1950)

Both rejection of and desire for security were inextricably bound up in Rhys's identity. She knew from experience what it cost to be a social outlaw: 'It was a long time before I learnt that when you are safe you are very rarely free. That when you are free you are very rarely safe' (MS fragment: 'I think I fell in love with words', UTC).

She understood early the ways in which money rules the world. In Europe, her first husband Jean Lenglet offered a comfortable, interesting life which made her happy, but this ended in their flight and eventually his arrest. Then Paris saw a young woman with a child, without financial support or apparent close family, living on the very edge of respectable bohemian society.

Rhys lived for years in her mature life with financial insecurity but she still had the title of writer, which secured her to the professional and artistic world of England: she never looked for sustained work of any kind which would secure her some measure of steady financial support over a long period, not even the hack work which supports many full-time writers in lean periods. A writer, particularly a bohemian writer, would be considered déclassé in the context of the English class system in Rhys's day, so though her income mostly kept her in poverty, her literary work raised her status. There is an interesting parallel here with the white Creole character Lilla, in Robert Antoni's novel *Blessed Is the Fruit* (1997), who continues to live in her crumbling house, without visible means of support, maintaining her outward self-construction as a white lady, complete with a servant, when there is clearly no way this is a reasonable reflection of the truth. Rhys strongly identified with the ways in which poor black West Indians were constructed in English culture in the 1950s when she created Selina in 'Let Them Call It Jazz' (first published 1962).

The subversive identity of the artist was familiar to her not only in herself but in her husband Jean Lenglet. He was a brave Resistance fighter during the Second World War and inspired his daughter to be the same, both at great personal risk: he barely survived brutal treatment in a concentration camp (Angier 1990:

436–7). But in his trading of money and goods after the First World War he cut corners which led to his arrest, separation from his wife and child and ultimately cost him marriage to Rhys. He was equally careless about immigration and nationality paperwork (Angier 1990: chapter 4), which meant Rhys suffered statelessness: 'Once Jean had no nationality (I mean my first husband) so of course I had none . . . I will never forget the expression on the British official's face when I presented a *Japanese* laissezpasser instead of a passport' (letter to Diana Athill, 7 February 1967).

England, and to a lesser extent France, were both difficult for Rhys but also gave her literary success. Both Paris and memory of Dominica inspired her writing (*L*: 171). In a period informed by high nationalism and two world wars, Rhys belonged to no single national identity and began to forge a textuality which speaks to that condition, most poignantly in the description of Sasha, in *Good Morning, Midnight*, as having 'no pride, no name, no face, no country' (*GM, M*: 44). In this, she anticipates the extensive migrations of the later twentieth century which have so much intensified a general experience of plural national identity and in which Caribbean people figure very importantly.

Rhys made many hostile statements in her published and unpublished writing about the English and Anglo-Saxons. She rarely mentions Britain or the Celts in her surviving texts, but there is no doubt she constructed herself as Celtic in the context of British society.[43] The Celts, and most especially the Welsh, have historically been the colonised people of Britain. This was complicated by the deculturation of the entire working class, Celt and non-Celt alike, across the country in urban centres during the Industrial Revolution. Marx worked on *Das Kapital* in the British Museum Reading Room, shocked by the social conditions in London, the first culture to exhibit the human cost of technological advancement. Rhys's father was of course not working class and his feeling of tension with his own father made his Welsh connection more tenuous.[44] In *Smile Please* Rhys also refers to 'Irish Granny', who was born Sophia Potts (Angier 1990: 6).

It was her father's Welsh and her mother's Lockhart Scottish ancestry which meant Gwen Williams could choose to consider herself a colonised Celt rather than a colonising Anglo-Saxon,

Anglo-Saxon being Jean Rhys's most frequent hostile textual definition of the British. Welsh people are often dark-haired and dark-eyed, testament to their probable Phoenician ancestry. But her fair skin, her blue eyes and her name Gwendoline pointed to a more stereotypical identity within Caribbean culture. She did not know England or the English as a child except through representations in books and her society: the pervasive notion of the beautiful English woman was fair-skinned and blue-eyed.

She was however clear about the confluence of cultural identities which fed into her Caribbean childhood: 'I'm a bit depressed today so forgive scrawl. It always takes me that way. (I'm only half Creole and haven't any lightness or gaiety to pull me through the black days. Or not much)' (*L:* 108). Even as a Celt, she must have felt that surviving Celtic cultures in the UK were partitioned by centuries of turbulent history and colonisation as well as class and cultural divisions within, and she perhaps had a sense of the divisions symbolised by the very different emotional qualities of her parents, her father Welsh, her mother Creole of Scottish descent: 'As I've been so personal I must end by telling you that I am not a Scot at all. My father was Welsh – very. My mother's family was Creole – what *we* call Creole. My great-grandfather was a Scot' (*L:* 172). She understood how the Welsh, in their own cultural space, have managed to sustain their separate identity. From Pembrokeshire, to her daughter, she wrote in 1953: 'It is astonishing how different they are from the English. They speak mostly Welsh here and their voices are very soft and gentle in English – I do like that. Also the men are very polite to women, make way for them and will do little things to help with the shopping. In short a different race' (*L:* 113).

In her manuscript, 'Essay on England' (UTC), she describes the definitive English geography book which confidently constructed national characteristics and managed to provoke unceasing thought about England, the colonial child's first battle with erasure of self. She assigns the root cause of her hatred of England to the idea that 'the white people should have eveything and the black people nothing, in money' (p. 2), a parallel with Dominican society as she knew it. But the real disappointment in England is that there is dirt, poverty, a greyness about the light and weather and a failure to live up to the fairy-tale promise created by a colonial English education, especially to a romantic white child whose beloved father was from Britain. Similarly, in an untitled manuscript, 'I FEEL so sick . . .', (UTC) she expresses a hostility towards an England of class hierarchy: 'the smug snobs and the prancing prigs and the ones who just aren't anything and they are nearly everybody, and . . . the ghost of a dead place that lives in the trees . . .' (p. 1). England has no 'current of life . . .' (p. 2).

In 'The Bible Is Modern' (UTC), England is the real target: 'it is a great crime to feel intensely about anything in England, because if the average Englishman felt intensely about anything, England as it is could not exist; or, certainly, the ruling class in England could not continue to exist' (p. 2). It is tempting to think that Rhys's real target here was the wealthy, well-educated but emotionally undeveloped Lancelot Smith, whose money shielded him from emotional involvement.

Rhys's protagonists, most evidently Antoinette in *Wide Sargasso Sea*, share a view of England as deadening, grey and emotionally destructive. England is a place of hypocrites, and the English have a 'bloody, bloody sense of humour'. With a West Indian accent, she goes on, 'and stupid, lord, lord' (*SP*: 134). But it remains Rhys's place, the source of those English books which provided an early contribution to her construction of herself as writer. The idea of definitive national origin and affiliation is a source of anxiety for Rhys's protagonists. For Rhys herself nationality was complicated by her exile and her race: also England did not value her Caribbean origins.

For Rhys's women, as perhaps for herself, England is also a place where human emotions, especially those associated with sexuality, are outlawed or repressed; she described sex in a letter of 1949 as a 'strange Anglo-Saxon word' (*L*: 66). Hemond Brown comments that Rhys's attitude to England remained remarkably consistent over her whole writing career: 'For those fifty-odd years, England meant to her everything she despised' (1987: 8). But despite this, she surely demonstrated in her characterisation of working-class English chorus girls and call girls and Rochester (perhaps informed by her important attachments to Lancelot Grey, Hugh Smith, Leslie Tilden Smith and Max Hamer, all upper- or middle-class Englishmen), that the poor Englishwoman and even the colonising, socially secure Englishman have their own areas of serious emotional damage. She may have blown off steam sometimes, but in her fiction she took pains to be fair to the country which had both given her sustained literary identity and denied her dignity.

Rhys's racial attitudes, as well as her sense of class and nation, clearly were partially transmitted by her white Creole childhood. But the ways in which she complicated them might well have been intensified by her difficult relationship with her mother, who finally gave up trying to change her daughter's defiant sympathies 'Re black people', though:

> I was always told that I was (a) showing off (b) mad or (c) a liar or all three. I had no answer except Dont care what you think dont care what you say. But I never stand much . . . and the end of my Liberty speeches was usually that I wept & they shouted. (BEB)

That Rhys at times separated herself from white Creole society is shown in her remark a little earlier in the same section, 'The white people in the West Indies are good and down. Serve them right too –' (BEB). What severs Rhys's account of Gwen Williams in *Smile Please* from the smugness of Roseau's white society is her willingness to admit to envy and jealousy of the black community, to expose the normally furtive underpinning of white racist supremacy as the need to define the self primarily as 'not the Other'. Her construction of black society was part of a private fantasy: since she felt as she grew older often repressed or alienated at home, hostile to her mother's severe physical punishments of her and to her apparent preference for other children over Rhys, as well as Rhys's memory that her mother once said she preferred black babies to white babies (*SP*: 33), she sometimes longed to cross over, making of the black community an image of all she felt she lacked. This was only possible of course because she lived as the face at the window, or more precisely behind the jalousies of the family's house on Cork Street, past which African-Catholic festivals and processions slowly moved. Her closest connections with the black community were those few servants who were willing to share their world with her.

She thought black society was warmer and more colourful than
white, and less bound by conventions, like the necessity to get
married (*SP*: 40). Planters discouraged marriage among their black
slaves, as this cemented family units and went against their attitude
that slaves were economic units. Offering their Christian blessing
on unions might have been therefore inconvenient for planter
self-interest (Walvin 1993: 210ff). Rhys understood that whites
were hated, even experienced it personally, as she writes in *Smile
Please* (p. 39), at her convent school and implicitly in her tense
relationship with her black nurse Meta (*SP*: 22–4). Veronica Gregg
links Rhys's self-conflicts about racial identity to general white
colonial self-constructions (1995: 64ff) and images of the Other.
She argues that Rhys makes Meta, for example, the 'bad nigger/
nurse/storyteller' and Francine the 'good nigger/nurse/storyteller',
the good native and the bad native being familiar constructions
of white racist ideology world-wide. But Rhys marks both women
as fundamentally influential in her cultural development: she was
so often engaged with both elements in a binary split.

She struggled to engage with her racial identity, sometimes
falling into white racial and class conventions, sometimes challenging them by trying to appropriate, in her writing voice, a black
identity. Selina in 'Let Them Call It Jazz', a black working-class
woman, has Rhys's own experience of being arrested and confined in Holloway prison for disorderly conduct. This is problematic: Rhys sought in Selina to express her own white English and
female underclass identity, choosing a black character's voice either
to mask her own or because being poor white Creole in England
was, to her, like being poor and black in Dominica – marginalised,
and therefore, if possessing of any spirit, hostile to established
authority and social hierarchy. As John W. Cell says in his study
of white supremacy in the American South and South Africa,
race is a relationship, not a fixed identity (1982). In another example
of white female appropriation of black female identity, Anna, in
*Voyage in the Dark*, thinks of a mulatto house servant called Maillotte
Boyd as she lies in bed with her seductive but inaccessible lover
Walter (*VITD*: 53, 56). She clearly associates Maillotte Boyd with
herself. Rhys herself directly assumed a voice as a black person only

once that we know of in her extant manuscripts and notebooks (draft essay 'The Bible Is Modern'): 'what is difficult for us black people to understand . . .'

Both Rhys's lapses into racism and her occasional appropriation of black identity for herself or her white characters are obviously problematic: they both seem to have begun in the self-rejection which Rhys reveals in *Smile Please*:

I was fair with a pale skin and huge staring eyes of no particular colour. My brothers and sisters all had brown eyes and hair; why was I singled out to be the only fair one, to be called Gwendolen, which means white in Welsh I was told? (*SP*: 14)

The opening of *Smile Please* deals with the child Rhys mourning an even younger self caught in a framed photograph: 'It was the first time I was aware of time, change and the longing for the past' (*SP*: 14). This is an unusual feeling for a child of nine: the child has realised and rejected her physical and racial appearance and longs for a previous time. Rhys chose as mature writer to find the core of her identity in the very skin colour which marked her in Dominica as member of the small, embattled caste of colonial whites. It is the Catch-22 of being white and morally aware of white history: being white cannot be denied or embraced without damaging consequences.

Rhys told an unnerving story of two dolls arriving from England, a present from 'Irish Granny' (*SP*: 30ff). One was dark and one was fair: Gwen Williams wanted the dark one but her mother told her to let her little sister have it. So she took the fair one out into the shadow of the big mango tree and smashed its face in with a rock. Though she remembered 'the satisfaction of being wicked' (*SP*: 30), as she narrated this story, in old age, she remembered clearly that the action seemed right and appropriate for her.

What her story signifies is the sense of self-rejection and outsider status within her own family circle which was fed perhaps both by her own subversive reaction to restrictive domestic conventions and her internalisation of the ways colonial whites were seen by others. She did not reach out to preserve and protect white supremacy, though she had perhaps deeply absorbed her mother's most characteristic ambivalent posture of generous sympathy for the poor black community and yet strictly maintained distance from them.

But self-rejection has to involve anger: to David Plante, often with the help of alcohol, Rhys offered both resentful and patronising accounts of the black community in Dominica. She refers here to the black community generally as 'they' or 'them' and is frightened by the power shift in Dominica. Whereas once, in her youth, she was 'on their side', she bursts out that 'They're taking over' (Plante 1984: 42). Her account of a Nigerian kissing her once in a bar leads to a thorough (and therefore racist) generalisation, 'I understand why they are attractive. It goes very deep' (Plante 1984: 22).

There is a fair amount of unreconstructed white colonialism in some of her statements, though given that these remarks were made by an elderly, drunk, frail Rhys to David Plante, who delivers them to us, and given her awareness of race and class, they often sound parodic, the very cliché of white colonial patronage and self-deception, 'We didn't treat them badly'; 'I'll never, never forget the dignity of that black man walking through the yard with his sixpence and the loaf of bread under his arm' (Plante 1984: 22, 21).

Rhys's comments on race make it clear that she was acutely conscious of being white: she remained so all her life. This in itself is a Caribbean or post-colonial white experience. White people living in predominantly white communities to this day too often feel little pressure to engage deeply with white racial history. For Rhys racial difference factored into painful childhood relationships at times. In *Smile Please*, Meta is 'very black and always, I thought, in a bad temper' (*SP*: 22). The young Rhys was terrified of this woman, 'who talked so much about zombies, soucriants and loups-garous', and also taught the child 'to fear cockroaches hysterically' (*SP*: 23). Meta's frustrations, no doubt, at being forbidden to discipline the rebellious child in the traditional West Indian way caused her to look for more insidious ways to punish. By telling stories which came out of her own African-centred oral tradition, she both made the young girl afraid and reminded her of her exclusion from the African world of the spirit. From time to time, Meta and Gwen Williams came to more direct forms of conflict:

She was forbidden to slap me and she never did but she got her own back by taking me by the shoulders and shaking me violently. Hair flying, while I still had any breath to speak I would yell 'Black Devil, Black Devil, Black Devil!' . . . Meta had shown me a world of fear and distrust, and I am still in that world. (*SP*: 24)

Suspecting that the subtext of Meta's hostility derived from race, the child hurled it back at her (Antoinette speaks in the same terms to Christophine in *Wide Sargasso Sea*). Race was already a powerful discourse. In 'Black/White' (*Smile Please*) Rhys's parents talk about 'the Riot', clearly much the same conversation as Annette, Aunt Cora and Mr Mason have in *Wide Sargasso Sea*. Mr Mason says of the black community, 'They are children – they wouldn't hurt a fly.' Aunt Cora makes her famous answer: 'Unhappily children do hurt flies' (*WSS*: 35). In *Smile Please*, Rhys's father says 'They're perfectly harmless' and her mother replies 'That's what you think' (*SP*: 37). Rhys worked from her own experience to text; then from text to experience.

It is this reading of black individuals only by a generally predictable stereotype which Rhys exposes in *Wide Sargasso Sea* as not only racist but evidently, in the sense that it blinds against elementary precautions, fundamentally against white self-interest. Mr Mason insists on speaking about importing labour to replace reluctant plantation workers in front of the house servants simply because he cannot believe he is risking anything by so doing. Even the imperial apologist for slavery, Mrs Carmichael, included more astute observations in her memoir of the Caribbean (1833). But she, too, like many Caribbean Creoles and English colonists, assumed a class- (and in effect, race) based hierarchy to be essential to her survival: 'The comfort of a family every one knows to depend greatly on servants' (1833, vol. 1: 20), an attitude Rhys's mother, with other white middle-class women in Roseau, might have shared.

There is also a good deal of reference in Rhys's texts to anti-white hostility. In *Smile Please*, it is a beautiful coloured girl, i.e. of mixed race, who rejects Rhys's overtures of friendship at school with a stare of 'impersonal, implacable hatred' (*SP*: 39). In *Wide*

*Sargasso Sea*, it is two children, an albino boy and a dark girl, who make Antoinette feel their hatred and from whom she is rescued by her mixed-race cousin Sandi.

In the Caribbean, complex racial narratives are the most powerful signifiers, although class inceasingly reverberates now. In England, in Rhys's lifetime, it was the class narrative which primarily constructed identity, though Rhys clearly writes the importance of race as a formative self-construction from her Dominican childhood. She sometimes sees race and class as equally important even in England, as in the case of Selina, who carries Rhys's own outlaw status during an important period of her life. In the two explicitly Caribbean novels, *Voyage in the Dark* and *Wide Sargasso Sea*, race is evidently a major source of identity. In *After Leaving Mr MacKenzie* (1931; 1990), it is a subtext: Julia's mother is Brazilian. Throughout Rhys's writing, race, class and nation signify as the major source of a female protagonist's placement in social hierarchy. Rhys was both racist and anti-racist, both hostile and sentimental, both patronising and egalitarian, reflecting the complex journey she made herself. It was always the repression of responsiveness which angered her most: she wrote of Dominica that it was extraordinary that white people there could not see its beauty. She conceptualised Dominica as an independent entity which was entitled to make a response to this violation of cosmic justice:

It's strange growing up in a very beautiful place and seeing that it is beautiful. It was alive. I was sure of it. Behind the bright colours the softness, the hills like clouds and the clouds like fantastic hills. There was something austere, sad, lost, all these things I wanted to identify myself with, to lose myself in it. (But it turned its head away, indifferent, and that broke my heart.)

The earth was like a magnet which pulled me and sometimes I came near it, this identification or annihilation that I longed for. (*SP*: 66–7)[45]

There is an important subtext here as well, which can be teased out by comparing Rhys's manuscript drafts. In her accusation in the manuscript fragment 'I FEEL so sick' she accuses England of having no current of life, because the 'wildness is gone' (p. 2). The wildness signifies resistance to control, to the 'suffocating ugliness' of urban living (p. 2), to 'the dreadful suburb' which

Rhys says white people in Dominica yearn for ('New Story', UTC, p. 1).

That the two teams hardly spoke to each other perhaps explains why Rhys could switch sides with apparently no conflict: she was at least brutally honest about the warring cultural identities which she experienced. In *Wide Sargasso Sea*, she dramatised these in the impossible relationship between Rochester, exiled from family, but English, white and male, and Antoinette, Creole and Caribbean and female. Once again, Rhys's unwillingness to take a single, linear position on major political issues marks a sensibility able to understand political and social currents of history with remarkable and uncomfortable honesty: she was entirely unable to be ideological, and fully determined to observe unpredictable contradictions of human behaviour; interesting details of consistent failure to live up to heroic ideals. She was herself sustainedly contradictory: she loved and hated both England and the West Indies; she both loved and hated money and privilege; she both loved and hated what black and white signified to her as racial identities.

CHAPTER 2

# *Registering protest:*
# The Left Bank *and* Quartet

I think French books helped me an awful lot . . . They had
clarity. Ford insisted – if you weren't sure of a paragraph or
statement, translate it into another language. And if it looks
utterly silly, get rid of it. Anglo-Saxon is rather messy, don't
you think?

(Jean Rhys to Mary Cantwell, Interview (1974) 1990: 24)

Cut it? Thats nearly always the answer. Cut bits of it
[CUT] . . . Ive looked up self-pity in my French dictionary &
cant find it. Only 'amourpropre' or 'egoism' [sic]. It can be
the start of a lot of things but can be tiresome too I know.
Perhaps there's too much in 'Postures'. That book could be
improved by cutting.

(Letter to Diana Atwell, 1 December 1966)

Rhys made an impressively swift transition from an amateur
writer of therapeutic diaries, with the instinct to use writing to
erase painful memories, to a professional and impressive writer
who was reviewed in powerful literary publications: a process
which took only three years. Furthermore, she reworked what
she learned from Ford, i.e. the prevailing style of European high
modernism and how to be a professional writer, in the light of
her writing instincts and what was important from her West
Indian experience.

A number of factors seem to have contributed to Rhys's decision
to attempt a writing path: her early instinct to write therapeut-
ically; her association with her first husband, Jean Lenglet, who
was a journalist and fiction writer, ultimately a novelist; and the
need to try to support herself and her child.[1] Rhys had by 1924,
the year she met Ford Madox Ford, some very rough manuscripts:

36

the notebooks in which she had recorded her relationship with Smith, and diary notes of her life since then. Some of this material eventually became an early draft of a novel, called 'Suzy Tells' by Mrs Adam, a journalist and a writer who befriended Rhys when she tried to sell some of Lenglet's stories she had translated into English. Mrs Adam passed the draft to Ford (Angier 1990: 130).[2]

This manuscript, which Ford titled 'Triple Sec' is described by Angier as 'pretty formless, its grammar and punctuation wild, its expression . . . naive' (1990: 130), though it was considerably more than the original diary Rhys had written in 1914.[3] Mrs Adam of course had somewhat organised the material for showing Ford, making chapters headed mainly though not exclusively by a man's name, reinforcing the impression that the novel was unpublishable by lurid content alone.[4] But 'Triple Sec' has many stylistic features, motifs and themes which reappear in Rhys's mature work, for example, the black velvet dress which the protagonist Suzy wears for the goodbye dinner with her lover Tony. Rhys's protagonists frequently identify a special dress, most often black, as Rhys herself also did.[5] The outlines of the Suzy–Tony relationship, Suzy's experience with Ethel the masseuse and an episode with a callgirl friend in a seedy hotel are reworked in *Voyage in the Dark* (1934), as is the letter which Tony's friend Guy writes to Suzy to explain Tony's desire to end the relationship.[6]

Already in this early attempt at writing fiction, ellipses are characteristic of Rhys's style: she already knew how effective it can be to create a serious hiatus in a text and give the reader just enough to be able to fill in the spaces.[7] This is particularly effective when the reader and the text occupy radically different social identities: as Iser theorises (1978; 1989), 'blanks' in a text provoke a reader to fill them in in order to make sense of the whole text. As a result, the reader supplies missing information out of his or her own location and experience. This may explain why Rhys has been popular with very different readers, in France, in England, in the Caribbean, in the United States.

Rhys's love of poetry is also evident in her use of figurative language to deepen and layer her spare prose: 'Sometimes London looks horrid at night . . . like a great black animal . . . that pounces . . .

and claws you up' ('TS': 24). In Rhys's fiction as a whole, imagery
provides an important connective code. Colour constitutes another
developed symbolic code both in this manuscript and in Rhys's
later texts: 'Such a hat! Alison all over . . . Pink velvet stuff made
like a turban with big white ospreys, or imitation ospreys, I suppose
. . .' ('TS': 37). Rhys's construction of both gender and nationality
is markedly political even in this early text: this is an early example
of her hostility to Englishmen, though the sense of national affiliation shaping character can drift into vehement stereotype: 'she
knows several Germans who are obviously gentlemen and well
bred, a little Dutchman of whom the same might be said, Jews
who ooze money, Americans who aren't bad, etc. – But the
Englishmen! Oh, Lord, they are second rate' ('TS': 47). Physical
detail is important in characterisation (in this Rhys followed Ford):
like Marya in *Quartet*, Suzy has 'slanting eyes', which make her
'strange' to the painter who is appraising her appearance ('TS':
135).[8]

Not only is Suzy in rebellion against conventions of acceptable
femininity but like many Rhys protagonists, she tolerates a degree
of masochism in her relations with men, 'I believe that Carl has
spoilt me so thoroughly that I only appreciate and understand
brutality' ('TS': 169).[9] There is also, as in Rhys's later texts set in
Europe, a subtext of West Indian identity interrelated with sexual
subservience or resistance: Suzy describes her 'price' as estimated
by her dependence on male support, 'My great grandfather paid
much more for a pretty slave' ('TS': 83). She needs a 'slight opera-
tion' (probably an abortion): under the effects of the morphia she
is given she finds herself 'floating to the West Indies – hearing the
palms rustle and the water gurgling over the rocks' ('TS': 195) just
as Anna retreats into memories of the West Indies in a similar
situation in *Voyage in the Dark*. Suzy's cultural identity is clearly
Rhys's, 'West Indian on the one side and Welsh on the other' ('TS':
201). Ford complained Rhys's portrayal of place was minimal in
*The Left Bank*: it is also here.[10]

As in later texts, the problem of representation, especially of
women, manifests as a major theme. Suzy feels a strong response
to the painting of herself which signifies to her a woman she does
not recognise: in *After Leaving Mr MacKenzie* (1931; 1990), Julia

speaks about a disturbing painting of a woman (*ALMM*: 52).
Clothes, makeup or simply disguising the feelings function as protective or deflective masks throughout Rhys's texts. Though the
tone of Suzy's narrative lacks the grimly comical edge which Sasha
demonstrates in *Good Morning, Midnight* (1939), Rhys protects against
the danger of sentimentality by giving her protagonist a strong
sense of wry humour, 'After all this time of saving and saving –
I've got exactly ten pounds. – It's simply laughable' ('TS': 139).
The importance of these details (and therefore of this crucially
important surviving ur-novel), is that Rhys clearly developed many
of what would become her major writing characteristics before
she submitted to Ford's training.

Rhys's writing apprenticeship took place in the midst of a
tangle of intense relationships between herself, her husband Jean
Lenglet, Ford and his companion Stella Bowen in the mid 1920s
in Paris. Since three of them were then or eventually professional
writers and the fourth lived with a writer for years it is not surprising that four books resulted, three novels, Rhys's *Quartet* (1929),
Ford's *When the Wicked Man* (1931) and Lenglet's *Barred* (1932)
(written over his penname of Edouard de Nève and translated
and edited by Rhys), and Bowen's memoir *Drawn from Life* (1941).[11]
In addition, of course *The Left Bank* (1927) was Rhys's graduation
from Ford's tutelage but owed much to his help and to his ability
to place her now excellent work in important literary locations.
What might actually have constituted the complex relationships
between these four will never be known: their interest derives
from the fictional versions which resulted. Rhys's autobiographical version of this period in *Smile Please* reduces Ford's intervention in her career to a couple of paragraphs, and the significance
of the publication of 'Vienne' is omitted. But Ford told her to keep
the exercise books from which 'Triple Sec' is roughly derived,
and not to worry with the novel ('Put It Away', UTC): this was
sound advice and she followed it. Though Ford definitely helped
her to get started as a writer, his *When the Wicked Man*, which
followed the affair, is ironically a very poor novel.[12]

It is worth exploring the connections between Rhys, Lenglet,
Ford and Bowen briefly because, in their hothouse literary and
artistic identities, they contributed greatly to consolidating and

intensifying the role of writing in Rhys's life. The bare bones of the story can be reduced to a few facts: Lenglet was arrested and imprisoned in 1924 and then had to leave France. Rhys, penniless, found shelter in the home of Ford and Bowen, and the resulting brief affair with Ford fatally wounded both her own and Ford's long-term relationships. According to Martien Kappers-den Hollander, *Quartet*, which was Rhys's highly fictional version of the affair and its consequences, caused a great literary scandal, especially in England, as Ford was so famous and many felt Rhys had behaved badly in exploiting the privacy of Bowen and Ford after being helped by them.

Gardiner (1982) comments that Ford is easy to read as an aesthetic mentor: he liked 'vivid and specific detail; clear, almost transparent prose; wry juxtapositions; elliptical dialogue; time shifts; a concern for the *mot juste*; and what Ford called "progression d'effet", a variable and climactic pacing of scenes' (1982: 69), and from Rhys's texts we can see she took his advice in developing many of these qualities. Yet Ford was the shrewd appreciator of literary talent in writers as diverse and original as Lawrence and Joyce, writers utterly unlike himself. He had a rare gift for reading. This is evident in his essay 'The Fox (D. H. Lawrence)' (ed. Killigrew 1971: 309ff), where he describes finding Lawrence's story 'Odour of Chrysanthemums' on his desk, 'the first words of a new author' (1971: 309). Also (as Gardiner (1982) realises) whereas Rhys learned many of the lessons Ford set out for her she rejected other aspects of his advice and set off firmly on her own writing way in *Quartet*.

Part of the development of Rhys's mature style came no doubt through her continual practice in translation. This began with her work on Jean Lenglet's stories, which was how she came to meet Mrs Adam, then continued under Ford's tutelage, and remained important to Rhys as a technique to detect weakness in a draft.[13] The story 'The Chevalier of the Place Blanche' (*Vogue*, 1976), one of the stories Rhys tried to sell to Mrs Adam, was included in Rhys's last short story collection *Sleep It Off Lady* (1976), with the note 'This story is a much adapted translation of one written by Edouard de Nève'. The value of translation and adaptation for a writer is enormous. First of all, language nuances are more appreciated, as are the demands of genre, internal structure and style, when a writer works between languages and works on someone else's imagination and craft in order to make it available to a different language audience. Rhys became, via Ford's agency, a professional translator of a novel, *Perversité*, by Francis Carco (1928), though the publishers accredited it to well-known Ford.[14]

One of the results of their relationship was that she reread fairly recent, important (as defined by Ford) French literature. In his introduction to *The Left Bank*, he comments that reading 'French writers of a recent, but not the most recent, date' was helpful (reprinted in Stang, ed., 1986: 244), because young French people were rejecting their past, which for Ford meant, 'neatness of form' (ibid.). Ford led her to Colette, whose work he set as a translation exercise for her, but though she remained a lifelong admirer of Colette's writing, her own style is quite different, much less evidently sensuous.[15] When Ford tried to make her pay more attention to setting, in the manner of Flaubert, Maupassant or Conrad, she became more rigid about excising it to the extent, Ford says, of 'even such two or three words of descriptive matter as had crept into her work' (Stang, ed., 1986: 245). Ford attributes her preference for Caribbean landscapes to the vivid memories of childhood, but still sounds puzzled. For him, the centre of the world was contained in the very places Rhys neglected to celebrate or critique even when she included an odd detail of street or building: Paris, London, Vienna, the very capitals of European modernism.[16] For her, the centre was the Caribbean, the only setting where, as Ford noted early, topography did matter in her work. Emery (1990) comments that Rhys was similar to other Caribbean writers in finding elements of European modernism useful, only in the service of her own cultural contexts and political affinities.

Such a complex definition of Rhys's modernism was not present when the novel first appeared as *Postures* in England, in 1928: where critics liked it, as with *The Left Bank*, they generally praised its style but did not locate that culturally.[17] Even in 1979, Thomas Staley defined *Quartet* unequivocally as a modernist novel because of 'its spare style, the author's gift for understatement and irony, the careful rendering of the heroine's preoccupations in a hostile, alientating urban environment' (1979: 35, 37), though Hanscombe and Smyers do not mention Rhys in *Writing for Their Lives: the Modernist Woman 1910–1940* (1987).[18] Modernism in the European context is identified with highly self-conscious subjectivity, aesthetic experimentation and often with poetic technique (Eysteinsson 1990). It is often linked to the collapse of idealism and self-confidence in the Europe between the wars. However Rhys's modernist construction of an isolated protagonist, sometimes complexly self-referential, is, as Gregg has pointed out, related to her own particular sense of alienation, 'In the Rhys canon, pastiche and parody represent an inbuilt aesthetic discourse with the literary traditions of Europe and the ideological framework which defines, constricts, and to some extent, distorts her as a woman, as an artist and as a West Indian' (1987: 35).[19]

Also, though Angier quite clearly thinks Ford was the critical factor in making the writer Jean Rhys (1990: 134; 175), the marriage to Jean Lenglet must have deepened the linguistic complexity she had known as a child in Dominica, where French patois and a continuum of English from British to Creole contributed. For several crucial years, whether she was with Lenglet in Holland, Austria or France, Rhys's linguistic world was truly European. She lived and thought as much in French as in English, and her husband wrote and thought in French and Dutch. Lenglet's multilingual identity is evident in the history of *Barred*, written in French, published first in English, via Rhys's translation, then in Dutch as *In de Strik* (1932), and finally in French as *Sous les Verrous* (1933).

Rhys learned in Dominica, as a child, from the political and cultural world of local newspapers that registers of language are highly political. A good part of English colonialism was established by the use of an imperial tone: 'Again the Antilles' (first published 1927; *TAB-L*, 1968; *CSS*, 1987) shows how well Rhys remembered the linguistic skirmishes over power and cultural identity, race and class which went on in the press in Dominica in her childhood. Perhaps her rejection of that imperial tone, in conjunction with Ford's influence and the new, bold styles of modernism she met in Paris, helped turn her towards a style which was clear, direct and unpretentious.

Rhys had a job for a few months with a rich and eccentric American woman as the affair with Ford was winding down, in which she took dictation for a book on reincarnation and home decoration.[20] This was another facet of the professional but impecunious writer's life: working for the rich and untalented as hired help but always practising and honing language skills. This difficult experience however probably ensured she was never interested in taking such a job again.

Rhys's first published piece of fiction was 'Vienne'. The version in *the transatlantic review* (1924) was revised by Rhys for both *The Left Bank* (1927) and *Tigers Are Better-Looking* (1968).[21] But all three versions, though substantially different from one another, are a series of sketches of impressions of time and place. This technique, as Ford was the first to suggest, places all the emphasis on feeling, but it is feeling which is acute and knowing without being explicitly intellectual.[22] Rhys conveys an emotional state through brief textual fragments strung together by ellipses, suggesting the fragility and transitory nature of any emotional state as well as capturing it. Rhys clearly understood however even as early as this that succinctly drawn character is the cornerstone of success in trying to establish a convincing narrative in a short space. Her longest and most complex version of 'Vienne' (*TLB*, 1927) establishes one character after another to anchor the loosely organised narrative.

All three versions of 'Vienne' (the third one, *TAB-L*, 1968, is called 'Vienna'), begin with the same fragments of the narrator's memory, with the elusive nature of past experience, 'Funny how it's slipped away, Vienne. Nothing left but a few snapshots – Not a friend, not a pretty frock – nothing left of Vienna' (1924: 639; *TLB*: 193; *TAB-L*: 188). This is followed by another free-standing impression: 'Hot sun, my black frock, a hat with roses, music, lots of music –' (1924: 639). The effect is of a deftly and quickly drawn picture, a pencil sketch or a water-colour, or indeed a snapshot – which by composition and emphasis draws the essential components out of a crowded scene for the observer. Although Rhys rarely demands historical knowledge of her readers, in 'Vienne', some knowledge of the aftermath of World War I in Europe is helpful. The Japanese were part of the Interallied Commission which oversaw disarmament in Europe, and of course, Jean Lenglet worked for the Japanese delegation for a while as secretary.[23] In her fiction Rhys rarely later engaged with historical events which might require explicit contextual explanation for the reader.[24]

Since she is so economical, each word has to be telling in this almost abstract mode of telling a story. When, for example, the narrator is trying to imagine the Geisha after Colonel Ishima has described them as 'war material' who served their country well, she thinks of 'big blond Russian officers and slant-eyed girls like exotic dolls stabbing them under the fifth rib' (*TAB-L*: 189). The impact of this lies in the simultaneous calling up and exploding of the stereotype of the submissive, delicate Oriental woman. There is the description of a Frenchman, a Parisian who can be recognised 'a mile off': 'Quantities of hair which he had waved every week, rather honest blue eyes, a satyr's nose and mouth' (*TAB-L*: 192). Here again the effect is achieved by contrasting the honesty of the eyes and the crude sensuality of the nose and mouth – as if physical features really do carry moral significance. There are many examples like this, such as Lysyl the dancer who has 'a wonderfully graceful body, and a brutal peasant's face' (*TAB-L*: 193). Rhys's subject matter is generally relations between men and women and she holds herself far off from the dangers of sentimentality or romanticising by constantly establishing a surprising contradictory quality in her brief portraits. Le Gallez argues that the portrait of Fifi in 'La Grosse Fifi' (*TLB*, 1927; *TAB-L*, 1968; *CSS*, 1987) is caricature, and also that Rhys uses clichés which are undermined cleverly with irony: Rhys stylises Fifi's speech to the point of parody. For Le Gallez, the indication of both awkward English and fluent French in Fifi's speech is inevitably funny and moves away from realism towards 'pure unreality' (1990: 13). But in the context of the Caribbean, such plural voicing would not be unreal at all. There is an important discussion between Mark and Roseau about Fifi in which Mark uses her as a comic butt and Roseau resents his attitude which again emphasises different interpretations of the same 'languages' which Fifi represents, verbal and semiotic. Fifi in effect mocks at established middle-class conventions of femininity. The undertow here is not against her but against assumptions that women are discreet, quiet, dainty and tasteful:

Her hat was large and worn at a rakish sideways slant, her rouge shrieked, and the lids of her protruding eyes were painted bright blue. She wore very long silver earrings; nevertheless her face looked huge – vast, and her voice was hoarse though there was nothing but Vichy water in her glass. (*TAB-L*: 173)

Furthermore, Fifi's gentleness and self-aware vulnerability is conveyed by the description of her small plump hands and her small plump feet, and the final irony is that it is her desire to enter into a heterosexual relationship, to play at being the ultimate feminine woman, which causes her death.

Interestingly the nearest character to a narrator is named after Dominica's capital and Rhys's birthplace (though Rhys came to see this as too obvious). Roseau proves to be quite subversive in her relationship to both Fifi and the world in general (Staley 1979: 22). A slyly subversive narrator permits Rhys to direct the reader's attention whilst still constructing a complex impression. In 'Vienne', this works well: 'For God knows, if there's one hypocrisy I loathe more than another, it's the fiction of the "good" woman and the "bad" one' (*TAB-L*: 194); 'Just prejudice to notice podgy hands and thick ankles – keep your eyes glued on the pretty face' (*TAB-L*: 195).

Rhys has a painter's awareness of colour, including of skin tone, shape and line; a sharp and connective use of imagery; a dramatist's economical and counterpointed dialogue; she communicates a strong awareness that language has multiple layers of meaning and hardly ever discloses one person fully to another, it rather serves as a protective mask or screen. It is not so much that she is ironical, though she sometimes does use irony, by which I mean a controlled divergence of signification – a surface level suggesting one direction, an underlying layer suggesting an opposite subverting tendency. In Caribbean language registers we see both clear indication of the power of surfaces and the reality which undermines them constantly. The Caribbean paradox is that stereotypes of race and gender and class and nation are the shapers of people, holding keys to their character, but also the most consummate lies and unreliable guides.[25]

A good example is the early story 'A Spiritualist' (*TLB*, 1927; *CSS*, 1987), which opens with a taut sentence, 'I assure you', said the Commandant, 'that I adore women – that without a woman in my life I cannot exist' (*CSS*: 6). The very construction of this sentence and the fact that the man is a Commandant, a military man, suggests a reliable, secure sort of fatherly figure. Yet as the story proceeds we discover that this man, far from loving women, needs their attentions, something quite different. His fox-like nature only comes into most characteristic play when he is with a woman, his favourite form of prey.

This subversive little story first permits the Commandant to tell his version of his relationship with Madeleine, who always agreed with him and let him have his way and who has died suddenly. On visiting her apartment to collect clothes and effects for the young woman's mother, he hears a very loud crash. There is a block of marble on the sitting room floor, but no indication of how it got there. Shaken, and retreating hastily, the Commandant thinks that this is a message for him because he has not yet bought the marble headstone he promised Madeleine. He confides that he told another woman the story and she said, 'How furious that poor Madeleine must have been that she missed you!' (*CSS*: 9).

The Commandant is French, and Rhys strengthens the sense that he is speaking in French by making the English sound at times like a slightly too literal translation, 'I opened quickly the sitting-room door' (*CSS*: 8). French words occur at times as well, so that the reader has an idea of translating the story as it is read. The Commandant thinks he controls the telling of the story but the mute Madeleine eventually undermines our belief in what he is saying. The convention is that an upright and proper old man knows how to treat a woman, how to love a woman. Rhys explodes it and in the process expresses the suppressed energy coming in from the silent margins of life, where women who have never had the freedom to live for themselves carry an immense burden of rage. Though the story is set in Paris in the 1920s, it is, like a good deal of Rhys's writing, quite contemporary. Here the subversion of a dominant discourse is enacted, playing with the idea of plural languages, signifying French in English and a woman's way of speaking volumes to a man who hears only himself.

Like a poet, Rhys uses linked chains of images or small descriptions or phrases over and over again. Rhys gives light blue eyes to the Commandant: pale shades of primary colours are never a good sign in Rhys's fiction. Cold blue eyes are of course commonly assumed to be the eyes of the white racist by Caribbean people and in Europe, the eyes of the Nazi. Rhys herself had, as she described, 'huge staring eyes of no particular colour' (*SP*: 14), though they were in fact blue. Pale blue eyes would become a familiar attribute in Rhys's texts of cold and predatory English or European men: Ford gives them, in a more vivid shade of blue, to Edward Ashburnam in *The Good Soldier* (1915), devoting a good portion of a paragraph to these extraordinary blue eyes, 'as blue as the sides of a certain kind of box of matches' (1983: 28). Some critical opinion, most notably Gardiner (1982) thinks *Quartet* harks back to *The Good Soldier*.[26]

'Illusion' (*TLB*, 1927; *TAB-L*, 1968; *CSS*, 1987), like 'A Spiritualist', encourages the reader into trusting a surface appearance, and then undermines it. Miss Bruce is a rather masculine English painter living in Paris. Rhys sets up the narrative trap by offering a national cliché: Miss Bruce is a 'shining example of what character and training – British character and training – can do' (*CSS*: 1). After seven years, she is totally untouched by anything 'hectic, slightly exotic or unwholesome' (*CSS*: 1), in other words by the normal complexities of life. But in Miss Bruce's closet, whilst she is ill, the narrator finds wonderful extravagant, brightly coloured dresses in all sorts of fabrics, and a box of makeup, even a carnival costume with a mask. Of course Miss Bruce is masked every day, pretending to a severity which belies her secret passion for frivolity and sensuousness. But there is another twist: Miss Bruce, once exposed, is not simply praised for having a secret life. She suffers rather from 'the curse of Eve', 'the thirst to be loved', and 'the search for illusion' (*CSS*: 4).

The whole story is about layerings of identity which correspond to coded levels of language: when Miss Bruce observes a young girl, she admires her hands and arms, leaving the exact meaning of her admiration for us to work out. She not only holds back her own love of sensuality but with it her own sexual identity. It is appropriate that she is a painter, not only because her love of colour and texture is therefore easily understood, but because the whole idea of painting, of illusion, so deeply involved with the construction of woman as beautiful object, is something which Miss Bruce can only enter into just so far. Her safety depends on her suppression of her full identity – and so she creates another illusion, herself as masculine and severe. This idea of masking, whether through makeup, clothing, gesture, voice, language or bodily response to say, sexual encounter, is central to Rhys's texts. On the one hand, it is disguise and protection and on the other a failure of nerve, a shyness or inability to commun- icate which can have serious consequences.

Of the four texts written after 'L'Affaire Ford',[27] *Quartet* was the first published so the others may be considered partly reactive to it. Several scholars (Mizener 1971; Kappers-den Hollander 1987; 1988; Angier 1990; Lonsdale 1992) have explored the tangled per- sonal and textual relationships of Rhys, Ford, Bowen and Jean Lenglet. The literary relationship between de Nève and Rhys continued long after their marriage was effectively over and, as Martien Kappers-den Hollander has demonstrated (1994; also Angier 1990), led to remarkable collaborations.[28]

Comparing the fictional portraits of Rhys in texts by Lenglet, Ford and Bowen throws into some relief Rhys's effort in *Quartet* to keep herself from being either simple heroine or simple villain. She already had a sense of the demands of the fictional text being more important than what happened in life, and her interest in the collision of multiple points of view, in the dramatic text, served her well in balancing the four major characters. The description of Stania in *Barred* has strong correlations with Rhys's central female protagonists, though the narrator is the husband. She is reckless in a calculated way, he says, capable of 'horrible cruelty' and has 'indolence and passivity' (1932: 86), so that he sometimes hates her. She is 'always tired when it was a question of corres- ponding with me' (1932: 96) and she asserts 'I'd go out with any- body rather than sit alone and think' (1932: 100). But Martien

Kappers (1987) points out that Rhys toned down Lenglet's original portrait of a faithless wife but as part of her extensive revisions of the novel: 'All in all, Rhys scrapped between six-and-a-half to seven thousand words from her husband's narrative . . . Hardly a paragraph has remained unchanged'.[29] Ford's version of Rhys occurs in *When the Wicked Man* (1931). In this novel, Lola Porter, alcoholic and tempestuous, who has 'a taste for toughs and low-life' (1931: 163), is from 'one of the West Indian islands' (1931: 163) with a voice which is 'extraordinarily soft and stealthy' (1931: 166). This melodramatic portrait, together with the thin characterisations of the rest of the novel, contributes much to making the book virtually unreadable.

Stella Bowen's memoir, *Drawn from Life* (first published 1941; 1984), reveals both resentment of Rhys, since she thought the relationship between Rhys and Ford caused the crucial 'cutting of the fundamental tie' between herself and Ford (1984: 166), and a certain amount of insight. Her anger came out in her response to the bohemian group which surrounded Ford in Paris as editor, writer, literary lion: she thought them 'dirty, drunk, a pervert or a thief or a whore' which was acceptable to Ford as long as they produced their creative work, or as long as 'you had a lively and honest mind and the courage of your instincts' (1984: 119). She still had an injured and superior air in her description of Rhys as a tragic girl who had written 'an unpublishably sordid novel of great sensitiveness and persuasiveness' (1984: 166), i.e. 'Suzy Tells', later 'Triple Sec'. Her most damning description despite itself captures what still impress as some of Rhys's strongest literary qualities: 'She had a needle-quick intelligence and a good sort of emotional honesty . . . she took the lid off the world she knew and showed us an underworld of darkness and disorder' (1984: 166). Bowen realised that her own part in this domestic drama was the worst role as the 'fortunate wife' and concluded from this that 'a powerful weapon lies in weakness and pathos' (1984: 167). Bowen's remarks, which could mostly be justifiably applied to Marya, give evidence of how Rhys managed to build a complex fictional portrait of her central character out of acute self-observation.

Rhys presented Ford in *Quartet* as Heidler, a repellent figure, physically unattractive and sexually inept, incapable of clear moral perception of any given situation, pretentious and self-indulgent: 'God's a pal of mine' (*Q:* 161). In the novel the wonder is that Marya can have any interest in him, since she is, unlike Rhys herself with Ford, not engaged in an intense relation between professional mentor and student artist. Gardiner describes Ford as 'self-dramatizing' and seeming 'to have inspired those close to him with an unusual zeal to tell the world what he was really like' (1982: 67). Rhys first wrote the Lenglet role as romantic, a man fond of his wife, 'Stephan was secretive and a liar, but he was a very gentle and expert lover' (*Q:* 22), by the end of the novel he becomes violent and utterly indifferent to Marya. Stella Bowen becomes Lois Heidler, vulnerable, confused, self-deceiving, capable of emotional callousness, and 'Obviously of the species wife' (*Q:* 97). But the dominant character is Marya, the Rhys figure, and the novel's success rests on Rhys's capacity to both expose her youth and confusions and yet balance them with the shortcomings of the other major characters, using a complicated narrative which shifts points of view.

The most impressive aspect of *Quartet* is the confidence with which Rhys handles the novel form and particularly how she deepens and extends her ability to handle multi-vocal narrative, an ability which was to become more developed and adventurous with each subsequent novel, but always achieving the same end, the destabilisation of the reader's easy moral judgement and the fracturing of confidence in a single narrative voice. The novel opens with a spare and taut description of Marya Zelli, who is the central character, just as it closes, equally tautly, with a description of a confrontation between Marya and her estranged husband and his departure and meeting with another woman. Rhys's prose constantly establishes uncertainty by the implied presence of a subtext and an unnerving understatement: it is quite highly dramatised, as befits a novel which began as a play. At the end of the novel, there is even a muted horror. Marya screams abuse at her husband and then they struggle:

He caught her by the shoulders and swung her sideways with all his force. As she fell, she struck her forehead against the edge of the table, crumpled up and lay quite still.

*Voilà pour toi*, said Stephan.

He straightened his tie carefully, put on his hat and went out of the room without looking behind him. He felt dazed and at the same time extraordinarily relieved. As he went downstairs he was thinking, 'The concierge; I must be careful of the concierge.' But the concierge's *loge*, when he passed it, was in darkness. (*Q*: 185)

Like a great deal of the violence which can occur in life, this scene is frighteningly convincing because it is so ordinary, and because Stephan's really chilling capacity is to feel no response to Marya's unconsciousness. He does nothing deliberately to hurt or kill her, but he does nothing to help once she is hurt. His last comment is an intimate form of address in French, '*Voilà pour toi*': he so declares his contempt, his separation and his casual vengefulness. Marya, who is English and remarkably without family connections, has come to Paris and married a Polish man. By the introduction of French from time to time into the narrative, Rhys ensures we understand that a significant origin of Marya's tragedy is that her life is conducted in a space where languages and cultures intersect and collide. Migration as an adult causes intense awareness of plurality: sometimes resulting in a feeling that it is impossible to communicate with those who do not share it.[30]

The spareness of Rhys's prose contributes very well to this effect, because it emphasises the silences and omissions which almost inevitably problematise a relationship conducted across evident borders. When Marya is with her lover Heidler, who is, though English, of a different class, comfortably off and a man, the spaces between their statements to one another suggest a subterranean level of miscommunication which finally makes their relationship intolerable and impossible. When Heidler makes a crass declaration to Marya of his determination to make sexual approaches to her in his own house, where he lives with his wife Lois, they both hear a noise upstairs. He says, 'There's Lois falling about' (*Q*: 101), and goes up to investigate. On his return he tries to explain:

'Poor Lois is quite seedy,' he remarked, putting the lamp down on the table with an expressionless face.
'She's been awfully sick, nearly fainted.'
Marya asked, without lifting her eyes: 'What's the matter?'
'Well,' said Heidler, 'she thinks it's the cassoulet. So do I, I don't trust this tinned stuff.'

Of course, there they were: inscrutable people, invulnerable people, and she simply hadn't a chance against them, naive sinner that she was. (*Q:* 101)

That inscrutability is of course the Heidlers' refusal to investigate the passions which drive them because of their commitment to a socially acceptable surface and to their own self-centred needs. When Marya visits Stephan in prison, she suddenly finds she cannot understand French at all (*Q:* 36), signifying that the intimate, multilingual world of their marriage is suddenly lost to her.

Rhys's complex narrative technique is a great strength in the novel. Chapter 16, for example, begins in the Hotel du Bosphore, which looks down on Montparnasse Station in Paris. Montparnasse was the centre of Paris for the American and English expatriates who frequented the bars there and so it is appropriate that Marya should be there for her encounter with Heidler which follows a few pages later. The chapter begins with Marya in her hotel room and her dialogue with herself about the affair with Heidler: '"What's the matter with you?" she would ask herself. . . . "No self-control", thought Marya, "That's what's the matter with me. No training"' (*Q:* 117). She thinks of Heidler's dislike of women and his sexual ineptitude, but the passage contains both information Marya could and could not know for sure:

He wasn't a good lover of course. He didn't really like women. She had known that as soon as he touched her. His hands were inexpert, clumsy at caresses . . . He despised love. He thought of it grossly, to amuse himself, and then with ferocious contempt. (*Q:* 118)

The strands which make up this section of the novel are characteristic of much of Rhys's writing. She uses the French form 'petite femme' to capture the nuance of Heidler's use of Marya, in the French bourgeois tradition. Dialogue is exceedingly important: in this short chapter of ten pages, there are numerous passages of dialogue, including talks Marya has with herself, with Heidler, with the patronne of a bar, with Lois and with Stephan, her husband.

The four, Marya and Stephan, Marya's lover Heidler and his wife Lois, make up the quartet of the title, and also assume, in their roles as faithless wife and mistress, betrayed husband, seducer and betrayed wife the stock characters of domestic farce.

That Rhys manages both to suggest the game of treacherous love and the complexity of actual people caught in this situation, both fatuousness and tragedy, owes much to her careful dramatic arrangements of dialogue, scene construction and ruthless paring of description. The reader learns quickly to measure a word or a phrase in a context carefully. The dialogue has economy and terseness, yet carries much of the information the reader needs to judge Marya's introspective narrative. There is a multiple point of view, as when Marya laughs loudly: 'Heidler looked at her sideways. He disliked her when she laughed like that' (*Q*: 121). The multiple perspective suggests Rhys had a theatrical instinct for the creation of strong characters working out their conflicting readings of a given situation. Rhys's dramatic sense is evident in her awareness that people are assigned roles and dramatic interest develops from their acceptance or rejection of those roles.

Marya recalls typical meetings with Heidler, 'They would be sitting in the Café de Versailles . . .' (*Q*: 120), meetings where she tries to tell him the truth about her feelings and meets with rebuffs, where she recognises she has become 'the villain of the piece' (*Q*: 120). Rhys likes to use clichés or commonplace figures of speech and refigure them acutely in a specific context.

Atmosphere is achieved partly by the use of telling images, often connected from text to text, touches of evocative colour, impressions from sight, smell, touch, the inner feeling of the body. When Marya lies in her hotel bed watching Heidler dress after sex, waiting for him to leave for a dinner with his wife and some friends, she thinks 'A bedroom in hell might look rather like this one. Yellow-green and dullish mauve flowers crawling over black walls' (*Q*: 119). This room smells of stale scent and she thinks then of all the women who had laughed or cried in the same bed. The colours themselves suggest sickly states of emotion, perverse combinations of feeling. Animal images, the first linked chain of signifiers to be used in a major Rhys text, inform *Quartet* strongly. The painter Miss De Solla and the Heidlers discuss Marya 'as if she were a strange animal or at any rate a strayed animal' (*Q*: 11). As Staley points out (1979: 47), the caged animal is a strong image which informs the text widely. Marya says to Stephan, when discussing incarceration, 'If anybody tried to catch me and lock

me up I'd fight like a wild animal; I'd fight till they let me out
or till I died' (*Q:* 136). Rhys's use of animal images began in *The
Left Bank*, where for example, in 'Vienne', Francine remarks how
she hates women in Vienna, who have cunning like animals, and
she went on to use them again in *After Leaving Mr MacKenzie*, where
an important picture which haunts the protagonist, Julia, is of a
naked woman lying on a conch, 'like an utterly lovely proud
animal' (*Q:* 52).

Chapter 16, like others, is punctuated by ellipses, another
common Rhys stylistic identity. Each break in continuity permits
another scene, another development in the drama, to be played
out, in the way that a curtain permits a short break in a play.
After the scene where she is with Heidler in the Café de Versailles, the chapter moves to 'the lonely night' (*Q:* 121), when
there is nothing to do but drink to deaden the pain and then walk
home to the hotel. During her time in a students' restaurant off
the Boulevard St Michel (the Parisian geography is exact), drinking Pernod, she notices a lady eating alone and 'copiously' (*Q:*
122). It is evident that Marya sees her own ineptitude in dealing
with Heidler and Lois, but even in her own inner dialogues,
there are crucial omissions and silences, which accounts for her
curious paralysis and resignation.

Walking back to the hotel, still full of Pernod, she feels as if
she is 'walking under water' (*Q:* 123), and that life 'was a dream'.
Dreams play a very important part in Rhys's fiction, along with
references to ghosts and other metaphysical phenonomena, and
they work as small poems, concentrated clusters of images which
see below the surface of an apparently realistic narrative.[31] Marya
dreams here much as Antoinette will in *Wide Sargasso Sea*, and
part of this dream-reality is 'tall dark houses'. These look askance
at Anna in *Voyage in the Dark*.

Chapter 6 also searches out Marya's sense of where and who
she is:

But when she tried to argue reasonably with herself it seemed to her she
had forgotten the beginnings of the affair, when she had still reacted
and he had reconquered her painstakingly. She never reacted now. She
was a thing. Quite dead. Not a kick left in her. (*Q:* 123)

Rhys is, as I have already pointed out, in some ways a very distinct literary foremother of Jamaica Kincaid, whose central characters are also brilliantly terse, stonily honest and sometimes, as a result, entirely unappealing. Like Rhys, Kincaid concentrates on the resentful, anti-colonial female consciousness[32] and in a brutally economical lyrical prose, her protagonists expose all who have the power to hurt or marginalise her. Marya vividly imagines violence against Lois and lies awake thinking coldly through her own entanglements with both Lois and Heidler, 'I love him. I want him. I hate her. And he's a swine' (*Q*: 124). It is this capacity for brutal honesty which saves Marya from becoming a cliché and the novel from sentimentality.

Rhys pays careful attention to the physical: the structural identity of a particular body; its transformation by states of emotion. Marya's torment over Heidler shows in her face:

Her eyelids were swollen and flaccid over unnaturally large, bright eyes. Her head seemed to have sunk between her shoulders, giving her a tormented and deformed look. Her mouth drooped, her skin was greyish, and when she made up her face, the powder and rouge stood out in clownish patches. (*Q*: 124)

Ford saw in the Rhys of *The Left Bank* a champion of the underdog, and connected that to her Antillean origins, absolutely rightly. Marya is the antithesis of noble and selfless fallen women with hearts of gold, of the popular bourgeois fictional hero in general:[33] in this she shares common cause with those who fall outside bourgeois concern for the virtuous poor and the worthy failed. Very often her narrators identify with social outcasts and offer sympathies to:

all the inmates of the prison, to the women who waited on her under the eye of the fat warder, to all unsuccessful and humbled prostitutes, to everybody who wasn't plump, sleek, satisfied, smiling and hard-eyed. (*Q*: 125)

The chapter ends on an uneasy note: Marya confesses her acceptance of money from the Heidlers. This difficult moment is done purely through a dialogue largely about evasion and lack of communication. Stephan does not know at this point about the affair with Heidler and thinks the Heidlers are 'chic'; Marya is entirely without introspection about the issue of money. Rhys's poetic economy of style is excellent in suggesting the layers of possibility for communication which are here ignored.

Rhys's style did not fundamentally change for the rest of her writing career, though it matured of course and became more flexible and assured: in *Wide Sargasso Sea*, the presence of Caribbean landscape makes a huge difference in the intensity and identity of the familiar components of style. Staley thinks Rhys had 'an uncanny ability to discover meaning in the selection of event or action' (1979: 20): it is more that her choice of words, her style itself, was entirely about the excision of unnecessary material and a determined focus on political goals. In very subtle and entirely literary ways, she registers her protest against elitism of speech and marginalisation of the powerless through the many layers of tightly constructed and counterpointed meaning which identify a Rhys text.

# CHAPTER 3

# A Caribbean woman lost in Europe?
# After Leaving Mr MacKenzie *and*
# *the question of gender*

Miss Dufreyne, for such was the Lady's name, was a weak, sentimental, very lazy, entirely harmless creature, pathetically incapable of lies or intrigue or even of self-defence – till it was too late. She was also sensual, curious, reckless, and had all her life aroused a strong curiosity in men. So much for her.

('In the Rue de l'Arrivée', *TLB*, 1927; *CSS*, 1987: 51)

Gradually passivity replaced her early adventurousness. She learned, after long and painstaking effort, to talk like a chorus girl, to dress like a chorus girl and to think like a chorus girl – up to a point. Beyond that point she remained apart, lonely, frightened of her loneliness, resenting it passionately. She grew thin. She began to live her hard and monotonous life very mechanically and listlessly.

(*Q:* 16)

But on some days her monotonous life was made confused and frightened by her thoughts. Then she could not stay still. She was obliged to walk up and down the room consumed with hatred of the world and everybody in it – especially of Mr Mackenzie.

(*ALMM:* 12)

Since Francis Wyndham observed in 1950 that Rhys heroines in *After Leaving Mr MacKenzie*, *Voyage in the Dark* and *Good Morning, Midnight* could be said to be similar women in different circumstances, the issue of 'the Rhys woman' has been alive in Rhys criticism, especially in feminist critical approaches (Baldanza 1978; Nebeker 1981; Le Gallez 1990). Also one valid approach to explaining Rhys's eminence is to attribute much of it to the feminist discovery of her: *Wide Sargasso Sea* and the legend of Rhys came to prominence just as the international feminist movement was beginning to gain ground, in the 1970s. The reprinting of *Voyage in the Dark* (1967); *Good Morning, Midnight* (1967); *Quartet* (1969) and *After Leaving Mr MacKenzie* (1969) brought Rhys's earlier texts to the attention of a new generation of readers.[1] The concern as to whether Rhys's protagonists are one woman, at different stages of development or separate women has also been connected to the critical debate about Rhys and autobiography: if 'the' Rhys woman is thought to exist, she is often connected to Rhys herself: my view is that Rhys created fiction out of her experience and eventually her autobiography owed as much to her fiction as to her memory.[2]

According to Molly Hite, the Rhys woman's 'defining characteristic is her financial dependency on a man . . . or men' (1989: 23). She is sometimes employed, sometimes 'unemployed', or engaged in various levels of sordid transactions involving men and money, such as prostitution. Hite quotes an earlier Rhys critic, Arnold Davidson (1984), pondering the difficult question of whether Julia Martin in *After Leaving Mr MacKenzie* is a woman who sells sexual favours or a woman who desires money gifts as proof a man loves her (*ALMM*: 23). Hite critiques Davidson's old masculinist assumption that women must be either good and worthy of love or unworthy prostitutes: as Hite summarises, 'either financially or emotionally dependent, but not both' (1989: 23).[3] For Hite, as a feminist critic, Rhys's marginal female character destabilises 'an inherited narrative structure', that is, precisely because she is marginal, is not a winner or a solver of problems, she challenges the conventions on which the bourgeois novel is built – conventions assuming 'free will' in major characters.[4] Reading Rhys's texts with assumptions from the bourgeois novel causes problems: Staley defines 'the Rhys heroine' as 'so suffocated and turned in by the wretched life she lives, there is little spirit of rebellion' (1979: 57). Hite is right to see that the Rhys woman is an important pivot for reader-response: a feminist reader generally sees Rhys's protagonists as quite subversive, if not able to secure any social change.

Leading feminist literary historians in the United States, Gilbert and Gubar (1988), mapped Rhys as a major reinterpreter of past and present women's literary history.[5] But only a few northern feminists (by which I mean British, North American and European feminists, predominantly but not exclusively white) have realised that the political identity of Rhys was shaped as much by Dominican racial and class culture as by gender issues. Even when this is realised, discussion of Rhys's protagonists is often limited to those of evident West Indian identity (Anna, Antoinette, Selina), (Casey 1973; Casey Fulton 1974; Moore 1987; Carrera Suarez and Alvarez Lopez 1990). Rhys's gender constructions are particularly striking in the context of twentieth-century white feminism because she so early saw the connection between different kinds of hegemony. But this is entirely because Rhys was of Caribbean origin. Interestingly, feminist critic Kloepfer (1989) discussed *Wide Sargasso Sea* without specifically locating it within Caribbean history and culture: later feminists like Gregg and Emery would do so.

In many ways, erasing Rhys as Caribbean is emblematic of the problems inherent in the period of high northern feminism, where the complex intersections of race and class with gender were often marginalised in favour of universalist constructions of 'the woman', 'the mother', 'the daughter', 'the father' which were far more comforting and avoided difficult questions of intra-feminist divisions, most especially those of race (just as 'the white Creole', 'the subaltern', 'the colonial', for example, offer a similar frame for some post-colonial criticism and theory). By 1981, when Helen Nebeker published the first evidently feminist book-length study of Rhys, feminist scholarship was beginning to be established as a major contribution to contemporary literary work. But the problem with much northern feminist writing is that the Rhys woman is set up as a universally applicable example. Baer (1981) includes Rhys in a study of female-authored quest narratives. Nebeker has an unconsciously ironical summary of Rhys which reads Rhys's formative education as Anglo-Saxon and the opposition of black and white in non-racial terms:

Many of Rhys's ideas are, of course, reaction to the Victorian Zeitgeist which was her reality. The turbulent history of social reform in late Victorian and Edwardian England – particularly the evolution of the socialist and women's rights movements – is common knowledge thanks

to much recent scholarship . . . what would have been the 'reality' of turn-
of-the-century Anglo-Saxons – the milieu in which a Jean Rhys would
have matured? . . . in this culture which Rhys would have inherited,
women lived in an Aristotelian oriented world of either-or, black-white.
Thus a woman was a 'respectable lady' or she was not. (1981: 4–5)

Nebeker clearly sees nothing important in Rhys's sixteen formative years in Dominica, where social and political parameters
were quite dramatically different from those of England and where
if there were any dominant female myths, according to Rhys
herself, they were of frightening spirits like the Soucriant and not,
as Nebeker assumes, elements of the Jungian collective unconscious or Western feminist reconstructions of the Great Goddess,
even if one of Rhys's major characters is called Anna.[6]

Rhys is no easy feminist heroine: she created marginalised
women who rebelled, mostly unsuccessfully, against society, and
the woman who declared suspicion of women, 'I'm not at all for
women's lib. I don't dislike women exactly, but I don't trust them
. . . I've never been intimate with them. It's not worth it . . . Women
are kind, but they do for you what *they* want to do, not what *you*
want to do' (Plante 1984: 40).

Adrienne Rich listed, in an essay on Anne Sexton (1979), dangerous tendencies in women writers: self-trivialisation, believing
that women are not capable of major creativity, not taking the
work seriously enough, finding the needs of others more important than our own. Rhys resoundingly defeated the forces which
thwart women's creativity, but she did display the fear and distrust of other women, addiction to alcohol with 'its blanket of
blankness' and perhaps also addiction to male approval, all of
which Rich saw as silencing traits. Rich commented 'Her head
was patriarchal, but in her blood and bones, Anne Sexton knew'
(1979: 122): in similar fashion, Rhys was both conventional and
entirely subversive about gender.

Sex in Rhys's texts is always heterosexual, but mostly, for the
female partner, a matter of absence, inertia, coldness or distraction, with the dramatic exception of Antoinette's early passion for
her husband. Sexual experience, despite its usual requirement of
the removal of clothing and therefore the possibility of revelation
of the person under the social mask, is for Rhys's protagonists

largely another arena for retreat and refusal to disclose. Howells remarks that in *Voyage in the Dark*, in which sex plays a central role, 'there is an almost total absence of female sexual desire' (1991: 76; also Le Gallez 1990). Though the sexual act can take place, there is very often little feeling, certainly an absence of joy, and often Rhys contributes to this by simply leaving out the details of the sex itself and paying more attention to the emotional state of her protagonist, usually one in which the sexual act has little or no relevance. In this, gender roles become an obstacle: Rhys interestingly suggested to Plante (1984) that everyone is bisexual: certainly the creative process often requires an ability to breach gender conventions in the imagination.

What fundamentally shaped Rhys's sense of sexuality and gen-der is clearest in the draft manuscript narratives of Mr Howard (BEB), which together form a story intertwining gender, sexuality, class, race and nationality with colonialism. Mr Howard was a family visitor from England, in his early seventies, still handsome, at least to the child Gwen Williams (Rhys) was at fourteen or so. He was a trusted friend of her mother. He asked to take the young girl out: they went to the Botanical Gardens in Roseau and there he touched her breast: though she wanted to refuse to go with him again, her mother became angry at her reluctance. Mr Howard concocted a seductive sado-masochistic 'serial story' of the girl serving him in his house, and waiting on his guests, sometimes naked, her arms covered in bracelets and her hands in rings: if she made mistakes she was punished. Though Gwen Williams evidently listened avidly to this tale, she had frozen at the actual touch of his 'old man's hand' on her body (BEB). Mr Howard had a wife travelling with him who ultimately became hostile to the girl: he returned to England and died 'nearly eighty respected and loved by all' (BEB). The fourteen-year-old Rhys, on the other hand, discovered that 'something in the depths of me said Yes that is true. Pain humiliation submission that is for me' (BEB). Clearly the victim was the one feeling guilty here: 'I only struggled feebly What he had seen in me was there all right . . . he could be nice too Mr Howard. Probably with someone healthier like water off a duck's back' (BEB). Thomas (1994–5), who offers the most detailed contextual account of the Howard story, points out that Mr Howard's exact indecent assault was just about legal in terms of the prevailing British laws of consent.[7]

Rhys's mother is important in this: her approval of Howard is set into the narrative of a difficult mother–daughter relationship outlined in the BEB. Just before the Howard narrative is a description of her resistance to her mother beating her, prefaced by 'I was just at this stage when it happened – the thing that formed me made me as I am the thing I want to write about' (BEB). In Rhys's texts, the mother–daughter connection is always very complicated and told from the daughter's point of view (Kloepfer 1989). O'Connor (1986) thinks the beatings the mother gave may have predisposed the child to submission (perhaps even masochism). She quotes Diana Athill remembering Rhys saying she hated her mother, and points out that Rhys may have held her mother responsible for the Mr Howard episode,[8] because of her encouragement of Mr Howard into the family and her pressure on her daughter to go for an outing with him alone. Such a betrayal, as it turned out to be, would go very deep. O'Connor concludes that Mr Howard was the source of Rhys's difficulties in relations with men for the rest of her life, and that this was reflected in the female masochism and dependency in Rhys's texts, especially in the construction of the woman as child by an older man.

A young female consciousness narrates quite a number of texts by Caribbean women who revision the popular form of the *bildungsroman*, charting a developing female identity from adolescence into young adulthood. This has been brilliantly utilised by writers as diverse as Erna Brodber, Paule Marshall, Merle Collins, Jamaica Kincaid and Joan Riley.[9] The usual expectation is that this subgenre is centred in a youthful consciousness, advantaged by honesty and lack of guile. Rhys gives a voice to her protagonists, regardless of age, which in some important ways remains adolescent, young and combative, concerned with the fragility of the ego, but also in the same way acutely, even brutally honest: however she increasingly works towards a multivocal narrative which gives the character's antagonists plenty of space to make their case. James comments that 'the sensitive child never leaves home', that 'the more contrasting the world into which the adult goes, the more the child is present' (1978: 33). For him the schism between England or Europe and the Caribbean in Rhys's texts is the chasm between childhood and 'the cruel compromise' involved in growing up. But part of the effect is that Rhys permits the reader to see how that young voice is framed, especially housed increasingly in an ageing body.

The daughter–mother relationship is problematic in Rhys's fiction and motherhood remains elusive for the Rhys protagonist: if experienced directly, it is brief and tragic, though it is evident from numerous letters between them that Rhys had an important relationship with her daughter, despite major disruptions. This was a very crucial and unresolved, often difficult, experience with someone who was younger and deserved her space: Rhys kept it out of her fiction.

Mother–daughter relationships in Rhys's fiction always position the Rhys protagonist as the daughter. As Kloepfer (1989) has argued, in all the novels, there is either an absent mother or censored space where the mother might be. Since she is alienated from her physical mother and far from her mother's culture, Julia in *After Leaving Mr MacKenzie* is double-divorced from a space where she might be known. By choosing Brazil as Julia's mother's origin, Rhys suggests the complex interrelation of white domination and defensiveness in a majority African space similar to the Caribbean.

As Julia witnesses her mother's cremation, she identifies with it in a curiously intense way, as Kloepfer notes, for she finds 'some essence of her was shooting upwards like a flame' (*ALMM*: 131), a moment which connects her with the old woman she fears resembling who has a 'flame of hatred' keeping her alive (*ALMM*: 15). The Rhys protagonist leaves home partly because her relationship with her mother or family is ruptured and conflicted: rather than leaving because she desires independence and maturity, which in the Rhys world means inevitable compromise, she leaves in order to be a bravely rebellious, even self-risking, child.[10] The Mr Howard passages, so centred on a child's responses to adults, seems relevant here. The older men who exert power over Rhys's protagonists are often drawn to their youth, which suggests little resistance as well as an appealing physicality. In

*After Leaving Mr MacKenzie,* Julia can seem at first sight younger than her actual age, although this impression vanishes all too quickly. But her emotional landscape seems to be still focussed in a childlike way on her inwardness: she only briefly manages an empathy which engages her own experience with her mother's, 'Her mother had said: "I can't rest in this country. This is such a cold, grey country"' (*ALMM*: 123). Similarly, she can only briefly feel compassion for her rather smug and martyred sister, Nora, before she (with some justification) accuses her of jealousy. It is Julia's feeling, appearance and self-justification which absorb her, sustaining an acutely honest, highly sensitive child's eye out to the world.

But Julia's inability to enjoy adult life may have to do in fact with an inability to be finished with the child's vividly felt apprehension of the impact of a situation on the self, and a resistance to the complexities of maturity, sexual or otherwise. Mature vision has to include a sense of other people. Julia looks back rather than forward, her consciousness centred on her own responses, thinking of 'the last time you were really happy about nothing' (*ALMM*: 159): significantly the first time she remembers being afraid. The narrator speaks directly to an old subjectivity, in which entangled with the sense of a childish but absolutely real power of life and death over a living thing is a sense of fear, surprisingly associated with the sun:

You were walking along a long path, shadowed for some distance by trees. But at the end of the path was an open space and the glare of white sunlight. You were catching butterflies. You caught them by waiting until they settled, and then creeping up silently on tiptoe and squatting near them. Then, when they closed their wings, looking like a one-petalled flower, you grabbed them quickly, taking hold low down or the wings would break in your hand. (*ALMM*: 159)

The butterflies are imprisoned in a tin so that the child can hear the wings beating against it, until they break. But the cruel child senses something huge and terrifying behind her, in this sunlight which is 'still, desolate, arid' (*ALMM*: 160). This memory is located here towards the end of Julia's story, where it counterpoints her role as victim and emphasises her capacity to inflict pain herself (Brown 1987). There is a powerful combination of guilt, fear,

aggression and the terror which might signify the onset of difficult and threatening sexual experience.

Certainly the Mr Howard narrative is a braid of strands which
inform Rhys's texts, such as Antoinette's dreams of a sinister lover
or pursuer in *Wide Sargasso Sea* (see also O'Connor 1986; Thomas
1994–5). There is a manuscript dated 4 December 1938 (the same
year that Angier rightly dates the BEB), 'Mr Howard's House.
Creole', which is an early version of the story 'Good-bye Marcus,
Good-bye Rose' (*CSS*), and in which the mother's role is very
important. Critics who have examined the Mr Howard elements
in the BEB, notably Thomas (1994–5), O'Connor (1986), Angier
(1990), Howells (1991) and Gardiner (1989), generally offer feminist socio-psychological analyses of Rhys. She herself wrote after
the Howard narrative that she read a book in a Paris bookstore
which dismissed claims by women that they had been seduced by
older men as fictitious (BEB): this has provoked discussion of
Rhys's response to Freud.[11] She saw through his authority to his
patriarchy.

We shall never know for sure whether Mr Howard was in the
habit of molesting teenagers, but he must have realised to do so in
Dominica provided him with an escape back to England. In his
eyes, young Gwen Williams was ready to fall, sexually: English
middle- and upper-class Victorian culture had already split the
sexual from the ideal in women, constructing prostitutes or lower-
class women or, in this case, perhaps Creoles, as available and
the mother/wife as the asexual, pure madonna. Howard's compulsion to talk about sex is clearly a good example of what D. H.
Lawrence called 'sex in the head', i.e. a neurotic withdrawal
from the physicality of sex, also he was after all in his seventies.

Rhys understood clearly, but from her own female perspective,
that desire derives from the mind: the mind shapes sexual response.
In *After Leaving Mr MacKenzie*, which is also an extended essay
on the politics of sex, Mr Horsfield is either sexually stimulated
or alienated according to how Julia behaves or how he happens
to respond to her physical self. Julia blows her nose loudly in a
cinema when they are watching a film together and he responds
by becoming more distant, conscious of being embarrassed and
annoyed (*ALMM*: 44–5). Though she seems sexually unaroused

and protests tiredness one night, he begins to stroke her hair 'mechanically', but then discovers it is very soft and warm and 'felt extraordinary pleasure' (*ALMM*: 152–3). He had expected the hair to be 'harsh to the touch, because he was certain that she dyed it' (*ALMM*: 152), when it is soft, it begins to arouse him, until Julia remarks that he is good to her. His seductive mood vanishes, then returns as he gives himself permission to be sexual with her without responsibility, '"She asked me up here" he thought. "She asked me"' (*ALMM*: 153).

The details of the sexual connection which will occur between these two people is caught here in the shifts of mental response to the idea of it: what the mind thinks, the body feels. Significantly, this episode is in the chapter called 'It Might Have Happened Anywhere', as if the woman and the man are generic, the confusions and evasions and finally the physical connection have no individuality.

The colonial dimension is also important: as Gilman argues, in the context of racism and colonisation, 'the sexuality of the black, both male and female, becomes an icon for deviant sexuality in general' (1985: 209). This works itself out in other colonial texts: Naipaul's *Guerillas*, for example, depicts the violence of the colonised man on the coloniser's woman, with an intense element of sadomasochism involved (Fido 1985). Dissanayake and Wickramagamage examine Naipaul's adoption of the 'colonial gaze' (1993) and suggest Naipaul internalised the norms of Western culture: since Fanon's work, we have been aware of the connection between colonial formations of identity and sexual neurosis.[12] In the case of Rhys's protagonists, their alien status within English or Parisian society marks them as prey for seductive men: because they have no money or secure social position, they are vulnerable to being constructed as sexually available. What has made Rhys so appealing to feminist critics has been her connection of sex and gender roles with hegemonic structures in a given culture, a connection which was clearly first established for her by the experience with Mr Howard.

It is evident from Rhys's writing narrative that writing itself became a means not only to exorcise the past and turn it into completely achieved texts, but also a kind of autosadomasochism, a pain to which she willingly surrendered. A draft passage about her self-immolation through drinking precedes the comment 'It has relieved me to write' (BEB).[13] Submission to the writing is somewhat like submission to Mr Howard, and it even provides some release from the need to forget by abusing alcohol. Although the Howard draft material was never fully utilised fictionally, in writing and keeping it, just as with the early diaries of the affair with Smith, Rhys set the pattern of experiencing writing as therapy and as accusation.

There is another detail worth noting in the Howard story: a mother would rather trust her adolescent daughter to an old white man (who betrays her trust) than free that daughter in the wider community across racial lines to find someone who really cares for her. This of course speaks to the issue of racial lines in the colony: a mother wishing to corral her young daughter within white racist culture would have feared the child's association with a local boy or man of colour: she may also have been denying her daughter's relative sexual maturity. England was often looked to for mates for the small white community: Rhys's father was immediately highly eligible on arrival in Dominica. This returns fictionally in *Wide Sargasso Sea* where Sandi would seem to be the right mate for Antoinette, but she stays with the English husband who destroys her. Biographical speculation has entertained the possibility that Rhys herself had a passionate interracial romance in her teenage years. Angier (1990) cites Rhys's brother Owen's fictionalised family memoir in which 'Missy' would seem to be Rhys and has an affair with a young man of African, Carib and white descent. As Angier points out, this is not supported by any other evidence.[14] Owen may have been at least partially writing out his own relationship with his daughter, Ena Williams's mother; Rhys's notes for a manuscript called 'Wedding in the Carib Quarter' were lost. If this experience occurred, she buried it. But she has given us Antoinette, who might have stayed in her beloved island if she could have defied racial codes and married her brownskin cousin, Sandi. Her fiction made clear that racial division cost a white woman her chance at life.

But the strand of the Howard story which becomes a pattern recurring over and over is one of a neurotic, sadomasochistic sexuality. Rhys says cryptically in *Smile Please* that shutting sexual experience in the back of her mind as a girl caused her to remember it in detail for the rest of her life. There are sadomasochistic elements in the relations between Heidler and Marya (*Quartet*); MacKenzie and Julia (*After Leaving Mr MacKenzie*); Walter Jeffries and Anna (*Voyage in the Dark*); both the gigolo and *commis* with Sasha (*Good Morning, Midnight*); Antoinette and her husband (*Wide Sargasso Sea*). The swing between passivity and aggression in Rhys's protagonists has been noticed (Angier 1990) as has the masochism (Emery 1990; Davidson 1985): in a wider context Williams (1993) argues in the case of D. H. Lawrence that 'traditional' feminist criticism reads his female characters as victims exploited by the author. She points out however that some Lawrentian women are quite sadistic, such as Gudrun in *Women in Love* (1993: 57), though she is seen from the male point of view, not as with Rhys's female protagonists from inside, justified in her desire to even things up. Ramchand argued (1983: 235) that Rhys 'does not see the fierce sexuality between characters as destructive' in *Wide Sargasso Sea*, but rather it is a means to abandon defences: but the sexual responsiveness between Antoinette and her husband turns to a sadomasochistic intensity before it ends, in which both parties play a version of gender conventions; similarly the last encounter with the gigolo in *Good Morning, Midnight* tempts Marya to unfeeling and rough games. The importance of this in relation to references in Rhys's texts to slavery, race, class and money is that in their context sexuality is about power and trade, and thus is connected to Caribbean racial and economic history. Rhys constructs Julia's narrative as a writing back to romantic fiction where the heroine finds love despite a struggle (Howells 1991: 64).[15] In this she takes her place in the line of Rhys protagonists: she is more wary and aware than Marya or Anna, less cynical than Sasha, less flamboyant and risk-taking than Antoinette. All of these women seek to find refuge from the hegemony of English bourgeois conventions and even romantic love and desire, when that means accepting English men. Though sharing such an anti-colonial stance with other Caribbean women, Rhys protagonists usually fail to support themselves financially.

The outlaw woman, outside conventional family or social structures, is freer to express her resentment towards men at times in
a distinct emotional cruelty.[16] This is especially towards those who
are kinder and wish to engage, though mostly tentatively, in a less
neurotic, or even a really affectionate relationship, such as Stephan
in *Quartet*, Mr Howard in *After Leaving Mr MacKenzie*, Joe in *Voyage
in the Dark*, the gigolo in *Good Morning, Midnight* and Sandi in *Wide
Sargasso Sea*. Each of these men, in their different ways and to different degrees, seeks to make a human connection with a Rhys woman,
despite knowing her emotional condition, despite experiencing her
capacity for abrasiveness. The pattern is most developed in *Good
Morning, Midnight* where Sasha's self-destructive emotional state leads
her to embrace the sinister *commis* and to reject the increasingly
emotionally sensitive gigolo René.

Casual aggression towards men occurs usually when the Rhys
protagonist is approached sexually, whether politely or crassly.
Julia meets a fat man on the Underground on holiday from
South Africa, he asks her to have dinner, gives her his card, she
drops the card to the floor when she leaves the train, letting him
know his unimportance to her. More openly, when a man with a
'low, slithery voice' accosts her on the street when she has been
drinking, she is 'possessed' with a fit of rage and wants to hit him
(*ALMM*: 59): she pushes a hotel swing-door in his face. Another
unknown man approaches her, she prepares to send him off.
Glimpsing each other under a street-lamp, he is clearly young
and she much older: she laughs at the joke against her, manifest-
ing the particular comi-tragic tone of the novel (*ALMM*: 187–8).

Rhys's major male characters also repeat a series of patterns
of behaviour from novel to novel: the older male seducer, such
as Heidler, MacKenzie, Jeffries, the *commis*, even the husband in
*Wide Sargasso Sea*; the more sympathetic but unassertive man, like
Stephan, Horsfield, Joe, the gigolo René, Sandi. Kraf argues that
it is the men in Rhys's novels who 'engage and mystify, who
propel the novels forward, and whose identities are often so shad-
owy that they call out for further study' (1985: 118). There are
some interesting questions which Kraf raises here. In relation to
Mr MacKenzie, she asks why Rhys's male characters have such
fragility that they are concerned about the opinions of strangers,

as when Julia confronts MacKenzie in the restaurant: it is not until Julia leaves that MacKenzie can feel some sympathy for her. Rhys clearly connects the loss of strong family bonds for Julia with a vulnerability which leads to association with other emotionally inhibited or damaged people: MacKenzie, Horsfield, men who ask for sex in exchange for money. They themselves may be trapped in a young man's conception of what a man is, or by fear of feeling, just as Julia is trapped in the box of her own self-defeating self-construction. The contradictions in dominant white men, such as their love of control but capacity for dependency, are observed without explanation. Nebeker (1981) sees Rhys's male characters as indicating the changing role of men in society, i.e. an increasing loss of certainty of their power, which seems far too simplistic. MacKenzie is believably complex. He published a book of poems in his youth; he is both distant and controlling as well as sympathetic and anxious with regard to Julia. He remains entirely in control of his dismally small universe.

Rhys's upbringing, through her convent schooling and her family's close watch over her, separated her from casual contact with boys or men, except for the disaster of Mr Howard. Clearly formative emotional experiences described in *Smile Please* were with women: her mother, Meta, Francine, the coloured girl at school who disliked Rhys, the three sisters with whom she was friendly, the nuns. The painting of her great-grandmother, the lovely woman Rhys thought might be a Spanish countess from Cuba, a lapsed Catholic, was much more interesting than the portrait of her slave-owner ancestor, Old Lockhart. There is a strong sense in Rhys's fiction of men being an unknown quantity, never quite close enough to be understood, and of older women as authority figures who have the power to do a good deal of damage: there is evidence that Rhys had difficult relations not only with her mother but with her sisters.[17]

Brown (1986) and Angier (1990) on the connection between Rhys's women were discussed earlier, but I should add in this context that Staley thinks that there is sensuality in those passages where a Rhys protagonist 'recognises sexuality in another woman' (1979: 82): one example of this would be when Miss Bruce, in 'Illusion' notices a young woman's arms and hands in a 'gentlemanly manner' (*CSS*: 5). But there is very little delighted, joyous non-sexual or sexual communication between people in Rhys's texts.

The ultimate unfeeling sexual role for a woman is that of prostitute. Predating the feminist movement, Rhys thought early on that the life of a prostitute was dangerous, exciting, even difficult and noble: she wrote back to Zola's Nana through her character Anna in *Voyage in the Dark* thus predating feminist controversies about the nature of prostitution (as to whether it is simply demeaning of women and facilitating of male hostility or a necessary means of support for working-class women, Faust 1980). The history of the plantation wove together sexuality and money in the ways in which people were turned into property (slaves, but also planter's wives, under English law, had little legal recourse as autonomous beings). Though Rhys's explicit treatment of prostitution takes place in England, she understood this relationship was not only related to the plantation but to every human relationship in which money played a major role, i.e. in very many. The prostitute is also a subversive, whose indifference and anger towards men can be exressed legitimately: she does not have to hide behind a feminine submissiveness at all times.

Both Julia's sexual relationships and her relations with family (which counterpoint one another, as Howells points out (1990)) have to do with Julia's value and the public, heterosexual, even familial value of a Rhys protagonist is almost always explicitly associated with money. Feminism has drawn attention to the relationship between sexuality and money, always hidden but nevertheless crucially important in defining everything from male prowess to feminine attractiveness. Before formal feminism, Rhys understood that the way money is used both reveals and further defines human relationships, whether they be sexual or familial. Rhys was evidently fully aware of the economics of slavery, in which human lives were commodified to an extreme and sexuality functioned always within that economic perversity: families existed or were separated, children were born or sexual connection established all too often only as planters dictated. Rhys protagonists have not declared full adult fiscal independence from family or lovers willing to provide: they are however well over the age at which such support is endless and unquestioning but seem incapable of providing for themselves. References to slavery or to a particular character's sense of exclusion from the society in which a Rhys protagonist lives connect money with a hierarchy of male, metropolitan power.

When Julia resists being paid off by Mr MacKenzie with a final fifteen hundred francs and returns it to him angrily in public, she still needs and ultimately obtains a replacement payment from Mr Horsfield, which makes Horsfield feel powerful (*ALMM*: 47). Indeed, Julia's life is financed by touching various men for money. She approaches her former lover, Neil James, and her Uncle Griffiths, with varying success. She is offered money freely only by men looking to buy her favours on the street. The men she is close to have their own sexual hangups: Horsfield is put off, sexually, first because Julia cries in the cinema and secondly because she takes off her hat without looking in the mirror and rearranging her hair, which would have signified her desire to please him. Some time later, after the effort of securing money from him and also telling some of her story, Julia simply feels the 'cold of drunkenness' (*ALMM*: 55), which has been the emotional anaesthesia of the transaction. Horsfield recognises that the hallmark of Julia and her relatives is 'No bloody money' (*ALMM*: 54), because 'They would be members of the vast crowd that bears on its back the label "No money"' (*ALMM*: 54–5). Horsfield thinks of himself as a decent man in conventional English terms but does not seem to be comfortable with the role of male provider, which is a part of that social identity. He also controls Julia's access to him and permits himself only on occasion to be ruled by feelings for her: he tries to draw back to his more comforting feelings for his cat.

For Neil James, money is a way of securing his emotional peace and distance from Julia. He plays the role of the absolute gentleman, agreeing to see her and to give her something, but glazing over when Julia tells her story of trying to raise money to bury her dead baby in Paris and accepting a loan and flowers 'from the tart downstairs' (*ALMM*: 112). By bringing in the role of the prostitute Rhys sets up an ironic opposition between cold charity and warm friendship, between an English gentleman's need for economic control over a woman and his ability to be sexual at all.

The coldness and greyness of the England of *After Leaving Mr MacKenzie* reflects the ways in which Julia's own feelings are dulled and deflected in the company of such men. This might be compared with another version of sexual anaesthesia in Antoinette at the end of *Wide Sargasso Sea* when she dreams a silent rage which burns down the house which has denied her sexual identity for so long.

The protagonists of *Voyage in the Dark* and *Wide Sargasso Sea* are of course explicitly West Indian whites: O'Connor speaks of Rhys's 'West Indian novels'[18] as a separate cluster of textual identity. But the Caribbean informs all of Rhys's writing. The Trinidadian/ British[19] novelist V. S. Naipaul commented in 1972 that the protagonists of Rhys's first four novels are in effect one: 'a woman of mystery, inexplicably bohemian, in the toughest sense of the word, appearing to come from no society, having roots in no society' (1972; repr. Frickey, ed. 1990: 54). But he argues that the reason that Julia Martin in *After Leaving Mr MacKenzie* has no past is because 'the West Indian background is excised' (1990: 57), which makes this novel particularly interesting in terms of Rhys's women.

The Caribbean subtext is so buried in this novel that critics have often had trouble finding it: it is the code which opens up the text fully. Emery's reading of the novel notes the indirect references to the Caribbean but finds they are not integral to Julia's sense of direction and do nothing to displace the 'ghost text', the strong connective device of reference to ghosts which make 'the plot, like Julia's life, an insubstantial series of "disconnected episodes"' (1990: 124). Ghosts emphasise the failure Julia experiences in existing in this foreign world in which she finds herself, where her past is ignored and silenced. After trying to explain herself to Ruth, who owns the Modigliani painting, Julia goes home and pulls out all the evidence of her life, photographs, letters, passport, proof of marriage, proof of the existence of the baby she lost. But to no avail, 'I was there, like a ghost' (*ALMM*: 54). When Julia writes to Neil James, her wealthy former lover, she signs off hoping he won't think of her as 'an importunate ghost' (*ALMM*: 66). Later in the narrative, after a cheerful opening to a

chapter where the narrator asserts that every day is a new day
and you are a new person, Julia finds her mind is like an empty
room 'through which vague memories stalked like ghosts' (*ALMM*:
157). Near the end of the novel, she comes across an old woman
near the statue of Henri IV on the Pont Neuf in Paris. This
woman looks 'transparent' in the sunlight, 'like a ghost' (*ALMM*:
181). Mr MacKenzie finds Julia 'pale as a ghost' when she walks
into the restaurant and accosts him and this is repeated later in
his recollection of the scene, when he admits to fear at first sight
of her. Ghostliness is then both frightening to women but also a
source of power over men.

To be a ghost means to be insubstantial in certain important
ways to those still living and unable, usually, to communicate
with them, something poignantly conveyed in the late story 'I
Used to Live Here Once' (*SIOL*, 1976; *CSS*, 1987). Neither ghosts
nor animals can converse with humans. Julia hopes if she 'could
get to the end of what I was feeling it would be the truth about
myself' (*ALMM*: 54). But her life seems insubstantial: 'the last ten
years had been a dream' (*ALMM*: 67). Later, when she walks on
an afternoon of pale sunshine, the streets of Notting Hill are
'strangely empty, like the streets of a grey dream' (*ALMM*: 117)
and she thinks that she may be walking in a circle until she sees
street names and knows she is not. The images of death, sinister
darkness, coldness and entrapment in this novel suggest, as Emery
has argued, that Julia is not only a ghost but a specifically Caribbean form of the living dead, a *zombi*. In such a figure, boundaries
between living and dead are suspended: Emery argues that Julia
as *zombi* can subvert definitive identities like gender conventions
or the restrictions of time (1990: 143).

We begin to discover the suppressed Caribbean subtext by reading Rhys's careful descriptions. Julia, for example, has a pale face,
deep shadows under her eyes, highlights in her rather wild hair
which are 'too red'; the detail of her hands, delicate and slender,
like the 'hands of an oriental' (*ALMM*: 13), carries a suggestion of
foreignness, of racial mixture, which is very delicate, but important.[20] Similarly Julia's mother is dark-skinned, black-eyed and
Brazilian. Julia's strong sense of the importance and power of the
sea acts as a general if subtle point of important reference. Julia is

not of England and is the more crippled in her social identity because she cannot reveal who she is and from where she came: we know only that she comes from limited financial means; that at least one parent has migrated to England; that she has an English uncle with whom relations are strained; that she moves uneasily between Paris and London; that the 'hallmarks' of nationality, class and even age have rubbed off her in an era where all three are very important in French and English culture. In her mother's last days, when she is dying of the aftermath of a serious stroke she mutters something which Julia thinks is 'orange-trees' (*ALMM*: 99): the very indecipherability of this term which has foreign connotations in England suggests that Julia's mother, like Julia, has lost connection to a whole range of linguistic codes and exists in a cultural limbo. Her paralysis and silence act as a physical embodiment of this social and emotional isolation.

The issue of slavery is problematically translated from the Caribbean to European women's condition as it is in *Voyage in the Dark* (something which white feminism gladly accepted for a while). Nora, Julia's sister, reads Conrad's *Almayer's Folly* (Le Gallez 1990) and notes especially a passage referring to a slave who has 'no hope, and knew of no change' (*ALMM*: 103). Nora's own sexuality has been repressed in the service of caring for her mother (*ALMM*: 103), about which she is deeply ambivalent. As Gregg comments, Nora's very conformity is imaged as slavery (but Gregg's claim that Julia's rich lover Neil James is also a slave is unconvincing (1995: 152–3)).

*After Leaving Mr MacKenzie* is a slimly plotted novel which explores in Rhys's now established spare, poetic language,[21] as I have argued earlier containing many elements influenced by her Caribbean childhood, the bleak and circular emotional journey of Julia Martin through difficult affairs with men and the traumatic experience of her mother's death and her fractured relation with her sister. Like *Quartet*, *After Leaving Mr MacKenzie* has a third-person narrative, though it is more complex and multivocal.[22] Gregg argues that this novel is 'perhaps Rhys's most enigmatic work', and 'a self-reflexive text engaged as it is with analysing the means and process of artistic production from a position of liminality in terms of the dominant metropolitan discourse' (1995: 146,

151). In other words, Rhys's narrative is prone to ask questions of itself and be conscious of its own identity and self-contradictions: one could say this is post-modern, but it has long been a Caribbean identity resulting from migration and the experience of living on the edges of a less than welcoming society. Julia, the protagonist, is constantly alienated from the social order and exists on the margins of community, even with regard to her own family: 'I felt as if all my life and all myself were floating away from me on smoke and there was nothing to lay hold of – nothing' (*ALMM*: 53). She is drawn into the emotional anaesthesia which characterises European city life: she meets a pathetic man and some miserable horses in Paris on a cold night, but she feels nothing 'indifferent and cold, like a stone' (*ALMM*: 188). She does not entirely dominate the narrative which offers insights into Julia, her opponents Mr MacKenzie and her sister Nora, as well as her troubled ally Mr Horsfield. There are even momentary insights into the thoughts of Julia's former lover and wary helper, Mr James. Narrative voice, who speaks what to whom, is an important issue in feminist as in post-colonial criticism, because of issues of representation, of who claims the right to define what or whom. Rhys knew, as early as the 1920s, that where you stand is what you think: objectivity, especially with regard to human relations, is next to impossible. This plural perspective is generally an important aspect of Rhys's fictional technique: no doubt the experience of noticing the strikingly different voices with which each constructed their reading of events, on ethnic, racial, class and gender lines in Dominica caused a very sensitive girl to always notice how hard genuine human communication is to achieve, especially given a divisive history.

*After Leaving Mr MacKenzie* is, as Angier (1990) has argued, indeed a thoughtful philosophical essay on identity and existential consciousness in which reality and illusion are constantly being redefined, whether by reference to art or life. The novel also critiques the connection between sexuality and money, desire and power, again something obvious to a young woman who had grown up in the Caribbean and been subject to Mr Howard's dubious attentions. Early in the novel, a kind of perverse still-life arrangement draws Julia's attention. In her cheap hotel room, a fantastic design on the wallpaper lives alongside a faded cheap pink satin quilt, a red plush sofa and 'a very spotted mirror in a gilt frame' (*ALMM*: 10). There is also an unframed oil painting propped on a ledge under the mirror. It is of 'a half empty bottle of red wine, a knife, and a piece of Gruyère cheese' (*ALMM*: 10). Julia considers the painting and decides everything in it is 'slightly distorted and full of obscure meaning' (*ALMM*: 10). She hates it:

It shared, with the colour of the plush sofa, a certain depressing quality. The picture and the sofa were linked in her mind. The picture was the more alarming in its perversion and the sofa the more dismal. The picture stood for the idea, the spirit, and the sofa stood for the act. (*ALMM*: 11)

At this point in the novel, it is not clear exactly what the significance of this passage will ultimately be. The room has a tawdry sensuality with its cheap pink satin quilt and its red plush sofa. The red sofa, standing for the act, surely in the context of the novel and Julia's experience, is the sexual act, and the picture, in its very 'perversion' of life, is the twisted and unhappy idea of sexuality which informs the novel. In the painting, what should be nurturing and pleasure-giving, wine and cheese, becomes intellectualised, unavailable, 'alarming' in Julia's word, as the sexual act itself is 'dismal'.

Like other Rhys protagonists, Julia sustains a complex interaction with the costumes and stage-sets which help instigate sexual desire – makeup, clothing, bedrooms, alcohol, but nevertheless, most of the time these props fail to help much except to reinforce indifference. Interestingly, many of these supports are associated with the stereotype of the febrile white woman (in the Caribbean and outside). Julia has a complex fascination with masking, most often as makeup (Sternlicht 1997). Though she uses makeup as protective cover, we learn early that she has ceased to enjoy it and now uses it as 'partly a substitute for the mask she would have liked to wear' (*ALMM*: 14). Yet other masks are unnerving: Julia's mother, when dying, looks to her 'horribly frightening, like a mask' (*ALMM*: 124) and masks have always frightened her. Emery (1990) discusses at length how masking in the Caribbean sense of playin mas', of tropes of Carnival, plays ironically in Rhys's texts in *Voyage in the Dark* and *Good Morning, Midnight* in relation to female identity. In *After Leaving Mr MacKenzie*, the masking devices are also about putting on a face for the world, one which suggests frivolity, youth, pleasure, attractiveness and which makes much more sense when read in the context of Carnival. That the explicit references to Carnival and the West Indies are omitted here does not mean they are not relevant.

After all, Julia seeks so many masks and evasions of daily reality. Clothes are important (Nebeker 1981): she feels her coat is too small for her at the beginning of the novel, spends precious resources on buying second-hand clothes to travel to England which do not look as good to her when she gets them home as they did in the shop. Most significantly, in relation to her lack of involvement in sexual connections with men, Julia feels 'passion' for new clothes of which she thinks 'with voluptuousness' (*ALMM*: 20). She can imagine the feel of a new dress on her skin, almost as if it were a lover. In a moment which is close to Sasha's use of a good coat as a disguise in *Good Morning, Midnight*, she feels if she had not sold her good fur coat, she would have more respect.

Alcohol is a particularly dangerous mask, for it can appear to create a different personality, a skin to slip into, which however pushes important feelings and self-definitions to the fringes of consciousness. It functions as an important subtext in the novel: almost all major encounters between Julia and the important people in her life are fuelled or lubricated by it. A number of important scenes in the novel are in restaurants or bars where alcohol is sold, but people also produce it in their houses and offer it when dealing with Julia, often, clearly, as both a distraction and a way of coping with discomfort. It is not only Julia who is masked or self-deceived by it: 'To his own ears his voice sounded slightly thickened. Yet he was not in the least drunk. He simply felt that he understood life better than he understood it as a general rule' (*ALMM*: 42). Very early in the novel, Julia's landlady disapproves of her for coming home with a bottle – a man would have been understood. When Julia confronts Mr MacKenzie in the restaurant, she pours herself some of his wine in an empty glass.

Julia needs to mask herself partly because she is already terrified of the ageing process. Rhys wrote about this extensively (Hagley 1988) and with brutal honesty. In the 1930s, in which the novel is set, the mid thirties were still quite old for a woman, especially if she was single. Numerous references point out the seriousness of tiny signs of ageing and the fact that men notice age. This does not only affect Julia: when their mother is dying, her sister Nora looks 'old, old, old' (*ALMM*: 121). Uncle Griffiths notices how Julia looks no longer young when he sees her on the street and takes the decision to avoid her. She thinks if she ceases to care about hiding her age, she will have been finished by Mr MacKenzie and will look as hideous as the woman who lives on the floor above, lets her hair grow out into two inches of grey above the dyed portion and has malevolent eyes because she is 'old and forsaken' (*ALMM*: 15).

Of course the most prevalent reminder of the ageing process is the mirror, also important for Antoinette in *Wide Sargasso Sea*.[23] After the unpleasant encounter with the man who seizes her arm and tries to offer her money for sex, Julia retreats to her hotel in Paris and looks into the mirror, and thinks 'After all, I'm not finished' (*ALMM*: 59). Later, arriving in London, a young man who carries up her luggage appears knowing about her. She stands by the mirror when he brings up her trunk. She looks into it again after she has tipped him and he has smiled for the first time.

Mr Horsfield looks at her whilst she is drinking brandy and thinks she looks older and less pretty in London than she had in Paris. The 'suggestion of age and weariness' fascinates him and he begins to wonder what happens when such a woman looks into the mirror and how she sees herself. He assumes she must have some 'pathetic illusions' about herself. But then she takes out her small box of face-powder and attends to her mirror. He actually says to her 'If only you'd stop worrying about how you look and tell me what's the matter' (*ALMM*: 92). Her reply reveals how acutely she does see the reality of him – she says she thought she must be looking 'pretty ugly' from the way he was looking at her. Horsfield witnessed Julia's meeting with Mr MacKenzie in the restaurant. Later, he finds this difficult to believe:

There had been something fantastic, almost dream-like, about seeing a thing like that reflected in a looking-glass. A bad looking-glass, too. So that the actors had been slightly distorted, as in an unstill pool of water. (*ALMM*: 37)

The use of the word actors here is significant.

The critical difference between Rhys and her protagonists is that the latter are not full-time writers, though women artists do occur in Rhys's texts. This line of characters begins with Miss Bruce in 'Illusion' in *The Left Bank* and includes Miss De Solla in *Quartet*, Ruth in *After Leaving Mr MacKenzie*. All three of these women are quite intimidating, even masculine by the standards of conventional social assumptions about gender. Miss De Solla is 'ascetic to the point of fanaticism' (*ALMM*: 6), Ruth is 'a bit fanatical', and had 'something of an artist in her' (*ALMM*: 51). Ruth also 'simply wouldn't believe that anything was true which was outside herself . . .' (*ALMM*: 51), something close to Rhys's declaration that she wrote only about herself and her experience. The woman artist is marginal in Rhys's texts and is often English (Miss Bruce and Miss De Solla); Ruth sounds English from her speech. It is therefore an important question whether it is the artist's role or the English identity which makes these women strongly determined, interested obliquely in other women and very much in control of their work and therefore their lives, in all these qualities strikingly different from the Rhys protagonist. Rhys herself of course was entirely in control of her writing, and so in this more like her female artist characters than her protagonists: so much for the often repeated assumption that Rhys's female protagonists are really herself. But they do try to tell their stories: Julia, for example, tries to tell Mr Horsfield her history. He finds her irritating, because she seems to speak like someone who is trying to 'recall a story she had heard' and he thinks that she should either know her life or if she is making up a story, 'you ought at least to have it pat' (*ALMM*: 50). Julia lacks the confidence of the professional story-teller and the sureness of the person who knows how to turn personal experience into narrative, how to spin a story as opposed to merely stumbling through it. Mostly, if the Rhys protagonist works, she does a job which shores up feminine conventions, like modelling or in a dress shop, jobs on the edge of the artistic world but not providing a creative outlet. Unlike creative artists, Rhys's women generally have no sense of control over their creative energies.

Association with art in Rhys men seems mostly to help them reach a level of sensitivity otherwise crushed by their effort to be manly. Mr James, in *After Leaving Mr MacKenzie*, enjoys showing Julia his collection of paintings. He loves these pictures, and becomes in their presence momentarily a more appealingly hesitant, human figure. Mr MacKenzie, who appears a very unimpressive man, has however been a poet in his past and so has the courage or emotional instability to be willing to take a slight risk in pursuing his encounter with Julia: the implication being that a man who has once involved himself in something artistic is prone to emotional escapades otherwise unlikely. Horsfield, who is an inattentive businessman, bent on enjoying his life with his father's money, dislikes a woman in the cinema who comments negatively on a film he is enjoying. Horsfield finds the film and the cinema building together give him a sense of 'the illusion of art'.

Rhys uses the English or Anglo-Saxons and animals in the novel to further contribute to the complexity of gender identity. The portrait of the English in *After Leaving Mr MacKenzie* is almost entirely negative and carries implicitly the Caribbean sense of resentment of the colonial centre: it is the most central symbol of hostile power in the novel and implicitly informs every character's self-location and identity, and therefore their sexual behaviour. Even Rhys's English characters can have trouble with English identity, and be seriously conflicted about it. To Mr MacKenzie, an Englishman who professes dislike of the French when in England and yet does not want to be identified as English when in France, it is painful nevertheless to hear the French make fun of the English. At root, he acknowledges a commitment and connection to England.

But Julia lacks that, indeed, like other Rhys protagonists, she lacks a strong connection to culture or place, so when Mr Horsfield remarks that Paris is a place where Anglo-Saxons find difficulty being sober, Julia counters by saying that 'no place is a place to be sober in' (*ALMM*: 48). In this she is different from Anna or Antoinette, who miss the West Indies, or Sasha, who loves Paris.

Julia actively dislikes England and the English as is evident in the short encounter she has with some English fellow passengers on the boat train to Calais from Paris. They, and the English newspaper she is reading, make her feel she is already in England and so she is 'strange and subdued' (*ALMM*: 60). Their conversation is amiable and tries to be inoffensive about their travels. But they are difficult to know and it is impossible to 'be quite sure whether they were very kind or very hard, naively frank or very sly' (*ALMM*: 61). As Julia falls asleep, she tries to reread the English paper, the 'doggy page'.

Animal imagery is important in Rhys's construction of gender and sexuality here as in *Quartet*. It gives Rhys an economical code for delineating environments and human personalities. Animals figure in paintings or decorations. The wallpaper in the first hotel room in Paris, where we meet Julia, has 'a large bird, sitting on the branch of a tree' and facing, 'with open beak, a strange wingless creature, half-bird-half-lizard which also had its beak open' (*ALMM*: 10). Mr Horsfield takes Julia to a restaurant in London where the walls had 'paintings of dead lobsters and birds served up on plates ready to be eaten' (*ALMM*: 144). A complex passage, following Julia's expression of urgency to get away from England, describes the painting by Modigliani of a woman lying on a couch, a woman with a lovely proud body, 'like an utterly lovely proud animal' (*ALMM*: 52). She has 'a face like a mask, a long dark face, and very big eyes. The eyes were blank, like a mask, but when you looked at it a bit it was as if you were looking at a real woman, a live woman' (*ALMM*: 52.) This woman ultimately seems to mock Julia and to assert her own reality as more definite than Julia's and 'at the same time, I *am* you. I'm all that matters of you' (*ALMM*: 53). Wyatt, the strong, rather masculine nurse for Julia's mother, lifts her head 'like a terrier' (*ALMM*: 97), a particularly intelligent and tenacious breed of dog. Julia's mother, dying, loses human intelligence, and her eyes seem like 'bloodshot, animal eyes' (*ALMM*: 98). Julia's sister regards her as 'something out of the zoo' when she first visits Julia in her hotel in London (*ALMM*: 73). Julia's uncle, who is barely cordial with her, responds to the news that a lady is waiting downstairs to see him as if he might have said, 'A zebra? A giraffe?' (*ALMM*: 79).

When Julia walks through London after leaving Uncle Griffiths and a humiliating encounter, she hears a human voice sounding like 'an animal in pain' (*ALMM*: 85). When Nora feels particularly angry with her lot, she wants to call those who admire her devotion to her mother beasts, even though with further thought, she recants this. Horsfield's cat appears sufficiently to become a minor character, always after an encounter with Julia. The cat is attentive to him and waits for him, even meets him like a dog would: in response he caresses it, though it still retains some malevolence. In a parallel image, a woman Julia sees walking along in the rain in London seems like a 'dog without a master' (*ALMM*: 145), and Julia thinks of the power of society against which 'she had not a dog's chance' (*ALMM*: 22). In the last sentence of the novel, we see Julia drifting away from us as the night settles down over Paris in 'the hour between dog and wolf' (*ALMM*: 191). Underneath the domesticated pet's calm and docile exterior lies its wild and proud predatory ancestor: Julia who has been less than a dog, in the English sense of a dog's protected and cherished space, may be on the way to a more aggressive, more alienated identity.

The Rhys woman is a subversive not just in intention and reaction to social conditions but in her very existence as a puzzling, riddling, self-questioning loose cannon who continually destabilises conventional values for women, sexuality and male behaviour towards women and easy definitions of national, class and ethnic identity. Rhys's collective portrait of women at different stages of life destabilises all easy definitions, racial, gender, class and national.

She herself stood her ground against 'Anglo-Saxon' conventions, and constantly reiterated her resistance to bourgeois values.[24] But she also constantly flirted with them, probably partly for the sake of her daughter, partly because of her own upbringing: similarly her female protagonists are both politically subversive and willing to play along with middle-class conventions which are essentially inimical to their survival. It is a difficult and exhausting game which one individual can never win: political resistance, as the Caribbean knows, as feminism also knows, is successful when individuals join together into effective groups. Both the Caribbean and the women's movement have had internal struggles between those who were willing to stand up against established authority and respectability and those who were willing to go along with it: Rhys's characters seem to incorporate and internalise this struggle, often as simultaneous attraction to and repulsion from male-centred England.

# CHAPTER 4

# Writing colour, writing Caribbean: Voyage in the Dark *and the politics of colour*

Being black is warm and gay, being white is cold and sad.

(*VITD*: 31)

I bought a bright red dress to celebrate – at Exeter – a cheap Christmas cracker dress . . .

(*L*: 209)

I wont say one word about Voyage . . . except this – its after all an often related story. The difficult thing is the only worth while thing. The girl is *divided*. two people *really*. or at any rate a one foot in the sea & one on land girl.

(Letter to Selma Vaz Dias, 17 September 1965)

Throughout Rhys's texts, more intensely in some than others but always significantly, colour functions as a symbolic code. Rhys provides depth and complexity by developing such poetic metaphors within her spare prose. By colour, I mean both a painter's palette and the consciousness of skin shade and the social construction of race which is so clearly an indication of a West Indian consciousness at work in Rhys's texts. By politics, I mean that colour conveys a complex and detailed sense of power relations, mainly to do with how the life force, libido itself, is repressed by hierarchical social organisation. Much can be said about complexities of race, culture, gender and nationality through this coding of colour, which repays close reading because it proves to be quite subtle and integral to Rhys's characterisation and settings.

Colours both carry connective meaning within a given Rhys text and also from text to text, in the way poetic images tend to connect a poem series, though individual texts tend to have their own palette.[1] *After Leaving Mr MacKenzie* (1931; 1990), for example,

85

is largely a canvas of black, white and grey, with a few splashes of colour, whereas in *Voyage in the Dark* (1934; 1982) and *Wide Sargasso Sea* (1966; 1982), both expressly describing the West Indies, vibrant colours are much more significant. Some critics have noted generally that *Voyage in the Dark* and *Wide Sargasso Sea* construct England and France as largely cold, dark, dull or pale whereas the Caribbean is full of strong colour. This is evidently not simply an observation of the difference between northern and southern locales but a reflection of a difference between feeling, activity and strength signified by vivid jewel colours on the one hand and stress, passivity, self-destructive hostility and inability to feel on the other. Dull or dark colours are often identifiable as specifically English.[2]

Rhys was fully aware of the importance of the right palette for a given text. Writing to Francis Wyndham, she mentioned a poem she had sold to a Dutch magazine which had the line 'Purple against Red': she commented 'But the colours are not right for this book' (*L*: 208).

We are all susceptible to colour, but our interpretation of it is substantially derived from culture.[3] For example, whereas black is the common colour for mourning in Caucasian England, white, purple and grey are also prevalent in Caribbean cultures.[4] Because of the history of racism and the anxiety of white minorities in the Caribbean to hold themselves separate and apart from the black majority, skin shade and eye shade became critical: the caste hierarchy within the black community of the Caribbean and the United States has also long been based on relative fairness of skin and possession of European hair or features, reflecting the internalisation of racist values.

Because of Rhys's particularly complex cultural identity, her use of colour, both painterly and as skin shade, not surprisingly, is idiosyncratic.[5] Few critics however have paid extended attention to colour coding in Rhys's writing, although James Lindroth explored what he called 'The Whistlerian Moment' in Rhys's short stories (1985). For Lindroth, Rhys's colour language is 'narrow, achieving its effects as much by the withholding of hues and tones as by their inclusion' (1985: 128). Rhys works patterns of certain colours: silver and grey, yellow and black, green and gold.

Lindroth argues that in the story 'Tigers Are Better-Looking' (1962; *CSS*), black and yellow signify the absent tiger, associated with the emotional turmoil in Mr Severn. At the end of the story, Lindroth argues, the colours modulate into grey, white and silver and a muted yellow and he can return to his peaceful and solitary writing after a 'psychic transformation' which renews him.

But colour as race also signifies in this story.[6] Mr Severn, after two double whiskies, meets up with two young women, one of whom he knows 'fairly well' and 'if fair is fair' (*CSS*: 178) would have on her epitaph that she never made anybody nervous on purpose. 'Fair is fair' would not strike a racial chord except in someone who has lived formative years in a racially divided society: the words carry a double meaning. The English pride themselves on fairness, but have not yet dealt fully with race or class and their language still contains racial insensitivities. Linguistic echoes of this England enter into the 'mulatto playing the saxophone' and Mr Severn's noticing that one of the young women has, in British, casually racist parlance, 'a touch of the tarbrush', a little non-Caucasian blood: he approves of her, but asks himself 'Why is it that she isn't white – Now, why?' (*CSS*: 181).

Yellow is important: they are in a club in London guarded by a man 'with a yellow face' (*CSS*: 179). Mr Severn draws on the tablecloth with a yellow pencil. Yellow here is generally unpleasant and associated with threat: Maudie stands in a 'yellowish, livid light' in the street after appearing in court with Severn.

We assume, from the opening of the story, that Severn isn't sexually interested in women but he has strong views on how they should appear and behave. Drunkenly, he comments on a tall woman in a backless evening gown: he thinks she has an ambition 'to get a job as a stewardess on a line running to South Africa' (*CSS*: 181). He is clearly critical of that – and South Africa resonates as the apartheid regime was at its height in 1962, the date this story first appeared in the *London Magazine*.[7] He comments on a 'lovely dark brown couple' at the bar with whom he has had a conversation. They want to know where he lives: his comment is 'darkest, dingiest Bloomsbury' (*CSS*: 181). But the woman comments 'I didn't come to London to go to the slums' and speaks 'in the most perfect British accent, high, sharp, clear and shattering' (*CSS*: 181–2). Severn is an outsider to conventional British society anyway, being gay, but he shies from having the courage to be bold and he earns his living writing 'tame' articles. However he allies with other outsiders, though he makes a mistake with the 'lovely dark brown couple' because the wife has adopted English (white) snobbish attitudes along with the accent.

Severn and his friend Maudie are taken into custody for being drunk and disorderly. He gives Maudie a 'black look', (the usual Britishism for a hostile look), when they part as she has insulted his age. When they talk after their appearance in court, Maudie describes a 'very dark girl' who is highly respectably dressed, 'awfully nicely in a black coat and skirt and a lovely clean white blouse and a little white hat and lovely stockings and shoes' (*CSS*: 186). Clearly Severn and Maudie are acutely aware of race: darkness and fairness, black and white, function in Rhys's texts as a racial code.

Mr Severn (the title 'Mr' is a critical clue to a certain English reticence and constraint), the writer for an Australian (colonial) paper, has been imaged as 'a tame grey mare' or one of a band of 'timid tigers' (*CSS*: 176) by his lover Hans. The grey here is of a different order from the spectrum of skin tones from yellow to brown which inform the story: it appears to connote an emotional timidity and conventionalism. Severn's return to admiring his yellow-white brick wall, the silvered drainpipe, the grey steely sky and his silver oilcloth curtains is a return to the safe but dull world he was associated with by Hans. Though his writing cadence returns and he can work, he is back in the conventions of his society. Grey here hardly connotes beauty but rather a kind of elegant safety, reticence, withdrawal from danger. Perhaps the black and yellow pattern of the absent tiger signifies a willingness to be vivid, not pale, active, not greyly quiet, and to be able to assert identity.

Most of the time, colour coding is consistent throughout Rhys's texts (including her drafts and her letters) though a single colour often has a number of important meanings. For example, she exploits the conventional signification of red as passion, especially sexual passion, though there are many subtle uses to which she puts it. The small red flower pinned to the lapel of Nora's pale green dress in *After Leaving Mr MacKenzie* suggests an impulse towards vitality and sexual being barely surviving her generally repressed life. Similarly a touch of bright red often signifies Caribbean identity isolated in a hostile Europe, as in Antoinette's red dress or the red dress of the young Antillean girl in 'Trio' (*CSS*: 34–5).

Pale shades of primary colours are generally negatively coded in a Rhys text, such as pale or blue eyes. This is especially so when the character is an English or Frenchman with some social power, as with Hugh Heidler in *Quartet*, 'he had oddly shaped eyelids, three cornered eyelids over pale, clever eyes' (*Q*: 40).[8] In a 1934 letter to Evelyn Scott, Rhys writes from London of a 'yellow fog very cold' as 'more like hell than anything you can imagine' (*L*: 23). The yellow of London fog in the 1930s was a grey and sickly yellow, a smog-yellow, not the brilliant yellow of a flower petal in tropical sun. Yellow is a problematic colour in Rhys's palette often associated with emotional difficulty or stressful choice. Wolfe comments that 'yellow is the colour of fear' in Rhys texts (1980: 117), taking his cue no doubt from Rhys's story 'The Sound of the River' (*TAB-L*; *CSS*)

she had watched it fluttering up and down the window pane – a flash of yellow in the rain. 'Oh, what a pretty bird'. Fear is yellow. You're yellow. She's got a broad streak of yellow. They're quite right, fear is yellow. (*CSS*: 238)

At root, Rhys's dislike of pale colours and paleness itself seems to be directly connected to her dislike of her own paleness, i.e. white racial identity, which is most explicitly laid out in *Smile Please*, and which comes directly from her Caribbean experience. The Caribbean is generally associated in Rhys's texts with bright colours and vitality. This opposition, and an important conjunction of black and white, is marked in *Voyage in the Dark*.

*Voyage in the Dark* was originally called 'Two Tunes', signifying two quite separate and confrontational worlds of the Caribbean, Anna's childhood home, and England, scene of her unhappy present. Colour codes are critical in *Voyage in the Dark* for they convey very important signals as to how to read Anna's complex identity. It is this critical connection between emotions and the

perception of colour which is the fundamental key to this complex essay on race, gender, class and nationality as they play on
sexuality.[9] The narrative is told in Anna's first-person voice, but
her self-reflexiveness is tenuous. She is the youngest of Rhys's
protagonists, still a teenager.[10] She largely describes what happens
but not how or why it happens, just as she describes how she feels
and what she sees, smells, hears or touches in detail but does not
try to explain why this comes about. The use of colour helps Rhys
delineate Anna's moods in detail without explicit commentary.
Also references to race, class and gender are closely interwoven
in this novel and their interrelationship is emphasised by Rhys's
use of black and white.

This novel was developed out of some early notebooks in
which Rhys wrote out her pain and grief at the ending of the
affair with Lancelot Smith and which were carried along with
her for a number of years before she became a writer.[11] Though
the notebooks supplied the raw material for *Voyage in the Dark*, the
novel itself is her third. It was always her favourite.[12] She commented at length on its gestation to Francis Wyndham in a letter
(7 November 1968):

You know the exercise books (& Mrs Adam's version of them) weren't a
diary. They were written in diary form about a year after all the fuss
was over & I was living by myself in Chelsea.
     Writing relieved me a lot – I remember the first sentence and the
last. Then I hid them away in a trunk and didn't look at them for six or
seven years (But I kept them) . . . I think 'Voyage in the Dark' is more
true in its way than the exercise books (which have vanished) or the
typescript.

The novel is Rhys's *bildungsroman* which benefitted from waiting to be completed until she was an experienced and skilled
novelist. It follows the drift into prostitution of Anna Morgan,
white West Indian chorus girl, who has an affair with a much
older, well-to-do and emotionally damaged Englishman called
Walter Jeffries.[13] Eventually he ends the relationship and pen-
sions Anna off, and she begins a slow slide into prostitution. She
endures a dangerous abortion and, in Rhys's preferred version,
she dies as a result. However, the editor at Constable insisted
that the ending be more optimistic to make it easier for readers

to accept. Enough early reviewers were certainly sufficiently resistant to the novel's subject matter whilst praising the novel's
craft that perhaps in 1934 the editor was right in thinking a death
from an abortion was too shockingly graphic for the general reading public in England.[14] Why Rhys did not substitute the earlier
version when the novel was reissued is puzzling (Brown 1985). But
it is stronger: moreover I think reading the original for its colour
codes and their contribution to the novel as a whole strengthens
the argument for it even more.

Anna reads her world as dualist, the West Indies versus England, which signifies many subordinate oppositions:

It was almost like being born again. The colours were different, the
smells different, the feeling things gave you right down inside yourself
was different. Not just the difference between heat, cold; light, darkness;
purple, grey. But a difference in the way I was frightened and the way
I was happy. (*VITD*: 7)

The first impression we have of Anna is her vivid memory of
the sights and smells of her Caribbean home. She speaks of the
sea, 'When there was a breeze the sea was millions of spangles;
and on still days it was purple as Tyre and Sidon' (*VITD*: 7). Just
as in *Wide Sargasso Sea*, England seems to the Rhys protagonist
unreal, like a dream. It produces emotional stasis in her: an
absence of passion, liveliness and colour. As a chorus girl, Anna
has performed without much enthusiasm in third-rate theatres
and stayed in dismal lodgings in 'little grey streets' (*VITD*: 8) in
towns where the sea was 'grey-brown or grey-green' (*VITD*: 8).
Even the washing 'hung limp' on a line in the 'grey-yellow' light
(*VITD*: 9). Though England can certainly be grey for days on
end, it is clear that Anna concentrates on the drabness because
that is what she feels there. Louis James, rightly, comments that
Rhys's 'sense of colour was formed in the Antilles' (1978: 32): she
would be able to reproduce it until the end of her life.

Much has been made critically of Anna's reading Emile Zola's
*Nana* (1880; 1972) since this (and their similar names) connects
Anna early in the narrative with the romantic construction of the
prostitute as heroine. Maudie, who Rhys thought a simple young
woman, is however shrewd enough to know that *Nana* is 'a dirty
book . . . about a tart' (*VITD*: 10), and that 'a man writing a book

about a tart tells a lot of lies one way and another' (*VITD*: 10).[15]
Critics are not always so perceptive. Nebeker describes Zola's
Nana as greedy and 'utterly evil' (1981: 54); but from a summary
of Nana made by Zola outside his text, we see how he was working out of male fear of women and with grand mysogyny. Holden
(1972) cites Zola saying that at seventeen, Nana looked at least
twenty, and was:

> Blonde, pink, Parisian face, very wide-awake, her nose slightly turned
> up, her mouth small and laughing, a dimple on her chin, her eyes very
> blue and bright, with golden lashes . . . good-natured above all else.
> Follows her nature, but never does harm for harm's sake, and feels
> sorry for people. Bird-brain . . . superstitious, frightened of God. Loves
> animals and her parents . . . ends up regarding man as a material to
> exploit, becoming . . . a ferment of destruction without meaning to . . .
> The cunt in all its power . . . the moral will lie in the cunt turning every-
> thing sour . . . (*Nana*, ed. Holden 1972: 'Introduction' 11–13)

Zola here admits he built his novel on a woman of little intelligence, no education, no financial security, with only the unsoph-
isticated currency of youth and raw female sexuality. This is not
a woman with power of any kind, yet Zola makes her an agent of
male destruction and has her die at the 'height of her youth',
presumably as punishment for her hubris in bringing down men
of a superior class. This 'realism' is nothing more than heavy
class and gender bias: 'The fly that had come from the dungheap
of the slums, carrying the ferment of social decay, had poisoned
all these men simply by alighting on them' (1972: 452–3).[16] Nana
picks up 'poison' in the gutters, she poisons a whole people, and
then she rots herself, dying of smallpox.

Fantasies are spun when she disappears for a while just before
her death, drawing on the grossest of imperial and racist sterotypes:

> She had conquered the heart of the Viceroy, and was reigning, in the
> innermost precincts of a palace, over two hundred slaves, having one or
> two of them beheaded, now and then, for the sake of a little amuse-
> ment. Not a bit of it: she had ruined herself with a large Negro, satisfy-
> ing a filthy passion which had left her without a penny to her name,
> wallowing in the crapulous debauchery of Paris . . . (1972: 454)

Rhys's reply (in her original and preferred version of *Voyage in
the Dark*), revisions this pathologically hostile portrait: Anna dies

at the height of her youth, though not as punishment, rather, as Rhys said, to save her from endless pain and disappointment. Like Nana, Anna is an actress of sorts in a variety theatre. But in Rhys's version the men who use her youth and beauty are for the most part evidently cowardly or downright disreputable: Anna herself begins as naively trusting, passes through a stage of self-destructive hopelessness and passivity, and ends, in Rhys's pre-ferred, unpublished version, by dying from a botched abortion. Anna's ironic relation to Nana is important, and the earlier novel remains a fruitful companion to *Voyage in the Dark*, a kind of rehearsal for the relation between *Wide Sargasso Sea* and Charlotte Brontë's *Jane Eyre*. In intertwining gender, race and class iden-tities in Anna's narrative, Rhys replies to those elements in Zola's *Nana*, exposing the immorality of the men and women who prey on Anna and so reversing the image of Nana as a predatory force of nature.

The details of this effective fictional retort repay attention. Le Gallez points out that in the description of Anna with *Nana*, emphasis is on her looking at the cover, not on the story or the character. Anna remains elliptical in her response to Nana her-self (1990: 83). Le Gallez argues that the reader is left to interpret the visual meaning without Rhys's explicit intervention or Anna's: Anna proves to be reticent as her narrative proceeds. I would add to this that the colour of the cover and the text signify import-antly. The edition which Anna reads has a coloured picture of a 'stout, dark woman brandishing a wine-glass' (*VITD*: 9). The 'look of the dark, blurred words', not their meaning, gives Anna a strange feeling, 'sad, excited and frightened' (*VITD*: 9). Harrison comments that Anna's fascination with reading conveys a sense of words as talismans (1988: 73), rather than as language. But Anna also manages to 'read' London as a series of black and white con-trasting symbols, like a text. It is a great many white people and dark houses. It is the houses which seem to disapprove of her and not the people; the houses seem like characters, both human and in the sense of letters on a page. The pale people are backdrop and setting, the page on which the dark houses speak.

Chorus girls are particularly vulnerable, since they sell their beauty on stage, are poor and unchaperoned and long to escape their dismal lives. Anna and Maudie's landlady had not at first wanted to rent to 'professionals' (meaning chorus girls, whose reputation was chancy at best, and who might well be professionals in the other common meaning) but Maudie finds Anna always looks 'ladylike' (*VITD*: 10). Maudie and Anna pick up two men and Maudie tells them Anna was born in the West Indies and the other chorus girls call her 'the Hottentot' (*VITD*: 13). Walter Jeffries asks why and comments 'I hope you call them something worse back' (*VITD*: 13), thus reinforcing the name as a negative. This term reverberates through the novel, as does the opposition between Anna, the mysterious foreign 'dark' woman and Maudie, the rather worn and lascivious 'fair' woman, with her long white face, her pale yellow hair and her missing tooth.[17]

Sander L. Gilman remarks that in the iconography of the nineteenth century two apparently unrelated female images – the icon of the female Hottentot and the icon of the prostitute (1985: 206) are yoked together. He further points out that Manet's painting 'Nana' (1877) conveys the sexualized white woman without a black servant, whereas there had been a convention during the nineteenth century which paired a white woman and a black female servant as similarly sexual. For Gregg (1995: 117), Gilman's account of the Manet painting of Nana and the image of Nana on the cover of Anna's copy of the novel are similar, though it is not clear how Rhys could have arrived consciously at this connection.

The image of the Hottentot came to stand in British imperial discourse for Africans, for black people in general, and where female, to convey an intense sexuality conjured by the social fictions of racist imperialism: J. J. Virey, Gilman points out, argued that Hottentot women had much more developed sexual organs that those of whites (1985: 212–13). Most particularly, this pseudo-science stressed the large buttocks of the Hottentot.[18] Eventually, by the late nineteenth century, the sexuality of the prostitute was linked to these distortions of the physicality of the Hottentot woman: Manet's Nana has heavy thighs and buttocks. Manet's Nana of course developed from Manet's reading of Zola's novel *L'Assommoir* (1877): after Manet created his painting, Zola created his own version of this white male myth in *Nana*.[19]

Rhys's connection of Zola's Nana and the figure of the Hottentot is an interesting proof of the way in which the racist conception of the Hottentot was still lying around in popular British culture in the mid 1930s. Anna may seem ladylike and whilst Walter Jeffries, her seducer, may seem sexually discreet, not looking at Anna's body in an obvious way, eventually the transaction between them is understood fully on his side to be a promise of sexual excitement from a white woman whom he perceives as having an extra thrill presumably from association with racist constructions of black females in his culture. Anna's nice, clean English room with all 'the dirt swept under the bed' (*VITD*: 31) becomes a place from which she can escape through memory to the West Indies: the yellow afternoon light coming in through the wooden jalousies over the windows as she lies ill in bed, cared for by a black servant called Francine. She remembers 'I wanted to be black ... Being black is warm and gay, being white is cold and sad' (*VITD*: 31). Anna makes sure Walter knows how much she has wanted to be black. Later in the novel, a man speaks to her in the street and she feels violent towards him but sees a policeman looking at her, and the violence turns towards him, verbally. She makes him 'a damned baboon – a fair baboon too, worse than a dark one every time' (*VITD*: 148). This is a neat turning of the racist use of monkey imagery about dark or black people into an attack on whites – specifically white men.

When Walter takes her upstairs, he comments, 'you rum little devil' (*VITD*: 55), putting together presumably Anna's predilection for strong drink, her working-class identity as chorus girl and her desire to be black, with sexual stereotypes in British culture. Anna is of course inexperienced: her other dressing room nickname, given her by the worldly-wise Laurie is 'Virgin' (*VITD*: 16–17). She is sexually withdrawn with Walter, on one occasion thinking first of her childhood teacher, a nun, who spoke about lying down to think of death, judgement, hell and heaven as if you were dead. She then, problematically, appropriates the identity of a young slave woman, 'Maillotte Boyd, aged 18' (*VITD*: 56), being sexually used but accepting that: 'But I like it like this' (*VITD*: 56).

The opposition between fair-haired women who know how to manipulate the system and dark Anna who does not is sustained, and so is the opposition between obedient and willing women and Anna, who is capable of quiet but definite aggression. In her jamming of a lighted cigarette deliberately onto Walter's hand, she shows a moment of fierceness which intends harm and proves her entirely unlike Nana, because she is capable of a resistance which the text ultimately relates to the way the Caribs fought Europeans. Writing to Walter after he has ended the relationship, a little more than half-way through the novel, Anna gets drunk on vermouth and begins to sing a music-hall song. She is reminded of someone she heard sing the song, a 'plump girl with very curly pale-gold hair' and 'a long stupid face', who was very popular. As Anna tries to remember a line, and refuses to believe it can be 'Legions away from despair', rather 'Oceans, perhaps' (*VITD*: 105), she freely associates and thinks of the Caribbean Sea, then of the Caribs and their 'resistance to white domination', 'though spasmodic . . . fierce' (*VITD*: 105).[20]

As Emery (1990) comments, remembering the Caribs moves the memory of the song out of one phase of memory and into another. Inflecting an English music-hall song with Caribbean overtones makes it capable of subversion, just as Anna is clearly by this time not a typically willing or subordinated chorus girl or mistress, which makes her thought about Carib resistance connect: it also definitively identifies Anna with Dominica. It also separates her from the girl with the pale-gold curls entirely. Incidentally, later in the novel, Anna describes Laurie's neck coming out of her fur coat as 'pale-gold'. Laurie, like the music-hall singer, is a woman who knows how to make a success of pleasing an audience or a client. The colour-coding links these two women and places them. The stereotype of the poor white woman as passive and willing collides here implicitly with the stereotype of the tropical white high-caste woman as sexually inert. Anna draws on another stereotype she has absorbed: the passionate black slave woman who in this case will not respond to her seducer. The slave woman and Anna merge in their acceptance of their sexual role in Anna's mind, but by the statement 'I like it like this' she comes dangerously close to justifying acceptance of sexual predation, and extending this to all women, regardless of race or class.

Part of Anna's self-representation lies in her choice of the colour black for her clothing, which in Europe suggests sexual sophistication. She compounds this impression by her bright, brassy nails at her first private encounter with Walter Jeffries in London, her darkness and brightness contrasting with the waiter's 'pale, flat face' (*VITD*: 19). Here Anna is dressed in black and brandishing a wine glass, a younger thinner version of the picture on the cover of *Nana*, which has itself ignored the fact that Zola's character is blonde. Walter asks if she always wears black. Anna quotes a vaguely remembered remark from a book about a woman wearing black, 'that sable colour, or lack of colour' (*VITD*: 22). Black is of course all colours absorbed into one. It is counterpointed by red carnations on the table, and in the adjoining bedroom there are red-shaded lights. There are also 'heavy pink silk curtains' (*VITD*: 20) in the dining room. Pink in Rhys's palette generally is associated with a negative kind of sexuality, a kind of warped femininity.

But when Anna lies down on the bed, which is like ice, she feels 'as if I had gone out of myself, as if I were in a dream' (*VITD*: 23). Even the fire seems 'painted' with no warmth, elements which will recombine for Rhys's other evidently West Indian protagonist Antoinette in *Wide Sargasso Sea*. Because of her emotional retreat from Walter's seduction, even red flames have no life or capacity to provoke feeling.

When Walter summons her for a final meeting, Anna again dresses in black, though she wears more rouge than usual, combining the black and the red which signify a dangerously willing yet conflicted sexuality in a Rhys protagonist. When this black velvet dress becomes torn, Laurie, a practical call-girl friend, lends her a pink one with silver 'bits and pieces dangling here and there' (*VITD*: 123). It is rather tawdry, queasily sexual, but suggests a more malleable femininity. Joe dislikes the dress, but Laurie thinks enough of it to demand that Anna take it off when she is drunk.

White clothing is associated for Anna with grief and with the repression of vitality which white Creoles imposed on their children (especially the girls), in order to preserve caste. Anna remembers a funeral, probably her father's, which she attended in a white dress with wreaths on her head and in her hands which made her white gloves wet.²¹ People were saying 'so young to die' (*VITD*: 97). Just before remembering this, Anna wants to tell Walter: 'I'm dying now really, and I'm too young to die' (*VITD*: 97) which connects her directly to her father's premature death.

On a Sunday when London seems dead, there is no sun, but a 'glare on everything like a brass band playing' (*VITD*: 41). This light is somehow military, somehow sound which is controlled and controlling, not comfortable or relaxing for Anna. When she retreats into childhood memory here she thinks of the colonial white assumptions about respectable Sunday clothes with which she grew up: wool next to the skin; 'white drawers tight at the knee and a white petticoat and a white embroidered dress – everything starched and prickly'. Also black ribbed-wool stockings and black shoes which the groom Joseph (named as the groom is named in *Wide Sargasso Sea*) cleans with a pot of blacking and his spit. Brown kid gloves from England, 'one size too small' (*VITD*: 41). The alienating effect of white racial identity on Anna is intensified by white or brown or black clothing, and by the agony of wool and gloves in the heat of the tropical day.

Black or black and white clothes in this text often indicate a disguise. Ethel, the would-be madam in *Voyage in the Dark* cultivates the appearance of respectable middle-class professionalism on first meeting Anna: a white blouse and a dark skirt. But her skirt is stained, her chemise shows and is dirty and she bears the slightly sexual message of black stockings (*VITD*: 106). She will later wear black and white again, her signature mask of respectability (*VITD*: 148). Ironically, it is Ethel who expresses disgust at the 'soft, dirty way foreign girls have' (*VITD*: 109), though Anna whom she befriends is in effect foreign: she even disapproves of an actress in a film who adds false hair for the shoot: 'an English girl wouldn't have done that. An English girl would have respected herself more than to let people laugh at her like that behind her back' (*VITD*: 109).

Black and white memories from childhood can be a reminder of racial stress or of happy adventures. Anna remembers a Miss Jackson from childhood who spoke perfect French and taught it. She was an illegitimate daughter of a probably English parent, Colonel Jackson, determined to hang on to the colonial and racial privilege she imagined this provided. She wore black, had black glittering eyes and a dead-white face (signifying she avoided the sun at all costs), and Anna found her sitting room very dark with yellow pictures of men in uniform, and the banana tree's 'thick green silk' outside (*VITD*: 162): this woman seems to try to hold herself English by her severities of dress and lack of sun-tan, by ignoring the richness of Caribbean foliage outside.

Outside Anna's window at Ethel's the day she first sees it is a barrel-organ playing 'Moonlight Bay'. Popular songs are important in *Voyage in the Dark* as elsewhere in Rhys's texts.[22] The song acts as an ironical reminder to the reader of Anna's previous memories of moonlight on the bay and outings in a boat with Black Pappy, who wore a patched blue linen suit, and the stories of barracudas swimming along in the white roads the moonlight made, a moonlight which made shadows as 'dark as sun-shadows' (*VITD*: 53), a Caribbean experience as unforgettable as it is commonplace. When Anna knows the relationship with Walter is ending, she tries to simulate the idea of a waterfall in her bathtub, imagining again the heavy scented tropical white flowers which opened at night and which made Hester feel faint. There are crabs in the green-brown water which can be broken with stones so that white stuff bubbles out (this pool presages the one in *Wide Sargasso Sea*). These menacing, unpleasant or simply rich and heady references to white in the Caribbean context make the colour even more complex in Anna's experience: none have the degree of unpleasantness which the image of white people as woodlice conveys: 'The ones without money, the ones with beastly lives . . . They swarm like woodlice when you push a stick into a woodlice nest at home. And their faces are the colour of woodlice' (*VITD*: 26).

White and a subdued pink or red are dominant codes by which Ethel, the other major exploiter of Anna, tries to pass off her newly decorated flat as properly respectable, and so the wallpaper is white with stripes, the armchairs have a pattern of small rosebuds (I am assuming them to be red as most chintz rosebuds are), the furniture in Anna's room is painted white. Even Ethel, with her tendency to white overalls at times, and her red face, is sometimes coded similarly.

Red is often a detail of a threatening female hostile to Anna. Confined to her room by the flu, Anna finds her black-haired landlady's eyes little and red, like a Caribbean soucriant's eyes ('during the day they looked like ordinary women but you could tell them by their eyes', *SP*: 23). The touch of red suggests the passionate, aggressive nature of the soucriant (which is specifically mentioned late in the novel as having red eyes (*VITD*: 163)).

Anna buys new clothes, a dark blue dress and coat and a dark blue and white hat. The blue and white signify a grownup version of the child's innocence, the fact of dark blue coding England's environment as a muting influence and the need for a respectable appearance requiring a duller colour range. Blue, yellow and green in this Rhys palette are often mildly negative. The shop where she buys the clothes is run by two sisters, one has a 'yellow face', never a good sign in Rhys's fiction, as well as red lips. Laurie's face seems a clown's, when she and Anna are not getting on well: she is too obviously made-up, and her nails are very red.

Threatening red re-emerges as a detail of the artificial plant in the landlady's hall, which sits on a black table and to Anna's eyes looks smugly confident in belonging to the house and the 'spiked iron railings outside' (*VITD*: 34). Remembering being on tour with the music hall in dingy English towns, Anna thinks 'always a high, dark wardrobe and something dirty red' (*VITD*: 150), another negative red/black combination. When her relationship with Walter is ending, she lives in a rented room with a landlady this time who has a pink face and bulging eyes, 'like a prawn' (*VITD*: 103), suggesting a very weak form of the red threat she has found in women before. The fat woman who performs the abortion wears 'red, close-fitting' (*VITD*: 176) another example of the tawdry red which occurs so often in this novel.

Red, white and black become racial as well as personality indicators in the descriptions of Anna's relatives, such as her father's red moustache. Anna's stepmother, Hester becomes red in the face with exasperation as she criticises Anna's family and finally Anna: 'Exactly like a nigger you talked – and still do' (*VITD*: 65). Colours in the sense of the spectrum and colours in the sense of skin colour (red, white, black) come together when Hester fusses that Uncle Bo's outside (illegitimate) children are

'all the colours of the rainbow' (*VITD*: 63). Uncle Bo had 'exactly
the laugh of the negro' to Hester, who also disliked very dark
Francine, and wanted to think white people couldn't carry head-
loads. Francine, her eyes red with smoke from the kitchen fire,
makes Anna know she dislikes white people and Anna feels she
cannot say that she hates being white.

The major primary colours blue, yellow and green have a
complex identity here. Blue in England is domesticated and often
associated with situations of discomfort or insecurity, usually as a
small touch in conjunction with other colours. Ethel's purple and
white kimono is a mixture of the blue which can signify a con-
strained respectability and the red which signifies sexuality. The
sitting room of the house in which Maudie and Anna rent space
and where they take Walter and his friend has some pretentious
touches: 'two bronze horses pawed the air with their front legs on
either side of a big, dark clock. Blue plates hung round the walls
. . .' (*VITD*: 12). Maudie and Anna talk about their emotional
risks and scars in a room with a picture of a little girl (presumably white), fondling a dog and dressed in a white dress with a
blue sash. She is the conventional picture of European female
childhood innocence, erased by the colours of her dress, suggesting innocence (white) and compliance (the touch of blue). A brief
memory of Francine in the West Indies 'the blue cup and saucer
and the silver teapot' on a tray (*VITD*: 135) consoles Anna. Blue
was, in childhood, sometimes a comforting colour. Here in England, it is the colour of the flowers on Walter's sofa, signifying a
domesticated fake nature. It also signifies strained respectability.
Miss Jackson, the mixed-race French teacher Anna had as a child,
was a colonial who guarded her class and race position and who
used to sing 'By the Blue Alsatian Mountains I Watch and Wait
Alway' (*VITD*: 162), a song which could be taken to refer also to
the 'blue mountains' or Mornes of Dominica. The fence in her
garden looked a very cold blue to Anna.

The nightmare Anna has shortly before the abortion of being
on a ship, sailing in a 'doll's sea, transparent as glass' (*VITD*: 164)
has a blue theme. The ship sails close to an island which apears
to be home until the trees on the water's edge are English. There
is a 'little dwarf with a bald head' being carried by a sailor in a

child's coffin, and he wears a large blue ring on his third finger. His eyes are large and light in a 'narrow, cruel face' (*VITD*: 165). Anna struggles in the dream to go ashore but the deck heaves up and down and she wakes to morning sickness. Anna says it is funny that after this dream, she keeps dreaming about the sea. A blue lampshade over the bed is the one detail of colour she remembers from the first sign of sickness which announces her pregnancy: perhaps the feeling of being exploited, the sea crossed to come to England, and the semiotic fluid in which we begin life are connected here.

Yellow is muted in this novel, just a few details occur here and there, such as Maudie's hair. But the pills which Anna takes to try to end the pregnancy and which she believes will have caused birth defects in the child have labels, 'primrose', 'daffodil', 'orange' suggesting attractive flowers and fruits when actually they deal in death or mutilation. Again the natural in England is false or thwarted.

Pale primary colours or absence of colours generally means that Anna is feeling little or nothing. Even the early passion with Walter, and her visit to his forbidding and disapproving house on the ironically named 'Green Street' (*VITD*: 36), is almost without colour. Anna does feel 'on fire' for a moment or two, but when Walter mentions her virginity, she goes cold. Even when Walter sends roses for her birthday, Anna does not mention what colour they are, so they clearly have not signified in her emotional centre. This is perhaps because Walter cannot feel intensely himself. He also has the kind of reservations about 'not places' which Antoinette's unnamed husband in *Wide Sargasso Sea* would well understand (Hester, in her English way, hated the lushness of the tropical flowers too). So Anna retreats into private thought:

Sometimes the earth trembles; sometimes you can feel it breathe. The colours are red, purple, blue, gold, all shades of green. The colours here are black, brown, grey, dim-green, pale blue, the white of people's faces – like woodlice. (*VITD*: 54)

This is the clearest separation of the oppositional palettes of Anna's consciousness: though the two worlds are not always entirely separated in the vocabulary of colour Rhys uses, there is always a sense of acceptance even for difficult aspects of the

Caribbean memories which is quite different from the negative
responses Anna expresses about England. In the taxi after leaving Walter she remembers, not the sexual encounter, but 'how
sad the sun can be' at home, but quite differently sad from the
'sadness of cold places' (*VITD*: 56). The water in the bathroom
pool in her childhood house is dark green though Anna does not
record any hostility to it: a little later, Anna thinks with evident
distaste of a London street as being like stagnant water (*VITD*:
46). The 'rounded green hills' of her island contrast starkly with
England: 'white people white people rushing along and the dark
houses' (*VITD*: 17). The Caribbean's specific, strong colours are
important though some, like grass burnt brown in the sun, reminded of the dangerous power of the tropical sun. A hill had 'the
curve of a green shoulder'; there were 'pink roses on the table in
a curly blue vase with gold rings' (*VITD*: 70). The magazines kept
in the summer house had yellow pages from age and the tropical
air and a picture of the Virgin Mary on the wall of the kitchen
was dressed in blue. Above the house, where it was barren, there
were big grey boulders and the sky was 'terribly blue' (*VITD*: 73).
In another description, of the town house, the sky was a hard
blue, the stable-yard white-paved and hot, the bathroom dark,
damp and greenish. Green is important in the Caribbean descriptions: the 'cool and hot' hills where 'Everything is green, everywhere things are growing' (*VITD*: 151), by contrast with London,
where plants are tamed or artificial, emotions are truncated or
false. She remembers 'green, and the smell of green, and then the
smell of water and dark earth and rotting leaves and damp' (*VITD*:
151). This is a journey back into her personal Eden of pre-sexual
innocence where there was still a capacity for a natural sensuality
and connection to wilder aspects of nature.

Anna remembers small details which evoke the intense vitality
of her Caribbean experience: buying cloth: 'I'll take four yards of
the pink . . .' (*VITD*: 56); a hibiscus 'so red, so proud and its long
gold tongue hung out' (*VITD*: 56) and 'so red that even the sky
was a background to it' (*VITD*: 56). It is the red of intense feeling,
a feeling which ought to have survived into sexual passion and
attachment but which is cut off from Anna's sexual identity. But
she is also often reminded of the relation a white child was forced

to have with this richness and warmth. A white person cannot be too long in the vivid light of the sun: Anna once stood in the sun too long and became 'awfully thin and ugly and yellow as a guinea' (*VITD*: 73) afterwards: she could not will herself to be black or successfully will herself to die. She was forced through the church service, aided only by a fan with a faded blue and red picture on it of a fat Chinese woman falling over backwards. But she noticed the church windows were 'red, blue, green purple', on a walk through the churchyard 'through the still palms' that the light was 'gold and when you shut your eyes you see fire-colour' (*VITD*: 43).

Though there is one description of England at its natural best, in summer, the colours are still very much paler and more domest-icated than the Caribbean colours. When Walter asks Anna whether she has flowers like the ones they find in Savernake Forest in her island, she says 'Not quite like these' (*VITD*: 77). The flowers are red, yellow, blue and white, 'so many that it looked all colours' (*VITD*: 77): it is a brilliantly sunny day. Walter thinks this place proves his capacity for imagination (for feeling, actually, perhaps?), but Anna feels it has no wildness, that the 'hot blue day' is outside somewhere. Walter wants to be sexual with her here in the trees, after making it clear that he judges her 'perfectly satisfactory' from a certain angle. She, rightly, responds by being reticent, eventually simply by feeling cold: she tries to tell him of the flam-boyant tree in flower, though she does not describe it: the flowers are vivid lively red, with light green frondy leaves, against the Caribbean blue of the sky. This reference is Anna's appeal to a man she thinks she loves but who knows nothing of sexual love, only of the ways in which sexuality can be convenient and com-forting, like the comparative paleness and tameness of the English flowers. She finds this England beautiful, even somewhere out-side the trees, that the sky is hot and blue. But it is somehow lacking, as if the 'wildness' had gone out of it (*VITD*: 78).

Walter's cousin Vincent, who will eventually be the go-between as the relationship ends, is a handsome combination of colours: blue eyes, black hair, brown face. He is good-looking, apparently friendly, but has dubious attitudes to women and the blue eyes are generally a clue, in a male character in Rhys's texts, to a tendency for cruelty. When Vincent comes to see her about the money for the abortion, his eyes are 'like blue glass', though he gives the appearance of being 'very fresh and clean and kind' (*VITD*: 171). Anna's flowered dress, worn on the outing to Severnake Forst, seems an accommodation to the world Walter lives in, where nature is subordinated to his convenience. But she notices a moment of wildness, 'the shadows of the leaves on the wall', which move quickly, 'like the patterns the sun makes on water' (*VITD*: 80). This seems a subliminal Caribbean reference, for the drama of the sun on the sea around the shoreline of a steep and small island is constantly lovely and absorbing.

Rhys codes each room or apartment in England so that the colours are coherently suggestive. Ethel's room in the rooming house where she and Anna meet is similar to Anna's but the wallpaper is green instead of brown: the flat term for each colour provides no sense of brightness. The landlady's taste runs to practical, dark colours. Reunited with Laurie, Anna visits her flat where a red tablecloth and flowered wallpaper indicate the muted and calculating sexuality of the English world Anna inhabits.

More depressing is the heavy attempt at respectability in the larger of the two hotel rooms which Joe and his friend rent for sex with Anna and Laurie. Dark brown wallpaper, black painted mantelpiece and two huge dark-blue vases are an attempt to give the place a heavy propriety though it is clearly a place tolerant of prostitutes and clients (and it reminds of the bronze horses and blue plates of the room Maudie and Anna use to entertain Walter and his friend). The second room has no colour at all, being merely a bed with very little in the way of bedclothes. Anna ends up there very drunk, seeing black eyes staring at her from the ceiling (*VITD*: 127). When Anna has breakfast with her prostitute friend Laurie, served on a table with a white cloth by Laurie's elderly maid, the sun shines in onto the cloth, but Anna just continues to feel 'empty' (*VITD*: 13): English sun is powerless to warm her.

A picture with a begging dog, called 'Loyal Heart', over the bed at Ethel's reminds her of a hoarding which was at the end of Market Street in her childhood Caribbean home, advertising biscuits, with a picture of a 'little girl in a pink dress', the ultimate cliché of cooperative femininity.[23] There was a little boy in a sailor-suit (presumably blue), a 'tidy tree and a shiny pale-blue sky' and behind the little girl, a 'high dark wall'. It signified England to the young Anna, and still does.

Rhys preferred the original ending of the novel. Hemond Brown (1985) rightly argues that the new ending which Rhys cut by a thousand words, is much less dense. Though the Carnival procession is common to both versions, Rhys cut out a great deal, including the account of a childhood photograph being taken which would become the opening passage in *Smile Please*, in which the photographer has a 'black-yellow face'.[24] She also cut the exchange between Anna and her nurse Meta which would, in revised form, also become material for *Smile Please* and *Wide Sargasso Sea*: 'let me go you damned black devil you let me go you woolly haired devil . . .' (UTC: 5).[25] The original version has a more detailed stream of consciousness narrative with more intrusions on Anna's thoughts by her attendants, Laurie and Mrs Polo, and of course Anna dies at the end, from loss of blood after the abortion, whereas in the published version she responds to the doctor and seems likely to make a recovery. In both versions, there is an account of a horseride along the sea in Dominica, which ends in the first version when the horse stops suddenly and Anna falls, a fall which is the beginning of her death.[26]

In terms of colour codes, the ending of both versions is dominated by the vivid colours of the Carnival. Red and its weaker, more cutely sexual partner, pink, return in the dream of Carnival. We know Anna is beginning to have to live with pink, with a more willing and calculating sexuality, for after her rejection of Laurie's dress, she lives at Langham Street which has pink curtains, the only colour she notes in her description and without comment. In the Carnival, some masks are crude pink, with black squinting eyes, worn by men, but others, worn by women, are caricatures of white faces with blue eyes and little red heart-shaped mouths. In the first version, some masks are flesh-coloured, 'more like their faces than their faces were' (UTC: 11). These are similar to certain masks common in West African ritual and festival, which satirise and mock:[27] Carnival in the Caribbean, informed with

African traditions after Emancipation, became a briefly licensed space for challenging authority, providing relief of tension as well as an encouragement to cultural and political resistance.

In the first version, the men in the Carnival procession are described as sometimes painting themselves, again reaffirming African tradition, with red and black rather than wearing masks, a small but important repetition of this significant colour combination from earlier in the novel. Colour is very important here, for even Hester thinks (in the original version), that the colours are 'marvellous' (UTC: 12). People are dressed in 'red and blue and yellow', in 'all colours of the rainbow' (in the published version, Rhys adds, each time this phrase appears, 'and the sky so blue'). The dark arms of the women are dusted with white powder, again reinforcing their satirical impersonation of whites, their explicit resistance to racism and colonialism, which makes Uncle Bo's remark (included in both versions), that 'You can't expect niggers to behave like white people all the time' (*VITD*: 185) very ironical. Part of the material Rhys cut was conversation among the adults in Anna's house about slavery, and the comparative positions of the English and the white Creoles on Emancipation, so there was a sharper political edge to the longer version, which concluded earlier references to race, class and nationality.

Both versions (but especially the longer original version), weave references to earlier passages in the novel together as Anna relives moments of her previous experience. The man who has probably fathered Anna's child has, in both versions, a very white face. He is probably D'Adhemar, the 'slightly potty, but an awfully sweet old thing' who showed a book of Aubrey Beardsley's wittily pornographic, black and white caricatures of the sexual undertow of polite Victorian society to Laurie and Anna (*VITD*: 170). The concentration of black and white here is significantly in contrast to the complex colours of Carnival, again signifying the affective split in Anna's consciousness.

In the original version, yellow and black dominate the last moments of Anna's life:

and there was the ray of light along the floor like the last thrust of remembering before everything is blotted out and darkness comes ... (UTC: 20)

In the final version, Section IV opens with this yellow ray of light 'coming in under the door from the light in the passage' (*VITD*: 183) into the nearly dark room.[28] It returns at the end but not as the last line. Rhys inserted five sentences of fairly unconvincing resolution of Anna's crisis in order to please her editor. But it is appropriate that in the original version Anna, who longs to be black, finally drifts into welcoming darkness, a fitting ending to this complex coding of colour in that black is all colours together. The earlier version truly ends the novel by interconnecting the various strands of narrative, many of them reinforced and sharply focussed by reference to colour.[29]

# CHAPTER 5

# Dangerous spirit, bitterly amused:
# Good Morning, Midnight

There was that quite ordinary joke that made me laugh so much because it was signed God. Just like that – G-O-D, God. Joke, by God. And what a sense of humour! Even the English aren't in it.

(*GM, M*, 1986: 185)

Hardly anyone *in the village* reads you know many cannot Its an unbelievable place and they *do* put their faith in Black Magic – to tell you the truth it frightens me now – I've been really frightened & thought it sinister – several times lately. Not a pleasant feeling . . . They are a dour lot, very religious Low Church the older ones. The younger ones a complete vacancy. Poor devils. But why should I pity them? They pity *noone* – . . .

(Letter to Selma Vas Dias, 1963)

*Good Morning, Midnight*, published on the eve of World War II in 1939, is brilliantly achieved, very tightly and complexly structured (Byrne 1985), and is certainly the funniest of Rhys's novels. Rhys's humour can be understood better if viewed through the lens of Caribbean humour which is so often political, full of wordplay, sceptical of institutions and power and essentially survivalist. Though Sasha appears to set her spiritual survival in question by the end of the novel, her ability to deconstruct those social institutions and arrangements which threaten her, and often with hilarious humour, is a marked aspect of her resilience.

Rhys could be very funny, but she was always aware of the world's identities in terms of the moral map she received from Catholicism, a powerful influence in her childhood via her convent school: 'I decided firmly I would become a Catholic, and not only a Catholic but a nun' (*SP*: 65). In her fictional draft 'December 4th 1938 Mr Howard's House: CREOLE' (UTC), she creates her protagonist as both morally optimistic, 'Sister Marie-Augustine says that thoughts are not sins – they may be sent by the devil. As long as you drive them away at once, they are not sins', and as having the intense Jansenist Catholicism which sounds oddly almost Calvinistic: 'I hoped he would say something to me that would make it all right and as if I had not been wicked. The thing was I could never feel in myself that I had been wicked. That means, of course, that I am quite awful and damned' (p. 4). In old age, Rhys enjoyed alluding to herself as a witch, especially when she thought others so imaged her.

Rhys has left us plenty of evidence that she saw her writing both as gospel truth (not literally but morally accurate and honest) and a kind of personally invented obeah. In the Caribbean, obeah has historically signified a metaphysical means to address injustice, give support to the marginalised and challenge entrenched social power. Throughout her fiction, the metaphysical functions as an important chain of signifiers, including ghosts and masking, obeah or figures from Caribbean folklore such as the *souciant* (as Rhys spells it), and the *zombi* (Raiskin 1996). The power of possession or at the very least a doubling identity (Howells 1990) is important. At times the metaphysical has an explicitly Carnival context (Horner and Zlosnik 1990; Emery 1990; Gregg 1995). Death is prevalent in Rhys's texts, implicitly threatening all her protagonists.[1]

She offers in *Good Morning, Midnight* a subtle and damning demonstration of the bankrupt spiritual context of a Europe flirting with the threat of totalitarianism, an environment which all but destroys Sasha. Rhys was born into a morally bizarre world in which Christianity had clearly supported slavery and white people's self-designated respectability still rested on their refusal to respond humanely and as equals with people of colour: a world in which her colour and status marked her as culpable and in which the idea, learned from Catholicism, of confession and forgiveness may have seemed at times impossible in the sight of history. She also entered a European world in evident spiritual and moral trouble at home: two World Wars and the Depression between marked her early experience in Europe and the context of her first five books.[2] The casual talk of the educated and financially secure was to her at times enormously reductive of such concepts as the devil, God, damnation, hell: 'Nobody says now, "by the splendour of God". They say Jesus H. Christ. I often wonder what the H stands for. Hunted, harried, hypocrite?' ('I think I fell in love with words . . .' UTC). By her juxtaposition of serious moral and psychological crises in her fiction with the casual European terminology of the time, such as 'Oh, God', 'the little devil', she makes the latter suddenly emblematic of moral bankruptcy. Of course, like most middle-class people in England in her time, she also used such terms, but she also located them textually in reference to her own Caribbean and quasi-Catholic moral seriousness and commitment to language. Rhys had clearly a very great sensitivity to the specific perversities of morality which characterise high consumption societies, a willingness to be a part of them given a chance, and a determination to write about that participation.[3]

She played with the metaphysical in her letters, using her sharp-edged self-examination and her delight in being 'wicked': 'It is in fact a devil of a situation' (*L*: 249); 'really what a *devil* it's been' (*L*: 296). But at times, there was a serious respect for aspects of the spiritual, 'it was a very vague & silly "haunt" But a haunt –' (letter to Diana Athill 29 May 1964); 'This is not a place to be alone in', (letter to Selma Vaz Dias, 17/18 September 1965); 'they do put their faith in Black Magic . . . Ive been really frightened' (letter to Selma Vaz Dias 1963). To Francis Wyndham she wrote that *Wide Sargasso Sea* was a '*demon* of a book' and that she was sometimes sure that it needed 'a demon to write it' (*L*: 158) and to Diana Athill in 1966 that she was afraid Selma Vaz Dias was 'trying all she can to harm me' (27 December). Though she often joked that the villagers in Cheriton Fitzpaine thought her a witch, an identity she sometimes courted, it also worried her, because she took such things seriously. She trusted in luck and in symbols: in a letter where she said she mixed business and pleasure in an 'unholy way', she remembered a lucky dress which 'I hung on to through thick & thin & this started me on my literary career' (*L*: 256).

In the Black Exercise Book Rhys writes of her father after she
had done something as a child which she expected would make
him angry: 'I saw it in his eyes Good God the poor little devil's
frightened of me': given the context of her writing as a whole,
the line has a special significance, even in this rough draft.[4] Her
belief in religious terminology related uneasily to her modernist
scepticism in her texts from 1924–1939, culminating in *Good Morning, Midnight*, which plays off both as well as having a clear-sighted
and subversive humour.

In both Rhys's published and unpublished texts, the metaphysical or spiritual functions as a set of codes and metaphors
by which to interpret experience and puncture and expose the
amorality of power or the sterile arrogance of easy moral judgements.[5] The kind of religion or metaphysics which is approved
in Rhys's texts always has to do with subverting inhumane social
conventions and is therefore, almost by definition, outlaw, subversive, committed. This concern with the metaphysical is evident in most of Rhys's texts: it plays an important role in *Voyage
in the Dark* and *Wide Sargasso Sea* as well as some stories.[6] It less
obviously but still importantly informs the language and images
of *After Leaving Mr MacKenzie* and *Quartet*.

Also important to the young Gwen Williams's and adult Rhys's
sense of the metaphysical was the hidden (to white colonials)
world of African religious syncretisms and survivals known gen-
erically as obeah and feared as a source of political resistance by
the colonial authorities, as were other African-derived religious
beliefs held by the slaves (Simpson 1980).[7] The history of African-
Caribbean spirituality facing colonialism and racism has been a
history of respect for the power of words as weapons in resistance
to injustice. Not surprisingly, many Caribbean writers, such as
Kamau Brathwaite, Dennis Scott or Erna Brodber have found in
the metaphysical traditions of African-Caribbean society a touchstone for their most important political and social concerns.[8]
During the period of high colonialism and just afterwards, it was
not uncommon for writers to portray obeah in their texts as difficult or threatening and so reduce it to reactionary superstition
or evil destructiveness. But even in so doing, they kept alive its
importance in the collective Caribbean imagination.[9]

Of course even a renegade white child could only ever be outsider to the African-based traditions of obeah which were trying to deal with her own colonial power and that of other whites, yet Rhys was capable of hinting she was to some extent an insider, 'I seem to have forgotten my obeah. (I did know one thing)' (*L*: 240; see also Plante 1984: 44). Rhys was also both edgy about sanctioned religion and desirous of belonging somewhere at times: both isolated and individualistic.[10] Her sympathetic portrait of Christophine's reluctant efforts to help Antoinette through obeah in *Wide Sargasso Sea* marks her consciousness of the impossibility of whites ever entering fully into the circle of Caribbean African inheritance.

Among Rhys's critics, James (1978), Campbell (1982, repr. 1990), O'Connor (1986), Kloepfer (1989), Emery (1990) and Savory (1997) have all noted her use of the idea of obeah, which derived from West African religions during the time of slavery. It was often regarded by colonial authorities as subversive or evil, though it was mainly about healing and community strengthening. When approached by journalists bent on a story, Rhys suggested she knew something of obeah but also was outsider to it (letter to Oliver Stoner, 16 October).[11] Christophine in *Wide Sargasso Sea* says that obeah was not 'for beke' (white Creoles). Ann Tewitt, an obeah woman, was the family cook at Bona Vista (*Smile Please*). There is also Ann Twist in the story 'Mixing Cocktails' (*CSS*: 36–8). Campbell (1990) rightly argues that Twist, the first chronologically of Rhys's obeah women, was ancestor to Ann Chewitt in *Voyage in the Dark* and Christophine in *Wide Sargasso Sea*.

Another white outsider, much more outsider than Rhys, was Hesketh Bell, Administrator of Dominica during Rhys's childhood.[12] He wrote extensively on obeah. In his *Glimpses of a Governor's Life* (1946), Bell offers a colonialist reading: 'If Quashie finds, one day, an "Obeah bottle" hidden in the thatch of his little shanty or hanging to a tree in his garden he becomes filled with terror' (1946: 22). Obeah derives mainly from West African fetishism, Bell argues, but also seems related to the 'witch-pots' of South-West England – an interesting comment in the light of Rhys's own experience of Devonshire villagers believing in witchcraft. Rhys's construction of herself as witch is in effect the

European or white woman's equivalent role to that of obeah woman (Campbell 1982; repr. 1990). Rhys would have enjoyed the 'witch with blue eyes' image of her in Frank Delaney's 1984 article. She also left a significant number of references in fiction, autobiography, drafts and letters to her major characters or herself as ghost.

General references to religion or spirituality recur frequently in Rhys's published and unpublished texts as well as in her fiction: her childhood belief that God was a book; the spirits from Caribbean folklore of Rhys's hated nurse Meta's stories and her view that she was still, as an old woman, in the 'world of fear and mistrust' Meta had given her; her yelling 'Black Devil!' at Meta when the two of them engaged in a power struggle; the idea that drinking the water in a Dominica river would bring you back (Rhys was prevented from doing that by a guide on her visit in 1936 and she never went back); the satisfaction of being 'wicked'; prayers to God that she might be black; the thought that black Catholic people ought to have a better chance in eternity; fears of Carnival masks; curiosity about Milton's Satan; notes on her father's medical service to the clergy and convent and the Celtic cross which marks her father's grave; Sunday services in Roseau; race and class and the church in Dominica; Rhys's immature Manicheanism; ghosts.[13]

Her Manicheanism is interesting in the light of Fanon's comment that the colonial world is a 'world divided into compartments, a motionless, Manicheanistic world' (1969: 40). Rhys's childhood spiritual landscape, inhabited by permitted Anglicanism, forbidden obeah and her own seriousness about Catholicism, seems uncannily close to Fanon's insight into colonial selfhood, though he was evidently not thinking of a white colonial child:

In under-developed countries the occult sphere is a sphere belonging to the community which is entirely under magical jurisdiction. By entangling myself in this inextricable network where actions are repeated with crystalline inevitability, I find the everlasting world which belongs to me, and the perenniality which is therefore affirmed of the world belonging to us. Believe me, the zombies are more terrifying than the settlers . . . (1969: 43)

In *Smile Please*, Rhys connects her young consciousness of 'death, misfortune, poverty, disease' (and she might have added racism) to her Manicheanism, her passionate support of God yet helpless feeling, eventually thinking that both God and the Devil were 'far away' (*SP*: 71). In 'Mr Howard's House' (UTC), in the first-person narrative of the second section, she quotes a book saying good and evil, pain and happiness are the same thing. A nun is scathing about this view: but it is easy to see how a young white female's sexual awakening would be corralled in a colonial racist society by whatever means available.

But the most dramatic and important manifestation of both Rhys's absorption of Catholic morality, with its trust in the ultimate triumph of the good, and her Manicheanistic recognition of the power of evil comes in the extraordinary document which Diana Athill included in *Smile Please* after Rhys's death, 'From a Diary: At the Ropemaker's Arms' (*SP*: 129ff).[14] In this Rhys put herself on trial: it begins '*Do you believe in God?*' (*SP*: 131), and goes on as a moral inquisition. As O'Connor (1990) notes, Rhys's arguments about God and the Devil sound somewhat medieval. The defendant is accused of believing '*that human beings can be taken over, possessed by something outside, something greater; and that love is one of these manifestations*', therefore the accuser goes on, she must believe in '*God, or the gods, in the Devil, in the whole bag of tricks*' (*SP*: 131). But the defendant, struggling to express herself, asserts that what she believes is that all important moral qualities, 'Good, evil, love, hate, life, death, beauty, ugliness' are in herself (*SP*: 131). Indeed, when pressed, she says she will 'not have earned death' (*SP*: 133) if she stops writing.

Writing, and the 'good, evil and so on' within herself, are essentially connected. Hell she defines as coming to 'those who seek, strive, rebel', like herself, whereas heaven is for those who 'cannot think or avoid thought, who have no imagination'. Writers, then, by definition, live in hell. In this same piece, she defines her own failings by Catholic terms (mortal and venial sins). The first she lists as 'pride, anger, lust, "drunkenness??", despair, presumption, sloth, selfishness' but not coolness of heart; her venial sins as 'spite, malice, envy, avarice, stupidity, caution, cruelty and gluttony'

(*SP*: 141). Rhys thought moral distinctions and honesty crucially important: though people are likely to fail morally, she thought it essential to keep an acute eye on that failure.

It is in this context that *Good Morning, Midnight*'s telling of a complex moral fable should be read. Writing to Morchard Bishop (1939), in response to his comment that the newly published *Good Morning, Midnight* was depressing, she said she never meant it to 'be hopeless'. I think she thought the honesty of the exposure of Sasha's self-destructiveness could be understood as a dynamic: that even though Sasha does appear to have chosen a kind of spiritual suicide, she might ultimately come through it to another spiritual space beyond the novel's scope, precisely because of the courage of her clear-sighted humour.

Caribbean writers have been particularly emphatic about the writer's role as political or moral, but one of the strengths of Caribbean culture, as in calypso, has always been the marriage of acute political and moral insight with wordplay built on discontinuity and juxtaposition and therefore encouraging of a sharp, insightful humour.

Rhys's own sense of humour would appear to have been sparked by the edge of despair or by a puckish delight in matters ordinarily solemn or fearful. She joked to Selma Vaz Dias 'Do you know Selma I feel its very *tactless* of me to be alive. No savoir faire. (Damn little savoir vivre either)' (letter, 6 November 1960); to Peggy Kirkaldy about a 'rig' her husband Max had bought her for literary appointments in London, 'I hope I won't look like an ancient vamp . . .' (18 January 1953); to Selma in 1958 about getting 'back to being a Creole lunatic in the 1840's. Quite an effort. Sometimes am almost there, sometimes I think I'll stay there!! –' (*L*: 156). She had a wry sense of humour which she often turned on herself, but it was also often political, in the sense of being shrewdly aware of power and willing to engage with it. She wrote from Dominica in 1936 'everybody hates everybody else. But always for political reasons not moral. Such a lovely change' (*L*: 28).

But *Good Morning, Midnight*'s first audience was English, and dealing with the onset of war. Early reviewers felt this was a well-written but almost intolerably depressing tale, and her audience in the years 1939–45 had difficulty accepting a novel so focussed on negatives.[15] It has taken a long time for this novel to find its time – even now it is probably the most neglected of Rhys's major texts. Some recent criticism (notably Staley 1979, Wolfe 1980, Emery 1990) has understood that Sasha's grim story is contextualised by the shadow of fascism gaining ground in Western Europe.[16] *Good Morning, Midnight*'s modernist fabric has often been noted, modernism being an aesthetic which, in its embrace of fragmentation and alienation, identified the times.[17] But the subversive comedy of the novel has not received widespread recognition. A few analyses of the novel have seen how funny it is: Angier (1990) sees the importance of comedy conjoined with horror; Le Gallez (1990) traces the progression of Sasha's self-mockery into strong irony.

The Caribbean is a submerged text in this novel, even more so than in *After Leaving Mr Mackenzie*. To find it, the reader has to be alert to clues. Sasha's denial of national identity (she is supposedly English) is one such clue. If she truly were English, she would presumably have a sense of national identity, however conflicted, and even if she were English in France, her Englishness would still signify. But the issue of erased nationality is so important in the novel that it suggests something is being coded about erasure of the Caribbean which stands behind the English affiliation and gives Sasha her acute critique of the English and of power.

Sasha attracts other people, like the gigolo and Serge, whose national identity is complicated by migration. Serge, who is Russian and Jewish, is keen to demonstrate his connections with cultural traditions outside Europe, not only through masks he has made, but also his beguine music, Martinique music, to which he dances holding a mask over his face. Suddenly, Sasha escapes in her imagination to lie in a hammock looking up into the branches of a tree, listening to the sound of the sea, looking at hills which look like clouds and clouds like 'fantastic hills'.[18] For those familiar with Rhys texts, this is a sure code of the coastline of Dominica and Sasha's inheritance of memory of the island.

Race is also important in Serge's story of a mulatto woman he met in Notting Hill in London. European (white) inhumanity joins the victim's only and poignant defence of turning the joke

on the self. The mulatto woman looks at her unhappy life as the
mistress of a 'very Angliche' man and thinks it comical. But when
Serge looks into her eyes, he finds it is like 'looking down into a
pit' (*GM, M*: 96), an image of hell and damnation. To Serge, she
is a 'poor creature', and when he sees a child of seven or eight
putting her tongue out at the woman, he finds it proves Nature
tells such a young person how to be cruel and 'who it was safe
to be cruel to' (*GM, M*: 98), which he thinks '[o]ne must admire'
(*GM, M*: 98).

But this connection between suffering at the hands of the powerful, who were in colonial and immediately post-colonial contexts
Europeans (especially men), and turning the tables through laughter
is at the centre of comedy and humour in the West Indies. Thus
humour often works as a safety valve or releaser of stress, but
part of this function has often been constructed historically as
subversion of hierarchies and inequities protected by an unjust
political system. The very cultural complexity of the region, and
most importantly the fact that so many people easily move from
one linguistic register to another, facilitates the kind of wordplay
and interrelationship of linguistic systems which encourages clever
and socially biting humour.

Roydon Salick outlines the importance and identity of contemporary West Indian humour thus:

The distinguishing feature of the West Indian character, it seems to me,
is a unique brand of humour, that like its cultural provenance, is a wonderful combination of mimicry and originality, of the common and exotic,
and of the sublime and the banal . . . It may reveal itself in rib-tickling
laughter, or in an Anansi smile that steals across the face, or in a 'steups'
(sucking of the teeth), or in a gentle raised eyebrow . . . Humour is a
defining praxis; and, in a real sense, becomes the epistemological and
ontological point of reference for West Indian behaviour. (1993: iii)

Rhys's humour contains both excellent mimicry and acutely
painful originality and in the sense that her 'surface comedy'
masks 'an essentially tragic experience', her texts fulfil Salick's
definition of the kind of humour which emerges from centuries of
colonialism. Much of the most brilliant Caribbean humour, like
the tradition of the blues in the United States, has its source in
cultural strategies which slaves developed to survive and which

did not deny either pain or joy, nor turn away from political engagement. West Indian humour is verbal and performative, full of layered meaning, punning, irony and parody (Selvon, Keens-Douglas, St John, Bennett).[19] Though Rhys's ambivalent positions as white Creole and as exile both thwarted ready access to that tradition, she had a strong sense of the infinite possibilities in words, their sound, rhythmic pattern, multiple meaning, theatricality and always their political identity, and her humour is, like West Indian humour, acutely aware of the need to destabilise hierarchies.

In *Good Morning, Midnight*, with its title a quotation from the wry Emily Dickinson poem, there is an especially noticeable interaction between dangerous, self-destructive spirituality and bitter laughter. The novel's protagonist is an alienated middle-aged woman in the Paris and London of the 1930s, who is anything but passive, though some critics have so termed her (Amuso 1987). The mocking, ironic first-person narrative voice of the protagonist, Sasha Jenson, is the source of the novel's almost unbearable tension between humour and tragedy, between a bitterly mocking critique of society and a devastating and enervating spiritual chaos. Laughter, or the possibility of laughter, figures in many of Sasha's readings of her environment. She thinks a waiter can't be bothered to laugh at her; an old friend, Sidonie, who lends her money, smiles in a way which says Sasha is 'getting to look old. She drinks' (*GM, M*: 11). Sasha can imagine Sidonie thinking Sasha's hotel is appropriate, 'God, it's an insult when you come to think about it' (*GM, M*: 12). The casual reference to God just falls easily off the tongue. Sasha's self-definition demonstrates her characteristic acerbic tone, her bilingualism and her self-mockery: 'Quatrième à gauche, and mind you don't trip over the hole in the carpet. That's me' (*GM, M*: 12). This juxtaposition of humour and pain is characteristic of the novel. Sasha's English conversation lessons with a Russian are largely concerned with his obsession with torture and pain. Sasha concludes that 'God is very cruel . . . A devil of course. That accounts for everything' (*GM, M*: 140). She drifts off into thinking about a place where, like Anna in *Voyage in the Dark* she sees a 'dark wall in the hot sun' (*GM, M*: 140), a wall 'so hot it burned your hand when you touched it', and red and yellow flowers. Following this, a fat man in a bar tells Sasha a story about a man who loved a woman married to someone else and never had enough courage or clarity of purpose to go to see her when she was ill. By the time he went, she had died. The fat man's comment is 'Doesn't that make you laugh' (*GM, M*: 141).

It is that desire to laugh which saves Sasha's life over and over again: 'It shouts "Anglaise", my hat. And my dress extinguishes me. And then this damned fur coat slung on top of everything else – the last idiocy, the last incongruity' (*GM, M*: 15). Humour, of course, is largely a matter of incongruities. Laughter which Sasha can control, her own devastating way of puncturing the forces which will otherwise kill her, is a vital way she can deflect other people's cruel laughter about or against her. The young Sasha manoevred some money out of a Mr Lawson she had known a little before her marriage and had to give him a kiss in exchange: what she thinks of is how surprised he looked and then she cannot stop laughing. She can respond to conventional jokes at times: in a cinema she laughs 'heartily in the right places' (*GM, M*: 16). Her struggles in Paris are turned into a joke, as is herself: sometimes she can see she is not unusual. On her way back to 'the damned room', she inserts her laughter at a bit of misfortune which happens to a character in a film she watched because 'Exactly the same thing happens to me' (*GM, M*: 108).

She addresses the city: 'my darling, and oh what a bitch you can be! But you didn't kill me after all' (*GM, M*: 16). Even her memories of her previous life in Paris, years ago, when she was still young, are bitterly funny at times. The dummies on which dresses are displayed in the shop where she once worked are 'damned dolls', 'thinking what a success they would have made of their lives if they had been women' (*GM, M*: 18), because they are silk and satin, velvet and 'sawdust heart' (*GM, M*: 18). She can produce a sharply observed but gentle puncturing of sentiment: two young lovers in a restaurant make her feel that 'any moment you expect these two to start flapping wings and chirping' (*GM, M*: 49).

There's something about being a woman which is funny in itself in Sasha's cruel and capricious world, 'God, it's funny, being a woman!' (*GM, M*: 104). The examples Sasha provides are however disturbing: a girl washing dishes in a small *tabac* works in what is effectively a small cupboard, and Sasha asks 'how can she stay in that coffin for five minutes without fainting?' (*GM, M*: 105). Women who get drunk in bars (like Sasha), 'start crying silently', then go into the ladies and come out 'powdered, but with hollow eyes – and, head down, slink into the street' (*GM, M*: 107).

Masks, like makeup, clothes, even alcohol, can provide a refuge temporarily. Serge's ersatz West African masks, 'straight from the Congo. . . . I made them' (*GM, M*: 91), are part of the novel's mask motif (*GM, M*: 43, 90, 92). One of Serge's portrays a face with 'close-set eye-holes' (*GM, M*: 91–2), a face familiar to Sasha 'all faces are masks' (*GM, M*: 90). It reminds her of people like the solicitor, the representative of polite, secure society, who asked why she didn't drown herself in the Seine, or the ones who called her an old woman. But she depends on masking: happiness is the brief moment when money arrives from somewhere to repair evidence of time passing: 'money for my hair, money for my teeth, money for shoes that won't deform my feet' (*GM, M*: 144). She is nervous: 'Damn this light' (*GM, M*: 152), when making up her face. The lavabo at the Pig and Lily,[20] where there are many mirrors and 'not a soul' to watch (*GM, M*: 156) is both a kind of refuge and source of unease.

Sasha is something of a thinker, though a woman thinker too is also funny to her at times if she has no clear means of support. When she styles herself a 'cérébrale', she thinks how funny a book would be which was called 'just a Cérébrale or You Can't Stop Me From Dreaming' (*GM, M*: 161). René, the gigolo, thinks such a woman is unable to like anything except 'her own damned brain' (*GM, M*: 162), and Sasha immediately thinks 'So pleased with herself, like a little black boy in a top-hat' (*GM, M*: 162), presumably meaning, in this context, an excluded presence in a mask of belonging.

She remembers her old friend Lise saying that she wished there would be another war, so she might get a bit of luck and be killed. Sasha's response was 'My God, Lise, you've got a few more years, surely' (*GM, M*: 134). Both women were crying, arms round each other's waists, when Sasha's husband Enno[21] returned, commenting 'Oh my God, this is gay' and laughing loudly. In

response, both women began to laugh until they were 'rolling'.
The transition from despair to bitter laughter has once more
occurred: laughter is a mask or accompaniment to despair.

The most bizarrely subversive story here is about a woman
called Paulette, pretty, romantic, 'proud as Lucifer' when she
looks at herself naked in a mirror. She has a relationship with
a Count whose family have located her as not of their class 'je
ne joue pas du piano, moi' (*GM, M*: 136). After lunch with the
Count's mother, whilst walking out of the restaurant, 'Paulette's
drawers fell off' (*GM, M*: 136), something which Sasha remembers, '[c]huckling madly', happened to her also. She refuses a
man's sexual advances but he offers to see her to her bus, saying
'[s]tupid, stupid girl' and 'doing up buttons'. As they wait for the
bus, 'My drawers fall off' (*GM, M*: 136). Sasha looks down at them,
steps out of them 'neatly', rolls them up and puts them in her
bag. When she calls the man to apologise the next day, he offers
to send her a box of Turkish Delight and she says, hilariously,
'Well now, what is it, this Turkish Delight? Is it a comment, is it
irony, is it compensation, is it apology . . .' (*GM, M*: 137).

Unstoppable, hysterical laughter and a careless verbal reference
to the parameters of Christian theology have evidently always
been Sasha's major defences against pain: long ago, when Enno
quarrels with a friend of theirs called Alfred, she merely keeps
on saying 'Isn't this funny, isn't this funny?' (*GM, M*: 127). When
Sasha and Enno reach a very difficult stage of their relationship
and he gives her an order based on his provision of some money
for them 'My God, isn't it hot? Peel me an orange' (*GM, M*: 129),
she thinks 'Now is the time to say "Peel it yourself"', now is the
time to say "Go to hell", now is the time to say "I won't be
treated like this"' (*GM, M*: 129).

Sasha worked as a ghost writer for a rich woman who she
disliked a great deal, a woman who would 'raise hell if a spot
of wine fell on one of her Louis Quinze chairs' (*GM, M*: 168) and
whose mind was like a 'bilge hold of a ship, all washing about in
the same hold – no water-tight compartments' (*GM, M*: 168).
Sasha's portrait of this woman is very funny, with her belief in
reincarnation slipped in next to 'Samuel has forgotten to buy his
suppositories' (*GM, M*: 168).

Her humour is sometimes direct, brilliant social satire, attacking the wealthy, pompous and authoritarian Mr Blank (an obvious pantomime or English music-hall name), 'a real English type': 'Bowler-hat-majestic trousers, oh-my-God expression, ha-ha eyes ...' (*GM*, *M*: 19). Mr Blank summons her and she decides he must want to ask her whether she can speak German. She is quite evidently brilliantly verbal, and quite capable in French, though she says now, with meticulous honesty to us, 'sometimes, when I am a bit drunk and am talking to somebody I like and know, I speak French very fluently indeed' (*GM*, *M*: 20). What follows is very much like a comic skit. In her head, for Mr Blank, she makes up a string of German phrases punctuated by made-up Latin, 'homo homini lupus' and the notes of the scales 'doh ré mi fah soh la ti doh' (*GM*, *M*: 24). She exclaims, 'Jesus, help me!', but what she comes up with is a list of phrasebook German and a medley of linguistic scraps. Her silent soliloquy to Mr Blank is brilliantly political and hilariously funny:

You, who represent Society, have the right to pay me four hundred francs a month. That's my market value, for I am an inefficient member of Society, slow on the uptake, uncertain, slightly damaged in the fray, there's no denying it. So you have the right to pay me four hundred francs a month, to lodge me in a small, dark room, to clothe me shabbily, to harass me with worry and monotony and unsatisfied longings till you get me to the point when I blush at a look, cry at a word. (*GM*, *M*: 29)

Her cynicism frames his smugness, as she mocks his acceptance of gross inequities between people: 'There must be the dark background to show up the bright colours' (*GM*, *M*: 29), but in the end she can only resort to verbally cursing 'I wish you a lot of trouble' (*GM*, *M*: 29).

Rhys develops the idea of the 'ladies''', the public toilet or lavabo, as a hilarious essay in female social identity – she refers to the 'monograph' on lavabos. The joke is clear: fifteen women in a London queue to use the toilet, each 'clutching her penny', and 'not one bold spirit' willing to break the queue (a hilarious comment on British attitudes to queuing). Toilets in other places demonstrate their local character: in Florence, a pretty girl makes an affectionate fuss of the attendant; in Paris, the attendant peddles drugs 'to heal a wounded heart' (*GM, M*: 11). The lavatory is the ultimate comment on social hierarchies.

But as with the Mr Blank episode, the jokes about toilets contain Sasha's despair and make it accessible and tolerable for the reader. Drinking with strangers, Sasha feels like crying – so she retreats to the subterranean toilet in the first important scene where religious reference and humour interact. It is like a grimly funny Hades: a place for the living dead to hide, and eternally a source of ribald humour. Sasha stares at herself in the mirror. She considers her condition, sardonically, 'when I have had a couple of extra drinks and am quite sane, . . . I realize how lucky I am' (*GM, M*: 10), that she is not drowning in some dark river, alone, 'You jump in with no willing and eager friends around, and when you sink you sink to the accompaniment of loud laughter' (*GM, M*: 10).

Sasha's boss, Mr Blank, wants to send her on an errand, to carry an envelope to the 'kise', which turns out later to be a mispronunciation of 'la caisse', for the cashier (see Angier 1990: 378). Sasha, confused, walks straight through the nearest door into a lavatory (*GM, M*: 25). She tries another passage which also ends in a lavatory, and comments, 'the number of lavatories in this place, c'est inoui' (*GM, M*: 26). Along with the bitter humour of this episode, the numerous flippant references to the spiritual have a special significance: in Sasha's search, a kind of perverse spiritual quest, she gets lost, does not meet a 'soul' and is tempted to discard the envelope, 'the damned thing' (*GM, M*: 26). In response to Mr Blank's interrogation, she thinks she doesn't know 'a damned thing' (*GM, M*: 27).

Later in the novel, René, the gigolo, uses the image of a lavatory which played a tune to ridicule rich people, 'you have to be sorry for them' (*GM, M*: 169). Sasha feels prim for a moment and then 'goes down' to a lavatory in the basement of the Deux Magots café. Here, in her subterranean retreat, the mirror has a few words to say to her:

'Well, well', it says, 'last time you looked in here you were a bit different, weren't you? Would you believe me that, of all the faces I see, I remember each one, that I keep a ghost to throw back at each one – lightly, like an echo – when it looks into me again?' (*GM, M*: 170)

The comment follows: 'All glasses in all lavabos do this' (*GM, M*: 170). Ghosts are a significant detail here: this ghost is of course a memory of better looks, a younger face, which haunts a woman who allows herself to become afraid of getting to look old. René comments, after Sasha reappears, 'You're always disappearing into the lavabo, you' (*GM, M*: 170).

The references to deathliness here are characteristic of the muted but continuous horror of the novel's effect, always brought back to tolerable bounds by Sasha's humour. The kitten which had 'persecution mania' (*GM, M*: 54), who was attacked by male cats and finally run over by a car and killed, represents the kind of outlaw female Sasha is: her eyes, she sees, are just like the kitten's eyes. Her small legacy has made it possible for 'the end of me, the real end', as it has provided a safe place for her to die in, in effect, 'the lid of the coffin shut down with a bang' (*GM, M*: 42–3). But trying to drink herself to death doesn't work, nor does being slightly eccentric. Sasha cultivates under the 'agitation' of her surface, a 'bitter peace that is very near to death, to hate' (*GM, M*: 153). She knows those 'who prey upon the rich', is always capable of finding a wincingly funny way to describe the horrors of poverty and homelessness. 'Poor devils' without money are likely to be frowned upon, even crushed, by 'dark houses ... like monsters', 'Tall cubes of darkness with two lighted eyes at the top to sneer' (*GM, M*: 32). Her nihilistic description of one particular room is quite lyrical about death and dissolution:

flowers on the window-sill, and their shadows on the curtains are waving. Like swans dipping their beaks in water. Like the incalculable raising its head, uselessly and wildly, for one moment before it sinks down, beaten, into the darkness. Like skulls on long, thin necks. Plunging wildly when the wind blows, to the end of the curtain, which is their nothingness. Distorting themselves as they plunge. (*GM, M*: 130–1)

Rooms have the power to confirm the exact social value of their occupants: they are therefore both menacing, and, as shelters, consoling. Sasha lies in the bath in the communal bathroom and listens to the patronne trying to sell a room. The most elevated in price and status is the suite, where the second bedroom is a space which can permit emotional indifference: 'in case you don't feel like me, or in case you meet somebody you like better and come in late' (*GM, M*: 33). When she tries to move from one hotel to another, she finds the management is hostile to foreigners and the room she wants is already occupied, by someone she imagines has 'light-yellow' hand-luggage, a Rhys colour which generally signifies fear or anxiety. She remembers her room in London 'just off the Gray's Inn Road, as usual trying to drink myself to death . . .' (*GM, M*: 34). Sasha's sense of anxiety about a room of her own is exacerabated by her lack of secure nationality or self-placement, even pride (*GM, M*: 44). But she survives by scathingly observing her over-priced room: 'It shows that I have ended as a successful woman, anyway, however I may have started. One look at me and the prices go up' (*GM, M*: 34).

Rooms, as small enclosed spaces, are also Sasha's self-burial grounds: she eventually seems to live beyond her own death as a sort of *zombi*, speaking of the 'thin, frail ghosts in my room' (*GM, M*: 56), or a mad person shut into her own hell, as Antoinette will also be. She feels 'possessed by something' (*GM, M*: 62). She is also imprisoned and tormented: no matter how she tries to rise above her situation, every word she speaks 'has chains around its ankles', every thought 'is weighted with heavy weights' (*GM, M*: 106).

Living close to madness herself, she is sympathetic to madness in others. A customer in a hat-shop Sasha sees through a window seems as if she might at any moment start laughing 'the laugh of the mad' (*GM, M*: 68), and Sasha looks at her half-dyed, half-grey hair and wonders if she will be like that – indeed a page later she sees in her own face the 'same demented expression' (*GM, M*: 69). Sasha knows she is identified, often, as an old woman, a foreigner, mad. 'What the devil . . . is she doing here?' (*GM, M*: 54) is something she asks herself as well as thinking others are asking the same thing. But being a lost soul is not as bad as being damned. The 'smug, white, fat, black-haired one' trying to sell the hats looks to Sasha like 'the devil with a damned soul . . .' and she chooses to be instead like 'the hag' (*GM, M*: 68).

Her own construction of the world is as hell:[22] she associates with the 'damned gigolo' (*GM, M*: 163), 'this poor devil' (*GM, M*: 157), 'this damned old goop' (*GM, M*: 158), with whom she has dinner in a 'damned boîte' (*GM, M*: 156), 'swapping dirty stories' (*GM, M*: 163). The gigolo makes her think of 'the little grimacing devil in my head', a male who wears a top-hat and a cache-sexe and 'sings a sentimental song' (*GM, M*: 175). A valet de chambre makes her life hell. Even giving birth is contextualised as a hopeless, suffering space: a woman calls 'Jesus' in labour, Sasha identifies her son as '[p]oor little devil' (*GM, M*: 59); he is swathed 'like a little mummy' (*GM, M*: 60).

Religion, when it makes a formal appearance, is treated with the cynicism fashionable in educated pre-war Europe. She is asked 'what god do they worship in England, what goddess?' (*GM, M*: 47). Sasha responds, tartly, 'I don't know but it certainly isn't Venus. Somebody wrote once that they worship a bitch-goddess' (*GM, M*: 47). When very drunk, she remembers 'the Russian's' face, presumably her English language pupil, cursing Venus. Sasha dismisses Venus but the Russian says 'be careful of her' (*GM, M*: 187). Gods and goddesses walk in Paris with Sasha, 'Madame Venus is angry and Phoebus Apollo is walking away from me . . .' (*GM, M*: 187). But this is all illusion, because 'Venus is dead; Apollo is dead; even Jesus is dead' (*GM, M*: 187).

Years ago, starving in Paris, she made up her mind to kill herself, after the prepaid month's rent had been used up, 'and my credit for breakfasts in the morning' (*GM, M*: 86). It was a memory of a Catholic teacher, Sister Marie-Augustine, who said that 'eternity is in front of you' which gave Sasha the idea she could take her time about killing herself: death, then, is something to consider as a next step, a proper move.

Rooms and houses may have characters, but people can behave as machines, a particularly modernist construction of technologically developed society and highly functional in this story of a humanity depressed and degraded in the shadow of fascism. Sasha, like other Rhys protagonists, has vivid dreams, mostly in fact alcoholic visions: this way she distances difficult experience (*GM, M*: 121, 122, 186–7), as Antoinette will eventually do in *Wide Sargasso Sea*.[23] When she tries to look at the painting she has bought from Serge, she is so drunk she sees its subject, a man playing his banjo standing in the gutter, as having two heads and four arms.[24]

She dreams of the Paris Exhibition, in which she looks for the way out and asks a man to help her whose hand is made of steel: he simply points her in the direction of the Exhibition.[25] Machines are, when she has been drinking, capable of assuming human attributes, like the one made of white steel, with many steel arms, some of which have eyes at the ends with the 'eyelashes stiff with mascara' (*GM, M:* 187). In Rhys's short story 'Outside the Machine' (*CSS:* 189–209) the machine signifies what runs smoothly but inhumanly in society.[26] The mid to late 1930s saw a crisis within European humanism as fascism triumphed in Spain and then in Germany. Fascism, with its emphasis on authoritarianism and conformity was the polar opposite of Rhys's idiosyncratic anarchism.[27]

But perhaps the most chilling aspect of the novel's cruel humour is its portrayal of sexuality. Instead of being associated with desire, warmth, affection, enjoyment, sex is involved with money, power, self-punishment, coldness, exploitation. There are two important male figures here: the gigolo, René, and the *commis*.

Sasha meets the gigolo when she is masked by her new hairdo and hat, as well as the soothing effects of a good meal, wine and brandy. The irony of this meeting is greater of course if the reader has read Rhys's previous texts and knows that the Rhys protagonist has at times been forced into prostitution. She recognises how the gigolo must feel, approaching her as a potential source of income, 'You talk to them, you pretend to sympathize; then, just at the moment when they are not expecting it, you say "Go to hell"' (*GM, M:* 72).

The gigolo's script is one which Sasha, from experience, recognises, but she intends him, at first, no kindness, 'I had meant to get this man to talk to me and tell me all about it, and then be so devastatingly English that perhaps I should manage to hurt him a little in return for all the many times I've been hurt' (*GM, M:* 73). But there is a level of irony here which stops her short – her appearance, which she has gone to so much trouble to maintain, with the freshly tinted hair and the fur coat, signifies to him that she is a 'rich bitch' (*GM, M:* 75). It gets funnier as he asks her if she can help him get a passport, this woman who has already declared to herself and the reader that she has no nationality.

Sasha begins to laugh loudly: her life 'seems to me so comical that I have to laugh' (*GM, M*: 76).

Not only is Sasha's life comical (if you only look at it the right way), but for the first time, 'on these occasions' she doesn't care 'in the least what the man thinks of me' (*GM, M*: 76). Like the men who have, presumably, exploited her in the past, she only cares what the gigolo looks like. Everything rests on who has the money (or, in this case, is assumed to have it). But Sasha never deceives herself: faced with the gigolo's romanticism about a waiter's view of them, she comments: 'Yes, I expect he'll stay awake all night thinking of it. Like hell he will' (*GM, M*: 77).

The joke ends, brutally, movingly, as the gigolo pulls Sasha to him under a lamp-post and shrewdly declares he feels he is with a child. Sasha almost feels something in return, but the sardonic protection mechanism comes into play. There is nothing for it but for her to return to her room and to her complaints about the hotel management, to a state of mind which shuts 'the damned world out' (*GM, M*: 81).

The ending of the novel is brilliantly worked, and in the development of the role of the *commis* throughout the text many strands of the novel's metaphysical theme come together, counterpointed by Rhys's characteristic use of colour.[28] He has a white dressing gown, in which he floats about 'like the ghost of the landing', 'thin as a skeleton' (*GM, M*: 14). He eventually knocks on Sasha's door, in this garment, 'immaculately white, with long, hanging sleeves', which Sasha assumes 'some woman' must have given him. He smiles a 'silly smile', looking like 'a priest, the priest of some obscene, half-understood religion' (*GM, M*: 35). The idiocy of the smile and the power of the priestly presence are interconnected in the same unnerving way that humour and the spiritual are interconnected throughout this text.

Furthermore, he has, like some Egyptian god, a 'bird-like face' and his dark, sunken eyes have a 'peculiar expression, cringing, ingratiating, knowing' (*GM, M*: 14). Sasha thinks of him as a 'damned man' – the casual profanity here comes, as do many others in Rhys texts, to have a deeper significance. He is as much a part of this seedy hotel as the cockroaches who occupy the bathroom or the louse on the waiter's collar, but the patronne

speaks only of nice rooms.[29] When the *commis* stands in the doorway to Sasha's room, smiling, refusing to move, implying she is
for his use and he knows it, she puts a hand on his chest and
pushes him backwards out of the door, banging the door against
him. She remarks 'It's like pushing a paper man, a ghost, something that doesn't exist' (*GM, M*: 35). But afterwards, she lies in
her room and is 'frightened as hell' about the dressing gown
which looks like a priest's robes. This 'nightmare feeling' (*GM,
M*: 35) prepares us for the final encounter which ends the novel,
in which Sasha surrenders to a loveless sex with a total stranger.

Sasha knows quite clearly how she is both pathetic and comic:
'once again I have given damnable human beings the right to
pity me and laugh at me' (*GM, M*: 94). It is worth reading the last
section of the novel closely for Rhys's characteristic mode of inter-
relating the comic, the tragic and the metaphysical, the latter
being the major code in which the novel is presented.

Sasha has a moment of genuinely happy laughter with the gigolo, but a moment later she sees the *commis*'s shoes by his door,
a very bad omen.[30] But Sasha's room is 'laughing, triumphant'
(*GM, M*: 178), though later, when things start to go wrong, it is a
'damned room'. Her sardonic humour asserts itself as she suggests
a drink with the promise of sex before them: 'That's original. I
bet nobody's ever thought of that way of bridging the gap before'
(*GM, M*: 178). But she has been drinking and, with her fear of
opening up her emotions, she is brittle and hostile, 'Sparks of
anger, of resentment, shooting all over me . . . A comedy, what
comedy? A comedy, my God' (*GM, M*: 179). She tells the gigolo
suddenly to 'go to hell' (*GM, M*: 180), thinking he finds her 'easy
to laugh at' (*GM, M*: 180). So she turns on him: their sexual
wrestling is 'damned comic'; they are like 'English people', never
a compliment in a Rhys text (*GM, M*: 181). He is stung by her
indifference, 'women like you who pretend and lie and play an
idiotic comedy all the time' (*GM, M*: 182).

Death is very present: Sasha is 'as strong as the dead', with her
eyes shut, 'Because dead people must have their eyes shut' (*GM,
M*: 182). When the gigolo tries to engage her in sexual response,
she feels everything begin to hurt: 'it hurts when you have been
dead, to come alive' (*GM, M*: 182). She retreats from the possibility

of feeling into a callous, self-protective mockery. Laughter, and her conviction that men act out of a 'racial' feeling towards women (*GM, M*: 179), stand between her and feeling: 'I shall laugh every time I think about you . . .' (*GM, M*: 184).

Sasha acknowledges two selves at this point: the one who is crying and who managed that brief moment of happiness, and the sardonic one who 'isn't me' (*GM, M*: 184) and who now dominates: this self is the one who generates the most hollow laughter: 'Well, well, just think of that now. What an amusing ten days! Positively packed with thrills. The last performance of What's-her-name And Her Boys or It Was All Due To An Old Fur Coat. Positively the last performance' (*GM, M*: 184). It is this sardonic self who thinks the *commis* must have heard 'every damn thing . . . : and found it "quite amusing"' (*GM, M*: 186), and expects the gigolo to have taken all her money (he hasn't).

As with Rhys's previous novels, this one works its complex and tightly organised references up to a climax informed by the reader's previous experience. Like Anna with Walter in *Voyage in the Dark*, Sasha lies in bed as still as if dead, imaging the gigolo returning to her, a second chance for the less bitter and destructive self. But she realises eventually that it is the *commis* who has come. She at least manages a humane honesty: 'Thank God, he doesn't say anything. I look straight into his eyes and despise another poor devil of a human being for the last time. For the last time . . .' (*GM, M*: 190). After that, she pulls him down to her and we assume engages in loveless and demeaning sex. It matters that it is the white dressing gown he is wearing, which gives him an ironical priestliness (of what religion?). In calling the *commis* a 'poor devil of a human being' Sasha retreats from the challenge of a relationship of equals, as with René, to the sado-masochism of an old script. She despises him 'for the last time' not because she feels sorry for him, but because she is moving entirely beyond a place where she can understand feeling at all. Thus when she says 'yes-yes-yes', which critics have noted as a kind of parody of Joyce's Molly Bloom in *Ulysses*, she gives herself up most chillingly to a death-in-life, to a *zombi* state.[31]

This is Rhys's most contemporary novel, the one which seems to belong to the latter half of the century (its combination of humour and nihilism could be related to absurdism, for example).[32] As a fictional enactment of the worst possible fate for a woman of spirit and desire, it perhaps also functioned for Rhys as a kind of obeah incantation: a protection of the lost and a curse on the heartless and powerful in a morally culpable world, including their empty religious conventions.

# CHAPTER 6

# People in and out of place: spatial arrangements in Wide Sargasso Sea

> I cannot have stressed the poverty and isolation of that family at Coulibri (round about 1834) – Emancipation time etc) enough. They would not have been able to get to Spanish Town – far less to Granbois which is in another island (Dominica of course, my island, though I don't want to be precise about that).
>
> (L: 232)

*Wide Sargasso Sea* is Rhys's most celebrated novel and it has been extensively and variously discussed by critics.[1] Since its first publication, critics have been fascinated by its relation with Charlotte Brontë's *Jane Eyre*.[2] This remains a significant critical concern.[3] This relation has much to do with location, the Caribbean text writing back to the English one. Jane Eyre, in Brontë's novel, is poor and displaced within England. The novel's pivot is class, (underpinned by money), not national identity: Erwin (1989) argues that *Wide Sargasso Sea*'s absence of sure national identity is the most important difference between it and *Jane Eyre*. Although Rochester's mad wife, imprisoned in the attic, is clearly a stranger in England, her nationality and affiliations are repressed in the text. Jane eventually discovers herself an heiress, Rochester loses some of his physical ability and charm and some of his property: their marriage is at last possible.

Rhys's rewriting of Brontë not only privileges the Caribbean but does a great deal to move Rochester out of the realm of the Gothic romance and explain his capacity for cruelty. James comments that with this novel Rhys moved away from 'themes based on memory' (1978: 49) and into a more imaginatively free space, where the dramatic pacing and emotional intensity of the narrative offers a Caribbean markedly different from the Europe portrayed in Rhys's earlier texts. But *Wide Sargasso Sea* is very much informed by memory, not in the details of plot (although Rhys's imaginative reading of some of her family history is included), but in the construction of specific places such as the 'honeymoon house' at Granbois and Coulibri, places which evidently drew on her memories of childhood at Geneva and Bona Vista.[4]

The most provocative theme Rhys tackled in *Wide Sargasso Sea* is race: this too is a kind of placement, a political and economic identity which, driven by the history of white racism, can be the most difficult area for a white writer to try to unravel. Some critics, Spivak (1985), Hite (1989) and Gregg (1995), find Rhys's portrayals of the West Indies and race unacceptable: Gregg terms them 'racialist' (1995: 114) and remarks that every non-white character in *Wide Sargasso Sea* is drawn from the history of white stereotypes of black people: Tia as cheating, hostile nigger; Amelie as lusty wench; Daniel as hateful mulatto; Christophine as black mammy. White critics can also reinforce racial stereotypes, sometimes blatantly: Angier reads Tia as 'the strength and gaiety (and also the treachery) of the primitive' (1990: 566) and Daniel 'as the half-breed, neither black nor white but yellow', 'the wolf-like other' (1990: 566).

It is productive to compare Rhys with other writers both inside and outside the Caribbean who deal with race. Hawthorn (1983) argues that the plot summaries of *Wide Sargasso Sea* and Faulkner's *Absalom, Absalom!* are remarkably similar, and both 'offer fascinating accounts of the ways in which larger conflicts between societies and races generate internal contradictions in their members' (1983: 92). But when he states Rochester's use of strategies on Antoinette that were developed by planters for slaves, for black people, Hawthorn misses the complex irony of Antoinette's dual location as oppressor and oppressed. Much more useful is Blais's argument that Tia 'stands for all the ambivalence of Antoinette's identification across race lines' (1989: 105), an ambivalence which seems to be family to Rhys's own. Rhys certainly reflects the prejudices of her time, race and class, but she also marks a pathway for white writers, for whom too much liberal guilt and refusal to offend is as dangerous as racism itself. At least Rhys found an honesty which opens dialogue: she was in many ways ahead of her time in that willingness to deal with race. Her failings, that is her prejudices, capacity for patronage and limitations of vision, are, I would suggest, not more than most writers possess when writing across the borders of their own identity and social location. But it is imperative that critics, especially white critics, recognise and identify those failings, not glossing over Antoinette's ambivalent position nor the power structure which enables her to lack the 'spunks' which Christophine, as a poor black woman and slave, has had to find in herself to survive.

Though some critics have been interested to an extent in Rhys's construction of place, for example Margarey (1986) Nebeker (1981); Branson (1989); Griffith (1990); Casey (1974), few analyses pay extended attention to it.[5] Givner (1988) singles out *Wide Sargasso Sea* as the only Rhys novel in which landscape is used consistently to reflect the emotional condition of major characters, though this ignores the importance of the emotional connotations of place in other Rhys texts, notably *Voyage in the Dark* and *Good Morning, Midnight.* Nielsen and Brahms (1975) see the issue of how England is constructed as major in Antoinette's marriage.

I regard the issue of place and placement as crucial in all Rhys's texts and most particularly in *Wide Sargasso Sea.* It arises precisely because her protagonists are denied a firm and clear national connection, even a secure place to live, so that the absence of long-term connection is constantly a factor in a protagonist's state of being, as is the condition of a particular room in which she shelters for the moment.[6] Since Rhys's novels are minimally plotted, with the arguable exception of *Wide Sargasso Sea*, which works off the plot of *Jane Eyre*, the emotional condition of the protagonist is the novel's central concern and theme. For Sasha, in *Good Morning, Midnight*, a contributing factor in her crisis is the loss of 'hallmarks', or apparently unproblematic national and class indicators, placements in themselves. For Anna, in *Voyage in the Dark*, it is separation from her earliest national and cultural placement which is an important element in establishing the conditions for her seduction by Walter as well as encouraging a nostalgia for a Caribbean she has not grown to critique in an adult way. For Julia and Marya, in *After Leaving Mr MacKenzie* and *Quartet*,

cross-cultural experience tends to encourage an instability of identity. *Wide Sargasso Sea* markedly pits two opposing sensibilities against
one another, and a major expression of that opposition lies in
different responses on the part of Antoinette and her husband to
the same landscape.

Rhys's opening pages are famously complex but this novel is
especially compressed and multifaceted.[7] In just over two pages,
Rhys establishes the tension between white and black and between
Creole white and English over Emancipation, then between white
Jamaican society (colonial middle- and upper-class) and her narrator Antoinette's white family (Martiniquan widowed mother,
two children).[8] In addition there are the important contextual
details that Antoinette's mother was much too young for her
father, that a neighbour, Mr Luttrell, shot his dog and swam out
to sea rather than wait for the compensation promised planters
after Emancipation, that Luttrell's house was soon said 'by the
black people' to be haunted. In the isolation which Antoinette's
family comes to accept, an important factor is that the road from
Spanish Town to Coulibri Estate is poor and so few visitors come
to visit; Mr Luttrell's estate is the closest to Coulibri and, after his
suicide, abandoned. That the family lives so far from community
is important in what happens later on.

Rhys establishes a world in which everything rests on problematic and strained relationships: between people of different
nationalities, races, languages, classes, against which the struggle
to maintain connection even within a family can seem puny and
defeated.[9] After her horse is poisoned, Antoinette's mother thinks
of her family as 'marooned' (*WSS*: 18). She means that they are
cut off from human society, but of course, in the sense that
Antoinette grows up to become a subversive, maintaining defiance against a husband and culture which oppresses her, she
becomes a maroon in the Caribbean sense.[10]

A very important early set piece is Antoinette's description of
the garden at Coulibri, where she was a child, a garden which
was probably based on Rhys's memories of her mother's family
estate at Geneva. It marks childhood as taking place in a damaged Eden:

Our garden was large and beautiful as that garden in the Bible – the tree of life grew there. But it had gone wild. The paths were overgrown and a smell of dead flowers mixed with the fresh living smell. Underneath the tree ferns, tall as forest tree ferns, the light was green. Orchids flourished out of reach or for some reason not to be touched. One was snaky looking, another like an octopus with long thin brown tentacles bare of leaves hanging from a twisted root. Twice a year the octopus orchid flowered – then not an inch of tentacle showed. It was a bell-shaped mass of white, mauve, deep purples, wonderful to see. The scent was very sweet and strong. I never went near it. (*WSS*: 19)

This wild garden is a metaphor for Antoinette's family and ultimately for Antoinette herself. In the novel, wildness is constructed as a positive: Antoinette comments that all of Coulibri Estate had run wild like the garden, because after slavery, 'why should anybody work?' (*WSS*: 19), and that she was never saddened by this.

As in other Rhys texts, rooms and houses are major signifiers: the house at Coulibri, and Antoinette's room there, Christophine's room at Coulibri and house at Granbois, the room at Aunt Cora's where Antoinette recovers after the fire, the convent classroom and grounds, the house at Granbois and especially Antoinette's bedroom and her husband's dressing room, Daniel's small, hot living room and finally the cold room in England where Antoinette is confined with its high window, and the corridors and rooms she escapes to wander in that house at night. Narrating response to a particular room or landscape becomes a character's major way of communicating half-conscious judgements, emotional responses, cultural identity.

Antoinette's home, the great house, is described piece by piece as a series of settings for human tensions. Antoinette remembers her mother walking up and down the *glacis*, 'a paved roofed-in terrace which ran the length of the house and sloped upwards to a clump of bamboos' (*WSS*: 19). By the bamboos, the mother could see the sea but also be seen by passers-by and sometimes laughed at: Antoinette's mother registers such laughter long after in a deep frown. It is her mother's strange and sometimes hostile or indifferent behaviour which drives Antoinette to spend most of her time in the kitchen, 'which was an outbuilding some way off'

(*WSS*: 20). This is how she comes to be so close to Christophine, her nurse, whose room is next to the kitchen.

As a former slave-owner's place, the Coulibri great house carries with it the suppressed rage and agony of the past. It is in the house that Christophine speaks with her own authority to Antointette's husband. Christophine offers warning against the *glacis* as night falls: she offers Antoinette maternal warning from her culture, since Antoinette's mother has no advice to offer nor much interest in her child's activities. But although Christophine has tried to create security for Antoinette, and is associated with the house, we know from the way the fire starts at Coulibri that houses can be the most dangerous of all spaces.[11] Antoinette clearly feels safest in wild places which can suggest association with security, as when she sees the shadow of her house from a long way off but can smell ferns and river water: 'I felt safe again as if I was one of the righteous' (*WSS*: 33). But she enjoys the ruined beauty of the old estate house and garden only in the daylight, for after dark, 'the house was haunted, some places are' (*WSS*: 132).

In Antoinette's room in her husband's English house, her privacy and her identity have been taken from her, symbolised by the removal of the doors to her bedroom and the lack of a looking-glass: in Rhys's texts both mirrors and rooms offer critical reflections of psychological states in a female protagonist. Antoinette's small bedroom at Granbois has a large looking-glass as well as a window and a door: her husband knows this is Antoinette's territory and when things deteriorate between them he retreats from the room. Mr Mason's dressing room becomes his, though he hears how Mr Mason did not like the house and hardly came there. When he sleeps with Amelie, Antoinette's servant, he chooses this room, thinly divided by a partition from Antoinette's own room where he had once been passionate with her and from where she could hear him. In this way he violates not only her trust, but a house she has loved from childhood, and which now, as a result of the marriage, legally belongs to the man who has betrayed her.

Antoinette's Aunt Cora lives in Spanish Town, a distance from Coulibri. It is a source of colonial gossip and intrigue, and there are those who are hostile to Antoinette's mother's remarriage, which takes place there. Mr Mason thinks Aunt Cora did not do enough to take care of her brother's family after Emancipation but Antoinette defends her, on the grounds that she was married to an Englishman who hated the West Indies and so could not come home or help her family until he had died. Everything rests on where a person is located in terms of the central hierarchies of colonial Caribbean society. Aunt Cora's house becomes the haven of rest and kindness where Antoinette recovers from the effects of the fire which has devastated her family.

The ambivalence which characterises Antoinette's response to home also extends to the convent, which signifies both sunshine and death to her. The dormitory is a 'long brown room' full of 'gold sunlight' and the 'shadows of trees moving quietly' (*WSS*: 56), i.e. it is both inside and outside at the same time, both nature and nurture. Antoinette's memory of the convent is of contrasting light and dark, innocence and sin, from her Catholic teaching, with memories of her mother, who hated 'a strong light' and loved 'the cool and the shade' (*WSS*: 57). Though the nuns assure the blessing 'let perpetual light shine on them' is a different kind of light, Antoinette will not say it in case she is inadvertently wishing discomfort on her mother. The convent is all 'brightness and dark', grace and damnation and the actual tropical day and night, sunshine and shadow. Also:

The walls, the blazing colours of the flowers in the garden, the nuns' habits were bright, but their veils, the Crucifix hanging from their waists, the shadow of the trees, were black. (*WSS*: 57)

Displacement is a strong theme in the novel in relation to major characters such as Antoinette, her husband and Christophine (perhaps even Amelie who thinks of going to Rio to find a rich husband). But substantial displacement across racial and class lines severely affects coherent self-definition. Antoinette finds herself called white cockroach by black people, yet she has no place in white culture either. So she finds a place to be alone, outside human habitation:

When I was safely home I sat close to the old wall at the end of the garden. It was covered with green moss soft and velvet and I never wanted to move again. Everything would be worse if I moved. Christophine found me there when it was nearly dark, and I was so stiff she had to help me get up. (*WSS*: 23)

This child who is learning too much solitude is given a companion, the daughter of Christophine's only friend. Her name is Tia, and her relationship with Antoinette is conducted in certain particular neutral places: the turn of the road to the river, which is their daily meeting place; the bathing pool on the estate. Tia makes a fire and they boil green bananas in a pot; after eating they sleep. This home in nature is their only true meeting place, but it is quickly entered by the outside world when Antoinette has a few new pennies Christophine has given her and Tia makes a bet: she'll win them if Antoinette cannot turn a somersault under water. Though Antoinette manages the task, she comes up choking and Tia claims the money. Their ensuing quarrel marks them as placed firmly in their separate communities: Antoinette calls Tia a cheating nigger and Tia calls Antoinette a white nigger, a poor white, 'and black nigger better than white nigger' (*WSS*: 24). Looking for consolation, Antoinette goes off alone to parts of the estate she has never seen before, where if she is cut by razor grass or meets ants or rain, she still feels these things are 'better than people' (*WSS*: 28). Even in these relatively good times, when her mother is still sane, Christophine is irritated that Antoinette is running wild, a significant comment in the light of the importance of the idea of wild or tamed landscape in the novel; she warns that it is dangerous to sleep in the moonlight. A white girl child is supposed to be trained into submission to social mores which will give her status and privilege in exchange for her spontaneity.

The crucial issue for Antoinette is about where she belongs and can be happy. Her beloved Coulibri is burned down, her mother becomes mad and is shut away, and her convent boarding school becomes a 'refuge' (*WSS*: 56). But nothing can replace Coulibri, where she feels 'This is my place and this is where I belong and this is where I wish to stay' (*WSS*: 108). In this she is entirely different from Sasha or Julia in Rhys's earlier novels who have no substantial connection with any place.

Christophine's own placement in Jamaica is problematic as she is from Martinique, which makes her an outsider in a black community just as Antoinette's mother is in white. The fact that she was given as a wedding present, a piece of property, to Antoinette's mother by Antoinette's father, means that her own original attachments to family, community and country have been destroyed. She has not left the family after Emancipation, because by now, we might ask, where would she go? Antoinette's mother thinks 'we would have died if she'd turned against us' (*WSS*: 21), which in her mind would have been a better fate. The question of whether Christophine is an obeah woman becomes important as the novel proceeds, because such a vocation would position her automatically as an enemy to white hegemony: her protective stance towards Antoinette, to whom she acts as surrogate mother for a while, further complicates her position.[12] There is an ironic parallelism in Antoinette's ultimate fate: whereas Christophine finally retires to a little property she was given by Antoinette's mother and has her freedom, Antoinette will be carried away against her will and confined. For Antoinette's husband, the smug epitaphs of slave-holders on the walls of the church where he marries strike him more than the ceremony or his bride. Though he implicitly criticises them, he casts himself as Antoinette's owner by the end of the novel: 'She's mad, but *mine, mine*' (*WSS*: 166).

The very word 'place' occurs many times in the novel. Antoinette thinks of Coulibri as 'a sacred place' (*WSS*: 132). But after her trouble with her husband, she accuses him of having made Granbois, a place she always loved, 'into a place I hate' (*WSS*: 147). Christophine has seen much, 'in this place' (*WSS*: 151). Antoinette's husband says bitterly, 'I would give my eyes never to have seen this abominable place' (*WSS*: 161), by which he means either Jamaica or the unnamed island on which Granbois is situated, or both, and yet he has to admit Granbois and its surroundings are beautiful, 'however far I travel I'll never see a lovelier' (*WSS*: 164). He finds it on first acquaintance 'a cool and remote place' (*WSS*: 76), just as he finds the village of Massacre 'sombre people in a sombre place' (*WSS*: 68). After receiving Daniel's letter about madness in Antoinette's family and seeing Antoinette attack her servant after the servant, Amelie, is entirely provocative and insulting, he flees the house and finds 'a large clear space' in the forest where a ruined house is surrounded by rose trees

and orange trees run wild. It is 'a beautiful place' (*WSS*: 104). In
the end, Granbois becomes the 'hidden place' (*WSS*: 173), from
which Antoinette is taken by her husband, and he has every
intention then of reducing it to mere property, 'I'd sell the place'
(*WSS*: 173), for he has decided he hates it. England to Christophine
is a 'damn place' in which she hardly believes (*WSS*: 111).

What is important about a given place in the novel is how it
affects a narrating consciousness. An absence of attachment can
be so severe that it makes the place seem unreal, as in the case
of the house in England in which Antoinette is imprisoned,
'This cardboard house where I walk at night is not England'
(*WSS*: 181). The vivid colours of the tropics signify home to
Antoinette, whether as vegetation or sky or the colours of Aunt
Cora's patchwork silk counterpane (*WSS*: 56) or Antoinette's choice
of colours for her embroidery at the convent (green, purple, blue,
'fire-red' (*WSS*: 53)). But to Rochester, the very jewel colours
which Antoinette loves are oppressive, 'Too much blue, too much
purple, too much green. The flowers too red . . .' (*WSS*: 70). In
many ways, the emotional terrain of the novel is much as
Antoinette's husband defines the process of his marriage 'the
advance and retreat' (*WSS*: 65). The idea of safety is also critical
to the value of a place to Antoinette: she resents the nuns at the
convent when it is suddenly clear to her that they are safe, 'How
can they know what it can be like *outside*?' (*WSS*: 59). Antoinette
speaks of an England she has only known from books to
Christophine, but even at this moment, she knows somehow that
the house she will live in will be cold and the bed will have red
curtains. This awkward tie-in to *Jane Eyre* also introduces the idea
of being cold which is strongly associated with emotional inertia
and with fear or other trauma in other Rhys texts.[13]

Coulibri and Granbois are described in rich and careful detail
whereas England is vague and depressing, a prison for Antoinette.
Negative images of England begin long before the time Antoinette
experiences her traumatic confinement. She confides to her husband that she has heard England is like an unpleasant dream.
It is English law which denies Antoinette her property after her
marriage. The picture 'The Miller's Daughter' which hangs at
Coulibri is of an English girl: similar popular prints construct

stereotypical English images for other Rhys protagonists.[14] Antoinette sees Mr Mason as 'so without a doubt English' and her mother as 'so without a doubt not English' (*WSS*: 36). But the English connection is the defining one. Antoinette's husband stays with a retired English magistrate called Fraser in Jamaica just before the marriage, though his own relation to England is conflicted as he is the less-loved younger son and knows his marriage has been intended by his family to get him off their hands and give him Antoinette's money and property. He sees Antoinette as 'not English or European either', even if she is supposed to be of 'pure English descent' (*WSS*: 67).

Places are extremely alive in this novel: the menacing, lush garden at Coulibri, the mysterious bathing pool at Coulibri, sunset by the huts of the plantation workers, the road from the village of Massacre up to Granbois, the sea and sky at sunset from the *ajoupa* or thatched shelter at Granbois, the bathing pools at Granbois (the champagne pool and the nutmeg pool) the forest where Antoinette's husband wanders until he is lost, the road to Christophine's home, the trees and bamboos around the house at Granbois.

Sometimes a scene which is quite brief becomes deeply resonant because of the juxtaposition of landscape and people. As Antoinette and her husband prepare to leave Granbois for Jamaica and then England, he comments that she has now a blank look, for he has forced out the hate from her eyes and made her a ghost. But he is troubled by it, almost it seems tempted to wish she could be restored. Then a child cries, a child so low in the social scale that Antoinette's husband does not even know his name or care to: he is the boy who stands by the clove tree, waiting to do his job of carrying a basket. The child provokes him to ask hostile questions, exhibiting his power over everyone. Antoinette answers him very calmly and rationally. He goes on:

the nameless boy leaned his head against the clove tree and sobbed. Loud heartbreaking sobs. I could have strangled him with pleasure. But I managed to control myself, walk up to them and say coldly, 'What is the matter with him? What is he crying about?' . . . She had followed me and she answered . . . 'He asked me when we first came if we – if you – would take him with you when we left . . . He knows English . . . he has tried very hard to learn English . . .'

I was tired of these people. I disliked their laughter and their tears, their flattery and envy, conceit and deceit. And I hated the place. (*WSS*: 172)

The juxtaposition of the nameless boy with the named tree, together with the successful effort to control and conceal feeling, says much about this man's consciousness, much about his English cultural identity (the English love and know cultivated nature but the colonial and racist English dismissed those they considered inferior without knowing them at all). He finally realises how he has come to hate this landscape, because it signifies his wife and his failure to reach her, even to overpower or control her. That failure has made him negatively passionate, which absorbs his whole consciousness:

I hated the mountains and the hills, the rivers and the rain. I hated sunsets of whatever colour, I hated its beauty and its magic and the secret I would never know. I hated its indifference and the cruelty which was part of the loveliness. Above all I hated her. For she belonged to the magic and the loveliness. She had left me thirsty and all my life would be thirst and longing for what I had lost before I found it. (*WSS*: 172)

It is the location of Antoinette in the landscape which is significant. Similarly, the juxtaposition of the forest and lush vegetation around Granbois with Daniel's cramped living room sets out brilliantly and briefly his cruel and self-absorbed nature and his love of money. The table has a red fringed cloth, which suggests, in the manner of touches of red in Rhys texts, a suppressed and probably threatening passion in Daniel himself. Though Daniel puts a chair for Antoinette's husband near the door to catch some breeze, the room is still airless. A dirty white wall bears a framed text, 'Vengeance is Mine' (leaving out that God was the one speaking). Daniel is perfectly at home in this setting, wiping his nose revoltingly on a corner of the tablecloth. Outside his house, Antoinette's husband follows a path which ends out of sight and sound of the house, and there he stops, seeing 'The world was given up to heat and to flies, the light was dazzling' (*WSS*: 126) and feeling two levels of revulsion: one against Daniel himself and the other against the richness of vegetation and power of sunlight which have, in his reading of it, created the whole social maelstrom into which he has wandered.

The physical and spiritual landscapes of Caribbean topography and climate and cultural identity interconnect: in Antoinette's husband's mind there is fear of a brightness which is threatening because he cannot control it as he has learned to control himself. It is also a brightness which has no echoes in his imagination, 'It was all very brightly coloured, very strange, but it meant nothing to me' (*WSS*: 76), just as, much later, he sees Amelie's face as lovely but meaningless (*WSS*: 141). He can see loveliness but when it is disturbing, he retreats from it, and it is clear that what he cannot make his own is disturbing. More sinister is his colonising declaration that when he realises that the landscape, in this instance the bathing pool, hides something, 'I want what it *hides*' (*WSS*: 87). He insists on calling Antoinette Bertha, because that signifies his authority to name and control her (it is significant that Rhys never gives this man a name: he is only by inference Rochester from *Jane Eyre*).

When he first comes to Massacre, on the way to Granbois, it is raining, and he thinks 'It will all look very different in the sun' (*WSS*: 66), but when the sun does shine, and he rides along the 'wall of green' with 'a steep drop to the ravine below' (*WSS*: 69) on the other side, he soon begins to feel the colours of vegetation and sky are too much. He can appreciate the taste, clarity and beauty of spring water collected along a bamboo spout which Antoinette collects for him in a thick green leaf, but immediately afterwards, he tries to connect the redness of the earth he sees with red earth in England, to try to make it familiar. Antoinette is mocking, though he still sees the house at Granbois at first as 'an imitation of an English summer house' (*WSS*: 71), which proves to be his mistake in terms of the role he plays in it and the degree of resistance to him offered by servants loyal to Antoinette as well as to their own identity and identification with the house.

What gives productive tension to the narrative is that Antoinette's husband does in the romantic beginning of his marriage appreciate certain aspects of his wife's 'place', since he is alienated to an extent from his own family and location. He enjoys the sweetness of the air at Granbois, 'an intoxicating freshness as if all this had never been breathed before' (*WSS*: 73), full of the scents of trees and shrubs, cloves, cinnamon, roses and oranges, but he thinks the house 'neglected and deserted' (*WSS*: 73). This tension in him makes the attempted relationship the more interesting and dramatic, for he is not a simple conqueror, but a damaged child of English upper-class society trying to marry an injured and highly sensitive child of Caribbean upper-class society. Both Antoinette and her husband seek to identify to an extent with the injured or the wild, but draw back in their inability to extend their empathy beyond themselves. Not once does Antoinette's husband think of Antoinette as if he were her, nor she do this for him.

Perhaps the most dramatic instance of the relation of both of them to place occurs in dreams: the first nightmare and the second are reworked Mr Howard material.[15] Her mother is barely sympathetic, so Antoinette takes comfort in the location of her bed in a familiar room as well as in the tree of life in the garden and the 'wall green with moss' (*WSS*: 27). These things signify safety from strangers, more so than her mother's presence: the latter is conflicted and often a source of pain rather than strength or comfort. This first dream takes place before Coulibri burns.

The second dream takes place at the convent, after Antoinette has lost her home, her mother and brother after the fire. In it she is still at Coulibri, this time walking towards the forest, not in it. She is wearing a long dress and slippers, and can't walk fast, and this time she follows a man, holding her beautiful white dress out of the dirt. She is sick with fear but still follows the man. When they reach the forest, his face is 'black with hatred' and he asks her 'Here?'. He goes on, and she cries, letting her dress trail now. Then they reached an enclosed garden and she tries to hold onto a tree, which 'sways and jerks as if it is trying to throw me off' (*WSS*: 60), instead of going up some stone steps, presumably to a house.

The third time this dream comes, the flight of steps becomes steps to the room where Antoinette is imprisoned. She goes on to take the keys and let herself out into the house with a candle in her hand and discovers a room decorated in red, white and gold.[16] Then she knocks over a lighted candle and the fire spreads through the house. Remembering her childhood, she finally comes to see Tia beckoning and she calls Antoinette to jump over the edge of the parapet of the burning house. In this dream, the bathing pool at Coulibri is tempting. These dreams move from the forest to the garden to the house, in a progression which at the end returns to the wilderness where the bathing pool becomes the place Antoinette dreams of leaping to her death to rediscover.

Antoinette's husband also has a violent dream, that he is buried alive, after he takes the drink she has laced with Christophine's potion. Being buried alive is associated with earth, most often with the tradition of the Haitian *zombi*, who is buried and comes back out of the earth to serve an earthly power. Though it is Antoinette who becomes the ghost, perhaps her husband, in his living death of vengeances on her, becomes a *zombi* (Raiskin 1996).[17] We never hear from him again after he leaves Granbois for England with her: he is silenced and Antoinette has the last word, despite being erased in the world outside her small room. Her last vision brings the landscape of Coulibri into the grim, dull experience of England she has endured for so long. Our last image of her is as she dreams her escape, by flying off the roof to join Tia by the bathing pool, an impossible turning back of time and history, but one which locates her finally in the Caribbean and in nature.

Colette Lindroth (1985), in arguing that Rhys's fiction is 'haunted', sees a 'blurring' of details as a deliberate and effective strategy in all of the fiction and *Wide Sargasso Sea* as exhibiting only 'stasis, stagnation, alienation, and madness' (1985: 137). But the fiction, and especially *Wide Sargasso Sea*, is full of small but exquisitely described details of place which serve to illustrate the complex and subtle emotional landscape of major characters. O'Callaghan cites Tiffin (1978) in exploring a common 'theme of homelessness' in white Creole women's fiction (1993: 33), and argues that landscape in Bliss's *Luminous Isle* is said to be more real than people, drawing comparisons with Antoinette's preference for wild nature over people. I would argue further that Rhys has a most difficult relation to both the Caribbean and Europe.[18]

In terms of how it affected her writing, Ford Madox Ford was insightful about Rhys's relation to the Caribbean:

Her business was with passion, hardship, emotions: the locality in which these things are endured is immaterial. So she hands you the Antilles with its sea and sky . . . – the effect of landscape on the emotions and passions of a child being so penetrative, but lets Montparnasse, or London, or Vienna go. (Stang, ed. 1986: 245)

This raises an important question by suggesting that the intensity of Rhys's Caribbean landscapes might derive from the freezing of a child's vivid memory, the more so as a result of the separation from the region. His other suggestion is that, as a mature writer, she had little interest in locale. Of course Ford was making a generalisation based on her earliest professional work. As Rhys matured as a writer, she included limited but accurate geography of European places. Over and over again, her protagonists remember a street in Paris or London as a place where something important took place.

The issue of Rhys's construction of the Caribbean is intensified by the reluctance some readers have felt in placing her unequivocally as Caribbean. Her own ambivalence towards her exile from the Caribbean is markedly written into the negative weighting of complex cultural experience which she gives to her protagonists. Her conception of place grew out of her childhood connection with Dominica, her separation from the Caribbean, her difficult connection with England, her emotionally turbulent years in France. Caribbean identity is generally richly complex: Rhys's was also.[19] She knew the alienation of being white and resisting it to an extent; also she was half-British, though she refused affiliation despite making her home in Britain and finding her literary success there. People who are born and grow up in the Caribbean itself and those of Caribbean descent who are born and grow up in the Caribbean diaspora have different visions of their regional identity, but both are reinforced by Caribbean community. Rhys never knew such community, even as a child. Her natural mode of being was isolation, and the large migration which built the significant Caribbean presence in England did not begin until the 1950s, and would not have reached out to a white colonial. In any case, by the late fifties, Rhys was living in rural England, where she would remain, except for short visits to London, for the rest of her life. Harrison comments (1988), that Rhys would have agreed that she was displaced, and that people with no place are likely to be low in the social order.

Rhys's letters during the long period of the writing of *Wide Sargasso Sea* show her imagination to have been deeply engaged with displacement, absence, and the difficult construction of identity in permanent exile from origins, all experiences which intensified during her writing career. During the years of serious application to the novel Rhys's always marginal sense of settlement and affiliation had to have been further weakened by inadequate and temporary housing. In July 1957 she was living in Bude, in Cornwall, which she called 'Bude the Obscure' waggishly to a friend.[20] She could find pleasure there in a country walk, though as in *Voyage in the Dark* English flowers proved to be obedient to English human culture, 'all keeping primly to their place ...' (letter to Peggy Kirkaldy, 5 July 1957). Her house, 'This place', was surrounded in the summer by tourists and traffic, the sheep ate the spring flowers and the trees were few and fragile. In 1961, she wrote to Selma Vaz Dias:

This place, which I imagined would be a refuge, is a foretaste of hell at present – It has hardly stopped raining since we arrived, and I wish the bloody river Exe would make up its mind and wash this whole village and the damp fields and cows right away and finish (Me with cows). Instead of that it oozes and drips away ... Cambridge is a pleasant place ... Am always falling off things – Oh and Ely Cathedral. So lovely I thought it. I bet I wasn't wrong though a dreadful child I expect suspected by all (most unjustly) of being a Savage from the Cannibal Islands.

As a matter of fact I consider myself highly civilised – in some ways only I admit. (*L*: 200–1)

Though her own alienation from the bleak Cornish and Devon winter landscapes was intense, she admired writing which was sensitive to locale. She praised Colette for being able to capture country sounds, scents and feelings (letter to Peggy Kirkaldy, 30 July 1957). In the same letter she writes of a longing for 'leaves and shadows so that it hurts': she was thinking of a landscape other than that of deforested south-west England, which seemed to her 'Only rocks, sea, clouds, gulls & of course tourists Not a tree [sic]' (letter to Peggy Kirkaldy, 5 July 1957). Dominica's prevalent trees were evidently always missed: Rhys strongly disliked the new rich who she thought were responsible for chopping down

trees and farming the English south-west. In 1960, she wrote to
Francis Wyndham of her unhappiness that two bungalows were
to be built in the field next to her rented home in Perranporth,
intruding on her peace. She felt strongly that she needed 'a place
to live in' (*L:* 186), and she would complain of isolation, loneliness, hostility of neighbours and villagers, the climate, animals
and plants during her difficult years in Devon and Cornwall,
even after she had her own home.[21]

By contrast, there was never a question about her affection for
her childhood landscapes: she rejoiced that Wyndham had seen
the wild and majestic 'Dominica mornes', which she considered
had a chance of surviving as 'most people like smooth sands and
sea bathing' (letter to Francis Wyndham, 30 March 1964). Though
she thought Dominica difficult to love, she also thought if you did
love it, it was for a very long time. Dominicans as well as visitors
have always responded strongly to Dominica's dramatic topography. Lennox Honychurch writes that many travellers have
used 'the words "green", "blue", "wild", "beauty", and sometimes "melancholy"' to describe the island (1991: 3). There is the
famous statement of Alec Waugh, quoted by Honychurch and by
Louis James: 'I had never thought of green as being a colour that
could dazzle you' (James 1978: 1).[22]

Place in *Wide Sargasso Sea* is wild landscape and cultivated garden, houses and rooms which cannot protect against emotional
devastation, and also the placement which identity draws on and
reinforces, identity built out of crucial concepts like class, gender,
race and nation. Interactions between safety and danger, sanity
and madness are constructed in relation to cultivation of land or
people and refusal or lack of such cultivation. Rodriguez includes
Rhys in a general discussion of the idea of the wild garden or
wild place as a prototype for the idea of new nation which
opposed the cultivated plantation of English colonial culture. She
points out that in *Wide Sargasso Sea*, Christophine refers to the
unnamed island (evidently Dominica) as a free country whereas
other characters call it only 'place' (1994: 131).

Rhys's acute sense of the machinery of colonial power and
influence is evident not only in *Wide Sargasso Sea* but in her other
texts. In *Good Morning, Midnight*, Sasha describes the process of

dying hair in a way which suggests the process of colonisation: 'First . . . its own colour must be taken out of it – and then it must be dyed, that is to say, another colour must be imposed on it. (Educated hair . . . )' (*GM, M:* 52). For those, like Antoinette, who refuse to be educated (re-placed), in the ways of so-called cultivated society, there is only isolation and eventual madness.

The issue of where a protagonist is placed by social arrangements and how she places herself in response, a figure in a landscape, a room or a city street, is critical in all of Rhys's texts: they are in fact, collectively, an extended essay on identity.

# CHAPTER 7

# Brief encounters: Rhys and the craft
# of the short story

I will post you the story tomorrow nearly three weeks too
late . . . Its not right yet, too slow at the start too hurried at
the end . . .

(Letter to Francis Wyndham, 6 March 1961)

I will finish Leaving School & Mr Ramage A bit sentimental perhaps, and the West Indies as they *were* sound unreal,
but I cant help that.

(Letter to Olwyn Hughes, 25 February 1966)

Yesterday I posted a letter to Diana explaining the corrections I'm anxious to make in 'Fifi' and 'Vienne'. With 'Fifi'
its just a matter of deleting a few paragraphs but 'Vienne' is
more complicated.

The chapter headings must go of course and be replaced
by spaces but I want some of the 'chapters' left out altogether.
They are not good & only confuse what story there is.

(Letter to Olywyn Hughes, 7 March 1967)

Rhys's interest in and success with the short story form have
been compared favourably with that of other achieved writers,
most evidently Hemingway (Brown 1986) and Katherine Mansfield
(Wolfe 1980). Her first published text, 'Vienne', appeared in Ford's
*transatlantic review* (vol. 2, no. 2, 1924) immediately after Hemingway's
'Cross-Country Snow' and in the same issue as an extract from
Gertrude Stein's 'The Making of America'.[1] But whereas the
short story has long been marginalised in British literature, often
used as a practice run by writers intending to become novelists,
in the Caribbean, the literary short story, like its oral counterpart
is a major form, especially for women writers. For them, Rhys
stands chronologically as a kind of ancestor.

Many Caribbean women writers have excelled in the short story form, including Paule Marshall, Michelle Cliff, Jamaica Kincaid, Olive Senior, Velma Pollard, Pauline Melville, Christine Craig, Alecia McKenzie, Ramabai Espinet and Opal Palmer Adisa.[2] A number of writers, such as Olive Senior and Velma Pollard, have chosen both the short story and the poem, both genres requiring an ability to exploit the advantages and limitations of economy. Many of the most identifiably Caribbean forms of verbal artistry, such as calypso, require economy and highly developed verbal play which permits a depth of signification without a great many words.[3] I have argued that a good deal of Rhys's effectiveness as a writer comes from using such economical but richly layered poetic devices as linked chains of imagery. She constantly worked to eradicate any superfluous words in her texts: the economy of the story form was something she could therefore fully embrace.

Rhys's Caribbean is thematically visible enough in her stories for there to be a collection of them entitled *Tales of the Wide Caribbean* (ed. Ramchand: n.d.). Ramchand argues that Rhys gradually permitted 'repressed Caribbean experience' to emerge more and more forthrightly as her fictional career went on. Less than half of Rhys's published short pieces are included in Ramchand's collection. But Rhys's own vision of the Caribbean is encoded subtly in most of Rhys's shorter texts as important stylistic elements, just as I have argued it is in Rhys's longer fiction.

The direction Rhys took in 'Let Them Call It Jazz' (1962; *TAB-L*, 1968; *CSS*, 1987) in using a Creole or nation language speaker as narrator has become predominant in Caribbean writing.[4] Where locally accented international English is used for narration, nation language is very often essential for dialogue in women's stories, since many portray the dispossessed working woman. Kincaid, Cliff and Marshall portray the ways in which Caribbean speech and cultural identity survive the journey to another culture as a result of migration or are displaced or suppressed by it. Apart from resembling Rhys in her beginnings as an autobiographical short-fiction writer, her early exile and her ambivalence about the Caribbean, Kincaid's style in her early stories is economical and vividly precise in ways which recall

Rhys. Rhys's enthusiastic response to hearing from Wally Look Lai (letter to Francis Wyndham, 11 May 1968) that Caribbean writers such as Jan Carew were working together to launch a new literary magazine in Toronto called *Cotopaxi*, surely means she would have been delighted with the great quantity of extremely good writing which has come from the Caribbean since then.

Rhys tacitly drew on the tradition of story-telling so powerfully evidenced among poor women in the Caribbean in the folk traditions of 'tim-tim' and Nancy stories.[5] Her portrayal of Meta and Francine (*Smile Please*), clearly reveals Rhys's early connection of black women, Caribbean culture and a sophisticated oral tradition of vibrant, well-formed stories. Most of her stories are told by or on behalf of women who, even when passive, implicitly protest or expose a system which excludes or is indifferent to them. Her narrative complexity in the stories reinforces the difficulty of making oneself heard, or achieving any genuine communication, which, as I have argued earlier, owed something to her Caribbean sense of political, racial and class divisions being almost insurmountable, to which she added an acute sense of the particular marginalisation of women.

However her technique was of course also influenced by Ford, who clearly taught her a good deal about translating rough draft into crafted blocks of words, a process which understood that the process of writing itself supersedes whatever the writing is about. In that sense, Rhys understood from the beginning of her career that she was working words just as a sculptor might work marble or a carver wood. She worked as hard on her stories as on her novels, using the same techniques: drafting in notebooks, then revising and revising. Her letters show a continued concern for achieving the rightness of small details such as names in the stories.[6] She was also constantly self-critical.[7]

It is clear that a good number of the pieces in Rhys's later story collections are final reworkings of old manuscript material, sometimes from draft intended for novels. 'Night Out 1925' (*SIOL*, 1976) shares a protagonist called Suzy with the unpublished novel 'Triple Sec'; other examples include 'Till September Petronella' (1960; *TAB-L*, 1968) 'Vienne' (first published 1924). 'Mannequin', an early story included in *The Left Bank*, has a protagonist called

Anna: much later Rhys would make an Anna protagonist of *Voyage in the Dark*. She admitted to Francis Wyndham (27 September 1968) that 'Overture and Beginners Please' seemed part of a longer work.

Fortunately, a number of later stories have survived in multiple drafts which enable us to look at least at fairly advanced stages of redrafting and correction. Though some critics have thought that Rhys basically wrote the same story over and over again (Morrell 1979), as Malcolm and Malcolm point out (1996), the narrative variety demonstrated in the short fiction is impressive and extensive, ranging from an objective narrator to much greater subjectivity and the use of narrative devices such as letters. The Malcolms also interestingly suggest that the objective narrators' 'very reticence about themselves suggests that their own fates somehow parallel those of the characters they depict' (1996: 6).

In general, we can see from Rhys's surviving drafts and manuscripts that the process of fictionalising, whether in the story, novel, poem or autobiography, generally began for her with something close to diary or memoir and then moved through multiple drafts as she worked towards finishing a piece. She tried to eradicate every superfluity and awkwardness: the process is the same, whether stories are extremely short ('The Joey Bagstock Smile', 1977) or fairly long ('Rapunzel, Rapunzel', *SIOL*, 1976; *CSS*, 1987).

Rhys persistently expressed anxiety about the quality of her work in short fiction, though she was often far too hard on the work. 'Let Them Call It Jazz' is one of her finest achievements. She first called it 'They Thought It Was Jazz' (*L*: 184): it seemed to her 'a bit of a crazy story. For fun' (*L*: 184). It was her doubts and self-criticisms which propelled her to revise endlessly. 'Vienne', as I discussed earlier, has three clearly different versions. In two unpublished letters written 3 and 6 March 1967 to Diana Athill, as the reprint of 'Vienne' in *Tigers Are Better-Looking* was being planned, Rhys expressed her reservations about the second version, published in *The Left Bank*. It now seemed to her 'bitty'; it 'gives a feeling of untidiness & breathlessness because its in the *wrong* order'. She wanted the chapter headings left out (they were); she fretted over decisions: omitting certain chapters, trying to capture the feel of Vienna when only trivial things remained in her memory.

Similarly, she wondered if *The Left Bank* story 'Illusion' was good enough for inclusion though 'it is much how I wrote then'. She thought 'The Blue Bird' (*TLB*) sentimental; also 'some paragraphs of Fifi (*TLB*) ought to be deleted'.[8] She wanted 'Temps Perdi' (1967; *PMS*, 1969), one of her strongest stories, left out, because she had 'leaned on' it when she came to 'Part II of the book', presumably *Wide Sargasso Sea*, and that was because she had written it, or a version of it, whilst visiting the West Indies in the thirties. 'I Spy a Stranger' (1966; *PMS*, 1969) was 'too disgruntled', so that was left out also. On 4 April, she wrote again to Athill saying that 'Tea With an Artist' (*TLB*, 1927; *TAB-L*, 1968) was too sentimental (it was however included). Even after *Tigers Are Better-Looking* was published, Rhys had reservations, 'I think MacKenzie is better really' (letter to Francis Wyndham, 10 April 1970). The late stories cost her effort to complete, which she feared made some of them seem 'forced and toiled over' (letter to Francis Wyndham, Thursday 17 July), for she wanted to work on her autobiography.

She also worried about the fact that she mainly wrote about the past by the late sixties. Her stories about war seemed dated to her when she came to try to finish them. She admitted 'I was haunted by the War you see for quite a long time – only in "Petronella" did I reach farther back and get away' (letter to Oliver Stoner, 15 September). She was anxious that her vision of the West Indies would seem unreal to readers now. Rhys was always hypercritical of her own work, but especially when it came to the stories.

As if in response to Rhys's own doubts, the stories have been, relative to the novels, critically neglected until very recently though reviews of her three collections of stories were on the whole positive. Reviewers of the later two collections, *Tigers Are Better-Looking* (1968) and *Sleep It Off Lady* (1976) had of course the evidence of her outstanding success with *Wide Sargasso Sea*.[9] But as early as 1927, with the appearance of *The Left Bank*, Rhys's reviewers found her capacity to pare away unnecessary words and produce a sharp, evocative prose style was remarkable.[10] A. Alvarez's celebrated 1974 description of Rhys as the finest living English novelist certainly helped to minimise negative criticism. But even Carole Angier (1990), Rhys's biographer, chose for reasons of space to omit extensive discussion of the short fiction. Only a few critics have chosen to explore Rhys's short fiction in some depth, though there is now a full-length study (Malcolm and Malcolm 1996).[11]

Rhys paid relatively little attention in her short pieces to plot or character description, often depicting a state of being, often a feeling such as hunger or lonelines. Many of the stylistic effects, on which the success of a Rhys story depends, are exactly those which characterise the longer fiction. As we have seen in earlier chapters, Rhys always wrote economically, even in the novel, often using ellipsis and severe cutting, working with her poet's love of compression and parallelism and her dramatist's capacity for effective and weight-bearing dialogue. She established a semiotics of colour as consistently in the stories as in the novels. Placement, or more often displacement, is as evidently important in the stories as the novels. Very often in a Rhys story, communication must cross not only national boundaries, but those of class and race. There is a good deal of irony and a bitter humour, sometimes combined with an awareness of the spiritual as a source of resistance. Like the novels, the stories often have an evident political theme. As I have argued previously, a good deal of her writerly instincts drew on her own unique Caribbean experience and translated it into an idiosyncratic stylistic identity.

The volume of Rhys's collected stories (ed. Athill 1987) is the best way to see the development of her skill with shorter texts over her writing life.[12] *The Left Bank* (1927), as I discussed earlier, was the beginning of her achieved writing and is still mainly effective, even if, as Diana Athill comments in her introduction, there are one or two signs of a yet not quite mature style. By looking over the whole of the stories, the issue of Rhys's autobiographical fiction arises from a slightly different point of view. Though, like *The Left Bank*, *Tigers are Better-Looking* (1968) has a good deal of material which is evidently fictionalised but can be traced to Rhys's own experience, six of the sixteen pieces in *Sleep It Off Lady* (1976) have a first-person narrator and describe experience known to be Rhys's own, thereby provoking a good many reviewers to comment that the collection is autobiographical.[13] Carole Angier mines Rhys's later short fiction for biographical material though Rhys never wrote any version of experience which was not fictionalised and subdued and recast for professional reasons.

Towards the end of her life, Rhys was working seriously on her autobiography, and began to change her life-long habit of beginning from her own experience and fictionalising away from it, allowing the demands of her form and style to dictate what content remained and what was excised. Now, she often returned to old fictional drafts for her autobiographical material, or began to move towards what we now call the personal essay, or creative non-fiction, which is the process I will explore in chapter 9. She was herself aware of the risks involved in working so close to life: 'I think that scraps of obvious autobiography mixed with fiction are bitty' (letter to Francis Wyndham, 9 July). Most of the stories, of course have a basis in Rhys's personal experience, about which we are much clearer since Angier's research. But in a story, Rhys generally constructed the protection of a very clear narrative distance where she was using an intimate recollection ('Good-bye Marcus, Goodbye Rose', *SIOL*, 1976), or created the illusion of intimacy by giving a story first-person narration. But at times she in effect writes creative non-fiction, or the personal essay, in which the autobiographical element is clearly stated and understood, but also crafted, reinvented, as fictional material. Fiction gave Rhys an opportunity to work through the personal without exposing herself. The way she handled the personal essay allowed her to move ever closer to autobiography without identifying the material as her own life experience. The most evident personal essays I shall discuss with *Smile Please* in chapter 9, because they are not failed stories, but brave and innovative attempts to find a new fictional voice.

I have two major concerns in discussing the stories: firstly, how Rhys arrived at final drafts, which is evident from her extent notebooks and manuscript versions, and secondly, how her mature stories exhibit her signature stylistic traits, established first in *The Left Bank*, and which as I have argued in this study are often connected to her Caribbean experience as much or more than her European apprenticeship as a writer.

It is clear from variant drafts of stories that Rhys not only kept a good deal from first draft but also changed the construction of individual sentences over and over again, to get the right flow. She was always concerned with pace as well, with whether a story was too fast or slow in various sections, and it is clear that in the stories, as in the novels, she still heard Ford's advice that when in doubt, cutting would help. At times, she whittled away at the substance of a story until it became a slim fragment, sometimes remarkably effective, as in 'I Used to Live Here Once' (*SIOL*, 1976).

'Rapunzel, Rapunzel', one of Rhys's most disturbing late stories about female old age, exists in several typed drafts annotated in a hand not Rhys's, presumably that of a typist of the early 1970s, and although in this case the changes are very small ones, they show Rhys's concern for selecting and marshalling detail.[14] Tracking a few sentences through drafts 3, 5, 7, 8, 9, 10 and the final published version demonstrates the point. Draft 3 is heavily worked over in pen by the typist's hand. It is an early draft which needs to capture the memories for use, and includes a long description of an Indian woman patient, later totally excised because other than in the description of this woman's exquisitely shaped feet which could arguably contribute to the story's theme of the last feminine identities in old, ill women, it is not relevant.

The crisis around which the story is built in final draft is the cutting off of an old woman's lovely long silvery hair by a barber who does not pay attention to her request for the ends to be trimmed. This moment appears in an annotated version (draft 3) as 'Then to my horror I saw him produce a large pair of scissors. He picked up her hair in one hand. Snip, snip and half of it was lying on the floor.' In draft 5, the Rapunzel theme is missing, because the scene where the old woman's hair is cut has gone, and what is left is a much less tightly organised essay on a stay in a convalescent home. In draft 7, the scene is back, but the sentences about the cutting process now excise the narrator's feelings, 'He picked it up in one hand and produced a large pair of scissors. Snip, snip and half of it was lying on the floor.' This

remains unaltered through the remaining drafts, but in the published version, Rhys has added 'Then' to the sentence, 'Then he
picked it up . . .' Sadly, she omitted from the final version a lovely
image of the old woman as mermaid with her long, damp hair,
probably finding it too conventional or romantic. She was always
concerned to tighten and shorten and to find the best order, but
this was in the details, not usually in the grand plan of a story. A
paragraph which begins in draft 3 'We drove on for about forty
minutes' and ends with 'We stopped at 2 hospitals on the way to
pick up a couple of other patients' ends in draft 10 as 'We drove
for about forty minutes stopping twice to pick up other patients',
which is the published version.

'The Stepping Stones', a draft dated 24 Jan. 1974, which became 'I Used to Live Here Once' (*SIOL*, 1976) shows the same
attention to detail. A sentence beginning 'The only thing was that
the sky had a glassy kind of look that she didn't quite remember'
became 'The only thing was that the sky had a glassy look that
she didn't remember' (*SIOL*: 175). Rhys's excision of all unnecessary ambiguities from her prose makes her extremely good at
the very short, one- or two-page piece like this, but this of course
is the kind of attention to crafting a sentence which made *Wide
Sargasso Sea* so long in the final completion process but so perfectly finished that it remains a major example of a writer's fine
craft.

The story 'Goodbye Marcus, Goodbye Rose', (*SIOL*, 1976)
which is Rhys's only direct fictionalised version of the Mr Howard
incident, began as a story called 'The Birthday'. Comparison of
these drafts shows how Rhys worked when the autobiographical
material which was source for the story was particularly emotionally intense and difficult. The draft 'The Birthday' begins with
Phoebe waking on her thirteenth birthday. The first part of the
story contains material which would be reworked in later texts,
such as *Wide Sargasso Sea* and *Smile Please*. After Phoebe's attempt
to feel good about herself, which includes putting a rose behind
her ear, and her English aunt and father's comments about her
as a 'regular little creole', like her Spanish grandmother, she
remembers meeting an old man who claims to be an ex-slave
from her family's estate: 'With winks and leers and senile chuckles

he began to hint at, to describe in his primitive way, God knew what scenes of lust and cruelty . . .' (undated draft, UTC, p. 3). This is the pivot of the story, which then goes on to describe a young 'brown' girl from Martinique with whom Phoebe is friendly and whom she sees as 'a part of all the beauty . . . the blue of the sky and the crimson of a hibiscus against the blue the rustle of palm leaves in the evening and the mystery of a tom tom beating very far off, the heavy scent of certain flowers' (p. 5). The rather lurid, colonial construction of both the child and the landscape reveal that Rhys was right to restrain, by cutting, her desire to overly dramatise and stereotype the Caribbean. The final phase of the draft has to do with Mr Howard, the visit to the Botanical Gardens and his touching of her breast: this is the emotional core of the story. Rhys's tendency to laconic statement, even under-statement, and her rigorous exclusion of anything which might be considered sentimental makes those stories built of something truly powerful and alarming, like this kind of sexual assault, work much better than those built on something more trivial, where the kind of emotionally intense narrative which Rhys did not allow in her work would have substituted for lack of dramatic elements in the plot. For example, though some critics think 'Till September Petronella' one of Rhys's best stories, I find it tepid precisely because the narrator is so distanced from emotional involvement and the characters are all emotionally inert, yet the only action is their relationships with each other.[15]

Clearly the source for 'The Birthday' was a good deal of differ-ent childhood experiences combined, but by the time the story had become 'The Game and the Candle' (of which there are two extant drafts) Rhys had worked out a structure for the story. The second version begins with a Captain Cardo singing. This old man is a former war hero. He takes Phoebe to the Botanical Gardens, where he touches her breast.[16] But this time the story elaborates more, for the Captain talks ceaselessly of love, 'horrible, frightening and fascinating talk' (UTC, p. 4). The title of the story comes from the Captain's wife who makes a comment to her husband, 'Do you think the game is worth the candle?' The story ends with Phoebe's internalisation of guilt, and her acceptance of the fact that her dream of a virtuous future, with children called

Jack, Marcus and Rose, is now over, and a 'difficult and uncertain but far more exciting future' lies ahead.

There are two drafts of the version titled 'Good-bye Marcus, Good-bye Rose', which reorder elements from the earlier drafts as Rhys worked towards a line for the story which would make it coherent and tightly organised. The change of title neatly alters the focus from the Captain and his wife to the effect of the incident on Phoebe. By omitting Phoebe's birthday, her friendship with Tite Francine and her encounter with the old ex-slave, Rhys gives the story a narrow focus which then draws her closer into the Mr Howard narrative. Indeed she mined this for details such as Phoebe's self-flagellation. It is as if the various drafts were necessary stages by which Rhys was able to come closer to her experience whilst being able to retain the distance which enabled her to craft the writing. It is also interesting that the story was not finished until late in Rhys's career, when she had the will to add into it reference to Howard's sado-masochistic narratives which caused the real damage to her emotional development.

If working through variant drafts not only helped Rhys tighten a story but also find its lean lines, its true shape under the flab of too much detail in the early states, stories also helped Rhys establish her style, as I argued in chapter 3, and to practise it in the years between novels, especially during the long drought in her work from 1939–1966. 'The Blue Bird' is a mysterious and disturbing early story (*TLB*, 1927; *CSS*, 1987) which is set in Paris. Rhys's capacity to observe acutely and to bring a scene to life with small but vivid touches of colour is very evident here, 'The unpainted faces looked bald and unfinished, the painted – ochre powder, shadowed eyelids, purple lips – were like cruel stains in the sunlight' (*CSS*: 60). The details of a painter's palette applied to people, creating a scene through visual contrasts, are even more marked in Rhys's mature work. The next paragraph brings colour as race jarringly and yet whimsically into the narrative:

In the corner, to redeem humanity, sat one lovely creature, her face framed by a silver turban. Wisps of wooly hair peeped out from beneath it – a nigger – what a pity. Why a pity?

One becomes impressionistic to excess after the third kummel! (*CSS*: 60)

This is the only beautiful woman in the bar. Rhys establishes that first and so the brutality of having her loveliness caught within a racist term of abuse is intended to shock. This silent woman plays no more part in the story but there is here a latent presence of a Caribbean sensibility about race.

Rhys uses a good deal of dialogue, always her preference over action for conveying character. Her signature use of the careless ways in which Europeans drop the name of God or the devil is also already here, though it will be used in a more developed way, as we have seen, in *Good Morning, Midnight*. In 'The Blue Bird' such usage, 'Oh, thank God, thank God, it's hot' (*CSS*: 61), 'you poor devil of a blind and infatuated creature' (*CSS*: 62), 'It's funny, sometimes a devil talks with one's tongue' (*CSS*: 64), 'Oh, God, what a fool I was' (*CSS*: 64) is taken out of the possibility of being merely empty phrases by the shock of Carlo's story.

Carlo appears fairly quiet, 'such a *nice* woman really' (*CSS*: 61), but she wears a touch of red, a hat, which as we have seen earlier signifies some hidden passion in a Rhys character. She is an outsider in England, having 'lived so long in hot places and wasn't quite English to start with' (*CSS*: 62). She is the Rhys woman here, and it is her story which has the death-wish component which Rhys's female protagonists almost always experience. Her past includes a 'Bad Man' called Paul, and she tells the narrator how he took her into the forest near Barbizon and told him it would be wonderful to die, since she was so happy for that moment. He took her seriously and offered to help her to do so. Now she bitterly regrets that lost chance, 'To have been so close to a sweet death and to have pushed it away' (*CSS*: 64). Paul killed himself anyway, since he was in trouble with the police. In the context of what the narrator calls 'the Sufferers, white-faced and tragic of eye' (*CSS*: 61), denizens of Montparnasse who pour 'out their souls', and expose 'them hopefully for sale', Carlo's story is particularly poignant.

Her complexity of character is set out in physical descriptions, another Rhys stylistic trait. She is 'a mass of contradictions. Her voice is as deep as a man's; her shoulders and hips as narrow as those of a fragile school-girl; her eyes brown and faithful like a dog's (hence her name)' (*CSS*: 60). She even has the little black dress which so many Rhys protagonists favour, and her 'Bad Man' has a very white face and takes her into the forest, both components of later Rhys characters' lives in various versions and combinations.[17]

Although this story does not use different languages or registers of a language to indicate the difficulties of communication, unlike so many of Rhys's texts, the poetic coding of detail here conveys to the perceptive reader that surface meaning can be a disguise or deflection. Rhys's stories often tease the reader by this kind of subtle masking. Her stories are somewhat in disguise at times: her characters are also forced at times into public faces which betray their inner complexity.

The reader's sense of trying to read through conflicting evidence or to be able to understand the difference between lies and truth is the whole point of the very short piece 'Trio' (*TLB*, 1927; *CSS*, 1987) which Howells (1991) and Raiskin (1996) have both rightly seen as a mysterious and sinister portrayal of an apparent Antillean family group in a Montparnasse restaurant in which however the 'daughter' appears to have a flirtatious relationship with the 'father' and there is no guarantee that she isn't being exploited sexually and economically by both 'parents'. The ambiguity in this story may be related to Rhys's early desire to deal with the Caribbean only obliquely. Ramchand makes an interesting point in his introduction (n.d.) to Rhys's Caribbean stories: he says as Rhys matured as a writer, she tended less to have a 'peripheral but normative Black' and gave Caribbean fragments to her protagonists (but of course she also created Christophine and Selina, who are black women who speak for themselves, Selina much more than Christophine).

Rhys's Caribbean stories are frequently about racial and cultural self-constructions and collisions in the colonial period. In 'Pioneers, Oh Pioneers' (*SIOL*, 1976; *CSS*, 1987), the eccentric Mr Ramage who keeps himself apart from white colonial Roseau finally marries a coloured woman and retreats to isolation on a forested property on the Imperial Road, Hesketh Bell's experiment in attracting young Englishmen to develop Dominica. There he appears to have gone mad, at least appearing to a couple in the forest totally naked. Finally he is found evidently having committed suicide, though the rumours that he killed his wife prove

unfounded. Ramage's very resistance to both his own racial con-
stituency in Roseau and to general local social convention proves
self-destructive.

The core of the story was what Rhys herself described as a
'Dominican legend' (letter to Sonia Orwell, 1 May 1968, UTC).
The effect of any retold story lies in the mode of its retelling, in
this case in Rhys's manipulation of points of view. The story is
told as a composite of points of view and bits of information
offered by Rosalie, the little girl who admires him; her father and
mother; a passenger on the boat from Barbados with him; his
neighbours in the forest; people who go up to throw stones at
Ramage's house; his wife. These elements of mystery and collid-
ing narratives, telling a story of violation of codes of propriety
and ensuing personal threat are very important to Rhys's construction of story after story. It is evident from a series of letters
to Francis Wyndham (1975) that Rhys thought this story difficult
to write, especially with regard to point of view. Judith Kegan
Gardiner (1989), who regards Rhys as an undervalued 'master
of the twentieth-century short story' (1989: 19), finds that in the
later fiction, 'the disparity between texts and truth, language and
experience becomes a dominant theme that the narrative voice
dramatizes as well as reports' (1989: 44). A character called Jimmy
Longa is referred to at the beginning of the story. He returns as
the major figure in 'Fishy Waters' (*SIOL*, 1976; *CSS*, 1987) based
on another Dominican incident. In this case, multiple narratives
are managed partly through letters, a strategy Rhys used as early
as 'Again the Antilles' (*TLB*, 1927; *TAB-L*, 1968; *CSS*, 1987) and
which was clearly in her mind for this story from the earliest
drafts, to judge from the Red Exercise Book.[18]

Longa, working-class, British, a socialist, offends white colonial
Roseau much as Mr Ramage does, essentially by refusing to live
by the racial and class codes of separation and hierarchy: he
settled in the black community in Roseau. The issue the story is
built around is an accusation that Longa assaulted a little black
girl whilst he was drunk, but the story suggests from the beginning that this is a case where social prejudices are involved, and
eventually it becomes clear that white, middle-class Matt Penrice,
witness against Longa, is the reader's prime suspect.

It is this ability to play with points of view, at root learned out of Rhys's Caribbean childhood and time in Europe, which makes her stories successful. In 'La Grosse Fifi' (*TLB*, 1927; *TAB-L*, 1968; *CSS*, 1987), the story is told for maximum effect by Roseau, who has her own experiences to tell and who can only guess as to the last moments of her friend. In the late story, 'Sleep It Off Lady' (1976), an old lady's fondness for the bottle leads to her being scorned and abandoned when she needs help. Thought of a mysterious rat scares Miss Verney to death, in effect, and the switch of narrative focus from her thoughts to an objective narrator's account of her lying dead gives a slight but definite sense of menace and mystery to the short piece.

But the most important of Rhys's Caribbean stories is set in London, 'Let Them Call It Jazz' (1962; *TAB-L*, 1968; *CSS*, 1987) and it demonstrates all of Rhys's most evident stylistic identities in relation to a portrayal of an exiled West Indian woman. Rhys creates a very natural if generic and exiled West Indian voice for Selina, proving her memory of West Indian speech acute over decades of separation. Ramchand comments that Selina's voice is done in 'remarkable and convincing dialect' because of Rhys's 'memory . . . of . . . West Indian society and speech pattern' (n.d.: n.p.). Rhys's achievement of this voice is the more impressive because of her isolation. Contemporary Guyanese story writer Pauline Melville differentiates brilliantly between the different West Indian voices of London, but she is a contemporary writer and part of the stong presence which West Indian culture has established in Britain now.[19]

Rhys evidently found Selina's voice quickly, as is proved by a scrap of surviving early draft of this story, with three alternative titles, 'They Thought It Was Jazz', 'Holloway Song' and 'Selina': 'I hear the place very old. It take up too much room, so its going to be pulled down and destroyed. Meantime it make all the other houses in that street look cheap trash' ('They Thought It Was Jazz', UTC): this survived in some form in the final draft, though rearranged and sometimes rewritten.

Most importantly, the voice is confident from the moment the published story begins, 'I have trouble with my Notting Hill landlord because he ask for a month's rent in advance' (*CSS*: 158): it locates the character, culturally and politically. It is not only in the verb tenses and certain constructions of sentences that Rhys captures a West Indian intonation, but in the use of certain phrases and words, 'She too cunning' (*CSS*: 158); 'tired to my bones' (*CSS*: 159); 'it have style' (*CSS*: 160); '[t]oo besides' (*CSS*: 170). One or two aspects of Selina's language suggest Dominica specifically, or at least a place where both French and English patois is spoken, as in 'a dam' fouti liar' (*CSS*: 167) and 'doudou' (French patois for sweetheart, dear), or when Selina says 'It sound good in Martinique patois too: "Sans honte"' (*CSS*: 168). Judith Raiskin observes that the voice is 'a Caribbean English distinct from the voice of Rhys's white Creole narrators' (1996: 157).

Rhys was anxious in case this story should be read as autobiography if she asked a typist in her locality to work on it. She had after all been in Holloway herself. She was willing to joke about it to her friend Peggy Kirkaldy, 'my career's been a little stormy & it all ended up in Holloway. Yes dearie – am now a distinguished Old Hollowayian' (letter, Friday 1949).[20] But she was not happy that hostile people in the village might get hold of something to hurt her with. She therefore asked her daughter Maryvonne to type the story (*L*: 187).

Carrera Suarez and Alvarez Lopez (1990) see Selina Davis and Antoinette Cosway as sharing significant experience and psychological response. In the sense that Antoinette finally does seem to move towards action, confused as it is, by the end of Rhys's telling of her story, she does share with Selina an ability to confront oppression in risky and ultimately self-destructive ways. But the story mainly captures a specific moment in 1950s England when West Indian immigrants were beginning to establish homes in a largely resistant, exploitative or indifferent place: displacement is an important theme in this story. Both Raiskin (1996) and Thomas (1994) stress the historical accuracy and resonance of Rhys's story. Thomas argues it is a portrait of an England beginning to have to come to terms with the frustrations of both women and a newly immigrant Caribbean population, marginalised economically and racially. Rhys's general historical accuracy is affirmed by Gregg (1995): Thomas finds it also in 'The Insect World' (*SIOL*, 1976) and 'Heat' (*SIOL*, 1976).

Many of Rhys's stories, including this one, demonstrate the
same complex relation of stylistic identities as the longer fiction.
Colours matter: the neighbour's window in the story is stained
glass, 'green and purple and yellow', a tiny detail but important
because Rhys protagonists respond to combinations of primary
or jewel colours. Here, as elsewhere in Rhys's texts, tiny touches
of colour are very important, such as the red flowers which are
the only aspect of nature to 'stand up to that light' (*CSS*: 161) the
glare of the English summer, strong sunlight diffused through
cloud; the 'dusty pink dress' which Selina buys her quieter, post-
Holloway self with the little money she gets from her 'Holloway
Song'. This she heard sung in prison and gave it to a jazz pianist
to use himself: he pays her a little money. Important textual
reference to songs is another Rhys hallmark. Characteristic Rhys
play on the language of religion, 'Satan don't lie worse' (*CSS*:
158); 'dam' English thief' (*CSS*: 165), 'the little devil' (*CSS*: 161) is
common in this story. It indicates both common speech in Britain
in the post-war period and also Selina's serious sense of moral
codes.

Even where there is no evidence of an explicit Caribbean presence, the apparently modernist experimentation with narrative
voice which marks some stories can also be read as informed by
Rhys's Caribbean sense of complexity and displacement. 'I Spy a
Stranger' (1966; *PMS*, 1969; *CSS*, 1987), like many of Rhys's stories,
tells only a tantalising fragment of a life-story, and centres around
a moment of interaction between a few people. Casey (1974a)
argues that Laura is different from Rhys's earlier protagonists in
consciously abandoning 'almost all human contact' (1974a: 267).
Rhys makes a private joke of her own when she provides a miso-
gynist neighbour of Laura's landlady with a dog named 'Brontë'
which he pretends to kick saying 'Here's Emily Brontë or my pet
aversion' (Casey 1974a: 268). The story constructs both desirabil-
ity and danger in women attempting independence. It is also about
the necessary dangers and difficulties of being transnational, and
in this sense once more returns to a common theme of Caribbean literature, that is, exile, and a central theme of Rhys, i.e. the
relation between human social placement and place as landscape
or locale.

This story demonstrates again her characteristic stylistic motifs. Roses act as a connective code: Mrs Hudson's, small and flame-coloured, are the touch of red which usually signifies some important but suppressed emotion in a Rhys character, though in this case, it is not Mrs Hudson but her guest Laura who gives the roses her empathy and constructs for them a rather human character:

... growing four or five on a stalk, each with a bud ready to replace it. Every time an army lorry passed they shivered. They started shivering before you could see the lorry or even hear it, she noticed. But they were strong; hardened by the east coast wind they looked as if they would last for ever. Against the blue sky they were a fierce, defiant colour, a dazzling colour. (*CSS*: 242)

Bright colours are associated with Laura later on, when her stuff is piled on the floor of her room for her to pack and Mrs Hudson sees it includes 'reels of coloured cotton' (*CSS*: 251). Italicised presumably to indicate Laura's own thoughts, there follows a list which includes an inkstand with violets on it, silk scarves in red, blue, brown, purple, a green box for jewellery, a gold key, a bracelet which looks like a stained glass window, an old flowered workbox with coloured cotton reels and a blue envelope with red chalk writing on it. When, finally, Mrs Hudson's household evicts Laura, struggling, she suddenly turns to the roses, and says 'One forgets the roses – always a mistake' (*CSS*: 254). Like the roses, Laura is both apparently dotty and fragile and actually extremely enduring.

Multivalent language in this story is involved with the multiple consciousnesses involved in its telling, specifically Mrs Hudson, her sister-in-law Mrs Trant and Laura, as well as the anonymous writer of the hostile letter to Mrs Hudson about Laura. Like many of Rhys's texts, this one constructs the English as unwelcoming, suspicious and, this being the war, endemically hostile to foreigners or anyone a little unusual. The anonymous letter refers to Laura as 'that witch of Prague' (*CSS*: 242). The narrative includes both oral testimony and written documents (the letter and Laura's journal). Though everyone in this story speaks English and a similar sort of English, Laura in her fierce suspicion of the English is apart, 'This Anglo-German love-hate affair' (*CSS*: 244). The villagers have found out that Laura 'lived abroad a long time and that when you had to leave – Central Europe, you went to France. They say you only came home when you were forced to . . .' (*CSS*: 244).

This construction of insider–outsider is also familiar from Rhys's novels: here it is the woman writer who is outsider. Rhys identified few characters as writers. Interestingly, Mrs Hudson exclaims in exasperation that Laura left 'the wretched book lying about', just as in *Smile Please*, there is a line in 'From a Diary' where the narrator hears a voice telling her *'be damned careful not to leave this book about'* (*SP*: 133).

The fascinating 'Temps Perdi' (1967; *PMS*, 1969; CSS, 1987) takes narrative complexity a stage further: it was also partially first drafted whilst Rhys was on her visit to the Caribbean in 1936, and is informed by that reconnection.[21] Structural unity is sustained by the use of a first-person narrator's recollections. Rhys's short fiction style is generally fairly terse but here the voice is very evidently so: the tension between reticence and disclosing in the narrative voice is of the strength of a character.

Place and placement are important in this story which was released by Rhys not long after *Wide Sargasso Sea*. The house is a blank canvas, neither ugly nor 'beautiful, impulsive, impetuous or generous' (*CSS*: 256). It does have traces of an ordered garden now gone to seed, some 'sad flowers', as well as the remains of a border of lavender by a gravel path. The army is in residence in the two houses nearby for the duration of the war, and so even the four bathrooms in different colours in one of them, pink, black, green and blue, will not last long. The narrator thinks 'This is the time of smash and grab' (*CSS*: 256) and that the bathrooms are the result of 'Some poor devil – or rich devil or stupid devil' trying hard with the house. Rhys has then established in a few paragraphs not only the first setting for the story but her characteristic codes of colour and of metaphysical language, a strongly opinionated narrative voice and a sense of fatalism, 'Death brings its own anaesthetic, or so they say', 'I thought there wasn't a living soul there . . .' (*CSS*: 256).

Like many other Rhys stories this one is more significant for its portrayal of a state of emotion, thoughtfully examined, than for plot. The narrator describes her delight in the snow falling, and remembers how her first sight of it was 'the only thing in England that hadn't disappointed me' – a strong suggestion that the narrator is from somewhere else, somewhere tropical, in short that there is a Caribbean subtext even in this first section of the story. It is important that the narrator is 'almost as wary of books' as of people, because they 'can tell lies' (*CSS*: 257). In a passage which recalls Antoinette's separation from the Caribbean and her transportation to Europe ('Temps Perdi' was first published in 1967, not long after *Wide Sargasso Sea*), the narrator expresses her hostility to England. She quotes from one of the very few books which does not try to overbearingly draw her into English culture:

'. . . to conduct the transposition of souls of the dead to the White Island, in the manner just described. The White Island is occasionally also called Brea or Britannia. Does this perhaps refer to White Albion, to the chalky cliffs of the English coast? It would be a very humorous idea if England was designated as the land of the dead . . . as hell. In such a form, in truth, England has appeared to many a stranger.' (*CSS*: 257)

This old English house belonged to an English public schoolmaster and thus is deeply associated with the heartland of Empire, specifically those educational institutions which trained young boys to be the servants of colonialism and to promulgate their own social power. The piano, which might have been the vehicle for the narrator's creative energy to be expressed, is out of tune and ghostly and complains 'like a hurt animal' when she plays it (*CSS*: 258). Here the first explicit mention of the Caribbean occurs, when the narrator finds playing on the old piano leads her back in memory through a particular song to relive the circus visiting her small Caribbean island. A lovely girl Nina on the trapeze is like a gold and black butterfly, the insect used here as a symbol of escape from convention.[22]

Like many other middle-class houses in Rhys texts, this house has a distinctly hostile and supercilious identity, watching the narrator 'haughtily', hiding its 'hate' under the same kind of 'beige mask' which English people wear, 'for all here is beige that can be beige, paint, carpets, curtains, upholstery, bedspreads. Everything wears this neutral mask – the village, the people, the sky, even the trees have not escaped' (*CSS*: 260). Like other Rhys protagonists, this narrator describes her room in detail, including the important detail of a looking-glass, so often significant in a Rhys text. This time the mirror is cheap and 'won't stay put' (*CSS*: 260). It is putting bolsters along the window-sills to keep out the cold, just as she used to do in Vienna years before, which takes the narrator back in time to a younger self in 'my new black dress' and the smell of lilac, both details characteristic of a Rhys narrative, a woman's memory of clothes, especially of the little black dress which haunts so many Rhys women, and of isolated, rare moments of sensuous pleasure.

This transition is sustained in the formally differentiated second section which constructs Vienna and the time of Jean Lenglet's work with the Allied Commission, here called the Japanese Commission. Rhys was able here to recycle, as she so often did, different drafts into a new combination. Here the tone is close to that of the personal essay.[23] Rhys, as usual, connected apparently disparate sections of narrative by motifs, as in poetry. For example, the narrator speaks of the 'Japanese mask' dropping, as the Japanese became more animated and sociable after a drinking session and were willing to exchange confidences with the Europeans. Characters have some of the same linguistic habits as characters in other Rhys texts, such as moving in and out of English, and speaking of 'The poor devil', enough to link this story with others and with the novels.

The final passage of this section describes the narrator's clothes and the narrative first-person voice becomes more intimately personal: 'I had a striped taffeta dress, with velvet flowers tucked into the tight waistband' (*CSS*: 266): Angier (1990) uses this as autobiography.[24] This passage is quite important here as it runs into the 'Carib Quarter' section which follows and acts as a link between the memories of young womanhood and memories of the visit to Dominica which Rhys made in her mid forties, thirty years after leaving the island. Rhys uses touches of colour to good effect: the 'coloured stones imitating a necklace' on a white satin dress, the green border on the three flounces on a black dress and its green sash, the white and blue muslin and the blue serge dresses with sleeves embroidered in gay colours with a tassel, the yellow and blue dress for lounging in which reminds the narrator of cornfields and sky. The narrator's dislike of England and the English is present even here, for she hates her English outfit. Casey (1974) points out that Englishmen are elided in Rhys's texts about world war with Germans and Japanese men as brutal and unfeeling oppressors or vandals. For the narrator in 'Temps Perdi' good memories are a refuge away from the cold and dark days in the house she dislikes and which she imagines disapproves of her. When she emerges into that hated climate, she will be 'a savage person – a real Carib' (*CSS*: 267).

It is this kind of linking device which fashions a group of separated memories into a workable story: the narrator, inhabited by the spirit of the Caribs, remembers a visit to Temps Perdi, an estate near to the part of Dominica where the Caribs live. The narrator explains that in Creole patois, 'temps perdi' means wasted time, and that 'this island', which is clearly Dominica, was said to resist human beings. Human effort and labour are constantly undermined by the climate or some natural scourge of a crop. What is impressive here, as in the description of the Coulibri garden in *Wide Sargasso Sea*, is the overgrown lushness of the island. The natural world fights back here against so-called civilisation: Charlie, the young guide, is entrapped by 'hideous, heavy boots' which he takes off after he has trouble with them in a river. The horses are thin and miserable, 'morose, obstinate', because, the narrator thinks, this is the 'price of survival in hostile surroundings' (*CSS*: 271). A flamboyant tree, which Rhys especially loved, is just beginning to blossom and the narrator knows she will miss its full glory since she must soon return to England. This though makes her 'giddy and sick' (*CSS*: 271). At this moment, it is a figure of a Carib girl as illustration in an old book which comes to mind, vividly and in detail.[25]

Rhys's fictional world as a whole maps the generalities of colonial power and post-colonial resistance, of male domination and female subversion, of the actualities of the West Indian history and the complex relation of colony to metropole as Thomas (1996a) has especially noted. The story of a lovely Carib girl who could not walk, and who the narrator thinks is more Creole than pure Carib, is itself a kind of allegory of the ways in which modern people are powerfully formed by the running together of cultural currents, often involving coercion and violence. The girl's mother looks Chinese and was working in service in Martinique before being 'taken to Paris', the phrase being very significant, for the allusions earlier in this piece are to those who have been taken in some way or another away from their primary affiliations. But the narrator thinks, whilst in the Carib Quarter, 'I am home, where the earth is sometimes red and sometimes black' (*CSS*: 274): home where she and her childhood friends would write on a plant similar to aloe and where now 'some up-to-the minute Negro' writes a bolder message. Time passing changes everything: home finally exists in memory, in the conception of attachment which a person maintains.

But in the narrator's desire to be 'a real Carib', in her treasuring the 'lovely sound' of the horses hooves in water, a memory separated from the present by 'so many damnable years' (*CSS*: 271), Rhys also reflects a late Romantic opposition of wild, free nature with corrupt and oppressive civilisation, the implication that the written word is suspect and it is safer to keep an oral language secret as the Carib women are said to do. Landscape becomes a trope for the narrator's emotional state. After the description of the 'brown girl, crowned with flowers' (*CSS*: 271), which the narrator remembers from 'the book about the Caribs', she drifts into a day-dream:

In the midst of this dream, riding through a desolate, arid, lizard-ridden country, different and set apart from the island I knew, I was still sensitive to the opinion of strangers and dreaded hostile criticism. But no, it was approved of, more or less. 'Beautiful, open, park-like country. But what an *extreme* green!' (*CSS*: 271)

The voice which resists the intensity of lush tropical vegetation in the sun may have been loosely based on Rhys's husband's response to Dominica.[26] It clearly also is the attitude Antoinette's husband is given in *Wide Sargasso Sea*. The narrator dreams of a different, arid country, hoping to avoid criticism, perhaps because criticism from a close companion makes a desert of the lush and loved emotional landscape. Rhys's fiction does brilliantly and quite before its time expose the grim scaffolding of oppressions and denials which supported British imperial culture and it also explores, even more extraordinarily, the compromises which explain the victims' participation in their own defeats. 'Temps Perdi' is not a story about a victim but about a complex consciousness which reads itself as much as it reads the hostile elements of the world.

Rhys's stories are remarkable also because her confinement to the arena of personal experience meant that she constructed voices ranging from youthful inexperience ('Vienne'), to old and weary age ('Rapunzel, Rapunzel'), something easily seen in the *Collected Short Stories*. Her stories about old age are devastatingly honest. 'Sleep It Off Lady' is a horrific commentary on the fact that old ladies are not often regarded as dear and acceptable but rather as unpleasant and deserving of indifference or worse. 'I Used to Live Here Once', in using the ghost image, manages in a page and a half to convey the devastating idea that once dead, a person is entirely forgotten, unable to communicate what their idea of a given place used to be: only occupation in present time is real. In this collection, Rhys weaves her Caribbean and early European past with her wartime memories.[27]

A good part of Rhys's effect in these stories, as in her longer fiction, is the economical manipulation of emotional complexity: humour, irony, pathos and anger by turns inform narratives which twist and turn according to the unresolvable tensions at the heart of a single consciousness. By paring emotional complexity down to its core, Rhys found a language and a form in the short story which served her very well.

In this she found a language which was essentially poetic, though she always, in her committed work, chose prose. The lean imagery of 'Sleep It Off Lady', the title story in her 1976 collection, is horrifically effective. The huge rat which manifests itself in Miss Verney's imagination is just as ordinary as the block of marble which falls mysteriously into the Commandant's apartment in 'A Spiritualist' – and just as disturbingly in touch with our deepest anxieties about age, helplessness, death or revenge.

From the beginning to the end of her writing career, Rhys understood how to pare down a story to its acutely striking bones in terms of plot, and to fuse this with the vividness of difficult emotional states. The stories therefore deserve to be read in their own light, not as rehearsals for the novels, although because of their subject matter and their characteristic Rhys style, they are also clearly part of the Rhys canon and benefit eventually from being read in that context also.

CHAPTER 8

# *Performance arts: the theatre of autobiography and the role of the personal essay*

'Smile please,' the man said. 'Not quite so serious.' He'd dodged out from behind the dark cloth. He had a yellow black face and pimples on his chin.

I looked down at my white dress, the one I had got for my birthday, and my legs and the white socks coming half way up my legs, and the black shiny shoes with the strap over the instep.

'Now,' the man said.

'Keep still,' my mother said.

I tried but my arm shot up of its own accord.

'Oh what a pity, she moved.'

'You must keep still,' my mother said, frowning.

*(SP:* 13)

I wanted to write my autobiography because everything they say about me is wrong. I want to tell the truth . . .

(Plante 1984: 19)

She said, 'Wouldn't what happened to us make a funny story? We should write it.'

I was somewhat amazed that she should so quickly think of turning the episode into a story . . .

(Plante 1984: 19)

Writers are in effect performers who do everything off-stage and away from the sight of their audience (except when reading in public). In the case of oral performers such as story-tellers, comics, calypsonians, or even the average person telling a joke decently, we are acutely aware of the difference between the raw material of experience and the theatrical and linguistic demands of a good performance which cuts to the bone of that experience or doctors it up for effect, but either way uses the transformative powers of theatricality to communicate what the experience can or does mean. Much of life is simply passed through without loading it into memory: aesthetic images single out for us the reverberative potential of tiny moments of experience. Performance intensifies this awareness even more by asking us to respond on multiple levels (e.g. aural, visual, linguistic play and social action): texts which employ theatrical strategies or referents demand of the solitary reader the capacity to reconstruct complex experience through that multiplicity of remembered associations.

The Caribbean is a particularly theatrical culture, in the sense that there is a great deal of the performative not only in folk rituals and festivals but also in common speech, as Rhys knew from her experience and which she translated into the voice of Selina in 'Let Them Call It Jazz' and Meta and Francine in *Smile Please*.¹ It is also clear as we shall later see that Rhys knew this, from her images of the culture contained in *Smile Please* and the ways in which she utilised songs and other theatrical elements in her other texts.

Autobiography is a special kind of literary enterprise, particularly for Rhys, who by the time she was seriously trying to finish it was in her eighties and frail. Furthermore she had already worked over her major memories as literary draft shortly after they happened, and then worked them over again and again, or thrown them out as unusable. A common experience in writing is to find a memory used for fiction is gone afterwards in its original form as completely as a dream vanishes on waking. So it is interesting to find what she chose (or what she could still remember) to convey a sense of her Caribbean childhood.

Importantly, Smith and Watson (eds. 1992) use the term 'performances' to describe autobiography which draws on 'exogenous and indigenous cultural practices' (1992: xxi). The idea of performance as a critical element in the construction of the 'I' who narrates or the transmutation of personal experience into fictional form is particularly relevant to the way in which Rhys constructed personal experience as autobiographical essay. Before *Smile Please*, Rhys's way of recording her experience was to distance herself from its actual shape (or lack of shape, as she understood the raw material of life), and to work at it to turn it into memorable story.

Though it is clear from the few surviving exercise books and early drafts that she often cut and pasted one experience into another, making a kind of quilt which reinforced a line of signification unable to be apparent at the time of the separate experiences which contributed to it, she always intended to cut down to the bone of the truth as she understood it and wanted it told.

My trope for this chapter is writing as performance, which in Rhys's case here means the autobiography itself was performative rather than informative. Rhys was strongly attracted to the stage as a young woman, went to drama school in London for a year and afterwards joined a musical comedy touring company, but was evidently fairly inept onstage. By her own account she managed to fluff her one-line time after time when she was offered a chance to get out of the chorus (Angier 1990). By contrast, she very rarely fluffed a line when it came to writing, and if she thought she had she would correct it, even years later if given a chance to revise formerly published work. She wrote in a very late letter (to Phyllis, 4 September 1978) that she was finding the autobiography very hard to do because the Dominica material was so long ago. She didn't want to argue in the piece, 'neither do I want to be too dull so it's a balancing act'.[2] She also worried that if she wrote 'truthfully of the West Indies as I knew them', the work would not be trusted, or would disappoint, since everything had changed (letter to Sonia Orwell, 2 July 1969). Perhaps this is why in *Smile Please*, she sticks closely to stories about people with relatively little descriptive material on Dominica.

She had a horror of being photographed, increasingly noticeable in old age.[3] She was also however willing to love some photographs she thought showed her wrinkles and all.[4] She retained a love of the idea of a public face, evident in her texts in the strong motif of masking, and the use her protagonists make of the disguisess of makeup and clothes.

She resisted the idea of performing herself. She wrote to Diana Athill in 1968 that she did not want to appear on television because 'I usually photograph badly also I'd be very nervous indeed . . . A bad performance on television would depress me dreadfully & I cant believe that it would help the stories' (letter to Diana Athill, 12 February 1968). But Rhys retained a strong

interest in the possibility of dramatic identities in her texts, especially *Quartet*, which she first saw as a play.[5] She also made extensive use of songs in her fiction, very often from music hall or
popular repertoires of the day in England or France (James 1978).[6]
She greatly loved poetry which she wrote herself or read and
copied out from other writers' work. The poetry she enjoyed most
was often formal enough to be close to song.[7]

In a fragment of outline for *Smile Please*, Rhys mentioned a
piece she was working on called 'Songs my mother didn't teach
me', which was not yet good enough for inclusion but which she
hoped to improve ('Part II', UTC). The Tulsa Collection now has
five versions of this piece (two titled 'Songs', of which one is
dated July 1978, and three 'Songs My Mother Didn't Teach Me').
They all begin with the same idea, though not exactly the same
sentence: 'All my life I have been haunted by popular songs', the
word 'haunting' being significant when used by Rhys even casually, as I have argued earlier.[8] Rhys sustains this idea of being
haunted by the music throughout the essay.

She goes on to argue that, as for most people, popular songs
evoke a particular period of life, 'sometimes I think I can divide
my life into neat sections headed by the songs I loved at the time'
('Songs My Mother Didn't Teach Me', UTC): these songs are
popular. She comments 'I still don't understand why I find popular and [deleted] street music so nostalgic ["compelling" written
above]' ('Songs My Mother Didn't Teach Me'). Though she can
enjoy 'better things', it is the old music-hall or popular songs
which haunt her which she imagines she might be 'tripping gaily
to my death to some tune . . .' ('Songs' July 1978, UTC).

It is therefore distressing to her to find old songs have been
given new words, especially those from the musical 'Our Miss
Gibbs' in which she performed for nearly two years ('Songs' July
1978). Of course in identifying with the popular songs which were
the stock in trade of the music hall where Rhys made her living,
she was identifying with working-class culture. In a letter to Francis
Wyndham (26 October 197?), Rhys recalls a 'lovely song the girls
used to sing in the dressing room', ''E doesnt wear a collar / Or
a shirt all white / 'E wears a tiny muffler / And 'e looks all right
/ . . . 'E pays his little tanner / In the gallery with Anna'. In the

longer version of the 'Songs' essay, Rhys ties in the story of her wartime service in a canteen for soldiers outside Euston Station, and then the post-war years, to her memories of various songs and pieces of music, even asking the question why so-called classical music generally only temporarily interests her. Rhys titled another fragment of draft 'Music and Words' (UTC). Some of her titles suggest music.[9]

Songs were important in Rhys's childhood as they are important in her major texts for her protagonist. She comments, 'These Edwardian songs, how they cling' (*SP*: 67). There is the memory of 'Braga's Serenata' and the score of '*Flora Dora*, an American musical comedy' on the piano at home. Rhys's father liked Welsh songs which reminded him of his own childhood. There are memories of Rhys herself trying to play the piano to accompany a reluctant violinist and misreading the music twice so he refused to try again.

Rhys's characters are occasionally chorus girls and do sing, but all of them are deeply concerned with the skills of the performer: makeup; costume as clothing; the feeling of being in performance when being out in public. Rhys herself thought clothing made a critical difference to a person. In a fragment of draft autobiography she remembers her amazement as a child that Kipling knew all about 'women's underclothes' ('The only time my father . . .', UTC). A writer needs to see through the surface image, but a woman's job in Rhys's world is to fashion protective masks from clothes and makeup.

Masking is important, as we have already seen, in a good many of Rhys's texts. If acting plays consciously and publicly with the idea of multiple or substitute identities, writing can suggest this idea with devastating subtlety by going inside a character's mind and laying out the fragility of a divided consciousness, something Sasha demonstrated in *Good Morning, Midnight*.

In the light of this, it is interesting to consider Rhys's resistance to the idea of a biography being written of her and her compulsion to finish her own version of her life to preempt anyone else from trying. She was old and infirm when she worked with David Plante on *Smile Please* but it does seem circumstantially convenient that the completed narrative stops after her years in Dominica, though some of the draft material, edited a little by Diana Athill, makes up the second part of the volume under the title 'It Began To Grow Cold'. Rhys was understandably protective of her adult life story, insisting that it was not the life or the writer but the text which mattered: in a letter to Sonia Orwell (Friday 4 April 1969) she writes 'I'm very much inclined to cut it off when I leave the West Indies and skip London Paris etc' (p. 2).

Athill, in her foreword to *Smile Please*, speaks of Rhys's anxiety about writing something which seemed, by its very genre, to demand that memory provide infallible evidence of what actually took place. Athill comments that Rhys's 'honesty was uncommonly strict, so she felt that the only dialogue she could use in such a book would be that which she was perfectly sure she remembered exactly' (*SP*: 3). Also, it is not unusual for old people to remember the far distant past more clearly than more recent times. Nevertheless, Rhys seems to have had a more than usual desire to establish her version of her life as dominant.

All autobiography is of course fictional, a textual representation of a vision of a time filtered primarily through one consciousness. In *A Poetics of Women's Autobiography* (1987) Sidonie Smith writes that autobiography 'is ultimately as complex as the subject it seeks to capture in its representation and as the rhetorical expressions through which, with the mediation of language, that subjectivity reads itself into the world' (1987: 3). This is particularly true of Rhys, whose texts work on the raw material of personal recollection, informed increasingly as her career continues by a strong element of self-scrutiny.

Norine Voss (1986) sets out the major challenges to a woman writing autobiography in an intentionally revelatory way: she includes 'saying the unsayable'; contradicting traditional definitions of womanhood; expressing anger; talking about female sexuality. Rhys described in her unpublished manuscript 'Triple Sec' (UTC) experiences which whilst no doubt fairly commonplace amongst troubled young women in the early years of the twentieth century were taboo subjects such as unwanted pregnancy, abortion, sex for money and emotional trauma in relation to sexual identity. In her published fiction she alienated some readers by being willing to explore female anger and sexual and financial outlaw status. But in her autobiography Rhys was very protective of herself. She presented a portrait of a bright, sometimes troubled young girl, omitting, for example, the crucial sexual narrative of Mr Howard and the details of Ford's role as seductive father–mentor, as well as her experience with Maryvonne.

Rhys always set her characters' experience into political contexts, even when the character was 'I', so that the particular kind of autobiography which Smith and Watson address in *De/Colonizing the Subject: The Politics of Gender in Women's Autobiography* is relevant to reading Rhys. In common with quite a few other post-colonial theorists, they have a tendency to be reductive and overly general: 'the colonial subject inhabits a politicized rather than privatized space of narrative' (1992: Introduction xxi). Political and private space are very interwoven in the case of Rhys, who was never, as I have insisted earlier, a generic identity of any kind: Rhys politicised the personal and personalised the political. Thus the personal is opened out to a more general reading but then the political is prevented from becoming stereotypical or generic by the sheer contradictoriness of Rhys's characterisation of herself as colonial subject.

Françoise Lionnet's definition of post-colonial autobiography emphasises its 'transformative and visionary dimension: by the convictions that writing matters and that narrative has the power to transform the reader' (1992: 322). In this sense, Rhys entirely fits the definition: what informs her autobiography more than anything else is the story of how she became a writer and what the writing has the power to transform, namely, a life which has not been lived in community nor with visible intent to contribute to community save through the power of the written word.

Phyllis Rose's review essay on *Smile Please* (1980) acutely observes that it is women writers who are found wanting by prejudiced readers when they write too close to their lives and especially if they write to relieve emotional distress. But she argues that Rhys's 'rather primitive distinction between fact and fiction' reduced her autobiography to a demonstration of 'how *not* to write an autobiography' (1980: 599). For Rose, *Smile Please* is 'pathetic, unconnected, insignificant fragments of memory of the sort only precious to the memorialist' (1980: 599). That the omissions protected Rhys's privacy in some very intensely painful and personal areas of her

life should not be surprising: the no-holds-barred confessional feminist writers of the post-1960s cultural era in America and Europe
are products of a very different time and place from Rhys, a late
nineteenth-century child of colonial white middle-class respectability and small-town unwillingness to disclose private business.
In preferring the fiction to the autobiography, Rose is responding
to an intensity and detail in the fiction which seems unguarded
and therefore gripping, as an early literary declaration of the
hidden life of women marginalised by their cultures and societies.

Diana Trilling, no less, writing in *The New York Times Book
Review*, thought *Smile Please* 'markedly disappointing' (25 May 1980:
1), at least as autobiography. For Trilling, it was 'her nonfiction
novel' (1980: 17), just as V. S. Pritchett found the writing loses
the reader 'halfway between "real life" and the novels' (1980: 8).
Though for Ronald Blythe (1979) the writing hinted at Colette,
he recognised that Rhys, unlike Colette whom he praises as an
unusually good woman autobiographer, was most uneasy with
self-revelation of the kind autobiography requires and he, like
Rose, found it unsatisfactory.

It should be said that some reviewers, such as Robert Nye (1980)
found the very fragmentary structure fascinating, 'full of amazing
statements made in a quiet, unsentimental, slightly astrigent, slightly
puzzled voice, as if the writer is always straining to catch some
music or conversation which she alone can hear' (1980: n.p.).[10]
Marina Warner, descendant of the Antigua Warners and a successful British writer herself, writes of *Smile Please*, 'Throughout
this economical, subdued, unflinching tale, the incomparable voice
of the novelist is heard' (1979: n.p.).[11]

Interestingly, reviews of Rhys's letters, edited by Francis
Wyndham and Diana Melly and published five years after Rhys's
death, produced less diverse reactions. Here was not only the
history of a writer's obsession and construction of priorities, but
also moments of insight into the woman who was Jean Rhys and,
as Mark Amory notes (1984), proof that hardly anybody else
came into focus for her.[12] Rhys mostly wrote not only her fiction
but even her personal letters about herself.

David Plante's involvement in the development of manuscript
material which Rhys left and Diana Athill published posthumously

as the second section of *Smile Please* is well known.[13] We shall never know whether Rhys would finally have agreed to leave in the most interesting parts of this material for publication. Her final versions were often quite controlled: 'It seems to me now that the whole business of money and sex is mixed up with something very primitive and deep. When you take money directly from someone you love it becomes not money but a symbol. The bond is now there' (*SP*: 97). This rather distanced and measured mature observation mutes the emotional reality which is being described in the passage from which it comes. Rhys is describing a moment of rage and grief at being paid by her lover through a solicitor, a moment which would have had greater force for being more extensively explored. She hovers here on the brink of describing the ironies of what most women need to feel is a crucial difference between financial dependency on a man who offers affection and being paid for services rendered: the difference is ability to keep self-respect, even pride, although feminist theorists have often argued that any financial dependency on a man is ultimately morally and emotionally reductive for any woman.

But if we approach *Smile Please* as performance, and the central theme of the autobiography, personality as theatrical invention, then the writing begins to make sense as well as taking its natural place along the complex continuum Rhys fashioned between life and art. I opened this chapter with a quotation from the opening passage of *Smile Please* which indicates the importance of the idea of performance in the development of Rhys's public constructions of self. The mother disapproves of the child's resistance to the pose, but the photograph is finally achieved and the child captured into an image 'in a silver frame' which stands by itself and not among the other photographs in the sitting room in the Rhys family house in Roseau. That construction of self suddenly seems distanced from the now older girl, dressed for school, who looks at the picture, 'the curls, the dimples surely belonged to somebody else. The eyes were a stranger's eyes' (*SP*: 13).

The theatrical is constantly present in *Smile Please*. Rhys constructs herself as self-rejecting child persona who hates her assigned role as the 'only fair one' of her family's children. A brief attempt at becoming less frumpishly turned out is defeated at home (the incident of the garter tightening) and afterwards there is a gloriously pursued slovenliness at school, in itself performance, for there is sport in trying to outdo the only other thoroughly untidy girl at school. Yet in the paragraph which follows this account, Rhys offers the memory of a 'magic dress' (*SP*: 15) given as a present on her sixth birthday, the very dress in which the photograph was taken which opens the narrative. A magic dress presumably gives power to the wearer: it is a costume, a mask, a protection, an identity. In this dress,[14] Rhys's fictionalised self watched her siblings begin a performance of a play about Red Riding Hood, though they soon abandoned it. Happiness, careful costuming and performance are connected together as are self-hatred and a defiant lack of care in dress and self-presentation in public.

Meta's performance as a story-teller terrifies the young Rhys, but connects her to a part of Dominican experience which as a white child she would not have been given by her own parents. Francine, a later story-teller/childhood ally, told stories 'full of jokes and laughter', using traditional African-Caribbean folk ritual. Ritual is very important here: as when the child Rhys in smashing a doll's face translates a disturbing moment of self-construction into an alarming and deviant performance, much more explicitly set out in the family view than is usual for a child's inner tensions.[15] It seems as if it is performance itself which becomes the silent companion of a child never able to simply relax into a comfort with herself or her surroundings.

Admiration for others who can put on successful masks is the core of the story the young Rhys tells her mother about a woman who dressed up as a working-class girl and worked in a jam factory, then wrote an article about it. The mother thinks this is spying and then making money out of it: 'Disgusting behaviour' (*SP*: 34): the daughter clearly admires and believes the writer, implicitly approving the masquerade, and perhaps already seeing writing as a part of role-playing.

The father expects his daughter to give out alms of bread and money to the poor, though her mother worries about this close contact with people who might be ill. This, too, is performance, a class-based role-playing which the child learns, describing the line of old men, 'no women', as a procession. Rhys writes one of her most offensively white observations here, 'One of them' (the 'them' reverberates with the 'they' and 'them' of colonial gener-alisations about Others), 'was very different . . . He bowed, then walked away through the garden and out of the gate with the loaf under his arm, so straight and proud, I couldn't forget him after-wards' (*SP*: 35). The man, too, is acting out a role, but the colo-nial child believes in it and the memory remains for Rhys that it was extraordinary for a member of the poor (and black) commun-ity of Dominica to be 'straight and proud'. In the description of Rhys's mother, which follows that of the old man, a certain stubbornness and pride is also described: she, too, evidently knew how to play her class and racial role.

Three important theatrical events are prominent in Rhys's recol-lection of public Dominica: the Riot, the Corpus Christi proces-sion and Carnival. People participating in the Riot sound 'like animals howling' (*SP*: 37), exactly as they do in *Wide Sargasso Sea*, for by the time of the autobiography, Rhys needed to recycle fictionalised experience from her earlier texts where her own memory had been preempted.[16] The Riot is hardly convention-ally theatrical since an important element of theatre is our assur-ance that whatever is performed is only pretend, and cannot harm us. However, it is an event larger than normal life, which draws strong responses in the young Rhys: she says 'a certain wariness did creep in' (*SP*: 38) towards black people as a group after this experience.

The Corpus Christi procession was fascinating to the young child because it was evident theatre, drawing out the Catholic, black community who dressed in rich clothes and followed the priest and his acolytes in their red robes. The costumes for this occasion were impressive: 'sweeping trains, heavy gold earrings . . . colourful turbans' (*SP*: 40). Women sewed paper in the hems of their dress and petticoat to ensure the 'desired frou-frou noise' (*SP*: 40), a sign of dress transforming into theatre. Witnessing this from behind closed wooden jalousies, peering between the slats, the child was a secret outsider, both as non-Catholic and as white.

Carnival made the white family audience, neither 'dressed up' nor participatory, but watching closely from the open window, commenting as audience. A memory of a woman playin' mas who visited Victoria, a family servant, and talked in a 'strange artificial voice', is terrifying because of her mask. Fears developed of meeting some of the male masqueraders on the street, but that never happened. There was one mask which the child Rhys did not fear, the stiltman or Bois-Bois. Carnival was, for the child Rhys, about wanting to be black and join that dancing in the sun, with all of its metaphoric significance and romantic distortion.

White Dominicans had their own performances: evenings of singing and music, which together with card games provided a popular form of entertainment. Rhys remembered the little concerts though as a child she witnessed them as an outsider, looking on only at a distance. She however involved her little sister in theatrical performances: the little sister played 'the princess' and Rhys 'the wicked old baron' (*SP*: 53), once more embracing the 'bad' role. Even family meals could be turned slightly to theatrical use when the finger bowls were played (presumably by the children).

Churches are of course full of ritual, but the Anglican church is known for its oddly suppressed services, neither accommodating the full ritual and costumes of Catholicism nor the intensely theatrical preaching of more evidently Protestant forms of the faith. Anglicanism came into being because Henry VIII needed a divorce and the Pope would not sanction it: it was a politically created identity and therefore had much of its source in worldly concerns and not those of the spirit. Not surprisingly, where it took root in colonial societies, it could feed elitisms, racism and other forms of social division. Racial division was part of Rhys's story of Anglican worship in Roseau in her childhood. High Anglican ritual betrays its Catholic origins, and some of the Roseau congregation were afraid of moving in the direction of becoming 'papist' through it. One Sunday morning, the marvellously uniformed Zouaves who came into the Anglican church broke the social code of racial segregation by being shown into one of the front pews. They were soldiers, members of 'the West Indian regiment' (*SP*: 73). Rhys fell in love with them, for their uniform was so theatrical and they had successfully challenged the social order they entered: 'Dressed like that it would be impossible not to be brave, impossible not to be bold, reckless and all the things

I admired so much' (*SP*: 73). There was also a woman in the church who was interesting to the young Rhys because she had made immensely theatrical scenes after being jilted by an Englishman who left Dominica suddenly and so terminated their engagement.

'Mr Hesketh', who was in life the Sir Henry Hesketh Bell who was Administrator of Dominica from 1899, had a costume ball and Rhys wanted to go as a Zouave. When her aunt thought this was impossible to make as a costume, she asked to be a gypsy, because of the bright colours, but gypsy colours were red and yellow which did not suit a pale girl. In the end, she went as 'yachting' in a blue-green which she loved and which brought out her eyes so they were no longer 'pale' (*SP*: 74). Even the nuns helped by offering a net flounce for the plain dress with golden red cut-out paper fish on it. The result was that Mr Hesketh asked the young Rhys to dance first and she very much enjoyed it.

It is a singing performance she gives on the ship going to England with her aunt which provokes someone to say she should go on the stage (a common enough and often meaningless remark which Rhys however seems to have taken seriously). Her ambition to train as an actress sent her to Tree's School or the Academy of Dramatic Arts, where she had little success. Angier comments that 'it was her voice, her "nasty nigger's voice", that had let her down. For some time now she would be defiant about it . . . but when she was a famous old lady people could hardly hear her she spoke so softly . . . She'd learned to hide' (1990: 50), i.e. to live in a disguise, adopting a surface mask.

The most powerful piece of writing in *Smile Please* about the nature of self is written as a short play in theatrical dialogue and called 'The Ropemaker's Arms'. Right from the beginning of this piece, the influence of film is acknowledged, 'You saw it in a film. Naturally', 'Yesterday at the cinema in the one and threes' (*SP*: 129, 130). Not only is writing constructed here as the only source of peace and absolution, but theatricality itself becomes ironically the only mode of penetrating to the truth which is masked by conventions. Inserting a popular song into the section of this chapter entitled 'About England and the English', Rhys counterpoints the reality of being 'Not a pretty little girl' with the myth of expected girlish perfection 'I'm in love with a sweet little girlie . . .' (*SP*: 137).

As a young woman, Rhys had her first taste of English theatre and was disappointed: 'I'd thought the scenery would be real because I'd heard it was, but I saw the backcloth move' (*SP*: 138). Along with other Rhys protagonists, this young woman finds England betrays her sure sense of where truth and falsehood each end: England becomes a metaphor for a dangerously unfathomable, amoral, disguised space in which 'most English people kept knives under their tongues to stab me' (*SP*: 138). But even so, despite her unhappiness, she remembers among the few things which impressed her, 'The theatre. The smell of greasepaint' (*SP*: 139).

The manuscript version of 'At the Ropemaker's Arms',[17] in a steady, level handwriting, shows Rhys to have written it at an early stage pretty much as it survived into draft in the David Plante period. There are some stage directions, as it were, to herself as writer, which have gone in the published version: 'Question and answer The method of Socrates . . .' 'At the Ropemaker's Arms', UTC: these show how Rhys conceptualised the piece in a dramatic way. Her sense of theatrical structure was clear in her writing *Quartet* first as a play: she wrote vehemently to her friend Sonia Orwell as late as 1966 that 'if anyone dramatises it *I* will' (18 November 1966). In 1973, she seemed surprised that a dramatisation of 'Outside the Machine' was tolerable, 'no need to get drunk afterwards' (letter to Sonia Orwell, 25 September 1973). It is tempting to speculate that had she been born half a century later, she would have turned to screenwriting: certainly the films of *Quartet* and *Wide Sargasso Sea*, the television adaptation of *Voyage in the Dark*, a planned film of *Good Morning, Midnight* and numerous proposed adaptations of her work for stage, radio, television and film suggest that her dialogue and dramatic structuring of fiction lend themselves easily to translation for performance.

Rhys's real contribution to literary strategies for self-construction did not lie in her contribution to autobiography, but in her early reaching out for a genre only now coming into its own, i.e. the personal essay, or creative non-fiction. What might seem at times failed fiction or autobiography works very well if reconceived as an attempt at personal essay or creative non-fiction. Nick Totton argues in reviewing *Sleep It Off Lady* that 'autobiography must be a work of creation as well as of reconstruction' and that in these stories Rhys 'treads the boundary between fiction (always with its sources in recollection) and history (always fictionalised by the pattern-seeking mind)' (1976: 22). The stories had often appealed to those who like a writer's evident detachment: Rayner Heppenstall (1968), reviewing *Tigers Are Better-Looking*, praised *Wide Sargasso Sea* and 'Let Them Call It Jazz' precisely because that detachment was not always found in Rhys's other works (1968).

In stumbling on a new possibility whilst walking the line between fiction and autobiography,[18] Rhys does not seem to have seen the distinction between fiction and creative non-fiction: working on one of her most important though still unpublished pieces of creative non-fiction, 'The Imperial Road', she described it as a story throughout the process.[19] The difference between the personal essay and short story is that the personal essay is the performance of personal experience, whereas the short story, even when it retells and dramatises that experience, sets out to establish a narrative voice demonstrably different from a fictionalised authorial identity; creative non-fiction advertises the autobiographical base of the writing without promising to stay with the shape of original experience. Creative non-fiction is part reportage, part interpretation and within the spectrum of the form can fall closer to journalism or to fiction. Lee Gutkind, editor of the journal *Creative Non-Fiction*, defines the genre as welcoming the subjective voice, building the essay out of well-established scenes and often using factual material in the way a journalist might. Those late stories which the Malcolms describe as 'acts of recollection of distant events' are the ones which begin to set out parameters of the personal essay, a genre which began, in the work of some outstanding early practitioners like James Baldwin, to come into its own in the 1960s, just as Rhys was entering her last sustained period of writing. Once more she predicted a trend.

To Francis Wyndham she writes in 1968 that her manuscript story 'Leaving School', an early draft of 'Overture and Beginners Please',[20] seemed to her too long for *The London Magazine* and was perhaps 'more part of an autobiography' (19 February 1968). He clearly agreed, as she repeats this idea, adding 'as you say', in a letter written ten days later to Francis Wyndham (29 February 1968). Though there is some evidence of the impulse towards a fictionalised personal essay in Rhys's work as far back as *The Left Bank* ('Hunger', 'Learning to be a Mother', 'Mixing Cocktails'), it is in 'Before the Deluge', 'The Bishop's Feast', 'Heat', 'Overture and Beginners Please' (*SIOL*, 1976), 'The Whistling Bird', (1978) 'Invitation to the Dance' (1975) and 'Kismet' (*CSS*, 1987), 'Whatever Became of Old Mrs Pearce?' (1975), 'My Day' (1975) and 'Making Bricks Without Straw' (1978), that the autobiographical impulse is channelled into story in an evident way.[21] In many other stories, Rhys's own experience is fully fictionalised.[22]

'The Imperial Road' is one of the most interesting personal essays Rhys wrote, though it remains unpublished.[23] Rhys ultimately felt it was rejected by publishers because she revealed unacceptable racial attitudes in it.[24] It was begun by her visit to Dominica in 1936, though she seems to have only worked on it in her late period, at the same time as she completed 'Making Bricks Without Straw' and 'The Whistling Bird' (Angier 1990: 631). As Teresa O'Connor tells the story (1992), it was rejected by, among others, Diana Athill, who thought it inferior to Rhys's usual writing on the grounds that it had the voice of Rhys the woman, not Rhys the writer. O'Connor agrees with this verdict, going on to say it 'remains an essay in memory and recollection' (1992: 407). But at the same time, O'Connor thinks it reveals 'perhaps more than Rhys's autobiography, some of her feelings in later life' towards Dominica (1992: 407). In other words, it was not as distanced and nuanced as her short fiction but it was not as guarded and fragmentary as her autobiography. In order to prove the point, O'Connor explains that the names La Paz and Violet in the piece are actual names referred to by both Rhys and Alec Waugh in their letters: the story was then not entirely fictionalised.

The piece has a first-person narrative and begins from an actual-life experience, namely Rhys's arrival in Dominica by boat in 1936. Even the name of the protagonist's husband, Leslie, is only changed into Lee. The internal unity of it is the weight of the narrator's excitement in returning to her childhood home and sharing this with her English husband for the first time. Her sense of the island is of course dependent on memory and memory proves a false guide, most critically when she encourages her husband and two reluctant guides to try to cross the island on the Imperial Road, not realising this was never completed.[25] The essay ends with her rueful wakefulness, 'asking myself if I could conceivably have imagined the whole thing . . . The band played, the crowd cheered as he declared the Imperial Road across the island open to all traffic. Now no trace of it?' (Draft 'Copy', p. 22, UTC). Other, presumably earlier drafts of the piece include descriptions of a visit to the Convent in Roseau which had been Rhys's school and to her father's grave in the Anglican cemetery in Roseau. But Rhys evidently realised that the piece worked better if it moved straight from the romantic arrival through an incident in the bar of the Roseau hotel, La Paz, where locals are rude to the visitors, to the trip to the north of the island and the attempted return via the Imperial Road.

Though the racial observations are frank and disclose the returning native as a white, still rather colonial outsider, their value is the confused notes of resentment and yet proprietorial apology which the narrator moves through as a white person not able to look at colonialism squarely through history without some jealous desire to repossess her lost childhood space. It is unfortunate that the writing is not quite as sharp as was usual in Rhys's texts, and that Rhys herself felt uncomfortable with the revelatory racial opinions she had offered in the piece and which she felt were the sole reason for its rejection, because it does seem to be a step towards a new kind of writing, between fiction and autobiography, and well ahead of its time.

In terms of the performative, it seems that Rhys is here trying something even more difficult than showing how vulnerable people can mask themselves (as in the fiction), or how important the theatrical was in her own life (her autobiography): here she tries to delineate the role-playing which characterises colonial and postcolonial societies particularly. One level of performance is race, but another powerful play-acting element in the piece is gender: various Dominicans take to the narrator's husband but not to her, most evidently when one woman washes the narrator's injured ankle in cold water but then insults her saying she does this for the husband, 'I know who you are and for one of your family I would do *nothing*' ('The Imperial Road', draft 2, March 1974, p. 13, UTC). Here she neither censures the embarrassingly personal nor unequivocally claims it as her own: the space between the two permits a good deal of new freedom. Perhaps this also explains the newly uncertain tone of the writing: also Rhys's experimentation must have been somewhat discouraged by the rejection of the story.

There are some draft essays in the Tulsa Rhys Collection which show Rhys's interest in writing the formal essay: 'The Bible is Modern', 'Essay on England', 'The Hanger-On'. In these, she constructs a first-person narrator who is both willing to share personal history and to relate it to currents of ideas: clearly this form permitted also the direct expression of anger against those institutions and cultural formations which had caused pain, such as the English middle- and upper-class, men and especially a combination of the two, 'It is great crime to feel intensely about anything in England because if the average Englishman felt intensely about anything, England as it is could not exist; or certainly, the ruling class in England could not continue to exist' (UTC). These essays were clearly outlets for Rhys's feelings which would be rewritten to the point that they could, as she felt, be publishable: she worked into 'From a Diary: The Ropemaker's Arms' a good deal of her feelings about England and the English. She also permitted fantasies: 'what is difficult for us black people to understand' ('The Bible is Modern').

'Clouds in Stone' (UTC) deals with Rhys's experience in Paris,[26] rather than her ideas on morality and culture, but begins 'She said', an opening for a long narrative which is clearly Rhys's own experience but cast as fiction into an unnamed character's voice. But there is a willingness to exhibit enthusiasm in the description of the Richelot family which is very engaging and unlike Rhys's usual narrative tone of subtle and distanced criticism. These two quite different kinds of writing came together in 'The Imperial Road', where history, disclosure of feeling and contained narrative were combined. Rhys was perhaps beginning to develop another fictional voice by the time she wrote this piece, but she had no time to pursue it.

Perhaps the only actual autobiography Rhys wrote, in the traditional sense of being self-revelatory, resides in her letters, both published and unpublished.[27] Some reviewers of Wyndham and Melly's excellently organised edition of Rhys letters (1984) found it a gripping tale. Everything, after all, in literary work, depends on the form of a piece of writing being appropriate to its intention of effect. It is only in her most intimate letters that Rhys lays claim to the complex, contradictory personality on which she had drawn for characters in her fiction for so long. Her earliest versions of autobiography, such as the draft entitled 'DOWN ALONG: Fragments of Autobiography', reveal how much she sometimes cut out of final version which was in fact good writing and far more vivid and detailed than what we have as final draft in *Smile Please*. It is clear that Rhys went to considerable lengths to prevent us from knowing the writer behind the text and that in fact the autobiography was doomed to a certain failure by that determination. Biographies of Caribbean writers are rare,[28] perhaps because Caribbean culture is not encouraging of the sharing of family confidences, the public revelation of what goes on behind closed doors, except in fiction. We are fortunate however, that in her last major performance as writer, *Smile Please*, Rhys left us as much as she did. She remains the consummate performer of words: she deserves a canny audience. She is, above all, a writer who understood what the new century ahead of us will emphasise: the contradiction of longing for home but probably exploring and embracing some kind of homelessness, a condition of complex affiliation, deep loss and the difficult freedom of redefining self over and over again. It enriches painfuly: it complicates the idea of home and family. That contradiction says, for millions of us, very centrally who we are.

# CHAPTER 9

# The Helen of our wars: cultural politics and Jean Rhys criticism

> So that when we run into a strait of binaries (versuses &/or viruses), we begin to recognise that we in the Caribbean 'stand' where we have always 'stood' & that Jean Rhys has become the Helen of the wars
>
> (Kamau Brathwaite 1995: 77)

As Terry Eagleton has pointed out (1983), literary criticism is always ideological and shaped by its cultural location. The history of Rhys's literary reputation is a conversation, consciously or unconsciously, on the relation between the Caribbean and Europe (especially England) and also within and between Euro-American, post-colonial, feminist and Caribbean critical positions. Rhys criticism is always informed, implicitly or explicitly, by the cultural location and politics of the critic, even in those cases where political commentary is explicitly avoided or minimised. Predictably, those who have avoided Rhys's racial, cultural or political implications have tended to focus on her eminence as a literary stylist, especially connecting the latter to European modernism. Caribbean models of culture emphasise plurality and complexity: adopting such a stance is very important in reading Rhys.

Three major currents in Rhys criticism emerged within a decade of her death in 1979. Jean D'Costa, in an excellent essay (1986) describes them by means of a telling image of cultural relations as shaped by the transatlantic slave trade: 'Critics at three corners of the triangular trade lay claim to Jean Rhys' (1986: 390).[1] By 1991, British critic Coral Ann Howells (1991), without reference to D'Costa, located modernist and Caribbean identities within feminism as her central discursive space. Rhys's career becomes 'a cautionary tale about the difficulties and dangers of a woman writing' (1991: 1) and 'the alienated Rhysian heroine' (1991: 2), using 'contemporary feminist theory, theories of colonial and post-colonial discourse, and revisionist studies of modernism which take gender into account' (1991: 2).

This approach complicated feminist critic Teresa O'Connor's choice (1986) of only the 'West Indian novels', *Voyage in the Dark* and *Wide Sargasso Sea*, which meant she left out Rhys's other texts with their more suppressed Caribbean references, though her work is provocative and interesting. Like O'Connor, Mary Lou Emery (1990) is Caribbean-centred: her very rewarding reading of modernism in Rhys follows Sandra Drake's study of Wilson Harris (1986) with its extensive and valuable definition of the ways in which Caribbean writing has redefined European modernism.[2] Emery's model is even more complex than Howells: it braids all three identities, each constructed 'outside the main current by reason of its participation in the other two' (1990: 8). Rhys is thus a writer of 'plural and often conflicting outsider identities as West Indian writer, European modernist and woman writer at the closing of the era of empire', and Emery is concerned with 'the ways in which she occupied the spaces in between such identities' (1990: 8).

There has also been a significant male emphasis on Rhys as an especially transnational, ignoring the way in which her gender emphases inform her textuality: Trinidadian novelist V. S. Naipaul, in *The New York Review of Books* (1972), located Rhys in relation to the portrayal of white West Indians during the heyday of sugar fortunes by British writers (Smollett) and white Creoles like Leigh Hunt.[3] He identified her as 'outside that tradition of imperial-expatriate writing in which the metropolitan outsider is thrown into relief against an alien background' (1972: 29), affirming her as alien within the metropolis. Though he concluded much more generally, making of Rhys a fine, stoic writer who has survived her life and made good writing from it, his reading was no doubt informed by his own complex identity as alienated Caribbean writer and, in 1972, increasingly establishment British writer. Similarly, Paul Theroux saw Rhys as transnational in a review in 1972 of the second American edition of *After Leaving Mr MacKenzie*. He even thought Rhys's lack of clear national placement might be inhibiting her literary stature.[4] Not surprisingly, given that most critical placements of writers have been national or, more recently, based in gender or ethnicity, Rhys's reputation has been advanced at various times by critics who have clearly positioned her in terms of only one of those options. Her texts however conduct important conversations between gender, national, racial and class positions. Though Theroux, who has suffered himself from the marginalisation of writing out of no one definitive place, understood how important a national or local placement can be to securing an audience and so to securing a writer's reputation, he did not read Rhys's complexity beyond this general assumption or really challenge it.

The narrative of Rhys criticism is the narrative of cultural and racial history: it is also clear that Rhys's elliptical and economical style permits readers to fill in the spaces according to their own perspectives, a specific case of Iser's theory (1978; 1989). Early Rhys critics in the global north discussed form often to the exclusion of politics: such was the prevailing concern of high modernist circles. Ford Madox Ford did acknowledge her West Indian connection in his Englishman's middle-class tone and manner which came close to mocking Rhys's agony of consciousness of the inequalities of power between European capital and colonial society: 'And coming from the Antilles, with a terrifying insight and a terrific – an almost lurid! – passion for stating the case of the underdog . . .' (Stang, ed. 1986: 244). He also announced, modernist mandarin that he was, that 'the technical side – which does not much interest the Anglo-Saxon reader, but which is almost the only thing that interests me – is the singular instinct for form' (1927: 24). Ford thus permitted the 'instinct for form' to be separated, even in serious professional readings, from the discussion of political content in Rhys texts. Most early English reviews of Rhys indeed did concentrate on form: despite Ford's assumption about Anglo-Saxon indifference to stylistic elements in the general reader, English reviewers generally found form a safer space than the evidently complex gender and class politics central even to her early work.

In her first novel *Quartet* (first published as *Postures*, 1928; as *Quartet*, 1929) Rhys portrayed her mentor Ford as a particularly repulsive self-deceiving seducer.[5] The novel was rejected by Cape, who had published *The Left Bank*, on the grounds that it might be libellous in relation to Ford: Rhys had to find another publisher.[6] Rhys's Antillean and woman's sense of the 'case of the underdog' might have come to stand between her and the success which a self-congratulating, largely male literary establishment could bestow on those who did not betray their codes and expectations. Ford's faults and strengths were pretty widely known, however: Herbert Gorman, who as Mellown (1984) points out was Joyce's first biographer, argued in a review of *Quartet* in *The New York Herald Tribune Books* (1929) that Rhys's characterisations were powerful and accurate. Gorman was known to be an intimate of the circles around Ford in Paris (Mellown 1984: 9). Robert Morss Lovett, in the *Bookman* (New York), admired the novel 'so powerfully wrought out of weakness, futility, betrayal, lust and fear' (Mellown 1984: 10). A number of northern reviewers found some connection between Rhys's work and Hemingway's: this was praise indeed, but missed the huge political difference between the two writers. Also, as Carole Angier points out (1990: 177), there were negative reviews which disliked the novel's moral climate, though frank writing about drinking, sexual experimentation and living on the emotional edge written by men were modernist commonplaces.[7] Angier argues that Rhys wrote for the slaves in the master–slave relationship (Hegel's paradigm), and so offended masters (1990: 178).

Similarly, *After Leaving Mr MacKenzie* (1931) and *Voyage in the Dark* (1934) attracted admiration from northern reviewers for their stylistic clarity and reservations about their subject matter and themes as if the two did not spring from the same sources. Margaret Cheney Dawson found in *After Leaving Mr MacKenzie* that only 'true art' could transform Julia into a character of some consequence to the reader, given her alcoholism and general state of mind (1931). There was little serious interest in the West Indian subtext of *Voyage in the Dark*, Rhys's West Indian identity was mentioned only in passing.[8]

By 1939, when *Good Morning, Midnight* was published, Rhys's former husband Jean Lenglet, in the first essay on her, 'Jean Rhys, Une Grande Romancière Anglaise Inconnue', as usual

signing as Edouard de Nève, argued that her clarity of vision
resulted in part from her experience of leaving behind an idyllic
Caribbean childhood for the brutal realities of London's disappointed and marginalised: he understood Rhys's change of class
status as critical in her writing.[9] He stressed her wide reading of
European and American literature, but did not suggest her Caribbean origins might have caused Rhys to read that literature in her
own subversive way.

Most reviewers found *Good Morning, Midnight* depressing and
quite brilliantly done, like earlier Rhys reviewers discounting the
way in which the subject matter informed the style. As Angier
reports, 'It was sparsely and grudgingly reviewed' (1990: 373).[10]
Frank Swinnerton in *The Observer* (23 April 1939) commented that
'Miss Rhys has written several ruthlessly disagreeable studies of
women whose lives, casual, improvident and inescapably draggled,
have fallen into misery', nevertheless he found the crafting of the
novel 'quite exceptional' (p. 6).

Of course the novel's timing was difficult, since it offered a
biting portrait of a morally compromised Europe and appeared
in 1939: in reducing the story to the apparently isolated chaos of
one woman's failure, such an implication was avoided at the time
Europe, already largely overrun by Fascism, slipped into all-out
war. It was not until feminism developed as a major cultural
presence after the mid century in Britain and the US that Sasha's
resistance to the ways in which her culture marks her ageing spoke
to a great many readers with acute political relevance. This despite
the fact that the suffragette movement, which began in Rhys's
teenage years, was strongest when Rhys arrived in England from
Dominica and achieved the vote for British women at twenty-one
by 1928. Universal suffrage was granted in 1918, but unlike men,
women could not vote until they were thirty. But whereas the vote
ended the formal suffrage movement, it did not end the marginalisation of women (Deckard 1983), and the feminist movement of
the 1960s and 1970s found important material in Rhys's texts.

In 1950, Francis Wyndham, soon to become one of Rhys's
most loyal and brilliant supporters, wrote an important introduct-
ory essay on her, 'An Inconvenient Novelist', at a time when her
early texts had been forgotten.[11] He praised Ford for noticing

both her aesthetic ability and her passionate championship of the dispossessed and marginalised: both to Wyndham being essential aspects of her achievement. Elgin Mellown (1984: 171) notes that Wyndham's essay has become enormously influential. It was Wyndham (with writer/publisher Diana Athill) who gave Rhys vital encouragement in her work on *Wide Sargasso Sea*. He eventually wrote the introduction to the novel, in which he locates Rhys primarily in Europe. The Caribbean he read from Rhys was an imaginative space, not a real world: in *Voyage in the Dark* and *The Left Bank* it was a lost Eden, 'an innocent sensuality in a lush, beguiling land', whereas in *Wide Sargasso Sea*, Rhys 'returns to that spiritual country . . . and discovers it, for all its beauty . . . to have been a nightmare' (1982: 12–13).

The success of *Wide Sargasso Sea* in 1966 gradually brought the earlier novels back into print and a slow but steady flow of articles in the last years of Rhys's life. Some of the novel's publicity reinforced as myths the old rumour of Rhys's 'death' and 'resurrection', and the story of the frail yet glamorous, hard-drinking old woman at the top of her writing form.[12]

The first two books on Rhys prefigured subsequent separate constructions of her as northern/feminist and Caribbean: James (1978) and Staley (1979). Staley found support for some of his most central views of Rhys's work from early reviewers in the established literary circles of Britain or the United States: his fourth chapter begins 'Few serious British novels prior to those of Jean Rhys . . .', a locational remark which does not even complicate the term 'British' in her case. His handling of Rhys as woman writer was often awkward and lacking in conviction: 'The range of her subject matter has never been wide, but her understanding of what it is to have been a woman in this century is comprehensive' (1979: 130). Similarly, when James importantly defined Rhys as Caribbean, he was occasionally too straightforwardly enthusiastic, missing her unique contradictions, as subsequent scholarly work has shown:

The speech rhythms of the different racial groups – whether Creole, mulatto or Afro-Caribbean – are unobtrusively distinguished, and *right*. The social and racial relationships are *accurate*. The sensuous data of colour, scent and atmosphere are heightened but redolent of the Antilles.

And the imaginative texture of the book *perfectly matches* the exploration of facts of Caribbean history. (1978: 66; my italics)

In the United States, Britain and France, the rise of feminism (and its adoption of Civil Rights strategies in the 1960s) meant that Rhys's female reviewers in the early 1970s were especially able to appreciate the importance of Rhys's outlaw women protagonists. Rhys as unwilling but effective feminist is generally acknowledged to have become noticeable as an identity in criticism after the publication of Helen Nebeker's *Jean Rhys: Woman in Passage* (1981).[13] Most important work on Rhys since the 1980s has been written by women, a significant amount of which can be described as explicitly feminist, by which I mean, at its simplest, a commitment to end women's oppression. Nebeker, in preparing to offer her own highly subjective vision of Rhys and her novels, critiqued male critics who have 'impos[ed] upon Rhys's character and themes their peculiar subjective experience' (1981: ii). But despite her reliance on Jungian archetypes, Freudian derivations and Western 1970s goddess myths, Nebeker did at least also extend the image of the Sargasso, though her general application of it betrays an absolute indifference to history.[14] She appropriates Rhys's culturally specific images as universally applicable and forces onto them Western late twentieth-century feminist iconography, with the worst kind of sentimental global constructions of women and repressed racial subtexts. Nebeker reads Christophine, 'in her blue-blackness' as 'the most primitive, ancient earth-mother image, older than even the earliest western mythologies . . .' (1981: 137).

Feminist criticism on Rhys in the 1970s and 1980s reflected major issues in feminist criticism as a whole, for example, Casey (1974) on the gradual evolution of serious resistance to male domination in Rhysian women; Miles (1974) on female and class struggles; Thurman (1976) writing in the feminist magazine *Ms* on Rhys's concept of the woman; Abel (1979), using R. D. Laing's psychoanalytic work to discuss Rhys's female central characters; O'Callaghan on psychoanalytic factors in relation to women in the Caribbean (1990); Thompson (1981) on literary bias against women writers as evidenced in the case of Rhys; Blodgett (1981) on the mother–daughter relationship in Rhys's work; Kraf on men in Rhys's fiction (1985). These studies, generally short, provide a mosaic of evidence of Rhys's usefulness to feminism, despite her own reservations about the term and the fact that feminist studies with Caribbean reference were very much in the minority.

But *Wide Sargasso Sea* had, in 1966, provocatively raised the question of Rhys's Caribbean affiliation visibly enough for those critics who ignored it to have to have been determined to read in a blinkered way. Kay Dick, reviewing *Wide Sargasso Sea* in the London *Sunday Times*, and clearly aware of the connection between Rhys and a major British woman writer, Charlotte Brontë, inexplicably wished Rhys had returned to writing 'an aspect of life she has observed and experienced rather than by annotating' the earlier writer (Mellown 1984: 69).

However the relation between *Wide Sargasso Sea* and *Jane Eyre* was to prove major in post-colonial readings. Because Rhys so dramatically relocates the 'mad woman in the attic' in psychological and political terms (cf. Gilbert and Gubar: 1979), she offers both important feminist and important post-colonial paradigms. Indeed the relation between the two works can be seen as a complex trope of the relation between northern, white feminisms and post-colonial feminisms.[15]

Thorpe (1977) argued that *Wide Sargasso Sea* is not entirely self-sufficient, but relies on the reader knowing something of *Jane Eyre*, in the same way that post-colonial theory requires some knowledge of colonialism. Discussion of Rhys's use of the Gothic tradition is also relevant to comparisons with *Jane Eyre* and nineteenth-century English literary traditions. Luengo (1976; 1990), thought Neo-Gothic could describe *Jane Eyre, Wuthering Heights* and *Wide Sargasso Sea*, but especially the last. Luengo's argument was convincing enough then but now of course we know also that some of Rhys's dream landscape menace in *Wide Sargasso Sea* came from the Mr Howard narrative and predated the influence of the Brontës on her.[16] Givner (1988), in her discussion of the Brontës' influence on Rhys, located Rhys's use of evocative place as deriving from Emily Brontë: but surely Rhys's sense of place derived first from the Caribbean.

Unusual amongst northern critics responding to the appearance of *Wide Sargasso Sea*, Alan Ross (1966), long associated with *London Magazine* and publisher of Rhys's short fiction, made a

connection between Rhys's novel and Jamaican Herbert de Lisser's
*The White Witch of Rose Hall* (1929).[17] This is a provocative and
interesting comparison: De Lisser's romance is Eurocentric in
racial terms and in its construction of obeah: but at least Ross
signalled that Rhys should be interpreted within the emerging
canon of West Indian literature. Neville Braybrooke (1967) outlined Rhys's West Indian background and regional constructions
of race: he deduced her constant concern with bitterness in the
fiction was informed by her West Indian background. Later, he
positioned Rhys's women, romantically, as caught between rich
and poor just as 'in the West Indies, the Creole belongs to neither
white nor black' (1967: 77).

But the substantive beginning of the debate over Rhys as West
Indian writer, indeed as a white West Indian writer, began in
1968, when Wally Look Lai, a Trinidadian critic, published an
essay on *Wide Sargasso Sea* in Trinidadian John La Rose's influential series *New Beacon Reviews*.[18] Look Lai pointed out that the
English literary establishment had claimed the novel as a master-
piece whereas West Indian literary critics had 'largely ignored' it
(1968: 38). He was unhappy about the lack of reviews of the novel
in the West Indies since he regarded it as 'one of the truly great
novels to have emerged out of the West Indies' (1968: 38), though
of course in 1966, there was not a lot of criticism of any kind yet
emerging on West Indian writing. Also the pattern of a West
Indian writer first becoming known in Britain or the United States,
an often necessary stage in finding a publisher and readership,
was commonly construed as a deliberative exile.

Although African writers in the 1960s such as Chinua Achebe
and Wole Soyinka were importantly contributing to a new stance
in criticism[19] which was willing to confront Eurocentric norms of
aesthetic judgement, writers were still likely then to be assigned
to a literary canon on the basis of an unconflicted reading of
place of birth and upbringing: fortunately recognition of our times
as marked by migration and cultural syncretism has strongly
informed recent post-colonial positions on national affiliation,[20]
even if some of the old definitive placements still prevail.

Look Lai confronted the issue of whether Rhys was a West
Indian writer at all, despite her Dominican birth, since her adult

life experience and reception of her previous novels might suggest she belonged to European literature: he regretted that the novel 'is being appreciated in England largely as a brilliant continuation of a theme which has tended to dominate all of Jean Rhys's work so far: the transience and instability of personal relationships' (1968: 39). He made the important claim for Rhys that whereas she had once again in this most recent novel portrayed the 'theme of rejected womanhood' (1968: 40), this time, the 'West Indian setting, far from being incidental, is central to the novel' (1968: 40). This male critic argued that in this case rejected womanhood was an important symbol, but not the central issue: it was rather a metaphorical vehicle, by which West Indian society itself was to be delivered as the principal theme.

Look Lai's construction of white Creoles was in terms of the emotional and psychic stress of separation from origins: Antoinette and Rochester are symbolic in this reading of the 'existential chasm which exists between the white West Indian and his ancestors' (1968: 41). The use of the conventional 'his' rings particularly ironically here. His reading of the novel was somewhat sketchy too: he thought Daniel Cosway was Antoinette's father. Finally, Look Lai read the ending of *Wide Sargasso Sea* as Antoinette's attempt to try to belong to the West Indies, and hope to hear Tia's voice as welcome, though her death might have resulted from madness or reading this apparent welcome as real when it was illusion. Following this line of thought, he argued, in what would provoke an important response, that white Creoles in general needed to make their commitment to the Caribbean: 'realization that personal salvation, if it is to come at all, will come, not from the destructive alien embrace of Thornfield Hall, but only from a return – however difficult – to the spiritual world on the other side of the Wide Sargasso Sea' (1968: 52).

In 1970, Kenneth Ramchand's groundbreaking *The West Indian Novel and Its Background* set out to show the historical origins of West Indian fiction in the culture of the region itself. He included Rhys in his chapter on white Creole writers called 'Terrified Consciousness'. For Ramchand, *Wide Sargasso Sea* was less overtly political than Phyllis Allfrey's *The Orchid House* (1953) and less hopeful about the possibility of racial harmony than Geoffrey

Drayton's *Christopher* (1959). It seemed rather to be 'essentially modern', and this proved, judging by Ramchand's allusions to D. H. Lawrence, to signify an appeal beyond the West Indies. Indeed, Ramchand concluded, 'In Wide Sargasso Sea at last, the terrified consciousness of the historical White West Indian is revealed to be a universal heritage' (rev. edn 1983: 236).[21]

The term, 'terrified consciousness', adapted from Frantz Fanon's discussion of white colonials in the context of the Algerian war against the French, was explicated by Ramchand's citation of Fanon's well-known chapter 'Concerning Violence' in *The Wretched of the Earth* (1961; 1969). This chapter has of course been the basis for much important post-colonial theory, such as Abdul JanMohamed's influential *Manichean Aesthetics* (1983): by so constructing White West Indian writers, Ramchand (paradoxically, as it would turn out), opened the door to general and global constructions of race as a fundamental creative location for a given writer. Ramchand's 1986 essay on Rhys however stepped over the issue of race to find Rhys's ability to hear and reproduce West Indian speech and landscape as the defining factor in her placement, unlike Irving Andre's *Distant Voices: The Genesis Of An Indigenous Literature in Dominica* (1995), which reads Rhys in national/racial terms: 'Rhys has delineated the emotional and psychological scars experienced by white Creoles as they encountered economic decline in the island. She depicts white Creoles clinging tooth and nail to their exalted status in the society' (1995: 49). Dominican scholars such as Andre and Honychurch (1975; 1984) have recently declared an interest in Rhys: Dominica may consider celebrating Rhys at some future time.

Caribbean-centred responses to Rhys would prove to be the only centre of awareness of her location of race during the 1970s:[22] a period when decolonisation was not only a political but a cultural goal in the region. Kamau Brathwaite included in his *Contradictory Omens* (1974) a passage which replied to Look Lai's placement of Antoinette and white Creoles and which has reverberated in West Indian criticism ever since:

White creoles in the English and French West Indies have separated themselves by too wide a gulf and have contributed too little culturally, as a group, to give credence to the notion that they can, given the present structure, meaningfully identify, or be identified, with the spiritual world on this side of the Sargasso Sea. (1974: 38)

Brathwaite so signifies that a white coloniser cannot move to being white victim in one straight line without some recognition of the place of white power in history. His work has been to restore subordinated African identities within West Indian culture[23] to their rightful place, but in 1974 he was working in a cultural climate in the West Indies in which, despite the immediate political impact of the US Black Power movement, education in the history and culture of Africa was still largely sketchy for the general public. In terms of Rhys's novel, he insisted that the socio-political realities of Caribbean culture would prevent Tia and Antoinette from having more than a childhood playmate connection, as opposed to a strongly affectionate relationship which would be deep enough to permit Antoinette a spiritual connection with Tia after death.

However, Brathwaite's reading of Caribbean culture in this essay also privileges complexity: he argues that differences of opinion are inevitable. Critics responding to Rhys's *Wide Sargasso Sea* are not obliged to share unanimity 'because here one's sympathies became engaged, one's cultural orientations were involved' (1974: 34). Racial self-identification is of course no more than a reflection of Caribbean social practice, and therefore in itself uncontroversial: the controversy lies in 1974 in applying the idea to Caribbean literary criticism, which was largely the offshoot of English cultural and colonial universalism at the time and just beginning to establish local paradigms which questioned British lit. crit. tenets still current like 'universality'.

In shaping Rhys in such a context, it was not just Brathwaite but all Caribbean critics who were contributing to a major forum on the nature of Caribbean culture and the way forward at the end of the period of formal colonialism.[24] Jamaican writer John Hearne's 1974 article on *Wide Sargasso Sea* spoke of Rhys's use of *Jane Eyre* as 'an audacious metaphor of so much of West Indian life' (Frickey, ed. 1990: 188), but he also stressed the novel's universality, signifying availability to readers beyond Caribbean experience. For Hearne, clearly, Rhys and Guyanese novelist and poet Wilson Harris, 'alone are the free fabulists', 'Guerillas, not outsiders' (Frickey, ed. 1990: 186). He chose them rather than the evidently

radical African-Caribbean writers he specifically mentions, George
Lamming, Roger Mais or Vic Reid. Hearne's own work has been
summed up by David Ingledew as reflecting the part of the West
Indies that 'while often of mixed racial heritage, frequently nur-
tures and values European connections over those of Africa' (1986:
20). Though Hearne saw Rhys's talent as 'troubling', he read
her as representing, uncomplicatedly, West Indian 'indomitable
self-awareness' (Frickey, ed. 1990: 190). Hearne's comment that
Antoinette's English husband has a 'terrified, and therefore cunning, consciousness' (ibid.) is very similar to Ramchand's attibution
of 'terrified consciousness' to white Creoles.

Though both *Wide Sargasso Sea* and the 1960s in America put
race clearly on the table, little Eurocentric Rhys criticism even
since the 1960s has been deeply committed to looking at it. Studies
such as Tarozzi's on Rhys's style (1984) as well as Kappers den
Hollander's bio-critical explorations of Rhys's European connections are scrupulous and valuable (1982; 1987; 1988; 1994): the
latter offers much invaluable detail about Rhys's early writing
years in Europe. But for the most part the absence of race critically limits readings of Rhys.

Elgin Mellown, Rhys's first extensive and important biblio-
grapher, claimed his 1972 essay (repr. in Frickey, ed. 1990) as the
first serious Rhys scholarship. In it he briefly described Rhys's
parents as 'a Welsh doctor and his English Creole wife' (Frickey,
ed. 1990: 104) an accurate detail, but one which marginalised
Rhys's self-construction in Dominican terms. For Mellown, her
style was more informed by continental European ideas than by
British aesthetic trends: 'Rhys . . . employed . . . the European
*Zeitgeist* – its new ideas in psychology, its aesthetic application of
certain philosophical ideas, and most of all, its between-the-wars
appreciation of the plight of the individual, the isolation of exist-
entialism' (Frickey, ed. 1990: 115). He saw Rhys as not quite
British, strongly connected to the continent, like New Zealand
writer Katherine Mansfield 'an ex-colonial' with complex affiliations. But he failed to explore the exact identities of each writer's
alienation or to see it as a major creative source. Wolfe (1980),
who also made a comparison with Mansfield, offered a crudely
colonialist reading of major cultural influences on both writers:

In keeping with their scorn for affectation is the candor with which Jean Rhys and Katherine Mansfield discuss their native island colonies ... Though infiltrated by European values both places respond to them weakly. Thus both places suffer from the loss of European law. Situated thousands of miles way from England, site of their cultural heritage, the Caribbean islands and New Zealand, lacking an indwelling system of legal controls, abound in brutality. This primitive terror is presented without apologies. (1980: 163)

Alvarez's highly influential piece in *The New York Times Book Review*, 'The Best Living English Novelist' (1974), invited readers to think of Rhys as uncomplicatedly English. Alvarez focussed on the elements which he thought made her style so effective, mentioning Rhys's emotional penetration, formal artistry and 'unemphatic, unblinking truthfulness' (1974: 6). His most impressive sentence captured the struggle which that truthfulness cost: 'Her prose is reticent, unemphatic, precise, and yet supple, alive with feeling, as though the whole world she so coolly describes were shimmering with foreboding, with a lifetime's knowledge of unease and pain' (1974: 7), but he never located that pain or attributed it to a cultural experience. Alvarez found Rhys the more impressive because she avoids drawing explicit attention to ideas, but he overstressed this element when he said she did 'absolutely nonintellectual' work and has 'no axe to grind, no ideas to tout' (1974: 7). This article, Mellown notes, was the most influential in encouraging American critics to take Rhys seriously: no wonder few Euro-American critics were willing to look beyond style to understand what formed and motivated it. Whereas Rhys's fiction avoids intellectualising, it is provocatively original and highly political.

In the 1980s, Euro-American feminism began, to some extent, to think through contradictions and shortcomings caused by the monolithic construction of global feminism in a Euro-American image. But feminist criticism generally continued to be only locally sensitive to power structures and women's textual construction of them. By the late 1980s, Euro-American feminist psychoanalytic and reading theories informed full-length studies of Rhys. Judith Kegan Gardiner's *Rhys, Stead, Lessing and the Politics of Empathy* (1989) pursued the trope 'the hero is her author's daughter' (1989: 1) and

feminist constructions of the therapeutic concept of 'empathy'.[25]
She grouped Rhys with Doris Lessing and Australian writer
Christina Stead as colonials. Her argument claimed common
ground for them in their ambiguous relation to England, the fact
that they each left home to find some artistic freedom in London
and her reading of them as feminist writers, of course reading
feminism from her own cultural location. But there are also very
important differences here: Rhys's chronological space is just one
of them (and in 1907, she was seventeen, not sixteen). By 1928,
when Stead arrived, the First World War's impact on imperial
Europe was already felt and by Lessing's arrival in 1949, the
Second World War was over and the Empire was already under
considerable attack. Furthermore, between British-descended Lessing's birth in Persia and childhood from five in Southern Africa,
Stead's Australian experience and Rhys's Creole lineage through
her mother are more significant differences.

Nancy Harrison used important feminist work on autobiography
and reading practice to interpret Rhys (1988), though along with
generalisation characteristic of some high feminist writing: 'Rhys
may be the first practitioner of a woman's writing who allows
women's language to reveal itself through overt dialogue with the
language and discourse of men' (1988: 57). Harrison made a comment which poses and answers the question that Judith Gardiner
(1988) construes, in her work on Rhys, as central to feminist
criticism: 'Who is there when a woman says "I am"?' (1988: 194).
The comment is valid, but the real question might be shaped
more exactly to include Rhys's cultural identity: 'Where is it that
a Rhysian woman can say "I am", signifying, "and here I belong"?'

Deborah Kelly Kloepfer's *The Unspeakable Mother: Forbidden Discourse in Jean Rhys and H. D.* (1989), like Harrison, worked out of the
rich if culturally restrictive theoretical centre of Euro-American
feminism, locating the absence of the mother or ambivalent mother–
daughter bonds in relation to writing in Rhys's texts. She read
*Wide Sargasso Sea* according to this line of argument, which both
illuminates and narrows it: 'The significance of *Wide Sargasso Sea*
is that Rhys attempts a new strategy in which she forces the son to
experience her own psychological and linguistic space, positioning
him where he can no longer confine the mother inside a repressed

oedipal rage but must see her released through the daughter' (1989: 158). This reading of Rochester's drawing of a woman in a house as a depiction of his mother is, I think, not convincing, but easily seen to result from Kloepfer's focus.

One of the most difficult questions for literary feminism to answer is whether there is such a thing as a female or feminist aesthetic and in the search for that, as for all other theoretical constructions, generalities tend to dominate individualities. Avril Horner and Sue Zlosnik (1990), two British feminist critics, read Rhys along with American, British and Canadian writers Edith Wharton, Charlotte Perkins Gilman, Kate Chopin, Virgina Woolf and Margaret Atwood. Their common ground was claimed as the metaphoric construction of women's responses to land, sea, house or rooms: despite some detailed discussion of West Indian elements in Rhys's *Voyage in the Dark* and *Wide Sargasso Sea*. There was no exploration of how Rhys's West Indian origin might have informed her use of common female imagery differently. Gertrude Berger's article 'Rhys, de Beauvoir, and the Woman in Love' (1985), was another feminist reading which overlooked the complex fractures within Rhys protagonists and their problematic and quite specific relation to issues of race, class and age. Barbara Ann Schapiro (1994) included Rhys in a discussion of relational structures in nineteenth- and twentieth-century European and American writers: she constructed Rhys's experience and fictional portrayal of race as part of a 'normative' Lacanian and post-modernist theorising of an 'alienated, illusory self', a remarkably reductive argument on all counts. For Nancy J. Casey Fulton (1974), *Wide Sargasso Sea* was more than a 'study of the clash of European and Caribbean cultures', it continued Rhys's 'study of the problems of women in a world they are unprepared to face' (1974: 349). But Casey Fulton did not examine how these two issues converse within the novel.

Rhys is of course problematic for feminists, since she denied affiliation with feminism, but portrayed women as subversives within male hegemony. Paula Le Gallez in *The Rhys Woman* (1990) got around this by investigating the 'unconscious feminism of a consciously non-feminist writer' (1990: 8) and questioning overtly feminist theory being applied to Rhys and her texts: 'Where Rhys' heroines are concerned, the struggle concerns itself not with a physical grouping together in solidarity against the oppressive forces, but rather in the more subtle way of each becoming her own maker of fiction' (1990: 176): so each Rhys woman becomes an agent in the political liberation of women through telling her story. Le Gallez's title refers to an important sub-theme in Rhys criticism which developed from Francis Wyndham's 1950 view that all of Rhys's protagonists in fact form one composite figure.[26]

Feminism rightly places importance on biographical and auto-biographical constructions of women's writing, which set out the terms and contexts of women's literary production. But this needs to be fully realised. Carole Angier, Rhys's biographer (1985; 1990), despite excellent research on Rhys's European connections and family, never visited Dominica during her research, which weakened her early chapters on Rhys's childhood, although she did consult Dominican sources. The Caribbean background to Rhys's life may however be supplemented by Lizabeth Paravisini-Gebert's biography of Dominican writer and politician Phyllis Shand Allfrey (1996).

Not surprisingly, feminist critics centred in or at least aware of the Caribbean context and also aware of Euro-American critical positions can offer the most complex and rewarding readings of Rhys: D'Costa (1986) saw that Rhys's vision productively under-mines 'comfortable ethnocentrisms' (1986: 391). She recommended 'complex reading which recognises both the peculiar nature of cross-cultural experience in her native Caribbean and the focal role of this in Rhys's perceptions' (1986: 399), a perception which deserves to be central in Rhys criticism. Anderson (1982), James (1983), Emery (1990) and O'Connor (1986) all argued for working from the Caribbean out to feminist readings. O'Connor's study pays particular attention to Rhys's biography. Bev E. L. Brown's 'Mansong and Matrix: A Radical Experiment' (1986) discussed Rhys's women protagonists as redefining their identities through Caribbean female mentors, 'seed matriarchs', rather than through relations with men. It is true that connections between women are crucial in Rhys's fiction (Angier 1990), but so are pairs made up of a woman and a man, as in Marya/Heidler, MacKenzie/Julia, Horsfield/Julia, Anna/Walter; Sasha/René, Sasha/Enno: most importantly Antoinette/Rochester. Rhys's fictional world is one where men can mark women for life by their carelessness or malevolence: men are not explicitly crippled by their relations with women.

Rhys's portrayal of strong black women mentors for her white female characters is interesting. Lucy Wilson's essay on Rhys's West Indian outcasts (1986: 1990) argued justifiably that especially Selina and Christophine show up Rhys's white protagonists as weakly passive and detached. But the basic outline of 'Let Them Call It Jazz' (1962) is based in Rhys's own troubles with alcohol, her neighbours and the law in 1948–50.[27] Selina's modes of resistance are not those of Christophine: she is the more convincing a character because she is not so idealised. Selina has weaknesses, Christophine appears to have none. But some questions arise: in the 1950s, working-class black West Indian women in London would more likely have been very much concerned with proper behaviour, making a living, supporting a family, sending money home, avoiding racial confrontations, trying to undermine negative stereo-types (Gilroy: 1994). Rhys's rebellions against a respectable England she hated, fuelled by alcohol, were rebellious actions of a woman born into privilege, not politically coherent protest: but nevertheless in Selina she creates a believable woman whose survival against the system has clear political significance.

One of the most sensitive Caribbean feminist essays on Rhys thus far is Jamaican poet Mervyn Morris's '"Oh, Give the Girl A Chance": Jean Rhys and *Voyage in the Dark*' (1989), in which he discussed Rhys's rewriting of the end of the novel and her version of the story of Michael Sadleir's demands, as publisher, that she so do. Morris commented, tartly, that in Rhys's account in *Smile Please*, Sadleir represents 'commercial instinct and genial male privilege' and Rhys, imaged here in contradistinction to her character Antoinette, is 'a woman misunderstood . . . who protests a little, but gives in . . . (she does not jam a burning cigarette in Sadleir's hand, she does not set the place on fire; but the ironic account is part of her revenge)' (1989: 3). Morris, rightly, placed Anna as a 'Caribbean exile' (1989: 6), and believed Rhys's original ending offered a 'fuller picture of Anna's Dominica' (1989: 6), including greater detail on race and slavery.

Though recent Caribbean critics have generally termed Rhys 'white Creole' (Gregg 1995; O'Callaghan, much more briefly, 1986), this signifies a number of identities and affiliations. Jamaican feminist critic Evelyn O'Callaghan, who critiqued Brathwaite's comment on Tia and Antoinette, argued that a composite figure of the white Creole woman can be deduced from the fiction of three white, female West Indian writers, Rhys, Eliot Bliss and Phyllis Allfrey. She constructed an intensely sympathetic insider portrait of the white Creole woman:

This figure is a second-class member of an already precarious social group; she's creole rather than 'real' (English) white, she belongs emotionally and spiritually to no group, despite efforts at partial integration. With neither blackness, nor money and 'Englishness' as a passport to identity, she's a lonely, withdrawn, isolated and marginal figure, subject to cruel paradoxes – such as having privileges with virtually no power, or being oppressed without the support and solidarity of fellow victims. (1986: 86)

This portrait focusses on those very few whites who are economically fragile in Caribbean communities. However, the differences between Allfrey, for example, and Rhys are crucial. Allfrey felt she belonged to Dominica and was deeply involved in politics there; Rhys became an exile whilst young and never quite discovered her place there. White racist ideology has, over generations, had the effect of isolating Caribbean whites, especially women. Veronica Gregg, in her study of Rhys's affiliation with Caribbean history (1995), found Rhys's portraits of black and mulatto characters reflect her 'profoundly racialised, even racist' imagination (1995: 37) and rightly criticised Rhys's recruitment of black models for resistance into 'the engendering of the Creole subjectivity' (1995: 37). Nevertheless, there is an important anti-colonial, libertarian, anti-racist, pro-woman thread running through Rhys's fictionalising, often thwarted, contradicted and undercut, but remaining as the root source of her political landscape. That she sustained this in her lifetime and social contexts makes her a mentor for contemporary white female writers whose creativity is especially bounded by history and whose writing must often simply take huge risks to face that issue.[28]

Post-colonial studies often establish connections between writers from different parts of the former British Empire: Judith L. Raiskin's

*Snow on the Cane Fields: Women's Writing and Creole Subjectivity* (1996) discussed South Africans Olive Schreiner and Zoe Wicomb, as well as Rhys and Michelle Cliff from the Caribbean, as Creoles. Concerned about the extension of the term Creole beyond the Caribbean or the Americas, 'a broader, more metaphorical conception . . . focusing not on the individual human body or on supposed biological difference but on cultural intersections and mixtures' (1996: 5), she argued both common ground between these writers and noticeable differences between them, and succeeded in large part in resisting the kind of comparison which is reductive, whilst extending the term 'Creole'.

As with European constructions of Rhys, some useful Caribbean centred work deals with particularities of cultural connection without paying attention to feminism. Margaret Paul Joseph's *Caliban in Exile: The Outsider in Caribbean Fiction* (1992) discussed Rhys, Lamming and Sam Selvon in the context of Caribbean constructions of colonial archetypes drawn from Shakespeare's play *The Tempest*.[29] Joseph defined Rhys as a cross-cultural 'Welsh-Caribbean' here: her interest, as with the other two writers, is the fictional portrayal of being outsider or exile in England. There has been interest in Rhys's use of religion, ghosts and obeah (Campbell 1990; C. Lindroth 1985; Savory 1996, 1997), some of which attends to Rhys's Caribbean inheritance. What is at the moment a small footnote in Rhys studies, but an important one, is the question of how French Caribbean constructions relate to English ones, since Dominica's French cultural identities have entered the culture strongly. Barber-Williams (1989) read *Wide Sargasso Sea* alongside Michelle Lacrosil's *Cajou* (1961). Lacrosil's protagonist is of mixed race, African and European. Barber-Williams compared Antoinette as white 'with a black consciousness' and Cajou as 'a coloured girl with a "white state of mind"' (1989).

There is now a considerable body of important socio-historical scholarship (Hulme 1993; Ferguson 1993a, 1993b; S. Thomas 1994–5; 1996a; forthcoming) which has sought to research Dominica (Hulme and Whitehead 1992) and thus contextualise and critique Rhys's family, personal history and British experience as well as to compare Rhys's historical vision with that of contemporary

Caribbean historians (Gregg 1995). Some very important footnotes to Rhys's version of history are being clearly set out: Lennox Honychurch's correction of Rhys's memory that the Geneva estate house was burned down in the 1830s is explored in good detail in Hulme's '*The Locked Heart: The Creole Family Romance of Wide Sargasso Sea* – *An Historical and Biographical Analysis*' (1993).

But occasionally, an exchange between critics or theorists throws a sudden and brilliant light on the ways in which cultural positions inform reading. I have taken as title for this chapter Kamau Brathwaite's recent use (1995) of a metaphor of Rhys as Caribbean Helen of Troy in the context of 'cultural wars', or emerging Caribbean discourses engaging with Western cultural imperialisms. Brathwaite chose an image for Rhys from the foundations of European literary tradition. It is appropriate here: Helen, or Rhys, has in effect been stolen or kidnapped from the Caribbean by Western literary taste, and as a white writer, as the symbolic white woman, is particularly desired by Europe. Whether to try to win her back is the Caribbean dilemma: she functions then as a symbol of a cultural battle between Europe (most often constructed as England, the general Caribbean code for the imperial identity of Britain), and the Caribbean or post-colonial world. These 'culture wars' are primarily fought with language: their outcome in the West Indies will determine which directions the culture will regard as important in the next century.

Brathwaite wrote this essay in response to one by Peter Hulme, 'The Place of *Wide Sargasso Sea*' (*Wasafiri* 1994), which surveyed major Caribbean constructions of Rhys and found Brathwaite's 1974 position took the argument of the identity of *Wide Sargasso Sea* and Rhys 'into a cul-de-sac'. He also took issue with Brathwaite's 'explicit indication that neither Look Lai nor Ramchand are black' (1994: 6). But in the Caribbean racial consciousness is a commonplace of everyday life: race matters, though it shifts base, and like many historically bonded communities, the Caribbean's microcultures can quickly unite across race against outsiders.[30] In the Caribbean, racial affiliation is acknowledged, mostly, to deeply shape reading of a given situation (or text).

There is an implicit collision between Hulme and Brathwaite in that Hulme's position is multicultural and Brathwaite's is anti-racist: the first, especially in white cultures, conceptualises equal space for each ethnicity, though white dominance may still be in place (perhaps unconsciously to whites but still a matter of assumed comfort); the second is a much more direct engagement with racism, i.e. with black–white history. Hulme raised the issue of race himself by citing Brathwaite's 1974 remarks: oddly he did not contextualise them historically. In the 1970s, the Caribbean saw some very important and necessary arguments over the relative place of African, Indian, Chinese and Caucasian identities, especially since the history of chattel slavery and colonialism so long forced African-Caribbean culture underground. White political power was beginning to be defeated, but white economic power remains to this day largely intact. Black Power was a current Caribbean issue after the 1970 Black Power insurgency in Trinidad (Bennett 1989), though in Trinidad and Tobago, where the Indian community was not brought into the movement, this added to racial/ethnic tensions between Africans and Asians. In the literary context, Indo-Trinidadian writer V. S. Naipaul's evident preference for white British culture and his negativity towards African elements in the Caribbean have added to the tensions surrounding the issue of how writing/writers are to be viewed in the context of Caribbean discourse about race and ethnicity.[31]

Brathwaite explained at the beginning of his introduction to *Contradictory Omens* that the essay came directly from his work on Caribbean Creole society and his study of white power in Jamaica during the slave period. He was also beginning then to challenge the idea that prevailing Western forms of academic discourse were uncomplicatedly appropriate for the articulation of Caribbean anti-colonial positions. The form of this essay met with some American academic resistance at a first reading in public. This confirmed Brathwaite's intention to work on imaging the philosophical bases of Caribbean thought. His conception of '*tidalectics*', a verbal play on dialectics, and the anti-colonial '*sycorax video style*' in which he now writes are rooted in Caribbean experience.[32] These important anti-colonial experiments with form attempt to bring into academic and poetic discourse the orality and political presence of African-Caribbean popular culture and, by extension, the African diaspora: the book is drawn within African space by which we are all influenced in the region. Though Rhys could not fully enter an African-Caribbean cultural space, she certainly indicated its importance and its transformational power over and over again in her writing. She makes us aware of the presence of Africa in her white Caribbean, and like Brathwaite, she regards race as painfully crucial, a result of history, though she evidently thought at times it was not an unbreachable category.

By entering into Caribbean cultural wars in his comments on Brathwaite's 1974 position on Rhys, Hulme ceased to be neutral, offered his own racial–cultural reading of Caribbean literary culture and so drew Brathwaite's fire. Matters were not helped by Hulme's statement that Brathwaite is Jamaican (he is Barbadian). His reading of the place of *Wide Sargasso Sea* combined Ramchand's argument for the novel's universality and Look Lai's for its particular West Indian identity, so he offered a final very broad project for critics: 'the pedagogical imperative to make it readable in circumstances very different from those which produced it and yet to remain responsible to its moorings in a very particular locality' (1995: 10).

In 'A Post-Cautionary Tale of the Helen of our Wars' (1995), Brathwaite set out in detail his construction of Rhys and criticised Hulme and others for writing on Caribbean ethnicity and culture without self-examination. Constructing both Rhys and her characters as icons and cultural metaphors, Brathwaite's essay offered his own reading of cultural politics. Rhys herself brought up the agonising issue of race in the Tia and Antoinette relationship, throwing a challenge which inevitably now exposes each critic's cultural affiliations. Brathwaite found Hulme glossed over, in academic fashion, some vitally important, still current, racial issues:

in S Africa the Tia/Antoinette relationship has not essentially changed despite 'post-colonial' and 'post-apartheid' efforts to assume that things have . . . Above all, can we treat a race-founded & race-foundered society as if it – looking back at its future – didn't xist? the specimen w/out its environment sticking to its wings its claws? . . . (1995: 73, 74)

Brathwaite was also offended by Hulme's reading of *Contradictory Omens*, which he took to signify resistance to '*a blk norm*' (1995: 70) for the Caribbean, but it is important that this provoked

Brathwaite's response and the chance for him to revisit Rhys: his original statement was after all more than twenty years old. The chasm between cultural locations and their corresponding intellectual visions is very clear here: Hulme seemed to desire a scholarly space beyond race for literary discussion; Brathwaite's reply implied as an ideal a society where the races are politically equal but each conscious of history, free to speak about it and fully aware of the ways each influences the other, a society not yet realised, even in the Caribbean.

It is clear that two major and very different positions are being held, not only over Rhys, in the debate over race as the century closes: race is perceived either as a major and permanent cultural/biological identity and experience or as a construct which can be dissolved with sufficient intellectual effort (Appiah 1992). Both are, I think, equally important. For Hulme, Guyanese writer Wilson Harris was preferable to Brathwaite, and part of this was that Hulme read in Harris that the 'colour of [the] author is irrelevant' (1994: 7) as long as Harris could see indications of West Indian history and legend in the mythic substructure of a given text. Here Hulme tries to divide Caribbean options and oppose them. But Antonio Benitez-Rojo has rightly called Caribbean culture a series of 'supersyncretic signifiers' (1992: 21). Both Brathwaite and Harris emphasise the creative fluidity of Caribbean culture. Harris emphasises his own multi-ethnic Guyanese inheritance and theorises from that. Brathwaite is from Barbados, 98 per cent of whose population are of African ancestry. Virtual apartheid was long established there. His work has been to restore the recognition of African cultural identities within Caribbean culture. This distinction between two great Caribbean writers in effect proves Brathwaite's point: ethnicity does translate into cultural viewpoint and that shapes aesthetic judgement. But Caribbean culture means there does not have to be a choice: poet-intellectuals have been of major importance in the development of anti-colonial Caribbean cultures.[33] For both Harris, whose prose fiction is highly figurative and who began as a poet, and for Brathwaite, *Wide Sargasso Sea* is a provocative metaphor of and contributor to Caribbean culture. Harris's desire that submerged fragments of ancestral cultures be recognised in Rhys's novel and

Brathwaite's willingness to confront painful fractures and wounds in Caribbean consciousness provoked into memory by *Wide Sargasso Sea* both testify to their search for a language which can capture Caribbean history and the complex identities which have resulted from it.

Post-colonial societies bear wounds not only from colonial domination, but also from what Brathwaite calls 'lateral creolization'. Tensions between subgroups of colonised peoples, such as between African and Indian in the Caribbean, were set up initially by the coloniser's intentions for and racial construction of them and by the historical context of their arrival in the Caribbean: they continue to be a part of Caribbean experience. Though Harris is more utopian than Brathwaite and Brathwaite emphasises African cultural identity as the predominant Caribbean space, essentially they are talking about working through the same reality and towards a compatible goal. In 1990, Harris offered a summing up of his position on Caribbean culture: 'There are complex flaws in all cultures that led to the breakdown of homogenous societies on every continent and to the dangers at the heart of the modern world, dangers as well as far-flung, regenerative, cross-cultural possibility' (1990: 176). In many ways, this is not far from Brathwaite's understanding of Caribbean discussions over culture as regrettably amounting to 'cultural wars'.

Harris's two analyses of Rhys's writing, in 'Carnival of Psyche: Jean Rhys's *Wide Sargasso Sea*' (1981) and in *The Womb of Space* (1983) expressed one of his most central ideas, that writers can be informed (one is tempted to use the word 'possess' in its Caribbean meaning) by ancient myth without necessarily knowing it: *Wide Sargasso Sea* 'varies the rainbow arc between cultures in profoundly intuitive spirit' (1981: 126; 1983: 49).[34] The fire motif in the novel is directly connected to the Arawak myth of a tree of life, reaching across the heavens from ancient time, which is set on fire during war and drives the Arawaks themselves into space where they become part of the fiery conflagration, and eventually stars. Harris saw Rhys as having 'imaginative insights' which could be read as both 'white' and 'black', reminiscent of Catholicism and obeah: he saw her, in effect, as an Africanised white, or as Harris might want to put it, a Caribbeanised white.

What Harris approved in the novel was a buried level of mythic connection which requires interpretation in the light of Caribbean legend and history. When he said that Antoinette had the 'passion to illumine by fire the other's essential humanity . . . with layers of the past that had tormented her' (1983: 54) he meant that Antoinette's self-immolation might have altruistic implications, implications which can only be understood through her transformation into mythic dimensions. Bertha and Antoinette are like spirit doubles:

Bertha doubles into Antoinette to secure a hidden surrender of being, a loss of soul to find soul, an overturning of ritual-for-the-sake-of-ritual to enhance sensibility and feeling, a disrupted voice of convention in order to find (or begin to find) the voice in the foodbearing tree. (1983: 54)

The hidden script is one of spiritual continuity, necessary for the survival of the culture.

Hulme's intention is to sort through criticism to find the place of *Wide Sargasso Sea*, and he follows traditional Western academic methodology by keeping himself largely out of the argument: but for Brathwaite, the issue of Rhys's cultural identity is more than academic. It is part of the political and social struggle of a region to recover from colonialism. Rhys herself has importantly, if conflictedly, contributed to this and using the his provocative *video style*, Brathwaite revisioned Rhys in 1995, marking her important contradictions. Underlying his concerns about Hulme's mapping of Caribbean literary contexts for Rhys and his citation of such sources as Tiffin (1978), Wilson (1986), Ferguson (1993a), is the role in general of post-colonial criticism and theory: Brathwaite's concern is that this can in effect be used to write white people out of their difficult place in history. For example, responding to Hulme's use of 'victors', which introduces the idea of warfare, deriving from a comment of Ferguson's, he wryly pointed out that if he or any 'IIIW Ninja' had mentioned that, it 'wd have brought thunders down upon our house' (1995: 73).

It is not that Hulme has not recognised many of Brathwaite's points: he is aware of the tensions inherent in Antoinette's location as central figure in the novel. He also insists that Antoinette has to be implicated in imperial power, however complicatedly, and acknowledges that the black rioters at Coulibri, Antoinette's

childhood home, would not have been impressed by a white
woman's claims to share their oppression. Hulme also argues,
uncontroversially, that Gayatri Spivak, in her well-known post-
colonial essay, 'Three Women's Texts and a Critique of Imperialism' (1985), is overly willing at times to co-opt *Wide Sargasso Sea*
into 'an international postcoloniality' (1995: 8). Spivak's critique
of northern feminism's embrace of 'the axioms of imperialism'
(1985: 243) is still important precisely because she theorises opposition to the narrowness of a feminist criticism which does not take
account of other power relations than male–female. But Spivak's
use of the definite article, '*the* European novelistic tradition', '*the*
white Creole', '*the* native', '*the* Other', '*the* imperialist self' (my italics)
unfortunately resolved the very contradictions, which I call 'productive contradictions', in Rhys's text and set an unfortunte pre-
cedent. Indeed, trying to find the grounds of Hulme's attack,
Brathwaite asked the question: what was the difference between
his questioning *Wide Sargasso Sea* and Hulme's comments about
the difference between the white plantation women and the black
rioters? Hulme argued similarly in his reply to Brathwaite (1996),
where his own sense of injury is apparent, and where he sounds
both angrily contemptuous and in need of making peace: 'Where
Brathwaite and I can certainly agree is on the dangers of taking a
book like *Wide Sargasso Sea* as representing the history of the West
Indies' (1996: 50).

It is clear that Hulme's critiques of the missteps of post-
colonial criticism could not offset Brathwaite's sense that Rhys
'becomes a kind of wishful metaphor for what these critics want
to "say", & a way of masking any element of *GUILT* . . .' (1995:
73): his own metaphor for Rhys, the lovely and complex Helen
who has journeyed in literature from Homer to Walcott, places
cultural politics at the forefront and challenges the post-colonial
critic to self-disclosure and self-exploration. What angered Brathwaite is clearly the implication that he and only he was putting
race on the table, and that doing so was in itself racist. The fact
is that race is on the table, whether white people want to acknowledge it or not, and we put it there several hundred years
ago, so it is disingenuous to step away from it until it is dissolved
as a powerful economic and social category. Rhys tells us exactly

that, along with her awareness of women's subordination. She opens up the kind of risky space in *Wide Sargasso Sea* where we are, if we face it, forced to begin to speak about the implications of history in our relations with one another and in our work. To try to retreat from this into the kind of theory which volunteers to remove us from recognition of experiential identities such as race, gender or class almost inevitably costs us our faith in language's potential to recast difference into a positive. The Caribbean is still logocentric: so is poetry. It is in Brathwaite's poetic practice that the heart of his cultural theory lies, and the importance of his recent intervention is to remind us that we invest ourselves in the way we read major literary texts as cultural signs. It is important to be well aware that we do this and exactly how our cultural locations and identities write themselves through us, even when we think we are being our most individual and self-aware.

As Brathwaite pointed out, Rhys brought race into the debate in the first place and that was because of her Caribbean experience. But Rhys's Caribbean-centred texts, like those of many other Caribbean writers, deconstruct all easy oppositions, without demanding the price of denial of history. The most productive readings of Rhys, therefore, must take into account the ways in which she was continually evolving textually in the direction of a never entire, infinitely complex but decidedly anti-hegemonic identity, whilst accepting her unique contradictions and her political failures. The collective aesthetic of Caribbean culture is made up of such individual struggles with and revisions of the meta-narratives of history, expressed by the remaking of received forms and influences, and offered back to the community to evaluate. In his 1963 essays, C. L. R. James (repr. 1983) understood that cricket suits the West Indies because a successful side is best made up of eleven powerfully individualistic players held together by a common goal but each needing individual creative space. It has been Rhys's fate to be hostage to other people's visions of her place on their team: the reality is that she is a Caribbean player, but she plays on her own terms. But, as I have argued at length, although she brings her own version of what Caribbean signifies, her engagement with language cannot be understood fully unless it is understood within the context of her Caribbean origins.

Having the Caribbean as a frame of reference helps us to place Rhys in comparison to other white female post-colonial writers such as Nadine Gordimer, Ruth Prawer Jhabvala or Doris Lessing, or white American exiles such as Henry James, T. S. Eliot and more temporarily, Ernest Hemingway. Reading from the Caribbean emphasises a philosophical and cultural acceptance of multiplicity and permits us to see important contradictions in Rhys's work which open up the complexity of powerful structures like race, class, gender and nation.

Gordimer, a brilliant and extremely important writer who has deconstructed white apartheid culture and supported anti-racist activism in South Africa, nevertheless does not capture the ambivalences and contradictions of the deeply inner workings of white consciousness as much as Rhys does. Gordimer's concern is social, with the political life of a state which has built itself on racial separatism and hierarchy, and with the practical and moral necessities of trying to combat apartheid within the white community. Since apartheid was formally dismantled, she has been concerned with how people of different racial identities in South Africa are beginning to deal with history and to form the new state. Gordimer's characters know they belong in South Africa. By contrast, Rhys's protagonists are displaced loners, marked by the inequities of present and past societies. Their consciousnesses are reflective of social constructions of race, gender, class and nation, but they are unable to formulate theoretical or practical political strategies to protect themselves from exploitation or other damage. Yet they cannot easily go home, even if they understand where home is.

Hemingway's achievement was to explore the inner life of white American males, most notably in a period of living overseas: they were expatriates, carrying their original culture with them and returning to it, and redefining themselves as males within the parameters of American culture. Similarly, the texts of Eliot and James, though transatlantic, are unequivocally white and Euro-American in their cultural identities: that does not mark them as wanting, but it certainly sets them apart from Rhys's concerns. Jhabvala's white and Indian characters seem to lead live parallel lives, hardly communicating: though she apparently portrays a complex cultural environment, the texture of her fiction is far less deeply exploratory of displacement than Rhys's. Rhys's characters are unable to locate their national or class affiliations comfortably, nor to escape others reading their gender or race negatively.

As we begin to work on the vexed question of how to read and how to write our increasing consciousness of cultural complexity, especially in the United States, where it must co-exist with a powerful climate of separatism and division, the case of Rhys, therefore, is very important. She was by no means always the most evident of culturally complex writers: that is why she has been able to be read monoculturally with some success. But her texts only open fully to a reading which can hear their multifaceted voices, their ultimately Caribbean source and her brutal honesty about the necessary contradictions of our attempts to place ourselves in the world within and against the scripts in which history has written us.

# Notes

PREFACE

1. See, for example, Carole Boyce Davies's argument (1994) on the complexities of African-Caribbean women's identities after migration and in relation to national origins.
2. See, for this distinction, the note on p. xviii.
3. See Knight and Palmer in Knight and Palmer, eds. (1989): 12–15. Though Labour movements began to be important in the Caribbean during the period 1880–1920, the first election with full adult suffrage was not held in Dominica until 1951 and anglophone countries began to be independent after Jamaica and Trinidad in 1962. Rhys revisited Dominica briefly in 1936. In 1938–9, the Moyne Commission, set up after widespread riots in the West Indies to investigate social conditions, found Dominica the most economically and socially depressed British territory. Dominica became independent in 1978, the year before Rhys's death.
4. See Boyce Davies and Savory Fido, eds. (1990).
5. Including *Good Morning, Midnight*, adapted for BBC radio, 1949, Selma Vaz Dias; film planned starring Glenda Jackson, 1973. *Quartet* was filmed by Merchant-Ivory Productions, 1981; *Wide Sargasso Sea*, by Fine Line Features 1993; also by Crossbreed Productions 1991 (the latter filmed in the West Indies). There have also been television and stage adaptations of *Voyage in the Dark*, 'Let Them Call It Jazz'; *Q*; '*Outside the Machine*' (see letter from Rhys to Sonia Orwell, 25 Sept. 1973); *SP*. In addition, there is a ballet of *Good Morning, Midnight*, a musical programme for piano and voice including extracts from *Quartet* and *Good Morning, Midnight*. Nora Gaines's bibliographies of Rhys material in the *Jean Rhys Review* contain sections on media adaptations of Rhys texts which are extremely helpful. Other information included here is culled from Rhys's letters, and from programmes, advertisments and reviews. There is, in Rhys's papers (UTC), evidence of numerous other plans for

adaptations of her major texts for radio, television and film. The vexed relation with Selma Vaz Dias began with the first dramatic adaptation of *Good Morning, Midnight* (1949) The difficult story of Vaz Dias's exploitative relation with Rhys over adaptations of Rhys's work for performance is told by Nudd (1984) and Angier (1990). See also Vaz Dias (1957).

6. Mrs Adam saw this early version of what would become first *Postures*, later *Quartet*. In 1966, Rhys returned to the thought of *Quartet* as a play following Selma Vaz Dias's interest in dramatising her work (letter to Olwyn Hughes, 6 May 1966).

7. Lois Mailou Jones, the very highly regarded African-American painter, was advised to go to Paris to study by Meta Warwick Fuller, the African-American sculptor, and Harry T. Burleigh, the composer of black spirituals: they had both found some success in France. Jones, who arrived in Paris in 1937, also found France a much freer and more creative space than the United States. See Tritobia Benjamin (1994).

8. Benstock positions Rhys firmly within the dominant male-centred Modernist movement: 'although Rhys explores in her subject matter the concerns of other women writers of the period, her lean prose style shares more with the poets of the Auden group than with Nin's expressionistic landscapes or Barnes's antiquated verbal modes' (1987: 441).

9. For further information on Caribbean writers see, for example, Dance, ed. (1986); Ramchand (1976, 1983); Lindfors and Sander, eds. (1992); Paravisini-Gebert and Torres-Seda, eds. (1993).

10. See Phillips's *Cambridge* (1991), which is partly told through the voice of a nineteenth-century planter's daughter who travels from England to the Caribbean and Antoni's *Blessed Is the Fruit* (1997), in which the two narrators are a black and a white woman, both living in the Caribbean. Both of these male writers have aroused some resistance in their willingness to speak in a voice not their own, but like Rhys, both have sufficient skill in writing to challenge the political assumption that a writer should not stray far from her or his own direct experience in constructing narrative voice.

## CHRONOLOGY

1. The first issue of Ford's journal appeared with a lower-case title, according to Mizener (1971), an accident and to Judd (1991) because there wasn't room for upper case. It was a useful accident, since Ford was to publish e. e. cummings and other modernist experimenters with linguistic conventions.

1. She did lose an important draft manuscript, *Le Revenant*, though Angier (1990) comments that when Rhys said an ms. was lost, it could mean she had deliberately destroyed it. Angier believes that the typed version of this novel was burned by Rhys during a row with her husband, Leslie. For *Wedding in the Carib Quarter*, another Dominican novel, notes exist, though Rhys claims a manuscript was lost (*L*: 213), but Rhys resisted serious work on this manuscript, because, as Angier infers from the note on the surviving outline and Rhys's evident caution about self-revelation, it had too dangerous a theme, perhaps interracial sexual relations. Angier (1990) discusses a fiction written by Rhys's brother Owen which might seem to suggest such a relationship. I absolutely do not agree with Sternlicht (1997) who asserts that Rhys had her first sexual experience at sixteen with a young man of mixed race, taking literally Owen's narrative via Angier's account. Owen's version would, I agree with Angier, have been known in the island if it were true.

2. History has written us, on one level, but on another, we constantly rewrite ourselves against it. See Ashcroft, Griffiths and Tiffin, eds. (1995). At times, post-colonial theory's tracing of representation solidifies categories.

3. See Paravisini-Gebert (1996: 6): Allfrey was extremely proud of her family's long and illustrious ancestry in Dominica. Lennox Honychurch has a story of Allfrey answering a child's question about how long she had been in Dominica. She said 'three hundred years'.

4. See Angier (1990). Williams seems to have felt much the same way as Rochester in *Wide Sargasso Sea* about his father's favouritism towards his more successful elder brother.

5. See Angier's account (1990), especially her discovery of the address in Acton where the majority of the female members of the Williams family lived in the late twenties and early thirties. Although Rhys seems to have had little to do with her mother or siblings in England, her brother Edward bought her a small cottage in Devon towards the end of her life.

6. See Frickey, ed. (1990): the article by Mellown (originally written 1969–70) is prefaced by corrections of biographical data, including his original birthdate for Rhys of 1894. Similarly, James (1978) says that Rhys was sixteen in 1910 (1978: 8); Staley (1979) also puts the birth in 1894.

7. Angier, who at the time of her biography had seen more of Rhys's papers than any other scholar, settles on Gwendoline. The name is, oddly, spelled Gwendolen in *Smile Please* (1979), the majority of

which Rhys prepared for publication. Gwendolen is adopted by Frickey (1990). The few official documents included in the Rhys collection (UTC) show variant spellings. This may seem a small point, but given the importance of names and naming in *Wide Sargasso Sea* and the significance of Rhys renaming herself as chorus girl and as writer, it seems important to consider Rhys's concerns about the spelling of her given name.

8. Angier's version (1990) is that William Rees Williams had loved the sea as a child and became First Mate in the merchant navy for a while before training as a doctor and emigrating to Dominica subsequently to take up a medical post as part of a Government scheme. But the *Dominica Dial* of 29 November 1884 stated he was a medical attendant on a telegraph repairing steamer when he got the job in Dominica (see here chapter 1).

9. Bell became Administrator in 1899 and left Dominica in 1905. One of his grandest schemes was to develop sixteen miles of what Lennox Honychurch rightly describes as 'thin, winding' road (1984: 117) which he called the 'Imperial Road'. His purpose was to open up the interior of Dominica to new colonial settlers for farming. At one point he planned to bring three thousand Boer War prisoners from South Africa to settle (Honychurch 1984: 117).

10. See chapter 8.

11. Daphne Agar, interview with Elaine Savory, January 1995, Dominica.

12. Along with Acton Don Lockhart, a nominated member of the Assembly, and prominent doctor Dr Henry Nicholls, Rhys's father was among those interviewed by the Royal Commission sent to find out about conditions in Dominica in 1894, following the serious La Plaine riot (1893) and various negative reports on the island filtering back from well-known travellers such as Anthony Trollope (1860) (see Honychurch 1984). Apart from complaining about the Assembly, Williams argued that there was too much expenditure on the poor house, with no work test for inmates or serious search for relatives able to support them. In both he sounds reactionary. He also thought the number of doctors in the island was excessive in terms of cost though clearly not in terms of providing adequate care for everyone.

13. Lennox Honychurch (1984) notes that the 'Mulatto Ascendancy' had control of the legislature for two generations. By 1853, following active attack on the planter elite by politicians of colour, a movement began among the English in Dominica to change the composition of the Assembly and so defeat this control. By 1863, the Assembly consisted of nine appointed members and nineteen electives. In 1865 it was propposed this be changed to a Legislative Council completely

nominated by the Crown, as Dominica would become a Crown
Colony by the same bill. Eventually the Crown Colony proposal was
withdrawn but the Assembly was now constituted as half-nominated
and half-elected, therefore giving the Crown much more power.

14. Lizabeth Paravisini-Gebert (1996) gives a good sense of Nicholls's
personality and impact on Dominica. Paravisini-Gebert suggested
early in my research that I look at Dominican newspapers of the
late nineteenth century. Nicholls wrote in them, and was written
about: here is the story of how a British white male professional
was immediately accorded high status in the colony. The papers
are of course also an excellent source for imagining the Dominica
into which Rhys was born.

15. Interview with Elaine Savory, Oxford, 1995.

16. Part of the reason for a campaign of criticism against Williams
was no doubt his role as a nominated member of the Assembly.
But there clearly was much to complain about in Williams having
manoevred to live in Roseau where there were already two doctors
but where more income was potentially available from private
patients. Doctors on Government salary, like Williams and Nicholls,
were seen as being employed by the Government in political terms
as well as medical (see 'Carpe Diem' the column in the *Dominica
Dial*, Saturday, 10 July 1886, where Dr Nicholls is said to be 'more
completely at the mercy of his employers than a Treasury porter'.)
The *Dominica Dial* 'Carpe Diem' columnist felt indignation that
Williams should have been appointed to the Board of Health, and
felt this was due to political connections.

17. An anti-British feeling was common in editorial attacks on white
immigration in the 1880s. For example, in the column 'Carpe Diem',
24 December 1887, 'The Hour Before the Dawn', the British were
thus described: 'The classes rule under the fiction of representing
the people, and the masses throughout the Empire are made to pay
the piper for the classes, both directly and in bloated salaries to
useless aristocrats and indirectly in the odium everywhere attached
to British rule by the imbecile ne'er-do-well relatives, distributed
throughout the Empire on the principle of scattering raisins in a
pudding, and dubbed euphemistically a civil *service*.'

18. Rhys's story 'Again the Antilles' (first pub. 1927) portrays Papa
Dom, the editor of the *Dominica Herald and Leeward Islands Gazette*,
as feisty columnist who gets into an exchange in the pages of
the paper with an Englishman, Mr Musgrave. The tone of this is
exactly that of the Dominica papers of the years just before Rhys's
birth and during her young childhood. Papa Dom was, as Sue
Thomas points out (1996a), a historical figure, A. Theodore Righton,

who owned and edited the *Dominican* from 1880 and was one of a group of intellectuals of colour active in political life in Roseau.

19. The persistent feeling in the liberal press in Dominica was that the doctors who came to Dominica were substandard. Williams was attacked virulently, sometimes directly and sometimes by association. For example, in the 'Carpe Diem' column of the *Dominica Dial*, 31 January 1885, it was asserted that the Colonial Office sent out doctors on a first-come, first-served basis, some of whom had bought their diplomas, though there were some brilliant exceptions. The pay of 'imported medical staff' was absurdly high and the Governor had divided the island into inappropriate medical districts, too difficult to get around quickly. Even in Roseau, the same men who sat on the Assembly, with 'benevolent anxiety' for the health of the poor, would not get to their poor patients quickly.

20. For example, the 'Carpe Diem' column 'A Good Man Gone Wrong', Saturday 10 July 1886, attacked Nicholls, provoking his 17 July long reply, which was clearly directed at the political motives of the *Dial*'s owner/editor William Davies, 'intoxicated with the success of your party, you have imagined you are ever to be the dictator of the people'. Two more 'Carpe Diem' responses and another reply from Nicholls continued through the month of July, including a sharp comment from the 'Carpe Diem' column of 24 July that Nicholls's letter of the previous week had used the 'personal pronoun no less than forty-four times'. Nicholls offered his political manifesto for the coming elections, including 'All Englishmen are peculiarly tenacious of their rights . . . I share in that feeling' (24 July 1886).

21. Sue Thomas points out (1996b: 1) that the editor of the *Dominica Dial* in the late 1880s to early 1890s was William Davies, 'organiser in 1880 of the Party of Progress which rapidly filled the elective positions in the Legislative Assembly'.

22. Lennox Honychurch points out that by 1905, when Governor Hesketh Bell left Dominica, the island was much improved: by 1901, the Treasury showed a surplus, something 'unbelievable in Dominica' (1984: 115). It was in 1904–5 that new colonists arrived to take advantage of Bell's settlement scheme along the Imperial Road. Honychurch also points out that between 1900 and 1914, agricultural revenues improved greatly. However Williams made his money again by 1910, his status then does not disprove he might have had difficulties in the late 1890s.

23. The Roseau house and the mango tree are still there today, though the house is a small hotel: there is a sign on the mango tree which acknowledges that Rhys lived there.

24. I was able to follow the family's route from Massacre to Bona Vista through the agency of Mrs Patricia Honychurch. It is a journey which enormously helps to locate the original landscapes.

25. Angier notes that 'His mother was Dutch . . . John always said his father, Jean, was French . . . and John's elder brother has a French name too . . . the truth seems to be that their father was Dutch . . . though his family had been Walloon, French-speaking Belgian' (1990: 103). See Kappers-den Hollander, (1982; 1987; 1988; 1994); Angier (1990: ch. 4) for a detailed account of Lenglet's life and literary collaboration with Rhys.

26. Hubert Devonish (1986) argued against the introduction of Standard Creole on the grounds that students should be able to speak and write in the classroom as they do outside: however Rhys's construction of Creole as a narrative voice is a very general, as we might say standardardised, Creole, non-specific enough to be understood widely, without evident local features, but acceptable to middle-class readers in the Caribbean. Perhaps the most influential term coined to describe Creoles is Kamau Brathwaite's 'nation language', which is best explained in his own words: 'the language which is influenced very strongly by the African model, the African aspect of our New World/Caribbean heritage. English it may be in terms of some of its lexical features. But in its contours, its rhythm and timbre, its sound explosions, it is not English, even though the words, as you hear them, might be English to a greater or lesser degree' (1984: 13). Each Caribbean territory has its own unique nation language.

27. In later life in England, Rhys had a generic middle-class British voice, but she sang West Indian songs for Selma Vaz Dias, which are on tape in the Tulsa Collection, and these show her to have retained a capacity to sound West Indian even in old age.

28. I refer here to the incident of Rhys, drunk and frail, having a problem managing the toilet and Plante's shamefully detailed story of this, tacked unconvincingly onto his general construction of himself as responsble writer and friend, with Rhys's encouragement to him to tell the story.

29. Lenglet was evidently a complex man: he was both careless about important paperwork and willing to live on the edge of legality (nationality papers, transactions in the aftermath of war) and a man of conscience and courage in opposing Fascism, to the point of seriously risking his life and probably damaging his health permanently (Angier 1990). His relation with Rhys after their marriage was over was clearly one of affection and support as well as literary association, but there were underlying tensions as well: perhaps it is

best understood in terms of the contradictions of Lenglet and Rhys. See also chapter 3.

30. Rhys's letter to Leslie's daughter Phyllis Smyser is an important source here (*L*: 36–8). In this, Rhys tries to explain how difficult it was to get help for Leslie as there was no phone in the isolated cottage in which they were living. But in her comments about 'wanting to be there at the last', as he was cremated, and 'the feeling Leslie had *escaped* – from me, from everyone and was free at last', (*L*: 37) there is a strong hint of the underlying stresses of the relationship, despite the evidence of their mutual affection. It is typical of Rhys that she would include in a letter the precise words which give this away, just as in the fiction, she confronted damaging and difficult aspects of personalities and relationships.

31. Early women writers in the Caribbean include English expatriates such as Lady Nugent or Mrs Carmichael. *Lady Nugent's Journal of her Residence in Jamaica from 1801–1805* (1839; 1907) and Mrs Carmichael's *Domestic Manners and Social Condition of the White, Coloured and Negro Population of the West Indies* (1833), as well as native-born writers such as Jamaican Mary Seacole (1857) or Mary Prince, who has been attributed with writing a slave narrative (1831). See O'Callaghan (1993) and forthcoming ed. Paravisini-Gebert on women travellers to the Caribbean.

32. Maurice Hewlett (1939): see Angier (1990: 60).

33. This assertion of Rhys's may be held alongside the apparent evidence of her knowledge of the ending of Joyce's *Ulysses* (1922), at the end of *Good Morning, Midnight*. A section of Joyce's *Finnegans Wake* was published in *the transatlantic review*.

34. Such as V. S. Naipaul, Sam Selvon, George Lamming. This continues to this day. Contemporary writers may have migrated as child or adult, for example, in Canada, Nourbese Philip, Pamela Mordecai and Cecil Gray and in the United States, Jamaica Kincaid, Glenville Lovell, as well as Olive Senior, who lives between Canada and Jamaica.

35. See Preface, note 4. Also Rhys made a comment in a letter to Francis Wyndham (27 November 1969), that there was some talk of *Quartet* as a play, but that 'it seems the ending isnt suitable – thats one thing'.

36. In a fragment of manuscript about old age and memory, 'I'm very often plagued . . .' (UTC), she complained of the way a 'scrap of poetry or prose' would sometimes haunt her: 'At present, it's "the chase had a beast in view" – a line of poetry obviously but when or where I read it I don't remember.' From the evidence we have of written-out poems among her papers, it is clear she deeply engaged

with poetry and also wrote it from an early age: in *Smile Please*, she describes being 'assaulted' by both English and French poetry. The latter remained a life-long pleasure. In a letter to Francis Wyndham (1 May 1964) she speaks of poetry as 'my first and last love and my refuge –'. See also chapter 2.

37. Rhys died before she approved for publication final sections of the manuscript: Diana Athill included a good deal of this material in *Smile Please* in a separate section.

38. There is as yet little substantive comparative analysis of Colette and Rhys, so Nora Gaines's work will be especially welcome.

39. Rhys commented 'I like this very much. It has helped me' above a passage copied out in French in her own writing from Colette's *Mes Apprentissages* (originally published 1936; 1973: 216). It is particularly interesting as Colette celebrates 'l'art domestique' as teaching her many important skills, rather than writing. But these skills, which include complex reconstruction and recollection, are of course enormously important in the writing process. Ultimately, this all has to do with a shifting but vital enjoyment of living. Not only was Rhys unusually resistant to 'l'art domestique', as evidenced by comments in her letters, but if there is a single major difference between herself and Colette, it lies in the fact that Rhys's texts manifestly lack expression of joy in living. But somehow, of all the fascinating passages Rhys could have found in Colette's memoir of her writing apprenticeship, this piece caught her imagination.

40. The draft notebooks are not necessarily fully grammatical or coherent, as they were, like all writer's journals, private spaces in which notes, hints and drafts for fiction interconnected with rough material closer to personal experience and diary form.

41. In a long letter to Diana Athill (1 December 1966), Rhys discusses republication of the stories in *The Left Bank* and her responses to them, 'I suppose La Grosse Fifi is the best. Yes the self-pity is too blatant & perhaps one could give the girl another name. Roseau is too obvious.' She was eventually to submit meticulous corrections or, in the case of 'Vienne', a substantial rewrite, to some of the early stories for their reissue in the volume *Tigers Are Better-Looking* (1968) (see chapter 8).

42. Rhys was in England from 1928. Mizener (1971) dates the ending of the affair with Ford as 1925. Angier thinks Rhys eventually left France in October 1927 and lived with Lenglet and Maryvonne in The Hague until early 1928. Later in 1928, she began to live with publisher's reader Leslie Tilden-Smith in England and subsequently married him.

43. This was as complex as her other self-constructions: to Francis Wyndham she wrote, in response to his repetition of the BBC's

*Radio Times*'s description of her as both Welsh and Scots, 'I am not a Scot at all. My father was Welsh – very. My mother's family was Creole – what *we* call Creole. My great-grandfather was a Scot' (*L*: 172). Taken together with her hostility to Anglo-Saxon culture and identity, it seems she saw herself as a Celt in the UK (her father's mother was Irish also); always as Creole in the West Indies.

44. See Angier (1990) for the story of Rees Williams's sense of being marginalised by his father, though favoured by his mother. As for Rochester, his sense of displacement from his father's affections as second son in conjunction with his training to suppress complex and disturbing emotion, contributed to his capacity for self-justifying cruelty.

45. The following passage in the BEB indicates how closely Rhys chose to stay in her final versions to much of her original drafts. The reductive common sense of her mother was eliminated when Rhys finally used this material: 'Its extraordinary of [sic] growing up in a very beautiful place & seeing it was beautiful [*here an erased phrase*] It was alive. I was sure of it. To me it was a austere ['*was a austere*' *lightly erased*] behind the bright colours was something very wild [*written above*: the softness grace] austere sad entirely male. I wanted to identify with it to lose myself in it but it turned its head away indifferent & it broke my heart. And yet something came near it. Sometimes Id think I understand the language the water speaks – It was so intolerable this longing this sadness I got from the shapes of the mountains, the sound of the [river?], the moment [*here an indecipherable word*] after sunset that one day I spoke of it to my mother & she at once gave me a large dose of castor oil' (my interventions in italics).

## 2  REGISTERING PROTEST: *THE LEFT BANK* AND *QUARTET*

1. This is a hidden agenda in Rhys's surviving accounts of her life in Paris: Angier has uncovered what probably happened to Maryvonne during her early years but it was certainly for Rhys a private issue which she never explored in her writing.

2. As Angier (1990) notes, it included characters called Ella and John (Rhys and Lenglet's names) and diary material including Rhys's marriage, and 'about Vienna, probably about Budapest, possibly right up to the present day' (1990: 130): some of this eventually contributed to the evolving of 'Vienne''s various versions. Angier speculates that Mrs Adam might have had a 'secret taste for romance' (1990: 130) which predisposed her to trying to help Rhys to place her rough manuscript.

3. She also states that 'one of the first people to see it' judged 'Triple Sec' 'unpublishably sordid' (1990: 130).

4. In relation to the subtitles, Rhys said that Mrs Adam divided the manuscript into parts and gave each one a man's name (*SP*: 125). But actually it is titled by both male and female names: 'Book xi' has sections titled 'Lady Marjorie' and 'An Air Raid'. This manuscript is one of the last of Rhys's major unpublished documents to be generally available for scholarly examination: its rough state and Mrs Adam's intervention seem to suggest Rhys would not have wanted it to be counted amongst her finished work, although of course much unfinished draft such as the BEB has been available for some years, despite containing very personal narrative such as the Mr Howard story.

5. Angier notes that Rhys gave Leslie Tilden Smith's daughter Anne a 'chic and expensive' black dress, 'she'd bought with money from Ford' (1990: 233), so evidently the little black dress became an icon of identity for Rhys as well as for her protagonists.

6. It is worth exploring this comparison further as an example of the intertextuality of this draft novel and Rhys's mature work. Guy's letter begins 'My dear Kitten – / This is a very difficult letter to write – for I shall hate hurting you and I'm afraid I'm going to do it. / It's about Tony. / He is very unhappy, my dear because there is somebody he loves and wishes to marry and he is afraid to tell you so' (p. 26). He goes on, 'Tony is still very fond of you but he doesn't love you like that any more. After all you must have known it could not go on for ever – These things don't, and you must remember, Kitten, that he is nearly twenty years older than you are' (p. 26). In *Voyage in the Dark*, Vincent's letter begins 'My dear Anna, / This is a very difficult letter to write because I am afraid I am going to upset you and I hate upsetting people' and goes on 'Walter is still very fond of you but he doesn't love you like that any more, and after all, you must always have known that the thing could not go on for ever and you must remember too that he is nearly twenty years older than you' (*VITD*: 92–3). The texts are remarkably similar, but the emendations which Rhys made for the finished novel show a surer grasp of the rhythms of Vincent's plausible charm and evasiveness. In 'Triple Sec', he fumbles 'Love isn't everything. – / In fact people make a jolly sight too much about love, I think' (p. 26). In *Voyage in the Dark*, this reads 'Love is not everything – especially that sort of love – and the more people, especially girls, put it right out of their heads and do without it the better' (*VITD*: 93). The change makes Vincent the more unpleasant because he sounds more authoritarian and crisp. The final

version of the letter is longer, and overall more tightly constructed to feed into the reader's growing apprehension of Walter's cowardice and Vincent's indifference to Anna's youth and emotional condition.

7. It is interesting to speculate on the contribution that her attraction to poetry and her desire to write out of personal experience whilst protecting large areas of her own privacy made to this early writing instinct.

8. For example, in Ford's novel *The Good Soldier* (1983; first published 1915), some details of appearance are similar to Rhys's own use of colour as code: 'The head waiter, a man with a face all grey – in what subterranean nooks or corners do people cultivate those absolutely grey complexions . . .' (1983: 24). See for other references to 'slanting eyes' in Rhys's texts, chapter 3, note 20.

9. This echoes the Mr Howard narrative, where the protagonist claims some of the blame is hers, 'I only struggled feebly What he had seen in me was there all right . . . But the terrible thing was the way something in the depths of me said Yes . . . Pain humiliation submission-that is for me' (BEB).

10. I shall argue however that it is critically important in *Wide Sargasso Sea* and also in the descriptions of Roseau and Dominica in *Voyage in the Dark* and *The Left Bank*.

11. It is important that Rhys's heavily edited translation of Lenglet's French manuscript was published first (1932) thus defining the novel for subsequent translations. It appeared in Dutch (1932) and French (1933).

12. Martien Kappers-den Hollander's 'Measure for Measure: *Quartet* and *When the Wicked Man*' (1988) explores the question of whether Ford sought vengeance in his novel not only on Rhys herself (as the lurid character Lola), but also on Lenglet. The numerous small details which resonate to those who know Rhys's work show Ford to have had some malicious fun: the title of Rhys's unpublished novel MS, 'Triple Sec' is one of the pieces of dead stock in the publishing house Notterdam, the central character, owns and, as Kappers argues, many elements of Lola's character are parodies of Rhys's protagonists. Ford's portrait of Lola Porter begins 'Creoles are as noted for their indolence as for their passion. On that basis, she became entirely comprehensible . . .' (1931: 192) and goes on to include a description of her and another woman, 'when they were near each other, they moved elegantly, much as he had seen waterspouts do in the Caribbean Sea. They talked . . . about banana or alligator pear plantations; about rum-manufacturing in Martinique where one was born and the other had visited long enough to

exhibit an intelligent interest' (1931: 193). But the novel has little interest now except for serious Ford and Rhys scholars.

13. That is, the exercise of translating a sentence into French to see if it still worked.

14. See Angier (1990: 164) on the anger Rhys felt towards Ford, as well as Ford's desire that she should get the credit for her work (the wrong attribution was a mistake, not deliberate). One of Ford's biographers, Arthur Mizener (1971), mentions Rhys as the translator of Carco's novel, whereas another, Alan Judd (1990) has no mention of this connection.

15. There are however some evident connections. Colette is fond of using a touch of colour to good effect, 'I've thrown my blue scarf over the lamp' (*Recollections*, trans. David Le Vay, 1972: 7; first published in French in 1922). Colette has, like Rhys, the economy and depth of a good poet and she can be tart and devastating, also like Rhys: a young man is insulted by a young woman and becomes enraged, 'He bent foward, bit the beautiful cheek' of his companion and 'bore her away, newly branded, like the elect heifer of the herd' (1972: 67). Colette's women and men however enjoy the sensual pleasures of life much more readily, and with a certain grace: 'Delicious deception, his back watches me, his neck listens to me, his care envelops me. O great man who has remained generous, continue to hold my hand, lay on my cheek your own rough cheek, shaven at dawn, when you say goodbye . . .' (1972: 249). It is clear that Colette was a strong influence on Rhys, however (see chapter 1, note 44).

16. It is enjoyable to trace Rhys's topography of Paris on an old map of the city current for the 1920s: Rhys was accurate as to the selective geography of both Paris and London relevant to her later fiction.

17. The novel was reissued as *Quartet* in 1929 in the USA. *The Saturday Review of Literature* reviewer (1929) is a good example of early responses to Rhys's texts, calling the novel 'beautifully articulated' and a 'close-knit study of mordant personality' (Mellown 1984: 11). Angier (1990) comments that the worst and best reviews of the novel began a trend in critical response which remained always evident, i.e. they stressed the sordid themes and or the excellence of the craft.

18. Their definition of modernism is however particularly appropriate in relation to Rhys: they argue that women writers shared 'that feature of early twentieth century *Zeitgeist* in which the traditional chasm between life and art is breached, so that experimentalism and autobiography become inevitably enmeshed and the aesthetic drives impelling the transformation of literature also power the need

to live anticonventionally' (1987: 7). Benstock (1987) includes considerable discussion of Rhys in her study *Women of the Left Bank*.

19. There is an important collective rereading of modernism in Caribbean, African and Indian literatures in English, where the trauma of colonialism and racism fractures identity and a sense of home and belonging. Rhys belongs to this neo-modernist canon even more than she does to the European version.

20. This was Mrs Richard Hudnut who lived in Chateau Juan-les-Pins (Angier 1990: 148–9).

21. The 1924 version is by far the shortest, just a few pages which however include the opening Rhys preserved for the subsequent two longer versions. In 1924 and again in 1927, Rhys used subtitles for sections of the narrative: she abandoned these in the final version (*TAB-L*, 1968). In 1924, the narrator's partner was called John: this section 'The Spending Phase' refers to the phase during which Jean Lenglet was making considerable sums of money in Vienna in the early days of the marriage, 'Don't worry' said John, 'soon I will pull it off and we will be rich, rich' (1924: 644): a revised version of this section survives but John is renamed Pierre in both the 1927 and 1968 versions. He is less important in 1927 as just one of a number of important characters such as Lysyl, André, Tillie and Colonel Ishima, who are each given a section somewhat in the manner that 'Triple Sec' is organised into sections, with male or female names, or in this case also sometimes thematic titles heading them. But in 1968, the narrative line of the relationship between the narrator and Pierre becomes again dominant. There were considerable other changes between the 1927 (*TLB*) and 1968 (*TAB-L*) versions. Rhys moved the 'War Material' section further forward for the 1968 version, thus creating an effective sense of contrast. The last paragraph of the opening section now opens 'Pretty women, lots', and Colonel Ishima's comment on Viennese women as 'war material' begins the next. Rhys inserted a couple of lines for the 1968 version ('"The innards of the hanimal, sir" said the waiter tactfully. All the Viennese waiters talk the best Cockney') which show her anxiety to have the last version flow more easily from moment to moment, but with enough detail to convey the scene in its complexity. In 1968, 'merde' (*TAB-L*: 190) was able to be printed whereas in 1927, it had to be suggested 'M—' (*TLB*: 211). Rhys omitted some passages which meandered somewhat in the 1927 version (e.g. *TLB*: 199–200; 215–20, 221–2), producing a tighter narrative for the last published version of the story (*TAB-L*).

22. This should be read against Alvarez's 1974 comment that Rhys had no 'ideas to tout' (see chapter 9).

23. See Angier (1990: 114–19) for an account of the relation of 'Vienne' to Rhys's biography. However, Angier makes one of her most indefensible fusions of autobiography and fiction in Rhys's writing when she comments about the first published version of 'Vienne': 'And in everything they do and everything they say, John is utterly John, Ella utterly Ella' (1990: 119).

24. Though *Wide Sargasso Sea* can be dated fairly accurately (the immediate post-Emancipation period).

25. Masking was a very important linguistic strategy, as well as role-playing, during plantation slavery, when a slave's survival might demand both placating a master and maintaining a sense of personal integrity. Masking strategies in Caribbean drama, notably in Walcott's plays, are particularly important as they draw on this important historical experience in complex ways: masking can both strengthen and subvert stereotypes.

26. Alan Judd says of *The Good Soldier* that the theme is passion, rather than sex, 'a gaseous mixture of dream and desire, of deceit, of self-sacrifice fuelled by ego, of guilt, fear and affection' (1990: 32). *Quartet* is about these very same elements in human relationships and, as with the Ford text, sex itself is of marginal importance.

27. I use here the title Rhys herself gave to the relationship in a draft manuscript intended for *Smile Please* though not finally included.

28. Kappers-den Hollander states directly that de Nève's publication of ten stories in Dutch in his collection *Aan den Loopenden Band* (1934), some of them assembled from apparent rejected drafts for *Quartet* or *After Leaving Mr MacKenzie*, some translated crudely and very freely from *The Left Bank*, was 'a trespass of copyright laws and a case of plagiary' (1994: 6). Kappers-den Hollander points out also that in 1937, de Nève borrowed parts of *Quartet* for his own fourth novel, *Schuwe Vogels*, as well as in 1938, claiming he was co-author of *The Left Bank*, *Quartet* and *After Leaving Mr MacKenzie*. Maryvonne Moerman née Lenglet, daughter of de Nève and Rhys, told Kappers-den Hollander that her parents tried to help each other after their divorce, Rhys giving de Nève pieces he was to publish under his own name and he supplying her with ideas for fiction. Rhys however said forty years after *Aan den Loopenden Band* was published that she knew nothing of it.

29. It is clear that Rhys improved the original manuscript, and as Kappers-den Hollander points out (1982), Lenglet acknowledged this by permitting her version to become the basis for the Dutch version, as opposed to his original French manuscript. He praised her immensely as a modernist writer (1939), clearly generously perceiving her talent: perhaps he saw it as so much more than his own

that he was tempted to merge the two to his own benefit whilst supporting Maryvonne.

30. For example, as does Rhys's character Selina Davis in 'Let Them Call It Jazz' (1962; *TAB-L*), a West Indian woman trying to settle in London. She finds herself unable to honestly answer a woman who starts up a conversation: she knows 'they' (white British people), can be kept at bay if you know 'what to say' (*TAB-L*: 62), the discourse which protects, conceals and evades confrontation.

31. See discussion in chapter 6 on dreams.

32. Kincaid's protagonists, like Rhys's, have difficult relations with their mothers and are prone to be isolated as well as carrying a good deal of suppressed rage. See especially *Lucy* (1990).

33. In the sense that this protagonist is not the heroic victim of unjust circumstances who triumphs in the end, nor the feisty anti-hero who defies conventional social mores but is of good heart. Rhys sees the role of protagonist itself ironically, much more so than do many Caribbean writers. V. S. Naipaul's Mr Biswas (1961), for example, is ultimately heroic, as are many protagonists in West Indian fiction.

3  A CARIBBEAN WOMAN LOST IN EUROPE?: *AFTER LEAVING MR MACKENZIE* AND THE QUESTION OF GENDER

1. Reviews of *After Leaving Mr MacKenzie* in 1931 tended to recoil from the subject matter and praise the style. The *Yorkshire Post* (4 Feb. 1931), did acknowledge the novel unusual in English fiction, but compared it favourably to French fiction. American reviewers similarly were anxious about the theme but found the craft of the novel outstanding. Several reviewers remarked that any less artistry would have made the novel impossible to read, given its story. In 1972, with the American reprint, reviewers found the novel was entirely contemporary for them. The feminist interest in Rhys is somewhat ironical given her own denial of the term for herself (see chapter 1).

2. Most notoriously by Carole Angier. The biographical school of Rhys criticism is important, though great care needs to be taken in the relating of Rhys's texts to her life.

3. Davidson, along with most of the other male critics on Rhys, reflects, understandably, a serious attempt to understand a woman writer without abandoning male assumptions about women common in the culture in which he writes. Pam Johnson, a clearly feminist writer, makes the point that 'the underworld of female relationships' is the most interesting aspect of Rhys's work: though the terms Johnson uses seem too positive to describe many of the

complex female–female connections in Rhys, 'kindness, disinterested generosity, love' (1980: 41).

4. A quick survey of famous novel protagonists in English, such as Tom Jones, Moll Flanders, Robinson Crusoe, Oliver Twist, David Copperfield, will indicate how prevalent was the assumption that a hero would make resourceful choices to defeat his or her troubles and arise eventually above them, usually to find both emotional and economic rewards. But a reviewer of *After Leaving Mr MacKenzie* in *The New York Times* (1931) used the title 'Twice-as-Naturalism' and related the novel to Flaubert's work.

5. Rhys's reuse of the image from Charlotte Brontë of the madwoman in the attic and Gilbert and Gubar's choice of Brontë's image as emblematic of the nineteenth-century woman in their first book (1979) made her particularly appropriate for this discussion.

6. Nebeker (1981) argues that the name Anna suggests Rhys was in touch with ancient Celtic mythology, since Ana (Irish) and Anna (Celtic), are both names for goddesses.

7. Thomas (1994–5) points out that under English law, the age of consent for indecent assault was thirteen; for carnal knowledge, sixteen.

8. O'Connor cites the childhood nightmare described in the BEB as evidence of Rhys's sense of the evident failure of her mother to protect her and the fact that she feared telling her mother about Mr Howard's abuse of her.

   Rhys's account of her mother's beating of her in BEB is connected to Rhys's sense that her mother saw something 'alien' in her which she was trying to root out. Rhys saw violence as informing Dominica, emphasised by her nurse Meta's phrase 'tears of blood': all these references in the BEB are connected and juxtaposed with a reference to the dramatic scenery of the island. Rhys then mentions the religious frames of her childhood, much of which eventually would inform *Smile Please*, and then the Mr Howard narrative begins. The moment of resistance to her mother was clearly important: Rhys records that her mother stopped beating her when she screamed 'God curse you, if you touch me I'll kill you' ('Fears' UTC). There is a poignant line in a draft beginning 'I WAS THE YOUNGEST . . .' (UTC) which suggests great sympathy towards her mother however (and may be related to Julia's moment of empathy with her mother dying in a strange country in *After Leaving Mr MacKenzie*).

9. See, for example, Marshall (1959); Hodge (1970); Brodber (1980); Kincaid (1985); Collins (1987).

10. In this context, Vincent's comment, 'How's the child? How's my infantile Anna' (*VITD*: 80) is very significant.

11. Sue Thomas notes that 'Rhys summarizes part of Sigmund Freud's account of his renunciation of his seduction theory of hysteria in 'On the History of the Psychoanalytic Movement' (1994–5: 67).

12. See also chapter 5.

13. See Plante (1984: 52): 'I don't think I know what character is. I just write about what happened. Not that my books are entirely my life – but almost.' This is of course somewhat ironical in the light of Rhys's substantial reordering and reconstituting of raw experience into fictional narrative, which does indeed take imagination and inventiveness. A draft 'I FEEL so sick . . .': UTC seems half-way between autobiography and the fictional rendition of the relation between Anna, her emotionally inhibited English lover and England itself.

14. Also Daphne Agar, in an interview with me (January 1995) insisted on the same scepticism, though the suggestion persists.

15. Howells links her in this project with other modernist women writers such as Woolf but unlike them, she does not provide her heroines with a new way to triumph or move forward.

16. Rhys understood very well that oppressed people carry suppressed violence in response to their oppressors. The newly freed slaves in *Wide Sargasso Sea* are not tractable and free of the emotional damage done them in slavery, but resist anything they think an infringement of their rights very strongly. So, too, Rhys was aware that women were not ideal, but capable of both aggression to their oppressors, and, again in common with other oppressed people, lateral aggression towards each other.

17. There is quite a bit of information about Rhys's mature relations with her family in Angier (1990): this makes evident that Rhys was not close to any of the women in adult life.

18. Meaning *Voyage in the Dark* and *Wide Sargasso Sea*.

19. I use the plural identity here because I think Naipaul has moved closer to being a British writer in recent years.

20. Marya in *Quartet* has long almond eyes. The reviewer of *After Leaving Mr MacKenzie* in *The New York Herald Tribune* (1931) referred to Julia as a long-eyed, alcoholic woman; indeed perhaps these are the two very evidently identifiable elements of Rhys's characterisation of Marya.

21. Rhys defined poetry as 'words that sing' ('Poetry and Poets', UTC): in that sense her fiction was largely poetry. Reviewers and critics have often recognised poetic elements in her fiction: *Good Morning, Midnight*'s title comes from an Emily Dickinson poem, 'Good morning, Midnight!'.

22. Le Gallez (1990) offers a reading of Rhys's narrative strategies as progressively more sophisticated: the ironical third-person voice

in *Quartet* becomes the alternative viewpoints of *After Leaving Mr MacKenzie*, the single first-person narratives of *Voyage in the Dark* and *Good Morning, Midnight* and the shared first-person narrative of *Wide Sargasso Sea*.

23. Indeed the ideal of needing identity reflected as in a comforting kind of mirror is important throughout Rhys's fiction. Howells uses the term as a verb, 'mirrors' to suggest that art reflects a different truth from personal experience (1991: 66). See Gregg (1990) on *Wide Sargasso Sea*; Lawson on Lacanian constructions of the mirror and identity-formation in relation to Rhys (1991); Leigh (1985), among others.

24. For example, in a letter (22 October 1951) to her daughter: 'But oh dear the middle way respectable ones – they can be the devil- . . . *Everyone must be exactly alike*' (*L*: 89).

## 4 *VOYAGE IN THE DARK*: THE POLITICS OF COLOURS

1. Wolfe (1980) identifies the Rhys palette as follows: yellow-grey signifies despair and yellow fear (*CSS*: 175); blue is dominant in both *Quartet* and Ford's *The Good Soldier*; the 'dusty pink dress' in 'Let Them Call It Jazz' is important. Angier (1985) notes the importance of the colour of clothes to Rhys in the *Smile Please* passage about being taken to shop by her aunt and the 'yellow-grey' sky of Cambridge as signifying no hope; James (1978) cites Alec Waugh on the intensity of green in Dominica and mentions Rhys's Caribbean sense of brightness; Nebeker (1981) thinks blue and white patterns in Rhys reflect a spiritual feminist identity; Curtis (1985) explores the significance of the black dress embroidered in bright colours in *Good Morning, Midnight*.

2. In *Quartet* and *Good Morning, Midnight*, Paris is also sometimes depressingly dull or dark-coloured in Rhys's spare descriptions.

3. In West Africa, dark green and sometimes a touch of red can signify rituals associated with death, as well as white.

4. In *What Colour Are You?* (1981), Bek and Wilson, both women, define love of violet as indicating artistic ability, appreciation of beauty and spiritual introspection, and indigo suggests the power to heal. But colour symbolism is evidently culturally specific. The Luscher Colour Test (1971) shows evident European racist overtones: black is the 'No', 'the absolute boundary at which life ceases and so expresses the idea of nothingness, of extinction.' In this code, white is 'Yes'. Purple, according to the study, is only preferred by emotionally immature people, children, 'Iranians, Africans and Brazilian Indians' (1971: 71). This amazing travesty of the impact of colour (how

would they explain the love of purple by Roman emperors, for example), may be contrasted with African-American Alice Walker's complex emotional landscape in *The Colour Purple* (1982). Rhys's use of purple tends to be associated with intense apprehension of nature and life in the Caribbean and with other bright, rich jewel colours. For example it appears as an element in glass windows, whether in England ('Let Them Call It Jazz', *TAB-L*: 167) or the Caribbean, (*VITD*: 43); as rich, slightly overwhelming flowers, (*WSS*: 19), and as an element in Aunt Cora's counterpane (*WSS*: 56). Lois, Heidler's emotionally confused wife, has a purple dressing gown in *Quartet* (*Q*: 105).

5. Brown is virtually absent from the Rhys palette as associated with her protagonists, though they are all to a greater or lesser extent rootless and dispossessed: a further proof of the arbitrariness of trying to universalise colour codes.

6. Rhys is able to explore race subtly through the use of oblique references. At times she includes a small detail which indicates the terms of racial discourse of particular locales in her lifetime. For example, the man known as 'Michel the nigger, a former soldier of fortune' is an off-stage, minor reference in *Quartet* (*Q*: 135–6); Miss de Solla in *Quartet* has 'the Jewess's hunger for the softness and warmth of life' (*Q*: 9). Rhys's own casual use of language reflected the common speech of the time in England, where such a phrase as 'slaving away' was unremarkable: it does however seem ironical when Rhys uses it about her own work (Letter to Peggy Kirkaldy, 11 July 1957). She commented she looked 'coal black' in a 'terrible' photograph (letter to Francis Wyndham, 5 January 1970): another casual British usage which has racist overtones. Rhys once said she 'felt negroid'.

7. Apartheid was first established as an explicit government policy in South Africa in 1948. The 1960s saw sustained resistance from the black majority as well as some white and mixed-race activists. Rhys's own attitude to race was complex, (see also chapter 1). She thought in old age that whites in Dominica of her time were misunderstood, 'so much abused, so lied about . . .' ('When I think of my parents . . .', UTC).

8. Rhys gave Marya in *Q* blonde hair and very pale skin (and long eyes slanted up to her temples – a significant detail). Heidler notices her face as strange at one point, seeming to have higher cheekbones, wider nostrils and thicker lips than before, '[a] strange little Kalmuck face' (*Q*: 131), a detail which connects Marya to stereotypes of racial otherness, reinforced by Heidler calling her 'savage' (*Q*: 131). By contrast, Heidler's eyes do not seem to suggest he is an outsider.

9. Perhaps Rhys's account of her childhood assessment of herself as inadequately coloured, 'fair with a pale skin and huge staring eyes of no particular colour' (*SP*: 14) is one important source of this connection. Rhys saw her siblings, brown-haired and brown-eyed, as a group and herself as 'singled out' for the hated fairness. But Rhys's stepdaughter Anne remembered Rhys as prettily coloured, with green eyes, white skin and reddish-brown hair (Staley 1979: 13).

10. Rhys's protagonists are of different ages: Anna and Antoinette being very young, Anna still a teenager, Marya in her twenties, Julia in her thirties and Sasha in her forties. Rhys went on to create old women protagonists in her later stories and essays.

11. See chapter 1 for a discussion of the similarity between Colette's memory of her beginnings as a writer and Rhys's.

12. 'I like it best, most of all my books' letter to Olwyn Hughes, 23 June 1966.

13. Anna's family name is of course Welsh, like Rhys's own.

14. Southron (1935) describes Anna as having to move through scenes of 'sordid greyness'; Soskin (1935), believes (incredibly) that 'wantons' should stay away from Rhys's novels as they may tempt 'the fog of passive unconcern, the half-conscious repudiation of all the moral virtues' (n.p.). By contrast, reviewers in the late 1960s, after the novel's reissue, saw it in relation to feminist advances and were more willing to accept the subject matter.

15. Rhys thought Laurie quite intelligent and complex by contrast with Maudie. Anna was less worldly than either. In a letter to Selma Vaz Dias, Rhys wrote of Anna, 'This girl is an innocent. Really without guile or slyness. Why should she live to be done in again over & over again?' (Friday 30th [no month] 1963).

16. Zola's research on the relation between science and literature, and his journalist's training suggested he was capable of accurate observation: he thought writers should record rather than imagine (Holden 1972). But clearly his portrait of Nana reflects his own prejudices and judgements about sexual mores and gender identities more than it does any accurate observation.

17. Le Gallez (1990: 85) suggests an echo of Chaucer's 'gap-toothed' Wife of Bath, with her wide spaced front teeth suggesting lasciviousness, but I am not convinced of this. It seems to me more to indicate the prevalence of poor dental treatment and care in Britain, which has long been evident in the working class, and which Rhys may well have observed: a missing tooth is not the same as wide-spaced healthy teeth.

18. Gilman also details the genital abnormalities supposedly shared by Hottentots and prostitutes and set out in various nineteenth-century

studies. He points out that Picasso, who was so influenced by African art, 'saw the sexualised female as the visual analogue of the black' (1985: 232).

19. Zola's *L'Assommoir* told the story of Nana's mother: both Nana's parents being alcoholics. Nana has begun her sexual career by the end of this novel. Gilman argues that Zola's Nana is influenced by Manet's reading of Zola's earlier version of Nana in *L'Assommoir*.

20. See Hulme and Whitehead, eds. (1992) for a history of Carib encounters with Europeans, including a number of accounts of determined Carib resistance to colonisation or, in the first days, fierce reaction to discovery of European treachery. Massacre, the fishing village north of Roseau, where Rhys's family would turn up a hillside track to go to their estate at Bona Vista, was named for a massacre of Caribs. In the late seventeenth century, (and I take this account from Honychurch: 1984) the Caribs had to work out their relationship with various European colonisers. Indian Warner, the son of Sir Thomas Warner, English Governor of St Kitts, and a Carib slave woman from Dominica, fled to Dominica after his father's death and his English stepmother's hostility. He became chief of the Dominican Caribs and also was made Deputy Governor of Dominica by the English, to whom he had given military assistance against the French. But the English were divided about Carib support. Eventually, the Governor of the Leeward Islands, Sir William Stapleton, responded to Carib raiding of Antigua in 1674 by a punitive expedition led by Indian Warner's half-brother Philip. Accounts differ as to Indian Warner's death, but the French said Philip betrayed his brother and massacred his people, giving the signal for his men by killing his own half-brother. Whether this is true, or there was an accidental drunken killing of Indian Warner which provoked Carib revenge on the English and an English massacre of them, surely the name Massacre, and the fact that Caribs died there, must have lodged in Rhys's imagination.

21. The text is inconclusive at this moment. Clearly Anna has lost both parents, as she refers to her father in the past tense and her stepmother is evidently widowed. But in the original version of the ending, there are several references to Anna's father having the blue lips which signify heart disease, and we know of course that it was Rhys's father who died suddenly after she had left Tree's School and was defiantly pursuing her life as chorus girl (Angier 1990: 49, 53). O'Connor (1986) comments that Anna's father's death and her identification of Walter with her father dominate chapter 5. On the other hand, the memory of wearing a white dress, white gloves and having to both carry and wear a wreath suggests a young child

attending a funeral, in Dominica, and this would concur with Kloepfer's reading of this as the mother's death (1989: 72), if we presume this would have occurred much earlier in Anna's life. Rhys commented in a letter (to Sonia Orwell, 16 June 1974), that 'White is so very nice to look at I think. In the sun.'

22. See chapter 8.

23. Pictures are metaphors in Rhys's texts, frequently reflecting popular culture and conveying a subtext of cultural commentary as well as a character's indiosyncratic response.

24. Thus confirming the absolute synthesis of fiction and personal essay or autobiography which Rhys created from the rough material which was her experience. See chapter 8.

25. In the original version of *Voyage in the Dark*, this passage reverberates along with Hester's criticism of Anna speaking 'Exactly like a nigger' (*VITD*: 65) and Uncle Bo's comments on the Carnival to indicate the racial discourse which was commonplace among whites. In *Smile Please*, the passage is more dislocated and suggests the protagonist is responding individually as opposed to reflecting the general level of racial commentary carried on between whites and blacks.

26. The description of this journey does not quite match the route from Massacre to Bona Vista (see chapter 1), but no doubt contains memories of Rhys's childhood journeys on horseback.

27. Satirical representations of white faces are common in various Nigerian mask traditions, for example.

28. The reference to the ray of light is strongly related to the memory of yellow light coming in through the jalousies at home in the Caribbean (*VITD*: 31). Incidentally, the yellow and black detail here is reflected also in the yellow-black face of the photographer in *Smile Please* (*SP*: 13) (see also REB opening passage titled 'The High Wall').

29. The complexity and subtlety of Rhys's narrative is essential to its effect: Rhys realised when she saw the television version of the novel done by the BBC in 1973 that if such complexity was reduced for dramatic effect the story became a 'tract really'. She complained that the BBC version was 'very moral', so that 'Poor Anna never even got a drink and Walter seemed a bit bored and bad tempered' (letter to Francis Wyndham, 14 October 1973). She blamed herself for the name Walter which would easily suggest pomposity. But in the end, what she was seeing was that with the complex verbal patternings removed, the novel lost its subtlety and interest: the same damage was done to *Wide Sargasso Sea* in the full-length film version (Fine Line Features, 1993).

5   DANGEROUS SPIRIT, BITTERLY AMUSED:
*GOOD MORNING, MIDNIGHT*

1. Marya is left injured and possibly dead; Julia is at least in danger of emotional and spiritual death; Anna in Rhys's preferred draft actually dies; Sasha sinks into a deathly kind of sexuality; Antoinette, we believe, will throw herself off the roof of the burning house.

2. Of course Europe had been in spiritual and moral trouble for several centuries, given the slave trade and colonialism, as well as the exploitation of the poor at home, but that had not generally been understood.

3. Even Stella Bowen, Rhys's natural enemy, thought Rhys to have 'a needle-quick intelligence and a good sort of emotional honesty' even though she also thought 'she was a doomed soul, violent and demoralised' (1984: 166). Bowen, Australian born, went to England at the age of nineteen after her mother died (she had lost her father at the age of three). Her beginnings thus have something in common with Rhys's own: she however was willing to make considerable compromises in her private and professional life to stay with Ford, which must have given her a strong sense of Rhys's far more risky but independent spirit.

4. Her attention to the reduction of language as a spiritual medium is clear in a page of draft manuscript for *Smile Please* where she complains that language doesn't seem as rich as it used to be and that she is alienated from new usage because she feels the new words are often ugly. She loved words, but in old age she lost interest in new English colloquialisms.

5. Rhys's scraps of draft manuscript are often revealing in terms of her finished texts. One brief passage reads:

   it is much nicer to think things because then nobody contradicts you and you can feel like God because you feel you are Right. God is a lucky person but I don't think he has sense of humour.
      Anyway who wants to be God. Living with the sense of a hell of a failure. And blaming it on a Snake.
      Id [sic] Eve hadn't done what she did, what fun would we have?
      And God knows everything. He must have known about Eve and that apple, long before it happened. But he was celver [sic] about it. So we blame the devil. God must be definitely BRITISH. He's got all the characteristics of the finest type of English gentleman.
      ('But it is I don't want to write anything' [sic], UTC).

6. See, for example, 'A Spiritualist' (*SIOL*, 1924; *CSS*) and 'I Used to Live Here Once' (*SIOL*, 1976; *CSS*).

7. Contemporary religions which descend from these beliefs or reinterpret African heritage in a similar way include the Shango cult

in Trinidad which reinterprets Yoruba ritual, Rastafarianism and Pocomania.

8. All three of these writers have made important reference to African-centred ritual and religious observance which expresses an oppressed people's desire for secure grounding of self in communal strength and integrity. See, for example, Brathwaite's *The Arrivants* (1973), Scott's *Echo in the Bone* (1985) and Brodber's *Jane and Louisa Will Soon Come Home* (1980).

9. In a number of important West Indian texts, such as George Lamming's *Season of Adventure* (1970), a character is brought to confront his or her opposition to African ritual and comes to be aware of its liberating effect in the face of colonial pressure towards a constricting and alienating set of mores based in European mores.

10. Rhys's written record of her response to religious concepts, language and behaviour ran the whole range through her life from intensely devout to sceptically witty. She described herself as having a 'sort of agnosticism' ('But of course I have often longed for the happiness . . .': UTC); as superstitious (letter to Sonia Orwell, 2 July 1969) But this document seems to express her personal reading of Catholic morality as applied to her life and might have an element of expiation, the hope that confession might restore the writing gift.

11. (in the same letter to Stoner), 'I've told them I was not an authority . . .'

12. See also chapter 1.

13. Ghosts were important in Rhys's self-construction as well as in her texts, and so are frequently mentioned. In *Smile Please*, she described sleeping 'as if dead' after the ending of the relationship with Lancelot Hugh Smith (*SP*: 97). *Smile Please* ends with a ghost story, in effect. Rhys wrote to her friend Peggy Kirkaldy that she had tried to work on an article about English Harbour in Antigua, 'I dont know about the ghost' (1 March 1949).

14. Angier dates this 1952 (1990: 460) whereas Rhys's note above the piece in *Smile Please* dates it 1947.

15. Frank Swinnerton (1939) thought the central plot line similar to *After Leaving Mr Mackenzie* and the novel 'not for optimists' though the craftsmanship exceptional. Despite the fact that he thought it was Rhys's 'misfortune that she so brilliantly achieves the effect she intended' (1939: 614), John Mair found the novel 'quite remarkably impressive'. Hilton Brown found the whole novel 'macabre' (1939: 106) but easy to read. Linda Talbot (1967) praised the details of a woman's life in the novel as well as the imagery: in the 1960s, feminism helped the novel find readers.

16. All these critics are concerned with the connection between the atmosphere in Rhys's novel and the climate immediately before World War II in Europe, and Emery especially provides a reading in which fascism is important. Her construction of the father figure in Sasha's dream, for example, signifies the paternalistic aspect of fascism, its violence and its suppression of women. Horner and Zlosnik (1990) also point out that women were clearly disadvantaged before the law in France in the late 1930s.

17. Howells (1991) specifically discusses the novel as 'female modernism', critiquing male domination of society in general and women in particular.

18. The description in *Smile Please* of Rhys lying in the hammock at Morgan's Rest (*SP*: 67) is interesting alongside this passage as well as *Wide Sargasso Sea*.

19. There is a strong tradition of subversive humour in West Indian common speech, especially in Trinidad and Tobago. Walcott's play *Pantomime* (1980) is an excellent example of a literary version of this. Sam Selvon's fiction, and the oral performance of Paul Keens-Douglas and the late Bruce St John are all major examples of the use of humour for entertainment but also for social observation and political commentary. Phyllis Allfrey remarked to Ramabai Espinet that Rhys had a great sense of humour (1993).

20. In a letter of 9 November 1949 to Selma Vaz Dias about the adaptation of *Good Morning, Midnight* for performance on radio, Rhys said that in that sort of shabby Montparnasse hotel, the drinks came up with a waiter, the breakfast with a chambermaid. She says it would have made the minor male character too important to have had him announce the name Pecanelli, as opposed to the reductive Pig and Lily.

21. The BEB (probably mostly dating from 1938: see Angier 1990), contains the Mr Howard narrative, and an early draft of the passage about Enno (GMM: 129–30). O'Connor (1986) comments that Rhys portrays Dominica as an Eden with Mr Howard as the snake who introduces dangerous knowledge and ultimately, by implication, exile and death. It is interesting that the BEB contains both material from *Good Morning, Midnight* (the passage about Sasha's husband is evidence of her ability to love someone) and the Mr Howard narrative. Both deal with the dangers of sexual adventure for a woman vulnerable to the power of men and money.

22. David Plante records Rhys asking him to write down a poem which she couldn't get out of her mind: 'Two hells have I/ Dark Devon and grey London – / One purgatory: the past –' (1984: 34). Once he had recorded it, she said, 'Thank God, now I can forget that'.

23. Tarozzi (1989) and Angier (1990) have pointed out the importance of dreams in *Good Morning, Midnight* and how these look forward to *Wide Sargasso Sea* and back to *Voyage in the Dark*. From her published and unpublished texts, we can see Rhys was quite contradictory about the value of dreaming, which seemed to her both childish and immensely powerful, even to the point of seeming to be God (which is how she characterised the book as a child).

24. Alcohol is not only an agent in the novels and stories, but also in Rhys's accounts of her life. It was clearly a factor at times in the drafting of certain difficult material, indicated by dramatic hand-writing changes and occasionally by Rhys's own comments in the notebooks.

25. See Emery (1990) for an extensive discussion of this in relation to *Good Morning, Midnight*.

26. She only very gradually acquired some of the basic technological supports, and often took help, from her husband Leslie Tilden Smith, for example, in typing manuscripts. Quite late in life, she still had no phone or television, and at one point, even a radio was out of her reach.

27. I use the term anarchism here because it best describes Rhys's individualistic resistance to centralised authority of all kinds.

28. Whether the *commis* wears a blue or white dressing gown is significant: both are ambivalent in Rhys's palette, signifying both positive and negative associations: both the possibility of a perverse kind of redemption for Sasha in her reaching out to him from her usual negation of human connection and a damnation resulting from intercourse with the Devil seem caught within the symbolism of the colours.

29. See chapter 6 for a further discussion of locations in Rhys's texts.

30. The happy moment is on the landing outside her room, in darkness. She sees a lighted cigarette and calls out 'Qui est la?' (*GM, M*: 177), just as the parrot is fond of saying in *Wide Sargasso Sea*. This small repetition, as with many other details of Rhys's style, links Rhys's texts together.

31. Critical opinion has often noted the relationship of this line to Joyce's and this has helped to make the case for Rhys as modernist. Harrison (1988), Gardiner (1989), Emery (1990) and Gregg (1995) all explore *Good Morning, Midnight*'s relation to modernism. In this novel Rhys revisions modernism as a Caribbean woman: Emery argues interestingly that the ending may signify Sasha's 'renewal of identity with other "poor devils" ' (1990: 170).

32. I am grateful to Elizabeth Wilson for reminding me of the similarities here.

6  PEOPLE IN AND OUT OF PLACE: SPATIAL ARRANGEMENTS IN
   *WIDE SARGASSO SEA*

1. Major approaches to the novel include feminist readings of content and/or narrative form: (Blodgett (1981); Scharfman (1981);
   Tarozzi (1984; 1989); Knapp (1986); Hemmerechts (1987); Kloepfer
   (1989); Summers (1985); Harrison (1988); Spaull (1989); Le Gallez
   (1990)); post-colonial readings (often also feminist), most notably
   Tiffin (1978), Spivak (1985), Anderson (1982); Smilowitz (1986); Gilkes
   (1987); Saakana (1987) Fayad (1988) Friedman (1989); Guiness (1989).
   Historical–cultural analyses include Hulme (1994); Ferguson (1993
   a and b); Gregg (1995). Comparisons with other fiction are quite
   common: D. H. Lawrence, Herbert de Lisser (Higdon 1984); Margaret Drabble and Doris Lessing (Nelson 1987); Naipaul (Thieme
   1979); *Macbeth* (Little 1996); Faulkner (Accaria 1989). Psychoanalytic
   readings include interest in Freud (Harrison 1988; Blais 1993) and
   the Lacanian mirror in Rhys (Lawson 1991); see also Koenen (1990);
   Schapiro (1994). The mirror image figures importantly in Joseph
   (1992). Some readings stress the novel's modernism: Emery (1990);
   Holland and Meyers (1983). Ashcom (1988) argues that there are
   two modernisms within Rhys's work, one associated with the 1920s
   and Joyce and one with the 1930s and Hemingway: Rhys's early
   texts belong to the 1930s and *Wide Sargasso Sea* to the 1920s. For
   Caribbean critical approaches to the novel and ensuing debates see
   chapter 2. For comparison between Rhys and Allfrey see Campbell
   (1978); Williamson (1986); Paravisini-Gebert (1996). For a discussion
   of French identity in the novel, see Barber-Williams (1989); of Rhys's
   construction of Creole, Todd (1995). For the novel's Gothic character, see Allen (1967); Luengo (1976); Nollen (1985). For discussion
   of variant extant manuscripts see Webb (1988). Many of these readings make no attempt to locate Rhys's text in the Caribbean.
2. *Wide Sargasso Sea* provoked some interesting reviews and articles
   early on. Howard Moss (1974), in a survey article on Rhys's work,
   thought the novel the most dramatic and the least significant of
   Rhys's texts, because Rhys's strength is in what precedes action or
   madness. Phyllis Allfrey (1967) preferred the Dominican scenes in
   the novel to those set in Jamaica. Allfrey's novel *The Orchid House*
   appears to have inspired Rhys and to have given her the names
   Christophine and Baptiste (Paravisini-Gebert 1996: 270–1).
3. Central to much of this has been the issue of the degree of dependency which Rhys's text has on Brontë's (Porter 1976; Thorpe 1977;
   Clara Thomas 1987; Staley 1979; Nebeker 1981; Codaccioni 1984;
   Oates 1985; Spivak 1985; Kubitshek 1987; Harrison 1988; Givner

1988; Friedman 1989; Angier 1990). Rhys herself worried at times about writing 'just another adaptation' (*L*: 159), and yet was also aware of 'what I lose by cutting loose from Jane Eyre and Mr Rochester' (*L*: 271). She was on the one hand admiring of *Jane Eyre* but on the other irritated by it (Givner 1988). She believed Charlotte Brontë disliked West Indians, and of course that her version of Bertha, the mad Creole wife, was absolutely wrong – the springboard into *Wide Sargasso Sea*. Rhys thought of her idea of Rochester as connected to Emily Brontë's character Heathcliff in *Wuthering Heights* but the Gothic intensity of Heathcliff is far from the mundane emotional limitations of Rhys's Rochester.

4. Some aspects of the story of Annette and Coulibri seem to be imaginative renderings of bits and pieces of family history about Geneva Estate and the Lockharts. Rhys said in a draft for *Smile Please* that she tried to write about Geneva in *Wide Sargasso Sea* ('At first I knew remarkably little . . .', (UTC). From another fragment of draft, it is clear that Antoinette's experience of finding England cold and dark was also Rhys's own ('When I went from room to room . . .' UTC) As with Antoinette. Rhys found 'the place I live in is terribly important to me . . .' (*SP*: 135).

5. See also, as tangentially relevant, Bowlby's discussion of the term 'impasse' at the beginning of *Good Morning, Midnight*; Horner and Zlosnik's *Landscapes of Desire* (1990), in which the term 'marooned' is extensively discussed, in relation to the Sargasso Sea and the becalming of ships as well as Antoinette and her family. They and Nebeker (1981) think Coulibri is particularly important, a Garden of Eden.

6. All Rhys's previous protagonists exist in rented rooms in cities in which they endure emotional trauma. Details of particular rooms are always important in a Rhys text, for those details contribute importantly as economical directives to a character's condition.

7. See, on *Good Morning, Midnight* Byrne (1985).

8. Annette's slightly foreign identity and her long black hair suggest Rhys's 'Spanish' great-grandmother (see Angier 1990).

9. In this language is a crucially important factor. There is surprisingly little discussion of Rhys's rendering of Creole except for that of the linguist Todd (1995). Every Caribbean writer since the early colonial period has grappled with the problem of how to capture the ever-evolving, highly creative continuum from African-informed, multicultural Creoles to international English (or French, Dutch or Spanish) which characterises Caribbean speech. Much linguistic creativity in the Caribbean is oral, not written, and there is little yet in the way of standardised grammars or handbooks of usage. Therefore every major attempt to create a written Creole is important,

achieved by writers such as Bruce St John, Kamau Brathwaite and Austin Clarke (Barbados); Samuel Selvon (Trinidad) and Louise Bennett (Jamaica), not to mention the many dub and calypso artists whose lyrics are often strikingly ingenious. These writers however work out of Caribbean community and hear Creole every day. Rhys had only her memory, and it is the more remarkable that her version of Caribbean language is still convincing to Caribbean readers today.

10. The Maroons were a community of escaped slaves who took to the hills in Jamaica (and elsewhere). In Jamaica, they eventually achieved a separate state, in effect, giving hope to the oppressed all over the region. But maroonage, or living apart from an indifferent and cruel society in order to survive, is at a general level what Annette and her family experience.

11. Erica Waters (formerly Smilowitz) has suggested to me that perhaps Antoinette herself caused the fire by letting her candle burn down. But it seems to me that the fire began at the moment when a chair seemed to fall over in the little room. Myra, who has abandoned her post of protecting Pierre, might be the culprit, or just the accident of the candle falling over. Once the small room is on fire, the crowd outside is quick to add to it.

12. Obeah being a focal point of colonial hostility because it was also a focal point of alternative cultural identity and resistance.

13. See, for example, *Voyage in the Dark*, where Anna feels cold as Walter approaches her by talking about her being a virgin (*VITD*: 36).

14. See, notably *Voyage in the Dark*. Pictures of various kinds are important in *Good Morning, Midnight* and *After Leaving Mr Mackenzie* and in *Quartet*, the symbolism of wallpaper design is significant.

15. Rhys utilised manuscript draft in interesting ways, often taking a small portion of draft out of its original context and inserting it brilliantly into a long narrative. Her corrections of the manuscript for the *Art and Literature* excerpt from the novel, published 1964, show her characteristic attention to details of sentence construction and nuances of meaning. This focus on writing itself moved her far from original experience.

16. This detail is one among many which connect the novel intertextually to *Jane Eyre*, over and above its theme and plot. A red room is important in Jane's young life, Jane Eyre feels like a spirit when young, and dreaming is significant. There are also many references to slavery and some to persons of English nationality and dark complexion, the mention of witchcraft and the use of French at times in the text.

17. Raiskin argues that Rhys's construction of the *zombi* transcends race and economic position: even white men can be *zombis* in the

sense of their inability to change the system or themselves. Though a little too strongly stated, this is an interesting idea. Rhys marginalises men in all her texts, but more so in *Wide Sargasso Sea* where Rochester seems powerless and therefore turns to cruelty and brute force to mask his weakness. Mr Ramage in 'Pioneers Oh, Pioneers' (*SIOL*, 1976) is explicitly called a white *zombi* and hit with a stone by a hostile member of the crowd which gathers outside his house: this seems to have triggered his appearance with his gun.

18. See O'Callaghan: Bliss was born in 1903 in Jamaica. Her novel (1934, reprinted 1984) depicts white Creole society in Jamaica. See, for Allfrey's response to *Wide Sargasso Sea* and the novel's intertextuality with *The Orchid House*, Paravisini-Gebert (1996).

19. By this I mean that even where a Caribbean person is not of mixed race, there is such a range of cultural influences which meet and recreate themselves syncretically that to be Caribbean is to be multicultural. Trinidad and Tobago's strong African, Indian, and among European, English, French and Spanish influences, make it especially so. Dominica has Carib, African, French and English influences. But the region is African in predominant identity: Africa is here syncretic, complex, multivalent, but the overall creative space.

20. An obvious play on Thomas Hardy's novel *Jude the Obscure*. Rhys often spoke about place in her letters, e.g. mentioning putting up a sign in her house, a Cornish saying, 'Remember the rock from which thou was hewn' (letter to Selma Vaz Dias, 1964).

21. Angier (1990) offers a lot of information on the cold, damp summer cottages which Rhys and her husband Max rented in the winter, and about the small cottage which Rhys's brother Edward finally bought for her in 1960.

22. Even today, Dominica's lush vegetation stuns the eye. No other Caribbean island has so much wild and luxuriant plant life.

7 BRIEF ENCOUNTERS: RHYS AND THE CRAFT OF
THE SHORT STORY

1. She arrived at first publication in the company of major literary figures, an amazing piece of good fortune, but also her work stands well beside theirs.

2. The majority of this work dates from the 1980s, clearly benefitting from not only the post-colonial cultural climate but from the Caribbean women's movement.

3. It is tempting to suggest that there is an ancestral relationship with African languages behind these forms, since tonal languages can

play with signification in highly complex and inventive ways whilst being very economical.

4. 'Nation language' is Kamau Brathwaite's evocative term for each of the Creoles which are spoken in different Caribbean territories. See *History of the Voice* (1984).

5. Rhys acknowledged the ritual opening of a Caribbean folk tale in *Smile Please*: 'Francine would say "Tim-Tim". I had to answer "Boissêche", then she'd say, "Tablier Madame est derrìere dos"' (*SP*: 23). Later, Rhys discovered Boissêche is one of the gods worshipped in obeah. Anancy stories crossed the ocean from the Ashanti culture of what is now Ghana and became 'Nancy stories' in the Caribbean. MacDonald-Smythe (1997) compares the narrator's opening ritual address and the audience response at the beginning of stories in St Lucia, Trinidad and the Bahamas, and mentions Rattray's excellent bilingual version of the original Anancy stories, *Akan-Ashanti Folktales* (1930) as containing a formal narrative opening addressed to the audience.

6. In a letter to Francis Wyndham (8 July 1959), Rhys notes the need to find a new name for a character in 'Till September Petronella' as the name she chose for her original draft is too close to her present married name of Hamer. She likes the idea of Marston (which she used in the final version), but wants some reassurance as to whether this is a good name for a painter.

7. Even after the Alvarez article in 1974, which praised her highly, Rhys wrote to Oliver Stoner (16 August 1974) that she had written a number of stories 'of varying merit'. She wrote him on 29 July (no year) that 'Rapunzel Rapunzel' was not quite to her liking, and again on 15 September (no year) that the stories were to be published in October (as *Sleep It Off Lady*, 1976), but that she thought 'only a few are any good'. Ironically, given her own early exercises in translation, she found the French edition of *Tigers Are Better-Looking* better than her own original (letter to Oliver Stoner, 3 November 1969). But her judgement was often right: she would keep a story for years, considering it inferior or unfinished and we have one draft manuscript 'Chinese Vases' (UTC) which is an example of a piece which was never finished: it has the hallmarks of a Rhys text, but is indeed not up to her usual standard. It was based on a difficult experience of needing to sell two Chinese vases supposedly brought by Max Hamer, her husband, from China (letter written to Peggy Kirkaldy, 28 May 1950). The sale was necessary because of Max's conviction for fraud. The draft manuscript story is dated 20 March 1974. However it is important to bear in mind that Rhys even thought she'd 'slipped up' at the end of

*Wide Sargasso Sea* (letter to Diana Athill, 3 January 1967): in that case she was certainly wrong.

8. Rhys was seventy-eight when *Tigers Are Better-Looking* was published but had lost none of her stylistic perfectionism. Her correction lists for 'La Grosse Fifi' and 'Vienne' run to four pages: they note tiny flaws she wanted eradicated, like the word 'bulging' because it was used too often.

9. Bailey commented that Rhys is unsentimental, a detached artist who denies herself any indulgences, so that especially her later writing is 'a deliberate paring down by a novelist of wide-ranging gifts' (1968: 111). Jebb says 'Few living writers are as gifted in their use of language as Jean Rhys' (1968: n.p.) Haltrecht (1968) saw that any 'novelettish' quality in the plots of the stories was turned back by Rhys's vision and voice. Sullivan noticed the extremely funny quality of many of the stories, 'without taking a single step towards the artificially comic' (1968: 549). A few critics were not impressed (for example, Higgins 1968), but for the most part *Tigers Are Better-Looking* enjoyed intelligent and perceptive praise.

   Bailey thought *Sleep It Off Lady* had a unity not apparent at first reading (1976: 1321). Sullivan noted her theme of growing old, detachedly and ironically observed (1976); Clapp (1976) thought the astringent tone of Rhys's writing saved her from self-parody; Hall (1976) enjoyed the precision of the small details which give depth to short, plain sentences. Most reviewers were genuinely supportive and took the time to notice specific details of Rhys's achieved style or themes: the only reservations tended to be about stories which seemed fragmentary, not much plotted and without varied characterisation. Wood (1976) accused Rhys of occasional sentimentality: she took great pains to guard against it.

10. Critics coming to the selection of *The Left Bank* stories in *Tigers Are Better-Looking* in 1968 often praised them. Baker (1968) thought the early stories had great vitality. Jebb (1968), like other reviewers, thought the author of both *The Left Bank* and the *Tigers Are Better-Looking* stories evidently the same woman.

11. Notably Gardiner (1989); Le Gallez (1990); Howells (1991); Gregg (1995); S. Thomas (1994; 1996a).

12. On the whole, Rhys's stories have been thought less than her novels, but she did complete a number of very fine short pieces, placing her idiosyncratic signature on the form: Malcolm and Malcolm's study is very thin (1996) but clearly by focussing on the stories alone delcares them to be as major an issue in Rhys's achievement as the novels.

13. Of the stories collected here which were not in *The Left Bank*, 'The Sound of the River' is an evident fictional version of experience,

i.e. the death of Leslie Tilden Smith, Rhys's second husband. The comparison may be made between the story and Rhys's letter to Phyllis Smyser, Leslie's daughter, 10 October 1945 (*UTC*) (Angier attributes this letter to Anne, Leslie's other daughter).

14. The very reason we have so many drafts from Rhys's later period is the fact that she needed typists who generally preserved each draft. Rhys herself threw manuscripts away, including the first full manuscript of *Wide Sargasso Sea*. However there are important early drafts of 'The Lotus' and 'The Insect World' in the OEB.

15. Angier (1990), for example, likes the story, but perhaps this is because she is impressed with the autobiographical honesty which informs the character Petronella.

16. In various drafts it is 'breasts' or 'breast', finally being 'one very small breast'.

17. Antoinette in *Wide Sargasso Sea* dreams she follows a man into a forest.

18. The REB contains a draft version of the story. It opens with a letter to 'Elsie [deleted] Ina' about Jimmy Longa. Elsie and Ina's exchange of letters continues to discuss Longa's story. Here the little girl who cries because of him is called Rosalie (the name given to the little girl in 'Dear, Darling Mr Ramage' which became 'Pioneers, Oh, Pioneers'). The GEB has a draft beginning of 'Pioneers, Oh, Pioneers'.

19. Her first book *Shape-Shifter* (1990) established Melville as a deft story-teller with an acute ear for different Caribbean and English voices. Melville was born in Guyana and moved to Britain in childhood.

20. In this long letter, Rhys says Holloway really 'ought to be bombed' and speaks of the women she met, some of whom she liked. She also mentions a song she heard at Holloway 'that haunts me' and that she felt she should write but nobody would want to publish it: indeed she did write about the Holloway song, and this story is one of her best: Lennox Honychurch, in conversation with me, suggested this is her version of Selvon's classic *The Lonely Londoners*. Most of her stories, like her novels, were painstaking revisions of her life: in a letter to Francis Wyndham (5 July 1964), she mentions her best friend in the village is a Sikh who sells women's clothes door to door and who appears in the thinly fictionalised story 'Who Knows What's Up In The Attic', (*SIOL*), a version of a visit paid to Rhys by Jan van Houts (see Frickey, ed. 1990: 28–34 for van Houts's version of the encounter).

21. She questioned this title in a letter to Francis Wyndham (27 November 1969), thinking, briefly, of 'Labour Lost' but she fortunately retained her first title. 'Temps Perdi' was not included in either of

Rhys's two later collections. It was first published in *Art and Literature* (1967) and was then chosen for *Penguin Modern Stories* (1969).

22. See *After Leaving Mr MacKenzie*, quoted chapter 4, where the butterfly is a fragile victim of the protagonist's immaturity.

23. Hulme and Whitehead (1992) include this section of the story, titled 'Visit to the Carib Quarter' in their anthology *Wild Majesty: Encounters with Caribs from Columbus to the Present Day*, marking thus the closeness of the piece to personal essay.

24. I mention this because it seems to me that by mining Rhys's fiction for biography to quite the extent that she does, Angier obscures the delicate continuum between Rhys's experience, developing drafts, personal essays and distanced fiction.

25. The interaction of books and experience, of books and Caribbean landscape, is significant also in *Wide Sargasso Sea* and *Smile Please*.

26. A letter survives in the Tulsa Collection from Leslie Tilden Smith to a member of his family which makes this connection clear.

27. Rhys wrote four wartime stories which remain to us: 'Temps Perdi', 'The Solid House', 'The Insect World' and 'I Spy a Stranger'. The last, like the first here, was published in *Penguin Modern Stories* (1969) and not in either of the two late collections.

8   PERFORMANCE ARTS: THE THEATRE OF AUTOBIOGRAPHY AND
     THE ROLE OF THE PERSONAL ESSAY

1. See, for information about West Indian theatre and drama: Stone (1994), King (1995) and for a wonderful account of the history of calypso, which has developed its own theatrical language, Rohlehr (1990).

2. The only Phyllis, apparently, close to Rhys would have been Leslie Tilden Smith's daughter.

3. There are numerous letters from the period of high publicity for her, after the success of *Wide Sargasso Sea*, in which Rhys frets about or dreads impending photograph sessions or discusses how particular photographs turned out. Her response to Ander Gunn's series of portraits of her (letter to Olwyn Hughes, 5 June 1967) is particularly revealing. Rhys liked some, but said 'one in particular . . . makes me feel quite ill. / The cheeks are puffed out & the eyes very small, the smile is so forced that its simply pitiful. / What is worrying me so much is that this is one you seem to like – Why?'

4. Letter to Francis Wyndham, 20 June 1967: 'I have got two by Ander Gunn rather sad and wrinkled but I like them very much and am trying to get copies.'

5. There are many references to proposed dramatisations of Rhys's texts in the period after *Wide Sargasso Sea*. What Rhys once wryly called 'The Adventure of the Drunken Signature' (the agreement she made to pay Selma Vaz Dias 50 per cent of all royalties from any dramatic adaptation of Rhys's work anywhere in the world, as well as giving Vaz Dias sole artistic control over them) which subsequently caused immense pain to Rhys, see for example letter to Oliver Stoner (5 September 1969) and was somewhat revised in Rhys's favour (Angier 1990: 500–1), followed Vaz Dias's shrewd early recognition of the theatrical possibilities in Rhys's texts well before *Wide Sargasso Sea*. On 17 October 1969, she wrote her agent Olwyn Hughes about 'a man called Patrick something or other' to whom she had given *Quartet* for three months to see if he could make a play out of it. In the same letter she mentions Dutch television's dramatisation of 'Let Them Call It Jazz', and a contract for *Good Morning, Midnight* to be made into a film. There are many more references in the Rhys papers to such projects, most of which came to nothing but which are evidence of the interest in dramatic potential in Rhys's work.

6. See James (1978: 13): 'Music hall itself was to shape her particular art. She took over its juxtaposition of fantasy and tawdry reality; she used its motifs and rhythms to orchestrate her fiction . . . Indeed there was a relationship between musical form and Jean Rhys's composition of prose.'

7. She herself wrote the lyrics for a George Melly song, called 'Life With You' (UTC). The poems typed out and left among her papers include calypsos, late Romantic lyrics and a good deal of French poetry, as well as Rhys's own poems, (often songs), some of which were eventually published. She said poetry was her first love and told Francis Wyndham of her use of poetry to restart *Wide Sargasso Sea* when it was giving her trouble (*L*: 261–6). See also letter to Francis Wyndham, 1 May 1964: 'went back to poetry, my first and last love & my refuge'.

8. Rhys, in her usual way, altered the sentence from draft to draft. In what I take to be the earliest drafts, she wrote 'All my life I have been haunted by popular songs', and then revised this to 'I have been haunted by popular songs all my life'.

9. For example, 'Let Them Call It Jazz', 'Overture and Beginners Please', 'Invitation to the Dance'.

10. Among the most interesting comments in reviews of *Smile Please* is Helen McNeil's remark that the work is a 'stylistic and narrative coda' to the fiction, since the life was already written into the fiction (1980: 254). Samuel Hynes's view that all of Rhys's work is 'played

on one string' (1980: 31) unjustly narrows her range. Ronald Blythe's sense of *Smile Please* as 'slight, initially rich and finally sketchy' (1979: 789) responds to the increasingly terse sections which conclude the first section. Rose (1985) thinks *Wide Sargasso Sea* more of an autobiography than *Smile Please*: an interesting conclusion.

11. Warner's novel *Indigo* (1992) rather unsuccessfully tried to mine her West Indian ancestry and retell the Caliban story from the point of view of Miranda.

12. The majority of reviewers thought the volume excellently edited and a major source for Rhys scholars, though several commented on the bitterness of many of the letters, and Gornick (1984) on Rhys's 'monumental' self-absorption.

13. Indeed it is because of this involvement that we have so much in the way of drafts from *Smile Please*: the awkward symbolism of this material being largely lodged in the Plante Collection in Tulsa, a few feet from the Rhys Collection, however reinforces Plante's claim to have been deeply involved in the actual construction of the book.

14. Evidently connected to the little black dress which is so important to Rhys protagonists: clothing as icon is important in many Rhys texts.

15. This episode should be connected to Rhys's racial self-rejection described in *Smile Please* (see chapter 1). In the draft of the passage which describes her childhood dislike of her fairness, she says, 'I thought only dark people were beautiful. I hated my white face': the directness of this is excised from the final draft.

16. The major exercise books which have survived (Black, Green, Red, Orange), contain fragments of drafts which are easily recognisable, as well as longer narratives like the Mr Howard story, which were mined less evidently for the most part. The newest one to be released, the OEB, contains quite a bit of material suitable for the personal essay as Rhys ultimately began to conceive it: opinion informing personal experience. She writes in the OEB: 'There is not one truth there are all sorts of truths./ yes but they dont admit it.'

17. Some passages are scratched out, but not sufficiently to hide very personal responses to the traumas of Max's trial and Rhys's own skirmishes with the law when drunk (see Angier 1990: 438ff). It is clear from these that Rhys resented her brother and sister for their response to her own behaviour, with the suggestion they thought her mad. Angier remarks that this essay was 'the hardest thing Jean ever wrote, because it was without the mask of fiction' (1990: 464).

18. Many reviewers of *Sleep It Off Lady* simply take a good deal of the stories as straight autobiography.

19. See, for example, Rhys's letter to Francis Wyndham (Thursday 17 July): 'I will try to make Imperial Road into two stories and suppress all prejudice. But I can't suppress altogether what I felt so strongly even then.' Rhys's view was that Imperial Road was never published because it revealed her own racial prejudice (see also O'Connor 1992).

20. The UTC has ten versions of this story, working from what seems the original in a small red exercise book to typed versions which show revisions, some by Rhys herself and some by someone else. The newly released OEB also has what is presumably the original draft (UTC). The later versions of this are dated September 1974 and February 1975 and by February 1975 the final title has been attached. The process of revision shows Rhys's characteristic method of working, beginning with 'Just before my sixteenth birthday' (this draft is subtitled 'Two Tunes', the first working title for *Voyage in the Dark*) and working away from this clearly autobiographical fact. Even a conversational opening 'It must have been very cold that December for Camilla and I spent a lot of time . . .' is honed to the final version 'We were sitting by the fire in the small dining room when Camilla said "I hate my parents, don't you?"' A fairly lengthy description of the farewell dance which was given by Rhys's father for her is excised almost completely from the finished story, remaining as a short speech by the narrator offered to Camilla in response to her declaration of hostility to parents: 'I don't hate mine. They gave a farewell dance for me before I left.' Some of the discarded material from the original notebook draft would become a source for the section of *Smile Please* which describes Rhys's first arrival in England, though Rhys reworked the material considerably. Her method of work can be seen also from the extant drafts of 'Before the Deluge' (first called 'Daisy'), also in the UTC.

21. Reading these pieces one after the other demonstrates the common texture they share which separates them from Rhys's fully fictionalised stories. 'My Day' and 'Making Bricks Without Straw' (first published 1978; Frickey, ed. 1990) are very evident personal essays on old age which are unusually frank. 'Whatever Became of Old Mrs Pearce' became 'Close Season for the Old?' which with 'My Day' and 'Invitation to the Dance' was published by Frank Hallmann (1975). But even the stories most distant from Rhys's own experience have a texture which differentiates them from the translations/adaptations she did of Jean Lenglet's stories, 'The Chevalier of the Place Blanche' (one of the original stories Rhys translated to try to sell to Mrs Adam), (*SIOL*) 'Vengeance' and 'The Poet' (both UTC).

22. By this I mean that the process of creating character, dialogue and setting has displaced the original intimacy of the personal experience which lies behind it. A good example is the story based on the death of Leslie Tilden Smith, 'The Sound of the River' (*TAB-L*; *CSS*): 'If I could put it into words it might go, she was thinking' (*CSS*: 236).

23. The UTC has seven draft versions of this piece, the last dated 24 March 1974.

24. The racial element is frank: Rhys expresses her colonial distance, romanticism and general suspicion that she was being set up or laughed at, or resented, because she was the returning white Dominican. When a centipede bites her, the narrator (Rhys) thinks a well-trained young servant girl is delighted. Since her husband likes the girl, the narrator says nothing.

25. See Honychurch (1984: 117–18) for the story of Hesketh Bell's project of the road as inducement for new settlement from Britain, the sixteen miles which were completed and which are still in use today, and the ultimate failure of the settlement scheme.

26. The detail with which the Richelots are described here is far more achieved as a piece of writing than the brief version which is published in *Smile Please*. Mademoiselle Richelot is a complex, lively character whose comments and insights are fully developed, whereas in *Smile Please*, she is a much less distinct figure. This draft is dated 1920–2 by UTC's catalogue. It contains a moving description of the Richelot family, 'half-Jewish – that's why I write this to pay a debt I can never pay', for their kindness to Rhys took place before the war and there was no contact afterwards (Angier 1990: 366–7). Ramabai Espinet says in her study of Rhys and Allfrey that Allfrey thought Maryvonne's husband came from a Jewish family. Rhys's attitude to Jews was complicated, as Angier's account of Rhys shouting anti-Semitic abuse during a drunken rage in public makes clear (1990).

27. From the letters we know of Rhys's wry attitude to her drinking bouts (for example letter to Sonia Orwell, 22 February 22 1968); and her relationship with Maryvonne, e.g. letter to Oliver Stoner, 14 June 1968, which summarises Maryvonne's involvement with the Resistance and also her father's and Rhys's pride at both; to Sonia Orwell, 14 November 1968, mentioning that Maryvonne doesn't have all her facts right about her mother and Rhys wishes she could explain; to Orwell, 3 May 1968, discussing Maryvonne's disapproval of her drinking, and describing at length the painful decision to let Maryvonne go to school in Holland and the consequences of the long separations.

28. Lizabeth Paravisini-Gebert's excellent biography of Phyllis Allfrey is an exception (1996).

9 'THE HELEN OF OUR WARS': CULTURAL POLITICS AND JEAN RHYS CRITICISM

1. Actually, there were four points to the transatlantic slave trade: the ships left from British ports with trade goods for West Africa, took the slaves across the Atlantic to the Caribbean, then took trade goods from the Caribbean to ports on the American east coast, and finally returned to Britain with trade goods from America: Rhys has not, as far as I am aware attracted much interest from African scholars on the continent, but British, Caribbean and American scholars have, in D'Costa's image, contributed greatly.

2. In Emery's definition, European modernism is redefined through both female and Caribbean lenses in Rhys's work and thus requires a reader versed in the subtleties which ensue.

3. Naipaul's own conflicted affiliation with the Caribbean, as with India, and his apparently less conflicted relation with British culture have produced resistance in Caribbean readers: this in turn appears to have made Naipaul the more aware of the ways in which racial and cultural identity are constructed. See, for Naipaul's notorious complaints about West Indian culture, *The Middle Passage*, where he says West Indian writers have mostly failed to do more than 'flatter the prejudices of their race or colour groups' (1969: 73). Naipaul has never been positive about African culture: his 'Michael X and the Black Power Killings in Trinidad' and 'A New King for the Congo: Mobutu and the Nihilism of Africa' (both 1974), show a concentration on the negative. He was savagely reductive about Black Power; outside the US, he thought it mainly 'jargon . . . a sentimental hoax' (1974: 73). When he wrote about Rhys, he connected her to a white tradition of British and Caribbean writing and self-construction.

4. Rhys can be productively read alongside other writers who, whilst they each have a unique complexity, share her transnational location, writers such as Jamaica Kincaid and Michelle Cliff. The question is which reading strategies are most productive, not only in terms of entering a text but also in terms of a self-reflexive reading strategy which permits the reader's complexities to be recognised. Homi Bhabha (1995) has warned against nativist claims for national culture since all anti-colonial cultural movements are essentially hybridised. However hybridity itself has no coherent identity, but is extremely unstable as a concept from place to place and time to time. Nor should it be permitted to inevitably marginalise self-definitions

which choose at a given moment to elevate one cultural identity above another. Feminism, for example, is an important reading, even whilst it ultimately needs to be put into conversation between a variety of positions based in race, class etc. It is such a complexity of interpretation which is most helpful for Rhys's texts and finds a major inspiration in the Caribbean's privileging of complexities of identity, both as separate and interacting with one another.

5. *Quartet* was Rhys's choice of title, but the novel was titled *Postures* only for British publication in 1928. See Angier (1990: 177).

6. Though the details of the relationship between Ford and Rhys after 1924–5 are hard to establish surely, we know Ford helped Rhys make connection with major British publishers and literary figures, such as Edward Garnett (Angier 1990: 230–1). But in the late twenties, Ford was very busy writing and travelling between Britain, France and America (Mizener 1971): Rhys left France, according to Angier (1990), for Holland. Ford's life with Stella Bowen was also over by early 1927 (Angier 1990: 172), and Angier wonders whether Ford and Rhys met again in Paris in 1927. Ford's *When the Wicked Man*, which satirises Rhys, was begun in late October 1928: *Postures*, i.e. *Quartet* appeared in September. See also Kappers (1987; 1994).

7. *The Left Bank* provoked less resistance: for example the *New Statesman* review (6 October 1928) thought the brevity of the stories helped emphasise the excellence of their style; the longer novel was not only less gripping but Rhys 'has no perception as yet of a beauty in life capable of dazzling her' (Mellown 1984: 8).

8. Where there is more than passing attention paid, it can be grossly parodic: 'The bewildered girl of eighteen, young for her years, uprooted from a tiny British West Indian island – she adored the hot tropical sun there and the warm-hearted blacks . . .' (Britten 1935: n.p.).

9. Lenglet and Rhys were in touch in 1939 as parents of Maryvonne and through their work, though Rhys was married to Leslie Tilden Smith and living in England and Lenglet was in Holland. Angier (1990) points out that in 1934, Lenglet and his future wife Henriette van Eyk published *An den Loopenden Band*, stories which owed a great deal to Rhys's own writing (1990: 288ff) and raise an important question as to whether Rhys knew or approved of such a use.

10. Angier goes so far as to say 'Jean had written her greatest novel so far and no one wanted to read it' (1990: 373). But when the novel was reissued in 1970, the women's movement had moved reviewers on to see its brilliance: Raskin (1970): 'Rhys was one of the first to begin decoding the secret message of female existence, and her

novel is an important emotional and artistic legacy for us' (Mellown 1984: 61).

11. In 1950, Rhys's solicitor husband Max Hamer was on trial for fraud and Rhys disappeared, according to Angier (1990) for most of a year. But she had been in touch with Selma Vaz Dias in 1949, when Vaz Dias tried to locate her for permission to perform an adaptation of *Good Morning, Midnight* at a time when many people thought Rhys was dead. Wyndham's article led to his sustained support of Rhys during the writing of *Wide Sargasso Sea*: his intervention was critical in Rhys's resumption of writing long fiction.

12. Rhys herself enjoyed the joke of having been thought dead and coming back to life as a writer: she also provoked a fascination in the London-based media for some time after *Wide Sargasso Sea* appeared in 1966. She modelled clothes in *The Sunday Times* (Parkin 1973), and a number of journalists exploited and therefore trivialised her as a still beautiful woman who liked makeup. See 'Londoner's Diary': 'She is now in her mid-seventies and is still astonishingly beautiful. She is spare, small-boned, with wide blue eyes and thick hair, loves expensive clothes and experiments with make-up and hair rinses' (1967: 6); Foster: 'As the ambulance came to take her to the hospital, the . . . old lady said to the nurse accompanying her: "Please my eye shadow"' (1979: n.p.); Hamilton: 'A woman to the last, her final utterance on her last journey in the hospital ambulance was to demand her eye-shadow' (1980: n.p.); Clayton, reviewing the *Omnibus* film on Rhys: 'at eighty still beautiful and animated and more famous than before. She is still writing busily' (1974: 11); Davies, on 'Rip Van Rhys': 'You've got to be dead before you can make a come-back to the literary world, which is probably one of the reasons for Jean Rhys's present success. For twenty years, she was presumed dead' (1966: 18).

13. Whilst Nebeker's book is extremely odd, it exhibits some interesting contradictions as a piece of early feminist criticism reacting to an established literary tradition, for example, it both reflects an important championship of the woman writer and a willingness at times to use the generic 'he' for the critical voice.

14. Nebeker sustains an eccentric argument that Rhys wrote a narrative of the feminist construction of the ancient Goddess, pre-Christian and 'Graeco-Olympian' (1981: viii) to the extent of reading into characters' names elaborate Celtic symbolism. But there are some interesting readings of portions of the texts and Nebeker wrote early enough to be in touch with Rhys.

15. In many ways, post-colonial feminisms received a collective text of feminism from the predominantly white and North American

women's movement from the 1970s and have sought to reconstitute their own local constructions of women's oppression and of desired gender and family relationships.

16. The Mr Howard narrative is the autobiographical account of sexual abuse which is in the BEB. Rhys first read *Wuthering Heights* during her early years in England and had as much admiration for Emily as for Charlotte Brontë. She reread *Jane Eyre* in 1957 in preparation for resuming work on an idea of a West Indian novel she had tried to finish years before (see *L*: 149ff).

17. Alan Ross published, for example, 'Till September Petronella' (1960), 'The Day They Burned the Books' (1960), 'Tigers are Better-Looking' (1962) and 'Let Them Call It Jazz' (1962) (all in *CSS*).

18. It is important that La Rose established such a space for intra-Caribbean literary debate. He remains a major facilitator, through his bookstore and publishing house, New Beacon Books, of Caribbean literary networks and intellectual analyses of Caribbean cultures in the region, Britain and North America. The contribution of Caribbean intellectuals in London to literary culture from the 1950s is very important: though most publishing outlets remained non-Caribbean, La Rose's example provided a supportive space for anti-colonial writers.

19. See, for example, Achebe's important essay 'Colonialist Criticism' (first published 1975; 1988) and Soyinka's major challenge to Cambridge's Eurocentrism, *Myth, Literature and the African World* (1976).

20. See, for example, Gates (ed. 1984; 1988), Appiah (1992), Gilroy (1993), Ahmad (1992) for very important discussions of the relation of concepts of race and nation to the postmodern and post-colonial and various constructions of the implications of theory for political reality.

21. Black and White (as opposed to black and white) denoted a consciousness and a political affiliation in the 1960s and 1970s and I have accepted this usage where relevant. Ramchand's use of the term 'White' (1970) was not surprising in the light of the Black Power movement's usage of Black at the time: such usage was fairly common in the 1970s.

22. There was very important work on African-Caribbean history and identity being produced from the Caribbean in the 1960s, immediately before or after *Wide Sargasso Sea*, for example, C. L. R. James's *The Black Jacobins: Toussaint L'Ouverture and the San Domingo Revolution* (1963), Walter Rodney's *How Europe Underdeveloped Africa* (1969) and Kamau Brathwaite's immensely influential epic poem cycle *The Arrivants* (1973). This began to overturn the widespread amnesia of colonialism among the middle class about African heritage, but also provoked considerable discourse on race by the early 1970s, a

discourse which also drew on the work of African-American intellectuals and writers, particularly from the 1960s.

23. The question here is what functions as the major signifier for a culture, however much this is transformed and redefined by its own self-questioning as well as other, outside influences: in America, for example, that signifier has always been white, English-speaking, though that whiteness is informed, most evidently in popular music forms, by an African presence as well as by many others. In colonial Caribbean culture, the major signifier was said to be European, and in the case of Hearne's Jamaica, English. Each Caribbean territory has a different population in terms of constituent racial and ethnic communities, as well as in terms of European colonising influence, but the major cultural signifier for the Caribbean as a whole is Africa. Trinidad Carnival, for example, which began as a French Creole festival has become an African festival, incorporating within that creative space influences from all the diverse communities within Trinidad and Tobago and even from outside. Knight and Palmer note that 'whites, mestizos and mulattoes form significant components of Cuba, Puerto Rico, and the Dominican Republic. East Indians comprise the ethnic majorities in Suriname, Trinidad, and Guyana', but admit most of the rest of the region's people are African-descended (1989: 16).

24. In 1960, Lamming's 'The Occasion for Speaking' in *The Pleasures of Exile*, saw West Indians as substantially colonised. Brathwaite, by the late 1960s and early 1970s, argued that certain West Indian texts were most productively read 'in aesthetic relation to jazz' (1993: 181), i.e. by turning towards genres and forms which derived their originality from African-centred affirmations of creativity and freedom. One of the most important debates of the early postcolonial period was about language: linguists Richard Allsopp (1972) and Mervyn Alleyne (1961), among others, began their defence of West Indian Creoles against the old colonial charge of being poor versions of English. Bruce St John's pioneering work in Barbados on the tonality of Bajan language during the 1970s was very important. Rhys's *Wide Sargasso Sea* appeared just as these major issues were beginning to be discussed.

25. Gardiner regards the psychological concept of empathy as often associated with women, and suggesting a capacity for 'bridging differences between self and other', moreover for female twentieth-century writers it is 'necessary to change history and so establish a meaningful female identity' (1989: 3, 18).

26. Le Gallez shows how each Rhys protagonist's relation to her story is different because of the varying narrative strategies Rhys uses: in

the process she refutes the usual charge of passivity in the Rhys woman by showing her active control over her story.

27. See, for the details of Rhys's life which inform Selina's confrontation with her neighbours and her time in Holloway, Angier (1990: 441–8).

28. Two very gifted white Creole women writers have published in recent years: Honor Ford-Smith (1996) and Rachel Manley (1996) and neither seems explicitly to acknowledge Rhys. White Creole Robert Antoni's *Blessed is the Fruit* explicitly works off *Wide Sargasso Sea* and raises some very interesting and difficult questions in so doing.

29. This has become an important Caribbean literary trope. See, especially, Lamming's *Water with Berries* (1971).

30. Already, it is clear that because of colonialism, some persons of African descent made an internalised commitment to European cultural norms and were seen, in the light of decolonising cultural developments, as having become white (Fanon 1968), or, in more contemporary terms, in the West Indies, 'Afro-Saxon'. The same process is perfectly possible in reverse, in a community where African cultural norms predominate, though it has been much rarer and, as a result of history, more problematised. I see Rhys as entering this process to a limited extent. Race in the Caribbean is both essentialist and non-essentialist: there are those who privilege Caribbean identity above racial or ethnic identity, but many people still accept race as a fundamental signifier.

31. For example, Carole Boyce Davies writes that black characters in Naipaul's fiction alienated her from Caribbean literature generally for some time (Boyce Davies and Savory Fido, eds. 1990: xviii).

32. See, for example, *Barabajan Poems* (1994).

33. Notably Aimé Cesaire, Edouard Glissant, Nicholas Guillen, Kamau Brathwaite, Derek Walcott. Many fiction writers began as poets, e.g. Lamming, or are also poets, e.g. Glissant.

34. Harris uses some of the same words in these two essays to describe *Wide Sargasso Sea*.

# Bibliography

## WORKS BY JEAN RHYS

### BOOKS

All references in the text to works by Rhys are to the latest editions cited here unless otherwise stated.

*After Leaving Mr MacKenzie* (London: Cape, 1931) New York: Carroll and Graf, 1990

*Good Morning, Midnight* (London: Constable, 1939) New York: W. W. Norton, 1986

*My Day*, New York: Frank Hallman, 1975 (includes 'My Day', 'Invitation to the Dance', 'Close Season for the Old?')

*Quartet* (originally published as *Postures*, London: Chatto and Windus, 1928; first published as *Quartet*, New York: Simon and Shuster, 1929), New York: Carroll and Graf, 1990

*Sleep It Off Lady* (London: André Deutsch, 1976) Harmondsworth Penguin, 1979 (includes 'Pioneers, Oh, Pioneers', 'Good-bye Marcus, Good-bye Rose', 'The Bishop's Feast', 'Heat', 'Fishy Waters', 'Overture and Beginners Please', 'Before the Deluge', 'Night Out 1925', 'The Chevalier of the Place Blanche', 'Rapunzel, Rapunzel', 'Sleep It Off Lady', 'The Insect World', 'On Not Shooting Sitting Birds', 'Kikimora', 'Who Knows What's up in the Attic?' and 'I Used to Live Here Once')

*Smile Please: An Unfinished Autobiography*, Berkeley: Donald S. Ellis/Creative Arts, 1979

*Tales of the Wide Caribbean*, selected and edited by Kenneth Ramchand, London: Heinemann, n.d.

*The Collected Short Stories*, Introduction by Diana Athill, New York: W. W. Norton, 1987 (includes 'Kismet' and a selection from *TLB* and *TAB-L*)

*The Left Bank and Other Stories*, London: Cape, 1927 (includes 'Illusion', 'A Spiritualist', 'Mannequin', 'Tea with an Artist', 'Trio', 'Mixing

Cocktails', 'Again the Antilles', 'Hunger', 'Learning to Be a Mother', 'The Blue Bird', 'La Grosse Fifi' and 'Vienne')

*The Letters of Jean Rhys*, selected and edited Francis Wyndham and Diana Melly, New York: Viking, 1984

*Tigers Are Better-Looking* (London: André Deutsch, 1968) Harmondsworth: Penguin, 1968 (includes 'The Sound of the River', 'Tigers Are Better-Looking', 'Let Them Call It Jazz', 'The Lotus', 'A Solid House' and a selection from *TLB*)

*Voyage in the Dark* (London: Constable, 1934) New York: W. W. Norton, 1982

*Wide Sargasso Sea* (London: André Deutsch, 1966) New York: W. W. Norton Paperback, 1982


STORIES, POEMS, ESSAYS, AND EXCERPTS

'A Solid House', *Voices*, London: Michael Joseph, 1963

'I Spy a Stranger', *Art and Literature*, no. 8 (Spring 1966), 4–53; *Penguin Modern Stories*, ed. Judith Burnley, Harmondsworth: Penguin, 1969, 53–67

'Let Them Call It Jazz', *London Magazine*, February 1962, 69–83

'Making Bricks Without Straw', *Harper's* 257 (July 1978), 70–1

'Obeah Night', *The Penguin Book of Caribbean Verse*, ed. Paula Burnett, Harmondsworth: Penguin, 1986, 147

'Our Gardener', *The Penguin Book of Caribbean Verse*, ed. Paula Burnett, Harmondsworth: Penguin, 1986, 146

'Outside the Machine', *Winter Tales*, no. 6, ed. A. D. McClean, London: Macmillan, 1960, 189–219

'Pioneers, Oh, Pioneers' first published as 'Dear, Darling Mr Ramage', *The Times*, 28 June 1969

'Sleep It Off Lady', *New Review*, June 1974, 45–9

'Temps Perdi', *Art and Literature* no. 12 (1967), 121–8; *Penguin Modern Stories*, ed. Judith Burnley, Harmondsworth: Penguin, 1969, 53–67

'The Chevalier of the Place Blanche', *Vogue*, August 1976, 94–95

'The Day They Burned the Books', *London Magazine*, 7 July 1960, 42–6

'The Joey Bagstock Smile', *New Statesman* 94, 23–30 December 1977, 890

'The Lotus', *Art and Literature*, no. 11 (1967), 165–74

'The Sound of the River', *Art and Literature*, no. 9 (1966), 192–7

'Tigers Are Better-Looking', *London Magazine*, October 1962, 24–34

'Till September Petronella', *London Magazine*, no. 7 (1960), 19–39

'Vienne', *the transatlantic review*, vol. 2, no. 2 (December 1924), 639–45

'Visiting the Carib Quarter', *Wild Majesty: Encounters with Caribs from Columbus to the Present Day*, ed. Peter Hulme and Neil L. Whitehead, Oxford: Clarendon Press, 1992, 299–305

'Whatever Became of Old Mrs Pearce?', *The Times*, no. 59401, 21 May
  1975, 16
'Whistling Bird', *The New Yorker*, 11 September 1978, 38–9
'Wide Sargasso Sea: with Introduction by Francis Wyndham', *Art and
  Literature* 1 (March 1964), 177–204


UNPUBLISHED MANUSCRIPTS: UTC

'AND PARIS – SINISTER'
'At first I knew remarkably little . . .'
'At the Ropemaker's Arms'
Black Exercise Book
'But it is I don't want to write anything . . .' (sic)
'But of course I have often longed . . .'
'Chinese Vases'
'Clouds in Stone'
'Daisy'
'Dear, Darling Mr Ramage'
'December 4th, 1938, Mr Howard's House/CREOLE'
'DOWN ALONG: Fragments of Autobiography'
'Essay on England'
'Fears'
Green Exercise Book
'Hurricane', poem
'I FEEL so sick . . .'
'I have typed out all the stuff . . .'
'I'm very often plagued . . .'
'I remember when it started . . .'
'IT HAD always been like that . . .'
'I WAS THE YOUNGEST . . .'
'The Imperial Road' (all available drafts)
'In the Looking Glass', poem
'I think I fell in love with words . . .'
'Just before my sixteenth birthday: two tunes'
'L'Affaire Ford'
'Language doesn't seem to me as rich as it used to be . . .'
'Leaving School'
'Le Revenant'
'Life With You'
'Music and Words'
'New Story'
Orange Exercise Book
'Poetry and Poets'
'Put It Away'

'Rain on the Roof', poem
Red Exercise Book
'Shak-shak', poem
'Songs' (all available drafts)
'Songs My Mother Didn't Teach Me' (all available drafts)
'Sunset', poem
'The Bible is Modern'
'The Birthday' (all available drafts)
'The Game and the Candle' (all available drafts)
'Then came the time that I wrote plays'
'They Thought It was Jazz'
'The Hanger-On'
'The Imperial Road' (all drafts, under several titles)
'The only time my father . . .'
'The Poet' (translation of de Nève story)
'The Stepping Stones'
'Triple Sec'
'Two Tunes'
'Vengeance' (translation of de Nève story)
'Voyage in the Dark' (original ending: Part IV)
'When I think of my parents . . .'
'When I went from room to room . . .'
'Wide Sargasso Sea' extract: corrected galleys, *Art and Literature*

UNPUBLISHED LETTERS: UTC

Morchard Bishop, 1 June 1939
Phyllis Smyser, 10 October 1945
Eliot Bliss, 13 October 1947
Peggy Kirkaldy, Friday, 1949
Peggy Kirkaldy, 1 March 1949
Peggy Kirkaldy, 28 May 1950
Maryvonne Moerman, 22 October 1951
Peggy Kirkaldy, 18 January 1953
Peggy Kirkaldy, 5 July 1957
Peggy Kirkaldy, 11 July 1957
Peggy Kirkaldy, 30 July 1957
Selma Vaz Dias, 6 November 1960
Francis Wyndham, 6 March 1961
Eliot Bliss, August 1962
Selma Vaz Dias, 30 Friday 1963
Selma Vaz Dias, 1963
Matron, Belmont Hospital, 4 July 1963 (signed Ella Hamer)
Francis Wyndham, 30 March 1964

Francis Wyndham, 1 May 1964
Diana Athill, 29 May 1964
Francis Wyndham, 5 July 1964
Selma Vaz Dias, 1964
Selma Vaz Dias, 17/18 September 1965
Francis Wyndham, 25 February 1966
Olwyn Hughes, 25 February 1966
Olwyn Hughes, 6 May 1966
Olwyn Hughes, 23 June 1966
Sonia Orwell, 18 November 1966
Diana Athill, 1 December 1966
Diana Athill, 27 December 1966
Diana Athill, 3 January 1967
Diana Athill, 7 February 1967
Diana Athill, 3 March 1967
Diana Athill, 6 March 1967
Olwyn Hughes, 7 March 1967
Olwyn Hughes, 5 June 1967
Francis Wyndham, 20 June 1967
Diana Athill, 12 February 1968
Francis Wyndham, 19 February 1968
Sonia Orwell, 22 February 1968
Francis Wyndham, 29 February 1968
Sonia Orwell, 1 May 1968
Sonia Orwell, 3 May 1968
Francis Wyndham, 11 May 1968
Oliver Stoner, 14 June 1968
Francis Wyndham, 27 September 1968
Diana Athill, 14 October 1968
Francis Wyndham, 7 November 1968
Sonia Orwell, 14 November 1968
Sonia Orwell, Friday 4 April 1969
Sonia Orwell, 2 July 1969
Olwyn Hughes, 16 May 1969
Sonia Orwell, 2 July 1969
Oliver Stoner, 5 September 1969
Olwyn Hughes, 17 October 1969
Francis Wyndham, 27 November 1969
Oliver Stoner, 3 November 1969
Francis Wyndham, 5 January 1970
Francis Wyndham, 10 April 1970
Sonia Orwell, 13 January 1972
Sonia Orwell, 25 September 1973
Francis Wyndham, 14 October 1973

Sonia Orwell, 16 June 1974
Oliver Stoner, 16 August 1974
Francis Wyndham, 11 August 1975
Francis Wyndham, 1975 (plural letters)
Francis Wyndham, 26 October 197?
Phyllis, 4 September 1978
Francis Wyndham, 9 July, no year
Francis Wyndham, Thursday 17 July, no year
Francis Wyndham, 29 July, no year
Oliver Stoner, 15 September, no year
Oliver Stoner, 16 October, no year

### ADAPTATIONS AND CRITICISM OF ADAPTATIONS

Blume, Mary, 1981, 'The Filming of *Quartet*: Jean Rhys' Slice of Paris', *Los Angeles Times*, 25 January, 25

Rorem, Ned, 1995, 'Three Women: I From *Quartet* and *Good Morning Midnight*' by Jean Rhys, for piano and speaking voice, 92nd Street Y Unterberg Poetry Center, New York City, 30 January

Savory, Elaine, 1994, 'A Creole of Pure English Descent?' Review of the film, *Wide Sargasso Sea*', *Jean Rhys Review* 6:2, 11–16

Thomas, Sue, 1997, 'Revisionary (post)modernist plausibilities? Paul Monaghan's staging of *Obeah Night* and the film of *Wide Sargasso Sea*: a commentary', *Jean Rhys Review* 8: 1 and 2, 30–4

### INTERVIEWS

Cantwell, Mary, 1974, 'I am a Person at a Masked Ball without a Mask', *Mademoiselle*, October, 170–1, 206, 208, 210, 213 (repr. Frickey, ed. 1990)

Carter, Hannah, 1968, 'Fated To Be Sad', *The Guardian*, 8 August, 5

### TRANSLATIONS

Carco, Francis, 1928, *Perversity*, Chicago: Pascal Covici
de Nève, Edward, 1932, *Barred*, London: Desmond Harmsworth

## SELECTED WORKS ABOUT RHYS

Abel, Elizabeth, 1979, 'Women and Schizophrenia: the Fiction of Jean Rhys', *Contemporary Literature* 20, 155–77

Accaria, Diana, 1989, 'History: the Stuff Nightmares Are Made of in *Wide Sargasso Sea*', *Sargasso* 6, 52–6

Allfrey, Phyllis Shand, 1979, 'Jean Rhys: A Tribute', *Kunapipi* 1, 6–22

Alvarez, A., 1974, 'The Best Living English Novelist', *New York Times Book Review*, 17 March, 6–7

Amuso, Teresa Rose, 1987, 'Crises of Survival: the Precarious "I" in the Works of Elizabeth Bowen and Jean Rhys', *Dissertation Abstracts International* 48: 2 (August), 395A (University of Massachusetts)

Anderson, Paula G., 1982, 'Jean Rhys's *Wide Sargasso Sea*: the Other Side/Both Sides Now', *Caribbean Quarterly* 28: 1–2 (March–June), 57–65

Andre, Irving W., 1995, *Distant Voices: The Genesis Of An Indigenous Literature in Dominica*, Roseau: Ponde Casse Press

Angier, Carole, 1985, *Jean Rhys*, Harmondsworth: Penguin

1990, *Jean Rhys: Life and Work*, Boston: Little, Brown and Company

Ashcom, Jane Neide, 1988, 'Two Modernisms: the Novels of Jean Rhys', *Jean Rhys Review* 2: 2 (Spring), 17–27

Baer, Elizabeth R., 1982, 'The Pilgrimage Inward: the Quest Motif in the Fiction of Margaret Atwood, Doris Lessing and Jean Rhys', *Dissertation Abstracts International* 42: 8 (February), 3606A (Indiana University 1981).

1983, 'The Sisterhood of Jane Eyre and Antoinette Cosby', *The Voyage In: Fictions of Female Development*, ed. Elizabeth Abel, Marianne Hirsch and Elizabeth Langland, Hanover, NH: University Press of New England for Dartmouth College, 131–48

Baldanza, Frank, 1978, 'Jean Rhys on Insult and Injury', *Studies in the Literary Imagination* 11: 2 (Fall), 55–65

Barber, Patricia, 1974, 'Rediscovering Jean Rhys', *Seattle, Wash. Post-Intelligencer*, 15 September, n.p.

Barber-Williams, Patricia, 1989, 'Images of the Self: Jean Rhys and Her French West Indian Counterpart', *Journal of West Indian Literature* 3: 2 (September), 9–19

Bender, Todd, 1990, 'Jean Rhys and the Genius of Impressionism', in Frickey, ed. 1990, 75–84 (*Studies in the Literary Imagination* 11: 2 (Fall 1978), 43–53)

Benstock, Shari, 1987, *Women of the Left Bank: Paris, 1890–1940*, London: Virago

Berger, Gertrude, 1985, 'Rhys, De Beauvoir and the Woman in Love', *The Review of Contemporary Fiction* 5: 2 (1985), 139–45

Blais, Joline, 1993, 'Qui est là?': Displaced Subjects in *Wide Sargasso Sea* and Le ravissement de Lol V. Stein', *College Literature* 20: 2 (June), 98–118

Blodgett, Harriet, 1981, 'Enduring Ties: Daughters and Mothers in Contemporary English Fiction by Women', *South Atlantic Quarterly* 80 (Autumn), 441–53

Bowen, Stella, 1984, *Drawn From Life*, London: Virago (first published 1941)

Bowlby, Rachel, 1992, *Still Crazy After All These Years: Women, Writing and Psychoanalysis*, London: Routledge

Branson, Stephanie, 1989, 'Magicked by the Place: Shadow and Substance in *Wide Sargasso Sea*', *Jean Rhys Review* 3: 2 (Spring), 19–28

Brathwaite, Kamau, 1974, *Contradictory Omens: Cultural diversity and integration in the Caribbean*, Kingston, Jamaica: Savacou Publications (repr. 1985)

　1995, 'A Post-Cautionary Tale of the Helen of Our Wars', *Wasafiri* no. 22 (Autumn), 69–81

Braybrooke, 1967, Neville, 'Between Dog and Wolf', *Spectator*, 21 July, 77–8

　1970, 'The Return of Jean Rhys', *Caribbean Quarterly* (December), 43–6

Brown, Bev E. L., 1986, 'Mansong and Matrix: A Radical Experiment', *A Double Colonization: Colonial and Post-Colonial Women's Writing*, ed. Kristen Holst Petersen and Anna Rutherford, Denmark: Dangaroo, 68–80

Brown, Nancy Hemond, 1985, 'Jean Rhys and *Voyage in the Dark*', *London Magazine* 25: 1–2 (April/May), 40–59

　1986, 'Aspects of the Short Story: A Comparison of Jean Rhys's "The Sound of the River" with Ernest Hemingway's "Hills Like White Elephants"', *Jean Rhys Review* 1: 1 (Fall), 2–13

　1987, 'England and the English in the Works of Jean Rhys', *Jean Rhys Review* 1: 2 (Spring), 8–20

Brownstein, Rachel, 1982, *On Becoming a Heroine: Reading About Women in Novels*, New York: Viking

Byrne, Jack, 1985, 'Jean Rhys's *Good Morning, Midnight*: The Boulevard of Broken Dreams', *The Review of Contemporary Literature* 5, no. 2, 151–9

Campbell, Elaine, 'A Report from Dominica, B.W.I.', *World Literature Written in English* 17: 1, 305–16

　1979, 'From Dominica to Devonshire: A Memento of Jean Rhys', *Kunapipi* 1: 2, 6–22

　1990, 'Reflections of Obeah in Jean Rhys's Fiction', in Frickey, ed. 1990, 59–66 (*Kunapipi* 4: 2 (1982))

Cantwell, Mary, 1980, 'Hers', *The New York Times*, 20 March, C2

　1990, 'A Conversation with Jean Rhys', in Frickey, ed. 1990, 21–7

　1997, 'Still at Work on a Self', *The New York Times Magazine*, 9 March, 57

Carr, Helen, 1996, *Jean Rhys*, Plymouth: Northcote House Publishers

Carrera Suarez, Isabel and Esther Alvarez Lopez, 1990, 'Social and Personal Selves: Race, Gender and Otherness in Rhys's "Let Them Call It Jazz" and *Wide Sargasso Sea*', *Dutch Quarterly Review* 20: 2, 154–62

Casey, Nancy, 1973, 'Study in the Alienation of a Creole Woman', *Caribbean Quarterly* 19: 3, 95–102

1974, 'The "Liberated" Woman in Jean Rhys's Later Short Fiction', *Revista/Review Interamericana* 4: 2, 264–72

Casey Fulton, Nancy J. 1974, 'Jean Rhys' *Wide Sargasso Sea*: Exterminating the White Cockroach', *Revista/Review Interamericana* 4: 2, 340–9

Codaccioni, Marie-Jose, 1984, 'L'autre vie de Bertha Rochester', *Actes du Congrès de Poitiers*, Societé des Anglicistes de L'Enseignement Supérieur. Paris: Didier Erudition

Cowart, David, 1993, *Literary Symbiosis: The Configured Text in Twentieth Century Writing*, Athens, Georgia: University of Georgia Press, 46–65

Curtis, Jan, 1985, 'The Room and the Black Background: A Reinterpretation of Jean Rhys's *Good Morning, Midnight*', *World Literature Written in English* 25: 2, 264–9

Davidson, Arnold E., 1984, 'The Art and Economics of Destitution in Jean Rhys's *After Leaving Mr MacKenzie*', *Studies in the Novel* 16 (Summer), 217

1985, *Jean Rhys*, New York: Frederick Ungar Publishing Co.

Davies, Hunter, 1996, 'Rip Van Rhys', *Sunday Times*, 6 November, 18

D'Costa, Jean, 1986, 'Jean Rhys', *Fifty Caribbean Writers*, ed. Daryl Cumber Dance, Westport, Conn.: Greenwood Press, 390–404

Delaney, Frank, 1984, 'The witch with blue eyes . . .', *The Sunday Press*, 17 June, n.p.

De Nève, E., 1939, 'Jean Rhys: une grande romancière anglaise inconnue', *Les Nouvelles Littéraires* no. 880 (26 August), 8

Emery, Mary Lou, 1985, 'The Paradox of Style: Metaphor and Ritual in *Good Morning, Midnight*', *The Review of Contemporary Literature* 5: 2 (Summer), 145–50

1990, *Jean Rhys at 'World's End': Novels of Colonial and Sexual Exile*, Austin: University of Texas Press

Erwin, Linda Lee, 1989, '"Like in a Looking Glass": History and Narrative in *Wide Sargasso Sea*', *Novel* 22: 2 (Winter), 143–58

Espinet, Ramabai, 1993, 'Adieu Foulards, Adieu Madras: the Place of the Euro-Creole Woman Writer with Particular Reference to the Works of Jean Rhys and Phyllis Shand Allfrey', PhD dissertation, University of the West Indies

'Every day is a new day', 1974, *Radio Times*, 21 November, 6

Fayad, Mona, 1988, 'Unquiet Ghosts: the Struggle for Representation in Jean Rhys's *Wide Sargasso Sea*', *Modern Fiction Studies* 34, 437–52

Ferguson, Moira, 1993a, *Colonialism and Gender Relations from Mary Wollestonecraft to Jamaica Kincaid: East Caribbean Connections*, New York: Columbia University Press

1993b, 'Sending the Younger Son Across the Wide Sargasso Sea: the New Coloniser Arrives', *Jean Rhys Review* 6: 1, 2–16

Ford, Ford Madox, 1986, 'Preface to Jean Rhys: *The Left Bank and Other Stories*', *The Ford Madox Ford Reader*, ed. Sondra Stang, New York: Ecco Press 236–45

Foster, Margaret, 1979, 'Getting to know her . . .' *Evening Standard*, 27 November, n.p.

Frickey, Pierrette, ed., 1990, *Critical Perspectives on Jean Rhys*. Washington, DC: Three Continents Press

Friedman, Ellen G., 1989, 'Breaking the Master Narrative: Jean Rhys's *Wide Sargasso Sea*', *Breaking the Sequence: Women's Experimental Fiction*, ed. Ellen G. Friedman and Miriam Fuchs, Princeton: Princeton University Press, 117–28

Gaines, Nora, *Jean Rhys Review* (ongoing)

Gardiner, Judith Kegan, 1982, 'Rhys Recalls Ford: *Quartet* and *The Good Soldier*', *Tulsa Studies in Women's Literature* 1: 1 (Spring), 67–81

1989, *Rhys, Stead, Lessing, and the Politics of Empathy*, Bloomington: Indiana University Press

Gilkes, Michael, 1987, 'The Madonna Pool: Women as "Muse of Identity"', *Journal of West Indian Literature* 1: 2 (June), 1–19

Givner, Joan, 1988, 'Charlotte Brontë, Emily Brontë and Jean Rhys: What Jean Rhys's Letters Show about that Relationship', *Faith of a (Woman) Writer*, ed. Alice Kessler-Harris and William McBrien, Westport, Conn.: Greenwood Press, 105–14

Gregg, Veronica Marie, 1987, Jean Rhys and Modernism: a different voice, *Jean Rhys Review* 1: 2 (Spring), 30–46

1990, 'Jean Rhys on Herself as Writer', *Caribbean Women Writers*, ed. Selwyn Cudjoe, Wellesley, Mass.: Calaloux Publications, 109–115

1995, *Jean Rhys's Historical Imagination*, Chapel Hill: University of North Carolina Press

Griffith, Glyne, 1990, 'Madness and Counter-Discourse: a dialogic encounter between *Wide Sargasso Sea* and *Jane Eyre*', paper presented at the Caribbean Women Writer's Conference, Trinidad, April

Guiness, Gerald, 1989, '*Wide Sargasso Sea*: Two Arguments', *Sargasso* 6, 43–7

Hagley, Carol R., 1988, 'Ageing in the Fiction of Jean Rhys', *World Literature Written in English* 28: 1 (Spring), 115–25

Hamilton, Ian, 1980, 'Jean Rhys: a Wide Uncharted Sea', *The Times*, 4 March, n.p.

Harris, Max, 1976, 'The Girl's Cult of Reportage', *Australian*, 4 September, n.p.

Harris, Wilson, 1981, 'Carnival of Psyche: Jean Rhys's *Wide Sargasso Sea*', *Explorations*, ed. Hena Maes-Jelinek, Aarhus, 125–33 (*Kunapipi* 11: 2 (1980), 142–50)

1988, *The Womb of Space*, Westport, Conn: Greenwood Press

Harrison, Nancy R., 1988, *Jean Rhys and the Novel as Women's Text*, Chapel Hill and London: University of North Carolina Press

Hawthorn, Jeremy, 1983, *Multiple Personality and the Disintegration of Literary Character*, London: Edward Arnold

Hearne, John, 1990, 'The Wide Sargasso Sea: a West Indian Reflection', in Frickey, ed. 1990, 186–93 (*Cornhill Magazine* no. 1080 (1974), 323–33) (repr. in)

Hemmerechts, Kristien, 1987, *A Plausible Story and a Plausible Way of Telling It: a Structuralist Analysis of Jean Rhys's Novels*, Frankfurt am Main: Peter Lang

Higdon, David Leon, 1984, *Shadows of the Past in Contemporary English Fiction*, London: Macmillan

Hite, Molly, 1989, *The Other Side of the Story: Structures and Strategies of Contemporary Feminist Narrative*, Ithaca: Cornell University Press

Holland, J. Gill and Robert A. Meyers, 1983, 'The Theme of Identity in the Works of Jean Rhys', *Revista/Review Interamericana* 13: 1, 150–8

Horner, Avril and Sue Zlosnik, 1990, *Landscapes of Desire: Metaphors in Modern Women's Fiction*, London: Harvester Wheatsheaf

Houts, Jan van, 1990, 'The Hole in the Curtain', in Frickey, ed. 1990

Howells, Coral Ann, 1991, *Jean Rhys*, New York: St Martin's Press

Hulme, Peter, 1993, 'The Locked Heart: the Creole Family Romance of *Wide Sargasso Sea* – an Historical and Biographical Analysis', *Jean Rhys Review* 6: 1, 20–35

1994, 'The Place of *Wide Sargasso Sea*', *Wasafiri* no. 20 (Autumn), 5–11

1996, 'A Response to Kamau Brathwaite', *Wasafiri* no. 23 (Spring), 49–50

Hulme, Peter and Neil L. Whitehead, eds. 1992, *Wild Majesty: Encounters with Caribs from Columbus to the Present Day*, Oxford: Clarendon Press

James, Louis, 1978, *Jean Rhys*, London: Longman

1990, 'Sun-Fire – Painted Fire: Jean Rhys as a Caribbean Novelist', in Frickey, ed. 1990, 118–28 (*Ariel* no. 3 (1977), 111–27)

James, Selma, 1983, *The Ladies and the Mammies: Jane Austen and Jean Rhys*, Bristol: Falling Wall Press

Johnson, Pam, 1980, 'Jean Rhys', *Spare Rib*, March, 41

Joseph, Margaret Paul, 1992, *Caliban in Exile: the Outsider in Caribbean Fiction*

Kappers-den Hollander, Martien, 1982, 'Jean Rhys and the Dutch Connection', *Maatstaf* 30, 30–40

1987, 'A Gloomy Child and Its Devoted Grandmother: Jean Rhys, *Barred, Sous les verrous* and *In de Strik*', *Jean Rhys Review* 1: 2, 20–3

1988, 'Measure for Measure: *Quartet* and *When the Wicked Man*', *Jean Rhys Review* 2: 2, 2–17

1994, 'A Case of Borrowed Plumes: Edouard de Nève, Jean Rhys and *Aan den Loopenden Band*', *Jean Rhys Review* 6: 2, 2–10

Kloepfer, Deborah Kelly, 1989, *The Unspeakable Mother: Forbidden Discourse in Jean Rhys and H.D.*, Ithaca: Cornell University Press

Knapp, Bettina L., 1986, 'Jean Rhys: *Wide Sargasso Sea*: Mother/Daughter Identification and Alienation', *Journal of Evolutionary Psychology* 7: 3–4 (August), 211–26

Koenen, Anne, 1990, 'The Fantastic as Feminine Mode: *Wide Sargasso Sea*', *Jean Rhys Review* 4: 1, 15–27

Kraf, Elaine, 1985, 'Jean Rhys: the Men in her Novels (Hugh Heidler, "The Gigolo", and Mr MacKenzie)', *The Review of Contemporary Fiction* 5: 2 (Summer), 118–28

Kubitshek, Missey Dehn, 1987, 'Charting the Empty Space of Jean Rhys's *Wide Sargasso Sea*', *Frontiers* 9: 2, 23–8

Lawson, Lori, 1991, 'Mirror and Madness: a Lacanian Analysis of the Feminine Subject in *Wide Sargasso Sea*', *Jean Rhys Review* 4: 2, 19–26

Le Gallez, Paula, 1990, *The Rhys Woman*, New York: St Martin's Press

Leigh, Nancy J., 1985, 'Mirror, Mirror: the Development of Female Identity in Jean Rhys's Fiction', *World Literature Written in English* 25: 2, 270–84

Lindroth, Colette, 1985, 'The Haunted Fiction of Jean Rhys', *The Review of Contemporary Fiction* 3: 2 (Summer), 135–9

Lindroth, James R., 1985, 'Arrangements in Silver and Grey: the Whistlerian Moment in the Short Fiction of Jean Rhys', *The Review of Contemporary Fiction* 3: 2 (Summer), 128–34

Little, Judy, 1996, 'Signifying Nothing: Shakesperian Deconstruction of Rhys's Rochester', *Jean Rhys Review* 7: 1 and 2, 39–45

'Londoner's Diary', 1967, *Evening Standard* 12 June, 6

Look Lai, Wally, 1968, 'The Road to Thornfield Hall: an analysis of Jean Rhys's novel *Wide Sargasso Sea*', London: New Beacon Books, 38–52

Lonsdale, Thorunn, 1992, 'Behind Bars: the Literary Relationship Between the Fictions of Jean Rhys and Eduoard de Nève', *Jean Rhys Review* 5: 1 and 2, 14–21

Luengo, Anthony, 1990, '*Wide Sargasso Sea* and the Gothic Mode', in Frickey, ed. 1990, 166–77 (*World Literature in English* 15: 1 (1976), 229–45)

Malcolm, Cheryl Alexander and David Malcolm, 1996, *Jean Rhys: A Study of the Short Fiction*, New York: Twayne

Margarey, Kevin, 1986, 'The Sense of Place in Doris Lessing and Jean Rhys', *A Sense of Place in the New Literatures in English*, ed. Peggy Nightingale, St Lucia: University of Queensland Press

Mellown, Elgin W., 1984, *Jean Rhys: A Descriptive and Annotated Bibliography of Works and Criticism*, New York: Garland Publishing

1990, 'Character and Themes in the Novels of Jean Rhys', in Frickey, ed. 1990, 103–11 (*Contemporary Literature* 13 (1972), 458–75)

Miles, Rosalind, 1974, *The Fiction of Sex: Themes and Functions of Sex Differences in the Modern Novel*, London: Vision

Mitgang, Herbert, 1979, 'Jean Rhys, British Novelist, Dies; Known for *Wide Sargasso Sea*', *New York Times*, 17 May, n.p.

Mizener, Arthur, 1985, *The Saddest Story: A Biography of Ford Madox Ford*, New York: Carroll & Graf Publishers Inc.

Moore, Judith, 1987, 'Sanity and Strength in Jean Rhys's West Indian Heroines', *Rocky Mountain Review of Language and Literature* 41: 1–2, 21–31

Morrell, A. C., 1979, 'The World of Jean Rhys' Short Stories', *World Literature Written in English* 18: 1, 235–44

Morris, Mervyn, 1989, 'Oh, Give the Girl a Chance: Jean Rhys and *Voyage in the Dark*', *Journal of West Indian Literature* 3: 2 (September), 1–7

Moss, Howard, 1974, 'Books', *The New Yorker*, 16 December, 161–4

Nebeker, Helen, 1981, *Jean Rhys: Woman in Passage*, Montreal, Canada: Eden Press

Nelson, Barbara A., 1987, 'The Anatomy of a Madwoman', *Dissertation Abstracts International* 47: 12 (June), 4389A

Nielsen, Hanne and Fleming Brahms, 1975, 'Retrieval of a Monster: Jean Rhys's *Wide Sargasso Sea*', *Enigma of Values*, ed. Anna Rutherford and Kristen Holt Petersen, Aarhus: Dangaroo Press, 139–62

Niesen de Abruña, Laura, 1988, 'Jean Rhys's Feminism: Theory Against Practice', *World Literature Written in English* 28: 2, 326–36

1990, 'Family Connections: Mother and Mother Country in the Fiction of Jean Rhys and Jamaica Kincaid', *Motherlands: Black Women's Writing from Africa, the Caribbean and South Asia*, ed. Susheila Nasta, London: The Women's Press, 257–89

Nollen, Elizabeth Mahn, 1985, 'The Gothic Female Experience: Female Imprisonment, Madness and Escape in Selected Texts by Women Writers', *Dissertation Abstracts International* 46: 13, 159A

Nudd, Donna Marie, 1984, 'The Uneasy *Voyage* of Jean Rhys and Selma Vaz Dias', *Literature in Performance* 4: 2 (April), 20–32

Nunez-Harrell, Elizabeth, 1985, 'The Paradoxes of Belonging: *The White West Indian Woman in Fiction*', *Modern Fiction Studies* 31: 2, 281–93

Oates, Carol Joyce, 1985, 'Romance and Anti-Romance from Brontë's *Jane Eyre* to Rhys's *Wide Sargasso Sea*', *Virginia Quarterly Review* 61: 1 (Winter), 44–58

O'Callaghan, Evelyn, 1986, ' "The Outsider's Voice": White Creole Women Novelists in the Caribbean Literary Tradition', *Journal of West Indian Literature* 1: 1 (October), 74–88

1990, 'Interior Schisms Dramatised: the Treatment of the "Mad" Woman in the Work of Some Female Caribbean Novelists', *Out of the Kumbla: Caribbean Women and Literature*, ed. Carole Boyce Davies and Elaine Savory Fido, Trenton, NJ: Africa World Press, 89–110

1993, *Woman Version: Theoretical Approaches to West Indian Fiction by Women*, London and Basingstoke: Macmillan Caribbean

O'Connor, Teresa F., 1986, *Jean Rhys: The West Indian Novels*, New York: New York University Press

1992, 'Jean Rhys, Paul Theroux, and the Imperial Road', *Twentieth Century Literature* 38: 4 (Winter), 404–14

Paravisini-Gebert, Lizabeth, 1996, *Phyllis Shand Allfrey: A Caribbean Life* New Brunswick, NJ: Rutgers University Press

Paravisini-Gebert, Lizabeth and Olga Torres-Seda, 1993, 'Jean Rhys', *Caribbean Women Novelists: An Annotated Critical Bibliography*, Westport, Conn: Greenwood Press

Parkin, Molly, 1973, 'Look! Fashion: Everything Makes You Want Pretty Clothes', *Sunday Times*, 25 February, 33

Petschek, Anna, 1976, 'The Shy Lady Novelist Who Went Missing For Twenty Years', *Daily Express*, 1 September, n.p.

Plante, David, 1984, *Difficult Women: A Memoir of Three*, New York: E. P. Dutton

Porter, Dennis, 1976, 'Of Heroines and Victims: Jean Rhys and Jane Eyre', *The Massachussetts Review*, 17: 3 (1976), 540–52

Raiskin, Judith, 1991, 'Jean Rhys: Creole Writing and Strategies of Reading', *Ariel*, 22: 4 (October), 51–67

1996, *Snow on the Canefields: Women's Writing and Creole Subjectivity*, Minneapolis: University of Minnesota Press

Raskin, Barbara, 1970, 'Classic Female', *New Republic* 63 (4 July), 27

Ramchand, Kenneth, 1976, *An Introduction to the Study of West Indian Literature*. Kingston: Nelson

1983, *The West Indian Novel and Its Background*, London: Heinemann (London: Faber and Faber, 1970)

Robinson, K. E., 1979, 'Rochester's Dilemma', *Durham University Journal*, June, 223–32

Rodriguez, Ileana, 1994, *House/Garden/Nation: Space, Gender, and Ethnicity in Postcolonial Latin American Literatures by Women*, trans. Robert Carr and Ileana Rodriguez, Durham: Duke University Press

Rose, Phyllis, 1985, *Writing of Women*, Middletown, Conn.: Wesleyan University Press

Saakana, Amon Saba, 1987, *The Colonial Legacy in Caribbean Literature*, Trenton, NJ: Africa World Press

Sage, Lorna, 1992, *Women in the House of Fiction*, New York: Routledge

Savory, Elaine, 1992, 'Jean Rhys', *Dictionary of Literary Biography* (vol. 117: African and Caribbean Writers), ed. Lindfors and Sander, Detroit: Gale Research, 258–77

1997, 'Jean Rhys and the Novel as Obeah', *Sacred Possessions: Vodou, Santeria, Obeah and the Caribbean*, ed. Paravisini-Gebert and

Fernandez-Olmos, New Brunswick, NJ, 217–31 (first published in earlier version *Jean Rhys Review* 7: 1 and 2, 1996, 26–38)

Savory Fido, Elaine, 1991, 'Motherlands: Self and Separation in the Work of Buchi Emecheta, Bessie Head and Jean Rhys', *Motherlands: Black Women's Writing from Africa, the Caribbean and South Asia*, ed. Susheila Nasta, London: Women's Press, 330–49

Schapiro, Barbara Ann, 1994, *Literature and the Relational Self*, New York: New York University Press

Scharfman, Ronnie, 1981, 'Mirroring and Mothering in Simone Schwartz-Bart's *Pluie et vent sur Telumée Miracle* and Jean Rhys's *Wide Sargasso Sea*', *Yale French Studies* 62, 88–106

Smilowitz, Erica Jane Sollish, 1986, 'Childlike Women and Paternal Men: Colonialism in Jean Rhys's Fiction', *Ariel* 17: 4 (October), 93–103

Spaull, Sue, 1989, 'Gynocriticism', *Feminist Readings/Feminists Reading*, ed. Sara Mills, Lynne Pearce, Sue Spaull and Elaine Millard, Charlottesville: University Press of Virginia

Spivak, Gayatri Chakravorty, 1985, 'Three Women's Texts and a Critique of Imperialism', *Critical Inquiry* 12: 1 (Autumn), 243–61

Staley, Thomas F., 1979, *Jean Rhys: A Critical Study*, Austin: University of Texas Press

Sternlicht, Sanford, 1997, *Jean Rhys*, New York: Twayne

Summers, Marcia A., 1985, 'Victimization, Survival and Empowerment in *Wide Sargasso Sea*', *Women's Place*, Vermillion: University of South Dakota Conference, 79–85

Tarozzi, Bianca, 1984, *La Forma Vincente: I romanzi di Jean Rhys*, Venice: Arsenale Editrice

1989, 'The Turning Point: Themes in *Good Morning Midnight*', *Jean Rhys Review* 3: 2 (Spring), 2–12

Thieme, John, 1979, 'Apparitions of Disaster: Brontëan Parallels in *Wide Sargasso Sea* and *Guerillas*', *Journal of Commonwealth Literature* 14: 9, 116–32

Thomas, Clara, 1987, 'Mr Rochester's First Marriage: *Wide Sargasso Sea*', *World Literature Written in English* 17: 1, 342–57

Thomas, Sue, 1994, 'Modernity, Voice and Window-Breaking: Jean Rhys's "Let Them Call It Jazz"', *De-scribing Empire*, ed. Chris Tiffin and Alan Lawson, London: Routledge, 185–200

1994–5, 'Jean Rhys, "grilled sole", and an experience of "mental seduction"', *nlr* 28/29 (Winter–Summer), 65–84

1996a, 'Conflicted Textual Affiliations: Jean Rhys's "The Insect World" and "Heat"', *A Talent(ed) Digger* (Festschrift for Anna Rutherford), ed. Hena Maes-Jelinek, Gordon Collier, Geoffrey V. Davis, Amsterdam: Rodopi, 287–94

1996b, 'The Labyrinths of "A Savage Person-a Real Carib": The Amerindian in Jean Rhys's Fiction', *Journal of West Indian Literature* 7: 1 (May), 82–96

1996c, 'William Rees Williams in Dominica', *Jean Rhys Review* 7: 1 and 2, 3–14

Forthcoming, 'Jean Rhys and Dominican Autoethnography', *Victorian Journalism*

Thompson, Irene, 1981, 'The Left Bank Aperitifs of Jean Rhys and Ernest Hemingway', *Georgia Review* 35 (Spring), 94–106

Thorpe, Michael, 1990, 'The Other Side: *Wide Sargasso Sea* and *Jane Eyre*', in Frickey, ed. 1990, 178–85 (*Ariel* 8: 3 (1977), 99–110)

Thurman, Judith, 1976, 'The Mistress and the Mask: Jean Rhys's Fiction' *MS* 4 (January), 50–2, 81

Tiffin, Helen, 1978, 'Mirror and Mask: Colonial Motifs in the Novels of Jean Rhys', *World Literature Written in English* 17 (April), 328–41

Todd, Loreto, 1995, *Jean Rhys Wide Sargasso Sea*, York Notes Beirut: Longman York Press

Vaz Dias, Selma, 1957, 'In Quest of a Missing Author', *Radio Times*, 3 May, 25

Webb, Ruth, 1988, 'Swimming the Wide Sargasso Sea: the Manuscripts of Jean Rhys's Novel', *British Library Journal* 14: 2, 165–77

Williamson, Karina, 1986, *Voyages in the Dark: Jean Rhys and Phyllis Shand Allfrey*, Occasional Papers in Caribbean Studies no. 4, Coventry: University of Warwick

Wilson, Lucy, 1990, '"Women Must Have Spunks": Jean Rhys's West Indian Outcasts', in Frickey, ed. 1990, 67–74 (*Modern Fiction Studies* 32: 3 (Autumn 1986), 439–47)

Wisker, Gina, ed. 1994, *It's My Party: Reading Twentieth Century Women's Writing*, London: Pluto Press

Wolfe, Peter, 1980, *Jean Rhys*, Boston: Twayne Publishers

Wyndham, Francis, 1950, 'An Inconvenient Novelist', *Tribune*, 15 December, 16, 18

1982, 'Introduction', *Wide Sargasso Sea*, London: W. W. Norton, 5–13

REVIEWS

*The Left Bank*

Aiken, Conrad, *New York Evening Post*, 1 October 1927, 10

Law, H. A., *Irish Statesman*, 27 October 1927, n.p.

*Saturday Review of Literature*, 5 November 1927, 2

*The Times Literary Supplement*, 5 May 1927, 320

## Quartet

Bailey, Paul, 'Bedrooms in Hell', *The Observer*, 18 May 1969, 30
Gorman, Herbert, 'The Unholy Four', *The New York Times Herald Tribune Books*, 10 February 1929, 7
Lane, Margaret, *Spectator*, 16 May 1969, 649–50 (also *ALMM*)
Lovett, Robert Morss, *Bookman* (New York), 69 (April 1929), 193
Hazzard, Shirley, *The New York Times*, 11 April 1971, 6
Mount, Gretchen, 'Hard, Chilly Cleverness', *Free Press*, 3 March 1929, (Detroit, Michigan, n.p.)
Nye, Robert, 'What man has made of women', *The Guardian*, 15 May 1969, n.p. (also *ALMM*)
*Saturday Review of Literature* 5 (20 April 1929), 936
'Shorter Notices', *The New Statesman*, 6 October 1928, 806


## After Leaving Mr MacKenzie

Dawson, Margaret Cheney, 'Unbearable Justice', *The New York Herald Tribune Books*, 28 June 1931, 7
Gould, Gerald, 'New Novels. All Sorts of Societies', *Observer*, no. 7289 (February 1931), 6
Graham, Gladys, 'A Bedraggled Career', *Saturday Review of Literature*, 8 (25 July 1931), 6
Naipaul, V. S., 'Without a Dog's Chance', *The New York Review of Books*, 18 May 1972, 29–31; repr. Frickey, ed. 1990, 54–8
Theroux, Paul, 'Novels', *Book World*, 13 February 1972, 6
'*Twice-as-Naturalism*', *The New York Times Book Review*, 28 June 1931, 6
*Yorkshire Post*, 4 February 1931, n.p.


## Voyage in the Dark

Britten, Florence Howe, 'Recent Leading Fiction', *The New York Herald Tribune Books*, 17 March 1935, 10
*New Fiction: Some Feminine Portraits*, *The Sunday Times*, 11 November 1934, 9
Southron, Jane Spence, 'A Girl's Ordeal', *The New York Times Book Review*, 17 March 1935, 7
Soskin, William, 'Reading and Writing: Intense Neurological Study; Fiddling in Spain', *Herald-Examiner*, Chicago, Ill., 13 March, 1935, n.p.
*The Times Literary Supplement*, 1 November 1934, 752
*The Times Literary Supplement*, 20 July 1967, 644

## Good Morning, Midnight

Brown, Hilton, 'Some Recent Fiction', *Nineteenth Century and After*, July 1939, 106

Mair, John, *The New Statesman*, 22 April 1939, 614

Raskin, Barbara, *The New Republic*, 163, 4 July 1970, 27

Swinnerton, Frank, 'New Novels. All Sorts', *The Observer*, 23 April 1939, 6

Talbot, Linda, 'Search for Security', *Hampstead and Highgate Express*, 14 July 1967, n.p.

## Wide Sargasso Sea

'A Fairy-Tale Neurotic', *The Times Literary Supplement*, 17 November 1966, 1039

Allen, Walter, 'Bertha the Doomed', *The New York Times Book Review*, 18 June 1967, 5

Braybrooke, Neville, 'Shadow and Substance', *Spectator*, 28 October 1966, 560–61

Dick, Kay, 'Wife to Mr Rochester', *The Sunday Times*, 30 October 1966, 50

Ross, Alan, *London Magazine* 6 (November 1966), 99, 101

## Tigers Are Better-Looking

Bailey, Paul, *London Magazine* 8: 3 (1968), 110–11

Baker, R., *Books and Bookmen* 13 (June 1968), 34

Haltrecht, Montague, 'More from Jean Rhys', *The Sunday Times*, 24 March 1968, 52

Heppenstall, Rayner, 'Bitter Sweet', *Spectator*, 5 April 1968, 446–47

Higgins, Aidan, 'Alien Corn', *Hibernia*, July 1968, 20

Jebb, Julian, 'Sensitive Survivors', *The Times*, 30 March 1968, n.p.

Sullivan, Walter, '"Erewhom and Eros" The Short Story Again', *Sewanee Review* 83 (1975), 537

## Sleep It Off Lady

Bailey, Paul, 'True Romance', *The Times Literary Supplement*, 22 October 1976, 1321

Clapp, Susanna, 'Bleak Treats', *The New Statesman*, 22 October 1976, 568

Hall, Sandra, 'Analytical Artist in Disenchantment', *The Bulletin*, 19 March 1976, 51

Sullivan, Mary, 'Down on Their Luck', *Sunday Telegraph*, 24 October 1976, n.p.

Totton, Nick, 'Speak, Memory', *The Spectator*, 30 October 1976, 22

Wood, Michael, 'Endangered Species', *The New York Times Book Review*, 11 November 1976, 30–2

## Smile Please

Blythe, Ronald, 'A Girl from Dominica', *The Listener*, 6 December 1979, 789

Hynes, Samuel, '*Smile Please*: An Unfinished Autobiography by Jean Rhys', *The New Republic*, 31 May 1980, 28–31

McNeil, Helen, 'Broken Heart', *The New Statesman*, 15 February 1980, 253–4

Nye, Robert, 'Jean Rhys: the real rare thing', *Scotsman*, 5 January 1980, n.p.

Pritchett, V. S., 'Displaced Person', *The New York Review of Books*, 14 August 1980, 8, 10

Rose, Phyllis, 'Jean Rhys in Fact and Fiction', *Yale Review* 69 (1980), 596–602

Trilling, Diana, 'The Odd Career of Jean Rhys', *The New York Times Book Review*, 25 May 1980, 1, 17

Warner, Marina, 'Jean Rhys: A Voyage in the Dark', *The Sunday Times*, 18 November 1979, 41

## Letters

Amory, Mark, 'Poverty and Rain', *Spectator*, 16 June 1984, n.p.

Gornick, Vivien, 'Making the Most of her Miseries', *The New York Times Book Review*, 30 October 1984, 3ff

Grumbach, Doris, 'Jean Rhys: Pleasures and Regrets', *Washington Post*, 7 October 1984, n.p.

Moorhead, Caroline, 'Spirit and the Letter', *The Times*, 21 May 1984, 17

Warner, Marina, 'The Art of Survival', *The Sunday Times*, 18 November 1979, 41

## 'Omnibus' film on Rhys, BBC

Clayton, Sylvia, 'Jean Rhys Heroines Seen in Vignettes', *The Daily Telegraph*, 25 November 1974, 11

BACKGROUND MATERIAL

Achebe, Chinua, 1988, 'Colonialist Criticism', *Hopes and Impediments: Selected Essays 1965–1987*, Oxford: Heinemann International, 46–61 (first pub. as *Morning Yet On Creation Day*, London: Heinemann, 1975)

Adisa, Opel Palmer, 1986, *Bake-Face and Other Guava Stories*, Berkeley: Kelsey St Press

Ahmad, Aijaz, 1992, *In Theory: Classes, Nations, Literatures*, London: Verso

Alleyne, Mervyn C., 1961, 'Language and Society in St Lucia', *Caribbean Studies* 1, 1–11

Allfrey, Phyllis Shand, 1997, *The Orchid House*, New Brunswick, NJ: Rutgers University Press (first published London: Constable, 1953)

Allsopp, Richard, 1972, 'The Problem of Acceptability in Caribbean Creolized English', paper presented at UWI/UNESCO Conference, University of the West Indies, Trinidad

Antoni, Robert, 1991, *Divine Trace*, London: Robin Clark

   1997, *Blessed Is the Fruit*, New York: Henry Holt and Co.

Appiah, Kwame Anthony, 1992, *In My Father's House: Africa in the Philosophy of Culture*, Oxford: Oxford University Press

Ashcroft, Bill, Gareth Griffiths and Helen Tiffin, 1989, *The Empire Writes Back: Theory and Practice in Post-Colonial Literatures*, London and New York: Routledge

   1995, *The Post-Colonial Studies Reader*, London: Routledge

Baldwin, James, 1964, *Notes of a Native Son*, London: Corgi

Bek, Lilla and Annie Wilson, 1981, *What Colour Are You?* Wellingborough: Turningstone Press

Bell, Hesketh, 1946, *Glimpses of a Governor's Life*, London: Sampson Low, Marston and Co.

   1889, *Obeah, Witchcraft in the West Indies*, London: Sampson Low, Marston, Searle and Rivington

Benîtez-Rojo, Antonio, 1992, *The Repeating Island: The Caribbean and the Postmodern Perspective*, trans. James Maraniss, Durham: Duke University Press

Benjamin, Tritobia Hayes, 1994, *The Life and Art of Lois Mailou Jones*, San Francisco: Pomegranate Books

Bennett, Herman L., 1989, 'The Challenge to the Post-Colonial: A Case Study of February Revolution in Trinidad', *The Modern Caribbean*, ed. Knight and Palmer, Chapel Hill: University of Carolina Press, 129–46

Bennett, Louise, 1979, *Jamaica Labrish*, Kingston: Sangster's Bookstores

Bhabha, Homi, 1994, *The Location of Culture*, London: Routledge

Bliss, Eliot, 1984, *Luminous Isle*, London: Virago (first published 1934)

Bowen, Stella, 1984, *Drawn from Life*, introd. Julia Loewe, London: Virago

Brathwaite, Kamau, 1967, *Rights of Passage*, London: Oxford University Press (reprinted as part of *The Arrivants*, Oxford: Oxford University Press, 1973)
  1984, *History of the Voice*, London: New Beacon Books
  1993, 'Brother Man', 'Jazz and the West Indian Novel', *Roots*, Ann Arbor: University of Michigan Press, 55–110, 171–89
  1994, *Barabajan Poems*, New York: Savacou North
Brodber, Erna, 1980, *Jane and Louisa Will Soon Come Home*, London: New Beacon Press
Brontë, Charlotte, 1941, *Jane Eyre*, New York: Dodd, Mead and Company
Brontë, Emily, 1988, *Wuthering Heights*, London: Routledge
Carew, Jan, 1958, *Black Midas*, London: Secker and Warburg
Carmichael, Mrs, 1833, *Domestic Manners and Social Condition of the White, Coloured and Negro Population of the West Indies*, 2 vols., London: Whittaker, Treacher and Co.
Cell, John, W., 1982, *The Highest Stage of White Supremacy*, Cambridge: Cambridge University Press
Cesaire, Aimé, 1971, *Cahier d'un retour au pays natal*, Paris: Presence Africaine
Clarke, Austin, 1971, *When He Was Free and Young and Used to Wear Silks*, Toronto: Anansi
Cliff, Michelle, 1990, *Bodies of Water*, New York: Dutton
Colette, 1972, *Recollections*, trans. David Le Vay, New York: Collier Books
  1973, *Mes Apprentissages*, Paris: Flammarion (first published 1936)
  1987, *The Claudine Novels*, trans. Antonia White, London: Penguin
Collins, Merle, 1987, *Angel*, London: Women's Press
Craig, Christine, 1993, *Mint Tea*, Oxford: Heinemann
Dance, Daryl Cumber, 1986, *Fifty Caribbean Writers*, Westport, Conn.: Greenwood Press
Davies, Carole Boyce, 1994, *Black Women, Writing and Identity: Migrations of the Subject*, London: Routledge
Davies, Carole Boyce and Elaine Savory Fido, eds. 1990, *Out of the Kumbla: Caribbean Women and Literature*, Trenton, NJ: Africa World Press
Deckard, Barbara Sinclair, 1983, *The Women's Movement: Political, Socio-economic and Psychological*, New York: Harper and Row
de Lisser, Herbert, 1984, *The White Witch of Rosehall*. Kingston: Macmillan (first published 1929)
de Nève, Edouard, 1932, *In de Strik*, Amsterdam: Andries Blitz; trans. Jean Rhys as *Barred*, London: Harmsworth
  1933, *Sous Les Verrous*, Paris: Librairie Stock
  (with Henriette van Eyk), 1934, *Aan Den Loopenden Band*, Amsterdam: Querido
  1937, *Schuwe Vogels*, Amsterdam: Querido

Devonish, Hubert, 1986, *Language and Liberation: Creole Language Politics in the Caribbean*, London: Karia Press

Dissanayake, Wimal and Wickramagamage, Carmen, 1993, *Self and Colonial Desire: The Travel Writings of V.S. Naipaul*, New York: Peter Lang

*Dominica Dial*, 1883–

Drake, Sandra, 1986, *Wilson Harris and the Modern Tradition: a New Architecture of the World*, Westport, Conn.: Greenwood Press

Drayton, Geoffrey, 1959, *Christopher*, London: Collins

Eagleton, Terry, 1983, *Literary Theory*. London: Basil Blackman

Espinet, Ramabai, 1991, 'Barred: Trinidad 1987', *Green Cane and Juicy Flotsam*, ed. Carmen C. Esteves and Lizabeth Paravisini-Gebert, New Brunswick, NJ: Rutgers University Press, 80–5

Eysteinsson, Astradur, 1990, *The Concept of Modernism*, Ithaca: Cornell University Press

Fanon, Frantz, 1969, *The Wretched of the Earth*, Harmondsworth: Penguin (first published 1961)

1970, *Black Skin, White Masks*, London: Granada

Faulkner, William, 1986, *Absalom, Absalom!*, New York: Random House

Faust, Beatrice, 1980, *Women, Sex and Pornography*, Harmondsworth: Penguin

Fido, Elaine, 1985, 'Psycho-Sexual Aspects of the Woman in V. S. Naipaul's Fiction', *West Indian Literature and Its Social Context*, ed. Mark McWatt, Cave Hill, Barbados: Dept. of English, 78–94

Ford, Ford Madox, 1931, *When the Wicked Man*, New York: Horace Liveright, Inc.

1971, 'The Fox (D. H. Lawrence)', *Your Mirror to My Times*, ed. Killigrew, New York: Holt, Rinehart, Winston, 309–322

1983, *The Good Soldier*, New York: Vintage Books

ed. *the translatlantic review*

Ford-Smith, Honor, 1996, *my mother's last dance*, Toronto: Sister Vision

Gates, Henry Louis Jr, ed, 1984, *Black Literature and Literary Theory*, New York: Methuen

1988, *The Signifying Monkey: a Theory of African-American Literary Criticism*, Oxford: Oxford University Press

Gilbert, Sandra M. and Susan Gubar, eds., 1979, *The Madwoman in the Attic: the Woman Writer and the Nineteenth-Century Literary Imagination*. New Haven: Yale University Press

1988, *No Man's Land: the Place of the Woman Writer in the Twentieth Century*, Yale: New Haven University Press

Gilman, Sander L., 1985, 'Black Bodies, White Bodies: Toward an Iconography of Female Sexuality in Late Nineteenth Century Art, Medicine, and Literature', *Critical Enquiry* 12: 1 (Autumn), 204–42

Gilroy, Beryl, 1994, *Black Teacher*, London: Bogle-L'Ouverture Press, (first published London: Cassell, 1976)

Gilroy, Paul, 1993, *The Black Atlantic*, Cambridge, Mass: Harvard University Press

Glissant, Édouard, 1985, *Pays Rêvé, pays réel*, Paris: Seuil
  1989, *Caribbean Discourse*, tr. Michael Dash, Charlottesville: University of Virginia Press

Goodison, Lorna, 1992, 'Lullaby for Jean Rhys', *Selected Poems*, Ann Arbor: University of Michigan Press

Gutkind, Lee, ed., *Creative Non-Fiction*, Pittsburgh: Creative Nonfiction Foundation (journal)

Hanscombe, Gillian and Virginia L. Smyers, 1987, *Writing for Their Lives: The Modernist Woman 1910–1940*, Boston: Northeastern University Press

Hardy, Thomas, 1978, *Jude the Obscure*, New York: Norton

Harris, Wilson, 1960, *Palace of the Peacock*, London: Faber and Faber
  1990, 'The Fabric of the Imagination', *Third World Quarterly* 12: 1, 175–86

Hewlett, Maurice, 1939, *The Forest Lovers*, London: Thomas Nelson and Sons

Hodge, Merle, 1970, *Crick Crack Monkey*, London: André Deutsch

Holden, George, 1972, 'Introduction', *Nana*, Emile Zola, Harmondsworth: Penguin, 5–17

Honychurch, Lennox, 1984, *The Dominica Story: A History of the Island*, Roseau: The Dominica Institute

Hulme, Peter and Neil L. Whitehead, eds., 1992, *Wild Majesty: Encounters with Caribs from Columbus to the Present Day*. Oxford: Clarendon Press

Ingledew, David, 1986, 'John Hearne', *Fifty Caribbean Writers*, ed. Daryl C. Dance, Westport, Conn.: Greenwood Press, 198–206

Iser, Wolfgang, 1978, *The Act of Reading*, Baltimore: Johns Hopkins University Press
  1989, *Prospecting: From Reader Response to Literary Anthropology*, Baltimore: Johns Hopkins University Press

James, C. L. R., 1963, *The Black Jacobins: Toussaint L'Ouverture and the San Domingo Revolution*, New York: Vintage Books
  1983, *Beyond a Boundary*, London: Hutchinson (first published New York: Pantheon Books, 1963)

JanMohamed, Abdul, 1983, *Manichean Aesthetics*, Amherst: University of Massachusetts Press

Joyce, James, 1961, *Ulysses*, New York: Vintage

Judd, Alan, 1990, *Ford Madox Ford*, London: HarperCollins

Kincaid, Jamaica, 1983, *At the Bottom of the River*, New York: Farrar, Straus and Giroux
  1985, *Annie John*, New York: Farrar, Straus and Giroux
  1990, *Lucy*, New York: Farrar, Straus and Giroux

King, Bruce, 1995, *Derek Walcott and West Indian Drama*, Oxford: Clarendon

Knight, Franklin W. and Colin A. Palmer, 1989, 'The Caribbean: a Regional Overview', *The Modern Caribbean*, ed. Knight and Palmer, Chapel Hill: University of North Carolina, 1–20

Lamming, George, 1953, *In the Castle of My Skin*, London: Michael Joseph
1970, *Season of Adventure*, London: Michael Joseph
1971, *Water with Berries*, London: Longman
1995, 'Occasion for Speaking', *The Post-Colonial Studies Reader*, ed. Bill Ashcroft, Gareth Griffiths and Helen Tiffin, London: Routledge, 12–17

Lawrence, D. H., 1980, *Women in Love*, Harmondsworth: Penguin

Lionnet, Francoise, 1989, *Autobiographical Voices*, Ithaca: Cornell University Press

Lindfors, Bernth and Reinhart Sander, eds., 1992, *Dictionary of Literary Biography*, vol. 117, Detroit: Gale Research, 199

Lovell, Glenville, 1995, *Fire in the Canes*, New York: Soho Press

Luscher, Max, 1971, *The Luscher Colour Test*, trans. Ian Scott, London: Pan Books

MacDonald-Smythe, Antonia, 1997, 'Kwik! Kwak!: Narrating the Self. A Reading of *The Autobiography of My Mother*', paper given at the 16th Annual West Indian Literature Conference, University of Miami, Coral Gables, Florida

Mais, Roger, *The Hills Were Joyful Together*, 1953, London: Jonathan Cape

Manley, Rachel, 1996, *Drumblair*, Kingston: Ian Randle Publishers

Marshall, Paule, 1959, *Brown Girl, Brownstones*, Old Westbury: New York
1983, *Praisesong for the Widow*, New York: Putnam's Sons
1984, *Reena and Other Stories*, Old Westbury: New York: The Feminist Press

McKenzie, Alicia, 1992, *Satellite City and Other Stories*, Burnt Mill: Longman

Melville, Pauline, 1990, *Shape-Shifter*, London: The Women's Press

Mittelholzer, Edgar, 1941, *Corentyne Thunder*, London: Eyre and Spottiswoode

Mizener, Arthur, 1971, *The Saddest Story: Biography of Ford Madox Ford*, New York: Carroll and Graf

Mordecai, Pamela, 1989, *Journey Poem*, Kingston: Sandberry Press

Naipaul, V. S., 1957, *The Mystic Masseur*, London: André Deutsch
1967, *A House for Mr Biswas*, London: André Deutsch
1969, *The Middle Passage*, Harmondsworth: Penguin
1980, *Guerillas*, Harmondsworth: Penguin
1981, 'Michael X and the Black Power Killings in Trinidad' and 'A New King for the Congo: Mobutu and the Nihilism of Africa', *The Return of Eva Peron with The Killings in Trinidad*, Harmondsworth: Penguin (essays originally published 1974, 1979), 9–92; 165–96

Nugent, Maria, 1907, *Lady Nugent's Journal of her Residence in Jamaica from 1801–1805*, ed. Philip Wright, Institute of Jamaica (first published 1839)

Phillips, Caryl, 1989, *Higher Ground*, New York, Viking

Pollard, Velma, 1994, *Karl and Other Stories*, Burnt Mill: Longman

Prince, Mary, 1987, *History of Mary Prince, a West Indian Slave, Related by Herself*, ed. Henry Lours Gates, *The Classic Slave Narratives*, New York: New American Library (first published 1831)

Rattray, Capt. R. S., 1969, *Akan-Ashanti Folk-Tales*, Oxford: Clarendon Press (first published 1930)

Reid, Vic, 1949, *New Day*, New York: Knopf

*Report of the Royal Commission to Inquire into The Condition and Affairs of the Island of Dominica*, 1894, London: Eyre and Spottiswoode for Her Majesty's Stationery Office

Rich, Adrienne, 1979, 'Ann Sexton: 1928–1974', *On Lies, Secrets and Silence: Selected Prose 1966–1978*, New York: W. W. Norton

Roberts, Peter A., 1988, *West Indians & their Language*, Cambridge: Cambridge University Press

Rodney, Walter, 1972, *How Europe Underdeveloped Africa*, London: Bogle-L'Ouverture Publications

Rohlehr, Gordon, 1990, *Calypso and Society in Pre-Independence Trinidad*, Port of Spain, Trinidad

Salick, Roydon, ed., 1993, *The Comic Vision in West Indian Literature*, Marabella, Trinidad: no publisher (date taken from introduction, n.d. on volume)

Scott, Dennis, 1970, *An Echo in the Bone, Plays for Today*, ed. Errol Hill, Burnt Mill: Longman, 73–137

Seacole, Mary, 1984, *The Wonderful Adventures of Mary Seacole in Many Lands*, London: Falling Wall Press (first published 1857)

Selvon, Sam, 1956, *The Lonely Londoners*, London: Wingate

Senior, Olive, 1989, *Arrival of the Snake Woman and Other Stories*, Burnt Mill: Longman

　　1986, *Summer Lightning*, Burnt Mill: Longman

　　1994, 'Meditation on Red', *Gardening in the Tropics*, Toronto: McClelland and Stewart, 44–53

　　1995, *Discerner of Hearts and Other Stories*, Toronto: McClelland and Stewart

Simpson, George, 1980, *Religious Cults of the Caribbean*, Rio Pedras: University of Puerto Rico

Smith, Sidonie, 1987, *A Poetics of Women's Autobiography*, Bloomington: Indiana University Press

Smith, Sidonie and Julia Watson, eds., 1992, *De/Colonizing the Subject*, Minneapolis: University of Minnesota Press

Soyinka, Wole, 1976, *Myth, Literature and the African World*, Cambridge: Cambridge University Press

Stang, Sondra, ed., 1986, *The Ford Madox Ford Reader*, New York: The Ecco Press

Stone, Judy, 1994, *Studies in West Indian Literature: Theatre*, London: Macmillan Press

Voss, Norine, 1986, '"Saying the Unsayable": An Introduction to Women's Autobiography', *Gender Studies: New Directions in Feminist Criticism*, ed. Judith Spector, 218–33, Bowling Green, Ohio: Bowling Green State University Popular Press

Walcott, Derek, 1962, *In a Green Night: Poems 1948–1960*, London: Cape
1980, *Pantomime*, New York: Farrar, Straus and Giroux

Walker, Alice, 1982, *The Colour Purple*, New York: Washington Square Press

Walvin, James, 1993, *Black Ivory*, London: Fontana

Warner, Marina, 1992, *Indigo*, New York: Simon and Schuster

Williams, Linda Ruth, 1993, *Sex in the Head: Visions of Femininity and Film in D. H. Lawrence*, Detroit: Wayne State University Press

Wynter, Sylvia, 1962, *The Hills of Hebron*, London: Jonathan Cape

Zola, Emile, 1990, *L'Assommoir* (1877), Paris: Pocket Presses
1972, *Nana*, trans. George Holden, Harmondsworth: Penguin

# Index

Abel, Elizabeth, 202
Accaria, Diana, 253
Achebe, Chinua, 204, 268
Adam, Mrs, 227, 233, 236
Adisa, Opel Palmer, 153
Africa, identity and traditions, 32, 63, 107,
    112–13, 121, 204, 207, 215, 217, 220,
    232, 239, 244, 247, 249–50, 254, 256,
    265, 268–70
Afro-Saxon, 270
*After Leaving Mr MacKenzie*, xx, 34, 38–9,
    54, 57–84, 85, 89, 112, 135, 197, 199,
    240, 242–4, 250, 254, 260
Agar, Daphne, 229, 243
Ahmad, Aijaz, 268
Allen, Walter, 253
Alleyne, Mervyn, 269
Allfrey, Phyllis, xx, xxi, 205, 212, 214, 228,
    251, 253, 256, 265
    *The Orchid House*, xx, 205, 253, 256
Allsopp, Richard, 269
Alvarez, A., 156, 209, 239, 257
Amory, Mark, 184
Amuso, Teresa Rose, 119
Anancy stories, 154, 256
Anderson, Paula G., 212, 253
Andre, Irving, 8, 206
Angier, Carole, 2, 7–8, 11, 20, 24–6, 42,
    48, 65, 68, 70, 76, 117, 134, 157–8,
    179, 189, 192, 199–200, 212, 227–8,
    232–5, 238–41, 243–4, 250, 252,
    254, 256, 259–60, 262, 264, 266–7,
    270
Anglicanism, 114, 188, 193
Anglo-Saxons, 81, 83, 198
animal imagery, 53, 82
Antigua, 247, 250
Antilles, 207

Antoni, Robert, xiii, 227, 270
    *Blessed Is the Fruit*, xiii, 25, 270
Apartheid, 245
Appiah, Anthony, 219, 268
*Art and Literature*, 255, 260
Ashanti culture, 257
Ashcom, Jane Neide, 253
Ashcroft, Bill, Gareth Griffiths and Helen
    Tiffin, 228
Assembly (Dominica), 229
Athill, Diana, 181–2, 192, 234
Atwood, Margaret, 211
Auden, W. H., 227
autobiography, 184, 187

Bahamas, 257
Bailey, Paul, 258
Baker, Josephine, xii
Baldanza, Frank, 57
Baldwin, James, 191
Baker, R., 258
Barbados, 165, 218–19
Barber-Williams, Patricia, 215, 253
Barnes, Djuna, 227
Beardsley, Aubrey, 107
Bek, Lilla, and Annie Wilson, 244
Bell, Hesketh, xix, 4, 113, 164, 189, 229,
    231, 264
    *Glimpses of a Governor's Life*, 113
Bennett, Herman L., 217
Bennett, Louise, 119, 254
Benjamin, Tritobia, 227
Benstock, Shari, xii, 227, 239
Berger, Gertrude, 211
Bhahba, Homi, 265
Black Power movement, 207, 217, 265,
    268
Blais, Joline, 134, 253

297

Bliss, Eliot, 16, 147, 214, 256
  *Luminous Isle*, 147
Blodgett, Harriet, 202, 253
blues, 118
Blythe, Ronald, 184, 262
Boer War, 229
Boissêche, 257
Bona Vista, 8–10, 134, 237, 247–8
Bowen, Stella, 39, 50, 249, 266
  *Drawn from Life*, 39, 49
Branson, Stephanie, 135
Brathwaite, Kamau, ix, xi, xiii, 11, 112,
    191, 206, 207, 214, 216–23, 232, 250,
    254, 257, 268–70
  *The Arrivants*, 250, 268
  *Barabajan Poems*, 270
  *Contradictory Omens*, 217
  *History of the Voice*, 256
  *Rights of Passage*, xxi
Braybrooke, Neville, 204
Britain, 87, 95, 150, 152, 174, 197, 200–2,
    204, 208, 211, 215–16, 230, 232,
    245–6, 264–6, 268
Britten, Florence Howe, 266
Brodber, Erna, xiii, 112, 242, 250
  *Jane and Louisa Will Soon Come Home*,
    250
Brontë, Charlotte, 22, 93, 203, 242,
    253–4, 268
  *Jane Eyre*, 22, 93, 142, 135, 142, 145,
    203, 254–5, 268
Brontë, Emily, 133, 203, 254, 268
  *Wuthering Heights*, 133, 203, 254, 268
Brown, Bev, 70, 212
Brown, Nancy Hemond, 28, 64, 91, 106,
    152
Brown, Hilton, 250
'Brown Privilege' Bill, 5
Budapest, 235
Burleigh, Harry T., 227
Byrne, Jack, 109, 254

calypso, 153, 177, 261
Campbell, Elaine, 113–14, 215, 253
Cantwell, Mary, 36
Carco, Francis, 238
Carew, Jan, xxi, 154
  *Black Midas*, xxi
Caribbean, viii, 14, 34, 37, 41, 45, 59, 63,
    65, 68, 73–6, 81, 83, 86, 89, 96, 99,
    103–6, 112, 114, 116–18, 145–8,
    152–4, 157, 159, 161, 163–4, 166,

168, 171, 174–5, 178, 195–7, 200–3,
    205–9, 211–26, 239, 247, 252–4, 256,
    265–6, 268–70
  African-Caribbean, 112–13, 186, 218,
    268
Caribs, the, 96, 172–3
Carmichael, Mrs, 33, 233
Carnival, 78, 106–7, 110, 114, 187–8
Carrera Suarez, Isabel, and Esther
    Alvarez Lopez, 59, 167
Casey, Nancy, 59, 135, 168, 173, 202, 211
Catholicism, 4, 9, 29, 109–10, 114–15,
    187–8, 250
Cell, John, 30
Celtic, 114, 235, 242, 267
Cesaire, Aimé, 270
Chaucer, 246
Cheriton-Fitzpaine, 111
Chopin, Kate, 211
civil rights, 202
Clapp, Susanna, 258
Clarke, Austin, 254
Clayton, Sylvia, 267
Cliff, Michelle, xiii, 153, 265
Codacionni, Marie-Jose, 253
*Collected Short Stories, The*, xxi, 42, 44, 46–7,
    71, 86, 88–9, 113, 128, 152–76
Colette, 19, 41, 184, 234, 238, 246
  *Mes Apprentissages*, 19, 234
  *Recollections*, 238
Collins, Merle, 153, 242
colonialism, 208, 239
Conrad, Joseph, 41
Craig, Christine, 153
*Creative Nonfiction*, 191
Creole language, 2, 20, 173, 232, 253–4,
    257
Creole, white, viii, 29, 35, 59, 65, 107,
    136, 173, 208, 210, 214–15, 222, 235,
    237, 270
Cuba, 269
cummings, e. e., 227
Curtis, Jan, 244

Dance, Daryl, 227
Davidson, Arnold, 58, 68, 241
Davies, Carole Boyce, 226
Davies, Carole Boyce, and Elaine Savory
    Fido, 226, 270
Davies, Hunter, 267
Davies, William, 8, 231
Dawson, Margaret Cheney, 199

D'Costa, Jean, 3, 196, 212, 265
Deckard, Barbara Sinclair, 200
Delaney, Frank, 114
De Lisser, Herbert, 204, 253
   *The Witch of Rosehall*, 20
Devonish, Hubert, 232
Dick, Kay, 203
Dickinson, Emily, 119, 243
Dissanayake, Wimal, and Carmen,
   Wickramagamage, 66
Dominica, xix, 2–4, 9–10, 22–4, 27, 30,
   32, 34–5, 42, 59, 65, 67, 96, 114, 116,
   148, 150, 164–5, 172–3, 181, 186–7,
   189, 192, 200, 204, 206, 208, 212–14,
   215, 226, 229–31, 237, 242, 244–5,
   247–8, 253, 256, 264
*Dominica Dial*, 6–8, 11, 229–31
Dominican Republic, 269
Drabble, Margaret, 253
Drake, Sandra, 197
Drayton, Geoffrey, 206
   *Christopher*, 206

Eagleton, Terry, 196
Eliot, T. S., 224
emancipation, 107, 136, 141
Emery, Mary Lou, ix, 41, 59, 68, 73–4,
   77, 96, 110, 113, 117, 197, 212, 252–3,
   265
England, viii, 22, 24, 27–8, 29–30, 34–5,
   63, 65–8, 71, 75, 80–1, 84, 86–7,
   89–90, 95–6, 98, 103–5, 111, 117,
   130, 137–9, 142–7, 157, 164, 171, 173,
   180, 189–90, 192, 194, 196, 198, 200,
   208, 213–14, 216, 229, 231, 235, 247,
   256
English language, 37, 42, 44, 66, 167–8,
   234, 254, 269
Erwin, Linda Lee, 133
Espinet, Ramabai, 153, 251, 264
Eysteinsson, Astradur, 42

Fanon, Frantz, 66, 114, 206, 270
   *Wretched of the Earth*, 206
Fascism, 200, 232
Faulkner, William, 134, 253
Faust, Beatrice, 71
Fayad, Mona, 253
Federation of the West Indies, xxi
feminist, viii, xii, 58–60, 66, 68, 71, 75,
   83, 185, 200–2, 209–12, 241, 250,
   253, 266–7

Ferguson, Moira, 215, 221, 253
Fido, Elaine, 66 *see also* Savory, Elaine
Flaubert, Gustave, 41
Ford, Ford Madox, xii, xx, 22, 24, 36, 39,
   40, 42–3, 47–9, 147–8, 152, 154, 159,
   183, 198–200, 227, 234, 236–8, 240,
   244, 249, 266
   *The Good Soldier*, 47, 237, 240, 244
   *When the Wicked Man*, 39, 49, 237,
   267
*Ford-Smith, Honor*, 270
*Forest Lovers*, 15
Foster, Margaret, 267
France, French influence, 24, 26, 37,
   40–2, 75, 81, 86, 89, 117, 180, 202,
   215, 247, 251, 253, 256, 266
French language and patois, 42, 44, 46,
   52, 98, 123, 167, 234, 238, 254
French Resistance, 264
Freud, Sigmund, 65, 202, 243, 253
Frickey, Pierrette, 207, 228–9
Friedman, Ellen G., 253–4

Gaines, Nora, 226, 234
Gardiner, Judith Kegan, 40, 47, 50, 65,
   165, 209–10, 252, 258, 269
Garnett, Edward, 266
Gates, Henry Louis, 268
Geneva (Genever), xix, 136, 216, 254
German, 123
Gilbert, Sandra M., and Susan Gubar,
   58, 203, 242
Gilkes, Michael, 253
Gilman, Charlotte Perkins, 211
Gilman, Sander L., 66, 94, 246–7
Gilroy, Beryl, 213
Gilroy, Paul, 268
Givner, Joan, 135, 253
Glissant, Edouard, 270
Goodison, Lorna, xiii–xiv
*Good Morning, Midnight*, xx, 22, 26, 39,
   57–8, 68–9, 78, 109–32, 135, 150–1,
   181, 190, 199–200, 226–7, 233,
   243–4, 251–2, 254, 267
Gordimer, Nadine, 224
Gorman, Herbert, 199
Gornick, Vivien, 262
Gothic, 253
Gray, Cecil, 233
Gregg, Veronica, ix, x, 3, 8, 14, 21–2, 30,
   42, 59, 75, 94, 110, 134, 167, 214, 216,
   244, 252, 258

Griffith, Glyne, 135
Guillen, Nicholas, 270
Guiness, Gerald, 253
Gunn, Ander, 260
Guyana, 269

Hagley, Carol, 79
Haiti, 147
Hall, Sandra, 258
Haltrecht, Montague, 258
Hamer, Max, xx, xxi, 28, 256–7, 262, 267
Hamilton, Ian, 267
Hanscombe, Gillian, and Virginia L. Smyers, 42
Hardy, Thomas, 256
  *Jude the Obscure*, 256
Harris, Wilson, xi, xiii, xxi, 207, 219–21, 270
  *Palace of the Peacock*, xxi
Harrison, Nancy, 14, 148, 210, 252–3, 253
Hawthorn, Jeremy, 134
Hearne, John, 207–8, 269
Hegel, 199
Helen of Troy, 216
Hemmerechts, 253
Hemingway, Earnest, 152, 199, 224, 253
Heppenstall, Raynor, 191
Hewlett, Maurice, 233
Higdon, David Leon, 253
Higgins, Aidan, 258
Hite, Molly, 58, 134
Hodge, Merle, 242
Holden, George, 92
Holland and Dutch culture, 42, 86, 232, 254, 261, 264, 266
Holland, J. Gill, and Robert A. Meyers, 253
Holloway Prison, 59, 167–8, 270
Homer, 222
Honychurch, Lennox, 4, 6, 8, 150, 206, 216, 228, 231, 247, 259, 264
Honychurch, Patricia, 232
Horner, Avril, and Sue Zlosnik, 110, 211, 251, 254
Howard, Mr, 61–3, 65, 67, 76, 146, 161–2, 183, 234, 242, 251, 262, 268
Howells, Coral Ann, 61, 65, 68, 71, 110, 164, 196, 243–4, 251, 258
Hulme, Peter, ix, xi, 215, 217–19, 221–2, 253

Hulme, Peter, and Neil L. Whitehead, 247, 260
Hunt, Leigh, 197
Hynes, Samuel, 261

Imperial Road, The, xix
India and the Indo-Caribbean, 217, 220, 239, 256, 269
Iser, Wolfgang, 37, 198

Jamaica, 136, 207, 213, 218, 226, 233, 254, 256, 269
James, C. L. R., 223, 268, 261
James, Henry, 224
James, Louis, ix, xi, 9, 62, 91, 113, 133, 150, 180, 201, 228, 244
James, Selma, 212
JanMohamed, Abdul, 206
  *Manichean Aesthetics*, 206
Japanese, 172–3
  *Jean Rhys Review*, xi, 19, 226
Jebb, Julian, 258
Jhabvala, Ruth Prawer, 224
Johnson, Pam, 241
Jones, Lois Mailou, 227
Joseph, Margaret Paul, 215, 253
Joyce, James, 40, 131, 199, 233, 252–3
  *Ulysses*, 131, 233
  *Finnegans Wake*, 233
Judd, Alan, 227, 238, 240
Jung, Karl, 202

Kappers-den Hollander, Martien, 40, 48–9, 208, 232, 237, 266
Keens-Douglas, Paul, 119, 251
Kincaid, Jamaica, xii, 55, 62, 153, 233, 241–2, 265
  *Lucy*, 241
King, Bruce, 260
Kloepfer, Deborah K., 59, 62–3, 113, 210–11, 248, 253
Knapp, Bettina L., 253
Knight, Franklin W., and Colin A. Palmer, 226, 269
Koenen, Anne, 253
Kraf, Elaine, 69, 202
Kubitshek, Missey Dehn, 253

Lacan, Jacques, 211, 244, 253
Lacrosil, Michelle, 215
Laing, R. D., 202

Lamming, George, xi, xiii, 208, 215, 233, 250, 269–70
  *In The Castle Of My Skin*, xxi
  *Pleasures of Exile*, 269
  *Season of Adventure*, 250
  *Water with Berries*, 270
La Plaine Riots, 4, 229
La Rose, John, 204, 268
Lawrence, D. H., 40, 65, 68, 206, 253
Lawson, Lori, 244, 253
*Left Bank, The*, xii, xx, 38–9, 41, 43–4, 47, 54–5, 57, 80, 201, 240, 258, 266
Le Gallez, Paula, 44, 75, 93, 117, 211–12, 243, 246, 253, 258, 269
Legislative Council (Dominica), 229
Leigh, Nancy J., 244
Lenglet, Jean (Edouard de Nève), xx, 10, 12, 25, 36, 39–40, 42, 44, 48–9, 50, 172, 199, 232, 234–5, 237, 240, 264, 266
  *Aan den Loopenden Band*, 240, 266
  *Barred*, 39, 42, 48
  *In de Strik*, 42
  *Schuwe Vogels*, 240
  *Sous les Verrous*, 42
Lessing, Doris, 210, 224, 253
*Letters of Jean Rhys, The*, xxi, 14, 17, 20, 22, 24, 26–8, 86, 89, 111, 113, 116, 133, 149, 150, 155, 167, 195, 228, 233–4, 244, 253, 261
Lindfors, Bernth, and Reinhard Sander, 227
Lindroth, Colette, 147, 215
Lindroth, James, 86–7
Lionnet, François, 183
Lockhart, Acton Don, 5, 229
Lockhart, James Potter, xix
Lockhart, Minna, xix, 5
London, 75, 103, 119, 148, 181, 200, 213, 238, 241, 268
*Londoner's Diary*, 267
*London Magazine*, 87, 191, 203
Lonsdale, Thorunn, 48
Look Lai, Wally, 154, 204–6, 216, 218
Lovell, Glenville, 233
Lovett, Robert Morss, 199
Luengo, Anthony, 203, 253
*Luscher Colour Test, The*, 244

MacDonald-Smythe, Antonia, 257
Malcolm, Cheryl Alexander, and David Malcolm, 155, 157, 191, 258
Mair, John, 250

Mais, Roger, xx, 208
  *The Hills Were Joyful Together*, xx
Manet, 94, 247
Manley, Rachel, 270
Mansfield, Katherine, 152, 208–9
Margarey, Kevin, 135
Maroons, 254
Marshall, Paule, xiii, xxi, 153, 242
  *Brown Girl, Brownstones*, xxi
Martinique, 117, 136, 140, 161, 174, 237
Marx, Karl, 26
  *Das Kapital*, 26
masking, 77–9, 82, 121, 181, 240, 248
Massacre, 10, 232, 247–8
Maupassant, Guy de, 41
McKenzie, Alicia, 153
McNeil, Helen, 261
Mellown, Elgin, 199, 201, 203, 208–9, 228, 238, 267
Melly, George, 261
Melville, Pauline, 153, 166, 259
  *Shapeshifter*, 259
Middle Passage, 265
Miles, Rosalind, 202
Milton, John, 114
Mittelholzer, Edgar, xx
  *Corentyne Thunder*, xx
Mizener, Arthur, 48, 227, 234, 238, 265–6
Modernism, 36, 41–2, 197, 206, 238–9, 252, 253, 265
Moore, Judith, 59
Mordecai, Pamela, 233
Morrell, A. C., 155
Morris, Mervyn, 213
Moss, Howard, 253
Moyne Commission, 276
'Mulatto Ascendancy', 229

Naipaul, V. S., xi, xii, xxi, 66, 73, 197, 217, 233, 241, 243, 253, 265, 270
  *A House for Mr Biswas*, 241
  *The Mystic Masseur*, xxi
  *Guerillas*, 66
  *The Return of Eva Peron with The Killings in Trinidad*, 265
nation language, 153, 232
Nebeker, Helen, 59–60, 70, 78, 92, 135, 202, 242, 244, 253–4, 267
Nelson, Barbara A., 253
New Beacon Books, 204, 268
*New York Times*, 242
*New York Herald Tribune*, 243

*New Statesman*, 266
Nicholls, Henry, 5–7, 11, 229
Nielsen, Hanne, and Fleming Brahms, 135
Nigeria, 248
Nin, Anaïs, 227
Nollen, Elizabeth Mahn, 253
Nudd, Donna Marie, 227
Nugent, Lady, 233
Nye, Robert, 184

Oates, Joyce Carol, 253
obeah, 110, 204, 254, 257
O'Callaghan, Evelyn, 147, 202, 214, 233, 256
O'Connor, Teresa, ix, 62, 65, 113, 115, 192, 197, 212, 242, 247
*Omnibus*, 267
*Our Miss Gibbs*, xix, 12, 180

Paravisini-Gebert, Lizabeth, 3, 7, 212, 227, 228, 230, 233, 253, 256, 265
Paris, xii, 24, 37, 43, 54, 66, 74–6, 81, 119, 148, 174, 181, 199, 227, 235, 238, 251
Parkin, Molly, 267
*Penguin Modern Stories*, 156, 168, 170, 260
Philip, M. Nourbese, xiii, 233
Phillips, Caryl, xiii, 227
Picasso, 247
Plante, David, 3, 12–13, 17, 19, 21, 23, 32, 60–1, 112, 177, 184, 190, 232–3, 251, 251
Pocomania, 250
Pollard, Velma, 153
Porter, Denis, 253
postcolonial, 196, 214, 216, 220, 228, 253, 267–8
postmodern, 268
*Postures*, xx, 41, 266
Potts, Sophia ('Irish Granny'), 26, 31, 235
Prince, Mary, 233
Pritchett, V. S., 184
Puerto Rico, 269

*Quartet*, xi, xx, 16, 38–40, 47–58, 68–9, 75, 80, 89, 112, 135, 180, 190, 198–9, 226–7, 233, 327–8, 240, 243–5, 254, 260, 266

race, 86, 131, 188, 196, 208, 213, 216, 218–19, 268, 270
Raiskin, Judith, 110, 164, 167, 214, 255

Ramchand, Kenneth, 68, 153, 164, 205, 208, 216, 218, 227, 268
*The West Indian Novel and its Background*, 205
Raskin, Barbara, 266
Rastafarianism, 250
Rattray, Capt. R. S., 257
Reid, Vic, xx, 208
*New Day*, xx
*Report of the Royal Commission to Inquire into The Condition and Affairs of the Island of Dominica*, 4, 6, 229
Rhys, Jean
  and ageing, 79
  and alcohol, 32, 67, 78, 121, 213, 252
  and Phyllis Allfrey, 253
  and autobiography, 177–95, 212
  birth, xix
  and class, 1–35
  and clothes, 179, 181
  and colours, 85–108, 126, 172, 237, 244–5
  and creative non-fiction, 177–95
  and criticism, 196–225
  and daughter, Maryvonne, xx, 13, 183, 234, 240–1, 264, 266
  and dreams, 146, 252
  and ghosts, 74, 114, 125, 147, 175, 215, 250
  and humour, 109–32, 251
  and Jewish connection, 264
  and landscape, 133–51, 174
  and makeup, 179, 181
  and Manicheanism, 114–15
  manuscripts (unpublished):
    'At first I knew remarkably little . . .', 254
    'At the Ropemaker's Arms', 194
    'Black Exercise Book', 14, 20, 29, 61–2, 65, 67, 112, 235–7, 242, 251, 262, 268
    'But it is I don't want to write anything' (sic), 249
    'But of course I have longed . . .', 250
    'Chinese Vases', 257
    'Clouds in Stone', 194
    'Daisy', 263
    'Dear, Darling Mr Ramage', 259
    'December 4th, 1938, Mr Howard's House/CREOLE', 65, 110, 115
    'DOWN ALONG: Fragments of Autobiography', 195

'Essay on England', 15, 27, 194
'Fears'
'Good-bye Marcus, Good-bye Rose',
    112
'Green Exercise Book', 1, 12, 259,
    262
'I FEEL so sick . . .', 28, 34, 243
'I have typed out all the stuff . . .', 21
'I'm very often plagued . . .', 233
'I think I fell in love with words . . .',
    111
'I WAS THE YOUNGEST . . .', 242
'L'Affaire Ford', 48
'Leaving School', 191
'Le Revenant'
'Life With You'
'Music and Words', 181
'New Story', 35
'Orange Exercise Book', 17, 23,
    262–3
'Poetry and Poets', 243
'Put It Away',
'Rapunzel, Rapunzel', 159–61
'Red Exercise Book', 165, 248, 259,
    262
'Songs My Mother Didn't Teach
    Me', 180
'Suzy Tells', 37, 49
'The Bible is Modern', 28, 31, 194
'The Birthday', 161
'The Game and the Candle', 161
'The Hanger-On', 194
'The Imperial Road', 164, 191–4,
    229, 262
'The only time my father . . .', 181
'The Poet', 263
'Then came the time that I wrote
    plays . . .'
'They Thought It Was Jazz', 166
'Triple Sec', 37–9, 49, 154, 181,
    236–7, 239
'Vengeance', 263
'Wedding in the Carib Quarter', 67,
    228
'When I think of my parents . . .',
    245
'When I went from room to room
    . . .', 254
and Meta, 15, 32–3, 114, 186
and mirrors, 253
and mother, 3, 29, 63–4, 67, 136, 187,
    228, 235, 264

music and popular songs, 99, 168,
    180–1, 189
names:
    Ella Gray, xix, 12, 22, 24
    Ella Gwendoline Rees Williams, xix,
        22, 27, 31–2, 39, 61, 65, 112, 228
    Ella Hamer, 12–13, 22, 257
    Ella Lenglet, 12, 22
and narrative technique, 52–3, 58
and nationality, 1–35
and obeah, 113–14, 215
and performance, theatre, music hall,
    177–95, 261
and Perse School, xix, 11
and photographs, 179, 245
and poetry, 16, 17, 37, 42, 47, 56, 81,
    164, 175, 180, 237–8, 261
and psychoanalysis, 253
published stories and essays:
    'Again the Antilles', 42, 165, 230
    'A Solid House', 260
    'A Spiritualist', 46–7, 159, 175, 249
    'Close Season for the Old', 263
    'Before the Deluge', 192, 263
    'Fishy Waters', 165
    'Good-bye Marcus, Good-bye,
        Rose', 65, 158
    'Heat', 167, 192
    'Hunger', 192
    'Illusion', 70, 80, 156
    'I Spy a Stranger', 156, 168, 260
    'In the Rue de L'Arrivée', 57
    'Invitation to the Dance', 261, 263
    'I Used to Live Here Once', 74, 175,
        249
    'La Grosse Fifi', 16, 44, 234, 258
    'Learning to be a Mother', 192
    'Let Them Call It Jazz', xiii, 25, 30,
        153, 155, 166, 178, 191, 213, 226,
        241, 244–5, 261, 268
    'Making Bricks Without Straw', 192,
        263
    'Mannequin', 154
    'Mixing Cocktails', 113, 192
    'My Day', xxi, 192, 263
    'Night Out 1925', 154
    'Outside the Machine', 128, 190, 226
    'Overture and Beginners Please',
        155, 191–2, 261
    'Pioneers, Oh, Pioneers', 256, 259
    'Rapunzel, Rapunzel', 155, 175, 257
    'Sleep It Off Lady', 166

'Tea with an Artist', 156
'Temps Perdi', 156, 170–3, 175, 259–60
'The Bishop's Feast', 192
'The Blue Bird', 156, 162–3
'The Chevalier of the Place Blanche', 40, 263
'The Day They Burned the Books', 268
'The Joey Bagstock Smile', 155
'The Lotus', 259
'The Sound of the River', 89, 258, 264
'The Whistling Bird', 192
'Tigers Are Better-Looking', 87
'Till September Petronella', 154, 161, 257, 268
'Trio', 89, 164
'Vienne', 43–4, 54, 152, 154–5, 175, 234, 235, 239–40, 258
'Whatever Became of Old Mrs Pearce?', 192, 263
'Who Knows What's Up in the Attic?', 259
and race, 1–35, 67, 68, 85–108, 239
and religion and spirituality, 109–32, 168, 215
and the Riot, 187
and sexuality, 60–1, 64–8, 95, 104–5
and the short story, 152–77
and siblings, 262
and son, William Owen, xx
and Tree's School (Academy of Dramatic Arts), xix, 24, 179, 189, 247
unpublished letters:
to Diana Athill, 26, 36, 111, 155–6, 179, 234, 258
to Eliot Bliss, 17, 23
to Francis Wyndham, 90, 111, 150, 152, 154–6, 158, 165, 180, 191–2, 233–4, 245, 248, 257, 259, 260–2
to Maryvonne Moerman, 244
to Morchard Bishop, 116
to Oliver Stoner, 113, 156, 250, 257, 261
to Olwyn Hughes, 27, 152, 246, 260–1, 265
to Peggy Kirkaldy, 25, 116, 149, 167, 245, 250, 257
to Phyllis Smyser, 179, 259
to Selma Vaz Dias, 85, 109, 111, 116, 149, 246, 251, 256

to Sonia Orwell, 165, 179, 181, 190, 226, 248, 250, 264
voice, 24
woman, the Rhys, 83, 212
and women's issues, 57–84
and writing, 1–22
Rich, Adrienne, 60
Richelot family, 264
Riley, Joan, 153
Roberts, Peter, 10–11
Rodney, Walter, 268
Rodriguez, Ileana, 150
Rohlehr, Gordon, 260
Rose, Phyllis, 183–4, 262
Roseau, 9–10, 114, 185, 193, 230–7
Ross, Alan, 203, 268

Saakana, Amon Saba, 253
Sadleir, Michael, 213
Sargasso, the, 202, 254
Salick, Roydon, 118
Savory, Elaine, 113, 215, 230, *see also* Fido, Elaine
Schapiro, Barbara Ann, 211, 253
Scharfman, Ronnie, 253
Schreiner, Olive, 215
Scott, Dennis, 112, 250
  *An Echo in the Bone*, 250
Scotland, 26, 235
Seacole, Mary, 233
Selvon, Samuel, xi, xiii, xx, 119, 233, 254, 259
  *A Brighter Sun*, xx
  *The Lonely Londoners*, 259
Senior, Olive, xiii–xiv, 153, 233
Sexton, Anne, 60
Shakespeare, William, 215
  *The Tempest*, 215
Shango cult, 249
Simpson, George, 112
slavery, transatlantic, 71–2, 75, 110, 118, 196, 213, 265
  abolition of, xix
*Sleep It Off Lady*, xxi, 40, 152–76, 191, 256, 257, 259, 262
*Smile Please*, xi, xxi, 1–2, 4, 8, 11–23, 26, 28–34, 39, 47, 68, 70, 89, 100, 106, 113, 115–16, 154, 158, 170, 177–9, 181–90, 195, 228, 234, 240, 242, 246, 248, 249–51, 254, 257, 259, 261–2, 264
Smilowitz, Erica (also Waters), 253–4

Smith, Lancelot Grey Hugh, xix, 24, 28, 37, 90
Smith, Sidonie, 182
Smith, Sidonie, and Julia Watson, 178, 183
Smith, Leslie Tilden, xx, 13, 28, 192, 233, 234, 236, 252, 259, 264, 266
Smollett, Tobias, 197
Smyser, Phyllis, 233, 260
Soskin, William, 246
*soucriant*, 110
South Africa, 87, 245
Southron, Jane Spence, 246
Soyinka, Wole, 204, 268
    *Myth, Literature and the African World*, 268
Spaull, Sue, 253
Spivak, Gayatri, 134, 222, 253
Staley, Thomas, xi, 41, 45, 53, 56, 58, 70, 117, 201, 228, 246, 253
Stang, Sondra, 148, 197
Stapleton, Sir William, 247
Stead, Christina, 210
Sternlicht, Sanford, 77, 228
St John, Bruce, 119, 251, 254, 269
St Lucia, 257
Stone, Judy, 260
Suffragette movement, 200
Sullivan, Mary, 258
Summera, Macia A., 253
*Sunday Times, The*, 267
Suriname, 269
Swinnerton, Frank, 200, 250

Talbot, Linda, 250
*Tales of the Wide Caribbean*, 153
Tarozzi, Bianca, 208, 252, 253
*The Left Bank and Other Stories*, 36–48, 154–6, 165–6, 192, 234
Theroux, Paul, 197–8
Thieme, John, 253
Thomas, Clara, 253
Thomas, Sue, ix, 6–8, 61, 65, 167, 173, 215, 230–1, 242–3, 258
Thompson, Irene, 202
Thorpe, Michael, 203, 253
Thurman, Judith, 202
Tiffin, Helen, 147, 221, 253
*Tigers Are Better-Looking*, xxi, 42–7, 89, 153–8, 162, 164–6, 191, 234, 237, 239, 241, 245, 257–8, 268
Todd, Loreto, 253–4
Totten, Nick, 191

*transatlantic review*, xx, 43, 152, 233
Trilling, Diana, 184
Trinidad and Tobago, 197, 217, 226, 250–1, 256–7, 269
Trollope, Anthony, 229

United States, 183, 200–2, 204, 208, 211, 217, 233, 267, 269

Van Eyk, Henriette, 266
Vaz Dias, Selma, 20, 227, 232, 261, 267
Vienna, 41, 172
Voss, Norine, 182
*Voyage in the Dark*, xx, 14, 16, 18, 22, 30, 34, 37–8, 54, 57–8, 61, 68–9, 71, 73, 75, 78, 85–108, 112–13, 119, 131, 135, 149, 190, 197, 199–201, 211–13, 226, 236–7, 242–3, 245, 248, 252, 254, 263

Walcott, Derek, xi, xiii, xxi, 222, 240, 251, 270
    *In A Green Night*, xxi
    *Pantomime*, 251
Wales, 26–7, 208, 235, 246
Walker, Alice, 245
    *The Colour Purple*, 245
Walvin, James, 30
Warner, Indian, 247
Warner, Marina, 184, 262
    *Indigo*, 262
Warner, Philip, 247
Warner, Sir Thomas, 247
Wales, 26–7, 208, 235, 246
Warwick Fuller, Meta, 227
Waugh, Alec, 150, 192, 244
Webb, Ruth, 352
West Indies, the, 36, 59, 78, 81, 85, 86, 119, 139, 156, 167, 173, 179, 181, 197–9, 204–7, 211, 213, 216, 218, 222, 232, 235, 241, 251–2, 254, 265–8, 269
West Indian theatre, 260
Wharton, Edith, 211
Wicomb, Zoe, 215
*Wide Sargasso Sea*, xi, xxi, 2, 8, 20–2, 28, 33–6, 54, 56, 65, 67–9, 73, 79, 86, 91, 93, 97–9, 102, 106, 112–13, 127, 133–47, 150, 156, 170–1, 173–4, 187, 190–1, 197, 201, 203–8, 210–11, 215–16, 218–23, 226, 229, 237, 240, 243–5, 248, 251, 253–4, 256, 257–62, 267, 269–70
Williams, Edward, 228

Williams, Ena, 67
Williams, Minna, 7
Williams, Owen, 67, 228
Williams, William Rees, xix, 5–6, 9, 26, 67, 228–31, 235
Williamson, Karina, 253
Wilson, Elizabeth, 252
Wilson, Lucy, 213, 221
witchcraft, 110, 113
Wolfe, Peter, 89, 117, 208, 244
Woolf, Virginia, 21, 243
World Wars I and II, xx, 44, 109–10, 210, 251

Wyndham, Francis, 57, 86, 150, 200, 212, 234, 267
Wynter, Sylvia, xxi
  *Hills of Hebron*, xxi

*Yorkshire Post*, 241
Yoruba, 250

Zola, Emile, 94, 246
  *L'Assommoir*, 94, 247
  *Nana*, 91–2, 95–7
*zombi*, 74, 110, 114, 126, 131, 147, 255–6